THE LOST PROMISE OF PATRIOTISM

D0100282

JONATHAN M. HANSEN

THE LOST PROMISE OF
PATRI★OTISM

DEBATING AMERICAN IDENTITY, 1890–1920

THE UNIVERSITY OF CHICAGO PRESS

CHICAGO AND LONDON

Jonathan M. Hansen teaches history and expository writing at Boston University.

The University of Chicago Press, Chicago 60637
The University of Chicago Press, Ltd., London
© 2003 by The University of Chicago
All rights reserved. Published 2003
Printed in the United States of America

12 11 10 09 08 07 06 05 04 03   1 2 3 4 5

ISBN: 0-226-31583-5

Library of Congress Cataloging-in-Publication Data

Hansen, Jonathan M.
   The lost promise of patriotism : debating American identity, 1890–1920 / Jonathan M. Hansen.
      p. cm.
   ISBN 0-226-31583-5 (cloth : alk. paper)
   1. United States—Politics and government—1865–1933.   2. United States—Foreign relations—1865–1921.   3. National characteristics, American.   4. Patriotism—United States—History.   5. Democracy—United States—History.   6. Political culture—United States—History.   7. United States—Intellectual life.   8. Intellectuals—United States—History.   9. Political activists—United States–History.   I. Title.
E661 .H316 2003
973.91—dc21   2002152992

⊗The paper used in this publication meets the minimum requirements of the American National Standard for Information Sciences—Permanence of Paper for Printed Library Materials, ANSI Z39.48–1992.

for Chip, in memory,
and
to Anne, with love

Give her the glass; it may from error free her
When she shall see herself as others see her

MARK TWAIN

CONTENTS

This book began as a dissertation launched in 1991, in the aftermath of the Persian Gulf War. It goes to press a decade later, in the wake of the September 11, 2001, terrorist attack and amid America's open-ended War on Terrorism. The question that inspired the dissertation animates the book: what does it mean to be patriotic in a nation founded on a set of putative universal principles and composed primarily of immigrants and their descendants? If the current political rhetoric is any guide, to be patriotic means to pledge uncritical loyalty to the U.S. government and military in wartime. But surely this definition fails to recognize important forms of civic devotion and leaves a lot of work undone. Such patriotism bears little relation to good governance, after all, and is out of date in an era in which local and national developments have global repercussions. What has patriotism meant in U.S. history?

I began to pursue this question amid renewed scholarly interest in American patriotism, once out of favor in academic circles. Initial accounts suggested that the current reduction of patriotism to militarism is a legacy of the national reconciliation struck by Union and Confederate veterans at the end of the nineteenth century.[1] These Americans subordinated the causes for which the Union and the Confederacy had fought to abstract martial valor. Thus Oliver Wendell Holmes Jr., addressing the graduating class of Harvard College on Memorial Day, 1895, could praise as "true and adorable" the "faith . . . which leads a soldier to throw away his life in obedience to a blindly accepted duty, in a cause which he little understands, in a plan of campaign of which he has no notion, under tactics of which he does not see the use."[2]

If Holmes's sentiment seems unremarkable from a twenty-first-century perspective, remarkable indeed may seem the fact that, in stark contrast to today, many of Holmes's contemporaries protested his reduction of patriotism to soldiering. "We are sometimes asked," Frederick Douglass remarked, back in 1871, "in the name of patriotism, to forget the merits of this fearful struggle, and to remember, with equal admiration, those who struck at the nation's life, and those who struck to save it—those who fought for slavery, and those who fought for liberty and justice."[3] Douglass himself would not abide the divorce of patriotism from liberal democratic principles. Nor would Holmes's lifelong friend, the philosopher William James. At the 1897 unveiling of the Shaw Memorial in Boston, James celebrated the war for having once and for all exposed the "truth" perverting American nationhood. "Our great western republic had from its origin been a singular anomaly," he wrote. "A land of freedom, boastfully so-called, with human slavery enthroned at the heart of it. . . . For three-quarters of a century it had nevertheless endured, kept together by policy, compromise, and concession. But at last that republic was torn in two; and truth was to be possible under the flag. Truth, thank God, truth! even though for the moment it must be truth written in hell-fire." James was as quick as anyone to recognize the valor of soldiers, North and South. But he insisted on distinguishing soldiers' "common and gregarious courage"—a product of mankind's inherent "pugnacity"—from the "lonely courage" exhibited by Robert Gould Shaw "when he dropped his warm commission in the glorious Second" Regiment to command the "dubious fortunes" of the all-black Fifty-fourth. Shaw's "lonely kind of courage," James continued, "(civic courage as we call it in times of peace) is the kind of valor to which the monuments of nations should most of all be reared, for the survival of the fittest has not bred it into the bone of human beings as it has bred military valor." Echoing Abraham Lincoln, James proclaimed that "the deadliest enemies of nations are not their foreign foes," but those who "dwell within their borders. And from these internal enemies civilization is always in need of being saved. The nation blest above all nations is she in whom the civic genius of the people does its saving day by day."[4]

This book is the tale of a group of Progressive-Era intellectuals and social critics, who, elevating James's civic courage to a par with military valor, enlisted American patriotism in the daily, never-ending struggle for social and political justice.

ACKNOWLEDGMENTS

Over the course of this project, I have incurred numerous debts to scholars, friends, and family. Principal among these are those to Anne Rosenfeld Hansen, my wife, and Richard Wightman Fox and James T. Kloppenberg, my exemplars. Anne did not type, edit, or troubleshoot the manuscript. As a physician at Boston Children's Hospital, she performed tasks far greater: nurturing sick infants, counseling grieving parents, training future doctors, all the while reminding me, in the words of William James, of what makes a life significant. Richard and Jim, meanwhile, provided a model of professionalism, fellowship, and grace. Always ready with wit and wisdom, they awaited the book with great patience and buoying faith. To Anne, Richard, and Jim I shall remain permanently in arrears.

I am likewise indebted to Ross Posnock and David Hollinger, whose readings of the manuscript, initially anonymous, ultimately uncloseted, improved the book immeasurably. I only wish the book could approach their exacting standards. Sayres Rudy gave the text a meticulous reading; at once uncompromising and sympathetic, he redeemed the book from numerous technical and conceptual errors. Bruce Schulman weighed in at various stages over the course of the project with trenchant criticism and advice.

This book began as a dissertation at Boston University. To fellow graduate students Cheryl Boots, Beth DeWolfe, Traci Hodgson, Joe Lucas, Sheila McIntyre, Neil Miller, Becky Noel, and David Shawn, among others, thank you. Thanks too to the faculties and staffs of the History Department and American Studies Program at BU, especially to Sydney Burrell, Jim Dutton, Jim Johnson, Bill Keylor, Fred Leventhal, Alan Taylor (University of California, Davis), and Shirley Wadja (Kent State University). Early in the project I received encouragement from Casey Blake, John Bodnar, Scot Guenter, the late Christopher Lasch, Stuart McConnell, and Robert Westbrook; my thanks to them as well.

Revision of the manuscript began in the heady precincts of the Committee on Degrees in Social Studies at Harvard University, where Seyla Benhabib, April Flakne, William Mazzarella, Pratap Mehta, Louis Miller, Glyn Morgan, Geoffrey Vaughan, and Judith Vichniac, among many others, provided support and stimulation. The balance of revision occurred in the hospitable surroundings of Harvard's Charles Warren Center. My year at the Warren Center was a young scholar's dream come true thanks to the generosity of its director, Laurel Thatcher Ulrich, the perspicacity of cochairs Ernest May, Akira Iriye, and Jim Kloppenberg, and the fellowship, wisdom, and humor of David Armitage, Jim Campbell, David Engerman, Donna Gabaccia, Jessica Gienow-Hecht, Jonathan Rosenberg, and Glenda Sluga. To Glenda, Jim, and the two Davids, I am especially indebted. In the final stage of the project I was fortunate to befriend Jeanne Follansbee-Quinn, Jenni Ratner, and Bob Brandfon, whose advice and example have been invaluable.

Authors who have worked with Douglas Mitchell and his colleagues at the University of Chicago Press know how much books benefit from their shepherding. Doug's patience and personal interest in the project, not to mention his humor, sustained me over the years. More recently, Drusilla Moorhouse and Mark Heineke have made the copyediting and promotion process almost pleasurable.

This project could not have been completed without the moral and financial largess of Anne's and my families. Heartfelt gratitude to Bertha and Marshall Cole and Roselyn and Arthur Rosenfeld for saving me from penury, and to my parents Alix and Chris Hansen for teaching me that patriots can be cosmopolitans. Final and ultimate thanks to Oliver Benjamin Hansen, Julian Arthur Hansen, and Nathalie Rose Hansen, simply for existing. You are my inspiration.

INTRODUCTION

On September 9, 1918, the Socialist leader Eugene V. Debs appeared in Cleveland Federal Court to answer charges that he had violated the Espionage Act in a speech at Canton, Ohio, the previous June. According to the district attorney, Debs had impugned the U.S. government, derided the federal courts, praised the Russian Bolsheviks, and mocked the idea of a war fought to make the world safe for democracy. Worse, from the district attorney's perspective, was Debs's "sneering attitude towards patriotism and his attempt to make patriotism as we commonly understand it, ridiculous and absurd by his biting sarcasm." Noting that Debs had discharged these remarks "in the open air" and in the presence of "women and young men," and taking into account his "forceful and earnest delivery," the district attorney concluded that Debs was a threat to "the morale of the people." [1]

After three days of testimony the government rested its case, whereupon Debs's counsel, Seymour Stedman, prepared to call his first witness. At Debs's insistence, Stedman informed the court that the defendant would plead his own cause. There was no point refuting the prosecution's report, Debs declared; it was entirely accurate. At issue, rather, was whether his Socialist critique was really un-American, as the prosecutor charged, or the very embodiment of patriotism, as he himself had been arguing for twenty-five years. Resolved that it was not Eugene Debs but American institutions on trial in Cleveland federal court, Debs believed that no one was more qualified to rise to their defense than he.

Debs began his plea to the jury by accepting full responsibility for his acts and utterances, assuring his peers that he harbored no guilt in his conscience. He then responded to the government's charges one by one: he had impugned the U.S. government for thwarting the advance of industrial democracy; he had derided the federal courts for persecuting the defenders of beleaguered workers; he had praised the Russian Bolsheviks for overthrowing the tyranny of the czar; and he had mocked the idea of a war fought to make the world safe for democracy because the people themselves had never yet declared a war. Renouncing the district attorney's patriotism, Debs invoked another model. Patriotism, he argued, meant more than shedding blood and upholding law. As manifested in American history, patriotism meant defending sacred principles and resisting tyranny and oppression, often in defiance of the law. The court of King George III had branded America's Founding Fathers criminals and traitors, Debs reminded the jury. "Isn't it strange," he remarked, "that we Socialists stand almost alone today in upholding and defending the Constitution of the United States."[2]

This book poses the problem of U.S. civic identity at the turn of the twentieth century: how does a country founded on liberal principles and composed of diverse cultures secure the solidarity required to safeguard individuality and promote social justice? The problem of American civic identity has received considerable attention of late from scholars and cultural critics concerned about the current state of liberalism and democratic participation. Rampant individualism, economic disparity, and the impression of a government for sale on the open market induce political cynicism and a consequent retreat from public life that transforms citizens into spectators.[3] Local political passivity coincides with the rise of religious fundamentalism and ethnic nationalism around the world, lending this problem urgency. As the United States confronts vexing social and political challenges at home and abroad, more and more Americans may be heard to wonder, in the words of historian David A. Hollinger, "How Wide the Circle of the 'We'?"[4]

Mine is the story of a group of American intellectuals who believed that the solution to the problem of American civic identity lay in rethinking the meaning of liberalism. Between 1890 and 1920, William James, John Dewey, Jane Addams, Eugene V. Debs, W. E. B. Du Bois, Randolph Bourne, Louis Brandeis, and Horace Kallen, among others, repudiated liberalism's association with acquisitive individualism and laissez-faire economics, delineating a model of liberal citizenship whose virtues and commitments amount to what I have labeled "cosmopolitan patriotism." While celebrating individual autonomy and cultural diversity, the cosmopolitan patriots exhorted Americans to embrace a social-democratic ethic that reflected the interconnected and mutually dependent nature of life in the modern world. From their perspectives, Americans could best secure the blessings of liberty and property by ensuring their universal distribution.

The cosmopolitan patriots constituted no discrete political or intellectual community. In independent but overlapping criticism, they attempted to reconcile American nationalism with the liberal principles undergirding the American republic.[5] Far from impinging on individuality, the cosmopolitans asserted, a nation genuinely committed to liberty could marshal the political, economic, and cultural resources required to safeguard individual autonomy from the illiberal outcomes of a corporate-industrial, mass-market society. Cosmopolitan patriotism maintained a critical tension between local, national, and international affiliations. Locally, the cosmopolitan patriots sought to revive the reciprocal face-to-face community relations once assumed to nurture and sustain individual autonomy. Nationally, they challenged Anglo-American cultural assumptions about the meaning of American identity. Just as individuals achieved self-realization in the context of community, so cultural, ethnic, and voluntary communities could realize their potential by contending in the public sphere. Internationally, the cosmopolitan patriots repudiated diplomacy that advanced Western interests at the expense of other nations. Democracy imperiled anywhere jeopardized democracy everywhere; what was good for America was likewise worthy of the world.

The subjects of this study did not refer to themselves as cosmopolitan patriots. By calling them *patriots,* I mean to accentuate their claim that critical engagement with one's country constitutes the highest form of love. The cosmopolitan patriots rejected the notion ascendant in their day that patriotism entails uncritical loyalty to the government and to the military in wartime. The cosmopolitan patriots were not blind to the magnanimity of soldiers sacrificing their lives on the battlefield; some of them endorsed America's entry into World War I. But all insisted that love of country, like sacrifice itself, could take many forms. At the end of the nineteenth century, the cosmopolitan patriots launched a vigorous critique of American corporate capitalism, sexism, and racism in the name of equal opportunity and equality before the law. Critical vigilance became the keystone of their patriotism. Loving their country, they vowed to extend its privileges and immunities to all Americans regardless of gender, class, ethnicity, or race. Exalting public duty in the interest of private right, they summoned fellow citizens to assist individuals whose political, economic, or social circumstances compromised their pursuit of happiness.[6]

The cosmopolitan patriots were devoted to America's founding principles, but they saw no reason why those principles could not extend over the entire earth. They regarded democracy as a universal impulse, hence they did not construe the U.S. Constitution as the final word on democratic institutions.[7] The cosmopolitans regarded as compatriots individuals of any nation whatsoever who shared their commitment to equal opportunity and equality before the law, just as they denounced individuals, institutions, and governments—at home or abroad—that compromised those fundamental tenets.[8] The cosmopolitan patriots expected American foreign policy to uphold the democratic ideals regulating life inside the republic. In a nation founded on putative universal values, promoting those values universally constituted the ultimate form of self-defense.

By adopting the adjective *cosmopolitan* to describe a group of patriots, I want to highlight their perspective on social and political affiliations. Liberals of their day are thought to have divided into two camps regarding the role of ethnoracial affiliation in people's lives. *Universalists* viewed ethnoracial allegiances as parochial and divisive, the source of untold misery the world over; *cultural pluralists* celebrated ethnoracial allegiances as wholesome and inviolable, the sine qua non of individual and collective agency. The cosmopolitan patriots recognized partial truth in both accounts. They shared universalists' commitment to individual self-realization but insisted that individuals realize themselves in local, national, and global communities. They acknowledged that communities and nations have historically inhibited individuality at home and abroad but argued that this need not be so. A nation genuinely committed to liberal individuality, they maintained, would view affiliation as a product of choice rather than a consequence of stultifying ascription.[9]

In appropriating cosmopolitanism as a middle ground between universalism and cultural pluralism, I cut against the grain of a historical tradition that has long associated cosmopolitism with what Oliver Wendell Holmes Jr. derided as "a rootless self-seeking search for a place where the most enjoyment may be had at the least cost."[10] To Holmes, as to so many critics, cosmopolitans did not recognize the culturally contingent character of their privileged moral and economic position. Cosmopolitans were social parasites, preying upon the work of others.[11] More recently, scholars have dismissed cosmopolitan patriotism as theoretically contradictory. Patriotism's passions are said to be corrosive of individuality and moral universalism, just as individuality and moral universalism are thought to weaken affective bonds.[12]

The cosmopolitan patriots of this study were neither parasitical nor theoretically naive. They recognized that affiliations change with context. The unvarnished claims of either universalism or cultural pluralism are plausible only in a political or moral vacuum. In real life, individuals maintain overlapping, often competing, allegiances—as Eugene Debs discovered when canvassing locally for international socialism, as Jane Addams learned when taking the measure of her "cosmopolitan" neighbors.[13] Most people do not or cannot strive for theoretical coherence in their workaday lives. Rather, individuals maintain dynamic equilibrium between their private and public, local and national, national and international affiliations—precisely the pragmatic response I associate with cosmopolitan patriotism. Which is not to say that sustaining such equilibrium is easy or pretty or perhaps even possible. But such is nevertheless what most individuals *attempt* to do.

The cosmopolitan patriots recognized the complexity of people's lives. Rather than regarding cosmopolitan patriotism as a means to reconcile universalism with cultural pluralism or liberalism with nationalism, we do better to view cosmopolitan patriotism as a site on which these and other ideologies conflict. Hence, readers seeking harmony will be disappointed by this book.

Cosmopolitan patriotism promises not harmony but historical insight into the moral and political dilemmas that confront individuals who love their country and yet refuse to separate the privileges and immunities Americans enjoy from the plight of individuals and communities around the world. As the cosmopolitan patriots observed, acknowledging the equal moral standing of all human beings need not entail renouncing the various private, local, and national institutions in which morally equal individuals find meaning.[14] Recognizing the range of affiliations individuals maintain, the cosmopolitan patriots worked through local, national, and international organizations to promote the political, economic, and cultural integrity essential to individuality.[15]

Besides refining our understanding of cosmopolitanism, this book expands our knowledge of American patriotism, a project initiated by historian Merle Curti half a century ago, but one that has remained largely dormant since the Vietnam War due to the recoil of the American Left from a sentiment seemingly indistinguishable from chauvinism.[16] Lost in the silence has been our awareness that patriotism once sustained a democratic critique of political, economic, and social injustice, a point especially worth preserving as it becomes increasingly difficult to distinguish democracy from mass consumption and mass consumption from liberalism.[17] This book also contributes to recent scholarship challenging Progressivism's tarnished image as an elite-driven, corporate-administrative push for social control. Though some Progressives were undeniably elitist, others—among them James, Addams, Debs, and Brandeis—shared John Dewey's conviction that radical, participatory democracy represented the only hope for self-realization in a radically polarized economy.[18]

Emanating from within the discipline of history, this project joins the current discussion among philosophers and political and literary theorists about "globalization."[19] The cosmopolitan patriots occupy a middle ground between contemporary liberal and poststructuralist positions on imperialism, for instance, by applying the discourse of political economy to the problem of cultural integrity. Where liberal scholars view political and economic independence as prerequisites of individual autonomy, poststructuralists deny a necessary causal link between politics, capital, and agency. Privileging culture over capital, poststructuralists have ostensibly restored agency to oppressed individuals and communities, highlighting their critical adjustment to and refashioning of conditions and customs once thought to be the source of their undoing. In an era of globalization, poststructuralists argue, individuals and communities construct evanescent identities from limitless cultural options—in conscious defiance of conventional claims like kin and country, and with no apparent concern for political or economic power.

The poststructuralist account of identity formation is valuable insofar as it highlights the dynamism and contingency inherent in cultural interaction. But scholars who uncouple cultural analysis from political economy risk constraining the freedom of those they seek to empower: first, by underestimating the importance of economic and political independence to individual and collective autonomy; second, by eroding cultural diversity itself. Surely cultures unable to perpetuate themselves scarcely warrant the name.[20] The cosmopolitans illuminate this important, if familiar, debate. Experience among dislocated laborers, immigrants, and African Americans convinced them that culture was no substitute for economic and political justice. With cultural vitality and self-realization as their goals, they summoned Americans to address the economic and political disparity that eroded individual and collective autonomy, and hence the social reciprocity on which culture, like democracy, depends.

The cosmopolitans' recoupling of culture, economics, and politics spawned an attitude of humility toward the non-Western world that contrasts markedly with current enthusiasm for globalization. They welcomed the cultural contact that characterized their era, but they did not lose sight of its cost. They opposed unlimited Western expansion and defended unfamiliar cultures and governments. They ventured abroad—whether physically or figuratively—out of curiosity rather than insecurity or avarice. The more Western the world, the less it interested James and Addams, especially. The cosmopolitans viewed contact as an opportunity for self-reflection rather than self-assertion. Not presuming to save the world, they evinced a certain wonder, awe, and humility in and about the world—which, had it caught on, might have prevented some of the injustice that conventional liberalism spawned and then sought, guilt ridden, to correct.

The cosmopolitan patriots propounded their critique amid a crisis of affiliation in American society. The influx of southern and eastern European immigrants at the end of the nineteenth century unsettled the Anglo-Saxon foundation of American citizenship, just as innovations in the retail and communications industries thrust individuals into a national marketplace, eroding traditional forms of local, voluntary, and religious affiliation. Along with women's suffrage and African-American civil rights agitation, these developments bred anxiety about the dissolution of an "American" consensus and engendered discussion about the nature, scope, and locus of national loyalty. To many politicians and cultural critics, America appeared a veritable Babel—its cacophony of voices and accents seemed to inhibit much-needed political reform.[21]

This crisis of affiliation occurred amid seismic economic change. The foreign and domestic emigrants inundating American cities in the second half of the nineteenth century hoped to capitalize on an expanding industrial economy and steadily rising wages and living standards. There was cause for optimism in the nation's technological and industrial development, but there was ground for consternation too, as those advances spawned innovations in the management of labor and capital that alienated industrial workers and exposed the economy to prolonged episodes of depression. Although America prided itself on being a refuge for victims of political and religious persecution and economic upheaval, immigrants hailing from the autocratic regimes of eastern and southern Europe made dubious republicans, from the perspective of many old-stock Americans, and appeared prime targets for corrupt politicians and demagogues.[22]

At a crossroads culturally and economically, America confronted troublesome political questions at century's end, to which Frederick Jackson Turner's pronouncement of the "closing" of the American frontier added urgency: could a burgeoning, increasingly disparate population perpetuate democratic virtues? where would America's growing economy find markets and natural resources? what was America's proper role in an increasingly connected world? Alongside the insurgencies of industrial and agricultural workers, women suffragists, and civil rights agitators, these questions demanded immediate responses. Debate over these questions recalled the dispute between Federalists and Democratic Republicans about the meaning of American liberalism a century before. Corporate elites justified inequality in the language of social Darwinism: a capitalist economy needed resources, labor, and markets, and was it not appropriate that the fittest survive and rule? Meanwhile, middle-class entrepreneurs decried the structural inequality inhibiting economic opportunity and social mobility for laborers, African Americans, immigrants, and women. Designed to strike the fetters of government tyranny, laissez-faire liberalism had come, by the middle nineteenth century, to impose severe economic restrictions of its own.

As long as labor remained unorganized, workers' dependence could pass unnoticed in a nation nurtured on the Protestant work ethic and buoyed by a misreading of Darwinism. But over the course of the late nineteenth century, labor conditions worsened, workers organized, and public tranquility shattered. The dislocations of unbridled economic development clashed with the humanitarian principles at the heart of the American republic, pushing liberalism toward a critical reckoning. National politics provided a reckoning of sorts. In a spirit of North-South sectional reconciliation, Democrats conceded to Republicans the policies of tariff, deflation, and empire in exchange for Republican acquiescence in the South's disfranchisement and segregation of African Americans. As the federal government turned legislation designed to curb business monopolies on striking workers, the representatives of labor, immigrants, and African Americans looked on with increasing alarm as a once-hallowed commitment to liberal individuality appeared to seep from American liberalism.[23]

In order to establish the broad cultural context of this study, chapter 1 explores the philosopher William James's response to U.S. imperialism. Among anti-imperialists, James was unique in linking American belligerence to a psychological malaise cause by a crisis in laissez-faire liberalism. From James's perspective, egoism and corruption had robbed American political economy of its association with transcendent ideals. By imbuing liberalism with a moral dimension missing from corporate capitalism, James hoped to channel the zeal of his compatriots away from war and toward a defense of equal opportunity and equal justice. James insisted that a commitment to democracy at home in no way mandated a policy of American isolation abroad; on the contrary, democracy compelled America's intervention in world affairs in the interest of national self-determination and individual self-realization. James's influence on his generation is manifest in the work of Addams, Dewey, Du Bois, and Kallen. But I have turned to James as much for what he has to offer us: by scrutinizing his commentary on democracy, liberalism, and war, we discover just what was at stake in the cosmopolitans' attempt to reinvigorate American patriotism.

The cosmopolitan patriots shared William James's concern about the fate of individual agency and creativity in the emergent corporate political economy. Disenfranchised women, African Americans, immigrants, and laborers occupied the margins of late nineteenth-century society and hence suffered the brunt of the social and economic shocks wreaked by the nation's industrial transformation. Chapter 2 examines the experience of three cosmopolitan patriots—Eugene V. Debs, Jane Addams, and W. E. B. Du Bois—who grew up on the margins of Victorian-era America and who, having successfully secured their own economic and political agency, identified their callings in defending their compatriots' freedom to aspire. Aspiration did not imply a repudiation of family claims and social strictures, from their perspectives. Indeed, their public-mindedness sprang from their sense of gratitude and indebtedness to their progenitors.

Chapter 3 explores the cosmopolitan patriots' thought in local contexts. Like James, they construed America democracy in both moral and material terms; with James, they wanted to replace liberalism's traditional emphasis on *negative* rights with a *positive* ideal of social obligation. But they went beyond James in describing a model of citizenship akin to what John Dewey called "associated living." According to the cosmopolitans, the good democrat was she who exposed herself most receptively to strangers; the good society was that which reveled in its diversity, and which compelled every individual, in Dewey's words, "to refer his own actions to that of others, and to consider the actions of others to give point and direction to his own." [24] The cosmopolitans' critiques of American society describe a breakdown in democratic reciprocity. Increasing disparity of wealth created corresponding social constriction, as individuals secure in there own private circles began to regard the public with hostility and suspicion.

Chapter 4 scrutinizes cosmopolitan patriotism in the context of an early twentieth-century debate about American civic identity among a cohort of liberal intellectuals—which, for the sake of precision, I have divided into three ideal types: "universalists," "pluralists," and "cosmopolitans." As we have seen, universalists denied the importance of national and cultural affiliations for individual development, while pluralists viewed culture as sine qua non of human life. Cosmopolitans rejected this dichotomizing, arguing that life comprised endless negotiation between local, national, and international allegiances. [25] I argue that Jane Addams's understanding of America as a "radically unfinished society," along with her respect for individual autonomy and interest in public community, places her squarely in the camp of the cosmopolitan Dewey as he confronted the pluralist Kallen in 1915. [26] I also suggest that beneath Debs's universalist rhetoric lay a sympathy for local allegiances and national belonging that brought him in practical terms closer to Addams's and Dewey's cosmopolitanism than to the formulaic universalism of orthodox socialists, just as Du Bois's civil rights agitation demonstrated a commitment to cultural reciprocity more reflective of cosmopolitanism than of pluralism.

Chapter 5 makes explicit a point that has been hitherto assumed: the cosmopolitan patriots' understanding of the United States as a liberal proposition did not lead them to renounce national allegiance in favor of a hollow universalism. Even Debs recognized intuitively that democratic principles mandate thick local commitment and increasingly thin foreign commitment the farther one moves from home. [27] Thin should not be mistaken for passive. In the case of the Spanish-American War, for example, the cosmopolitan patriots agreed with William James that the United States promoted the conditions of democracy by ending Spain's rule over Cuba, Puerto Rico, and the Philippines, but violated democracy's cardinal injunction against legislating in another's interest when it crushed the Filipino independence movement and annexed the archipelago. The cosmopolitans sometimes differed about the righteousness of specific policies, but they were alike in weighing the merit of foreign policy on the scale of national self-determination and equal opportunity and justice for individuals.

Despite agreeing broadly about the problems of American democracy, the nature of American identity, and America's role in the world, the cosmopolitan patriots responded very differently to the U.S. entry into World War I.

Debs continued his criticism of corporate capitalism and landed in federal prison. Addams campaigned for a negotiated end to the war but eventually fell silent before an avalanche of antipacifism. Du Bois supported American participation in the war and solicited a job in the War Department to the horror of many supporters. Dewey initially endorsed President Wilson's notion of a war to make the world safe for democracy, then became uneasy as wartime jingoism stifled democratic deliberation. The disparity between the cosmopolitan patriots' experiences in World War I does not expose any glaring incommensurability in their thought. Rather, it highlights the role of individual conscience and even faith in determining the shape of cosmopolitan patriotism. Nevertheless, the lessons from chapter 2 about the influence of culture on identity suggest that more than individual conscience was at work here. As a second-generation white male immigrant, Debs was able to consummate his critique of war, even if landing in jail, whereas Addams's precarious position as an un-enfranchised woman caught up in a moment of reaction led her to search despairingly for even the smallest niche from which to oppose the conflict, just as Du Bois's hyperconsciousness of his outsider status in America inspired him to suspend criticism of American injustice in a desperate attempt to gain inclusion. Only Dewey, secure in his Americanism, was able to chart his own course through the conflict virtually as he pleased. Chapter 6 compares the cosmopolitan patriots' experiences during the war.

PATRIOTISM PROPERLY UNDERSTOOD

In December 1898, the U.S. government established the Division of Customs and Insular Affairs as the first step in administering its new empire—Puerto Rico, Guam, Hawaii, and the Philippines. In January 1899, the Philippines declared independence from the United States, inaugurating a three-year war. The paradox of a republican government waging an imperialist campaign against a national independence movement largely escaped a nation one century removed from its own war of independence and flushed with the spirit of jingoism. For the philosopher William James, the contradiction was too egregious to ignore. "Hostile Natives Whipped," proclaimed the *New York Times,* in early February 1899. "I've lost my country," James remarked, upon hearing news of an American attack. To James the Philippine-American War seemed a "shameless betrayal of American principles" and exposed a spirit of "big'ness . . . sweeping every good principle and quality out of the world." The nation's "relapse into savagery" kept him awake nights, he wrote his brother Henry. " 'Terminata, terminata,' indeed is our ancient national soul!"[1]

James's *cri de coeur* partakes of a long tradition of concern about the effect of expansion, or "modernization," on republican government. Since the fall of the Roman Republic, republican theorists have trembled as modernization chipped away at local affiliation and loyalty, jeopardizing the principles and institutions on which republican government is based. James was no knee-jerk opponent of modernization. Guided by judicious leaders and guarded by a virtuous citizenry, modernization need not have endangered American democracy, in his view. The problem with late nineteenth-century American modernization, from his perspective, was that it imperiled Americans' virtue by eroding their autonomy and independence. Without the check of a vigilant citizenry, politicians were liable to succumb to temptations of personal ambition. American imperialism appeared to validate these concerns by undermining the capacity of citizens to monitor government policy, by appealing for justification to public passion rather than calm deliberation, and by contradicting the principles of self-government. In short, James argued, imperialism represented the interests of the few disguised in the rubric of the many. Imperialists read "America" wrong.

By claiming to read "America" right, James joined a contest to define American ideals and institutions that stretched back to the American Revolution. The rhetorical amplitude of the Declaration of Independence and U.S. Constitution engendered perennial debate about the scope and form of American government. Though putatively universal, the privileges of American citizenship remained the province of an Anglo-Saxon cultural majority through much of the nineteenth century. By the turn of the twentieth century, William James, Jane Addams, Randolph Bourne, Louis Brandeis, Eugene V. Debs, John Dewey, W. E. B. Du Bois, and Horace Kallen, among others, began to demand that the rights of American citizenship be extended to all citizens regardless of ethnic, racial, economic, or gender affiliation. If their civic ecumenicalism seems unremarkable from an early twenty-first-century perspective, it was hardly so at the time. When confronted by the paradox of republican principles, on the one hand, and imperialism, racism, sexism, and the alienation of labor, on the other, American elites did not merely justify this contradiction in terms of manifest destiny; rather, they suspended belief in those principles—consensual government, equal opportunity, and equality before the law—that did not accord with their interests. Thus, when William James responded to America's invasion of the Philippines by bemoaning the loss of his country, he posed a timely, perhaps timeless, question: absent a commitment to America's founding principles, what could hold this disparate country together?

In posing the problem of American civic identity, James did not cling nostalgically to a mythic American past. He knew American principles to be "something of a fiction," as he put it in a letter to his brother, Henry, "but one of those fictions which, once ingrained in traditions, grow into habits and realities." As long as those principles retained their salience, they might serve as the bar at which citizens could challenge injustice and chart the country's political, economic, and moral development. Absent those principles, Americans would be without recourse in the struggle between right and wrong. Worse, they might lose all capacity to discriminate between them.

This chapter links two late nineteenth-century debates about civic identity and foreign policy in an attempt to demonstrate how attention to U.S.-world relations can reframe and illuminate what have heretofore been treated as isolated or local historical phenomena.[2] If identity, as theorists since Hegel suggest, entails the continuous construction of "opposites" and "others," then contests over civic identity are bound to result in new global oppositions, just as new global oppositions will inevitably affect a nation's sense of selfhood.[3] The controversy surrounding U.S. annexation of the Philippines in 1899 reflects the dialectical nature of national consciousness. With whom should the United States ally itself in the company of nations?[4]

In opposing U.S. annexation of the Philippines, William James sought to recast American national identity on a cosmopolitan foundation. Both a staunch liberal individualist and committed nationalist, James rejected the Western dichotomy between civilization and savagery, along with the assumption that U.S.-world relations would follow a Western model. James's anti-imperialism marks a new epoch in the history of cosmopolitanism. Before James, cosmopolitans subordinated national allegiance to universal affiliation; since Diogenes, they denied ethical warrant for elevating the good of fellow citizens above the welfare of humanity at large. James rejected this affiliative hierarchy. Maintaining group, national, and global affiliations in equilibrium, he worked to cultivate an atmosphere of cultural and political reciprocity conducive to international justice.[5]

The force of James's cosmopolitanism emerges in comparison to the universalism of two of the most influential Americans of his era, Theodore Roosevelt and Woodrow Wilson. Roosevelt and Wilson endorsed America's annexation of the Philippines on the grounds that global cultural and political development must follow a single, universal model. As the fabled beacon of democracy, America knew best what was good for the Philippines, hence the Filipinos had no choice but to accept the United States as their master. James's disagreement with Roosevelt and Wilson about the Philippines is compelling in light of their common concern about the fate of American citizenship in industrial, mass society. Like James, Roosevelt, newly elected governor of New York in 1898, delineated a model of civic identity worthy of what he perceived to be America's exceptional commitment to liberty. Innovative, if not progressive, at home, Roosevelt proved reactionary abroad. Thrilled by America's new global status, he championed the civilization/savagery dichotomy emanating from the very European capitals whose cultures he admonished Americans not to imitate. Roosevelt's nationalism extended the logic of liberal universalism from the individual to the nation. Reading Roosevelt one is reminded that imperialists can think in racial categories without being racist. According to Roosevelt, every people had the potential to depart savagery for civilization. Civilization achieved its zenith in the Western nation-state.[6] Woodrow Wilson regarded America's civic identity in light of Anglo-Saxon destiny, defending American policy in the Philippines with allusions to Edmund Burke. Wilson viewed liberty as a profound burden and insisted that political institutions accord with culture. Peoples untutored in the arts of restraint could not endure the responsibilities of self-government. Hence, annexation of the Philippines was the only course for a responsible nation.

The ensuing discussion probes these political positions, as James, Roosevelt, and Wilson struggled, often at odds, to reconcile subjectivity and solidarity—the imperative of individual self-realization with the demands of political responsibility, mobilization, and efficiency—in the local and global realms. My purpose in what follows is to highlight dilemmas of local, national, and global affiliation posed by America's entrance onto the geopolitical stage as a major player. It is not my intention to offer solutions to these dilemmas. In James and his fellow cosmopolitan patriots, we witness the transformation of a cosmopolitan *ideal* into a cosmopolitan *politics* at the turn of the twentieth century. James serves as the pivot on which this distinction turns, as the crisis of the Philippine-American War put his philosophy to practical test. But this war was only one of a series of national and international events that forced turn-of-the-century Americans to define America's relationship to the outside world. The book as a whole recapitulates and extends the argument presented in this chapter: the demographic upheaval and political developments of the era spawned a cosmopolitan perspective on American identity that, at the hands of James, Addams, Dewey, and others, promised to reestablish American citizenship and international relations on truly universal moral principles.[7] Less discomfited by nationalism and cultural difference than their classical and Enlightenment predecessors, the cosmopolitan patriots proved more egalitarian, more ecumenical, less aloof.[8] Like cosmopolitans before them, James, Addams, and Dewey embraced an ethic of cultural exchange based on the latest models of scientific rationality; but, according to the cosmopolitan patriots, Filipinos, immigrants, African Americans, and women could be "scientists" too—testing the virtues of self-government at the bar of infinite experience.

Debate over America's Philippines policy raised questions about what it meant to be a national power at the end of the nineteenth century and about the nature of civic virtue. James and Roosevelt, particularly, shared the sense that a century of economic development had left America vulnerable to the material decadence Alexis de Tocqueville anticipated in *Democracy in America*. Roosevelt embraced imperialism as a way to revive republican virtues putatively imperiled by the closing of the American frontier. No less concerned than Roosevelt about the state of American citizenship, James interpreted national greatness in a manner unfamiliar to adherents of conventional geopolitics. Against a backdrop of scientific and moral discovery, old republican virtues seemed blunt instruments to James—incapable of meeting the epistemological and moral challenges confronting citizens of the modern world. James set out to define an ideal of virtue ostensibly more in tune with the times. This chapter begins by reviewing Tocqueville's observations about the possibilities for virtue and national greatness in an age of social leveling. Few writers have posed the problem of virtue in liberal society as persuasively as Tocqueville. Few have demonstrated Tocqueville's understanding of how a country's ideal of virtue informs its national enterprise. Such concerns may seem remote to the problems confronting contemporary Americans at the dawn of the twenty-first century. But the world Tocqueville scrutinizes is very nearly the world in which James, particularly, grew up. He was closer to Tocqueville than to us. I turn to Tocqueville to recover a sense of what was at stake in the republican tradition that James, Roosevelt, and Wilson saw slipping away. The challenge confronting James's cosmopolitan heirs, as we shall see in ensuing chapters, was to promote a sense of mutual obligation necessary to achieve political reforms in what looked to be an atmosphere of diminishing civic virtue.[9]

THE PROBLEM OF CIVIC VIRTUE IN LIBERAL SOCIETY

Thirty days after arriving in the United States on the tour that would culminate in *Democracy in America,* Tocqueville challenged his friend Earnest de Chabrol via letter to envision a society composed of disparate European peoples—"people having different languages, beliefs, opinions: in a word, a society without roots, without memories, without prejudices, without routines, without common ideas, without a national character, yet a hundred times happier than our own." Doubtful this hodgepodge could be bound by virtue conventionally conceived, Tocqueville wondered: what linked "such diverse elements? What makes all of this into one people? Interest," he concluded. "That's the secret. The private interest that breaks through at each moment . . . appears openly and even proclaims itself a social theory. In this we are quite far from the ancient republics, it must be admitted, and nonetheless this people is republican, and I do not doubt that it will be so for a long time yet. And for this people a republic is the best of governments."[10] This insight contains the kernel of Tocqueville's life work, notwithstanding some significant revision. By asking Chabrol to imagine a republic founded on interest rather than virtue, Tocqueville confronted him with an apparent paradox. Republics, according to convention, drew sustenance not from citizens' self-interest but from their transcending self-interest, from sacrifices undertaken explicitly for the common good. Chabrol would have shared his correspondent's awe at the thought of a republic established without common roots, memories, prejudices, and all that. For these were thought to spring from common blood, and blood was thought to bind society together. To contemplate a nation lacking these elements was to invite an image of disorder and disease—in which liberty lay exposed to passing fancy, and where standards of excellence and heroism receded before the flood of egoism.

But more was at stake here than virtue and law. Meaning, heroism, culture itself hung in the balance. "What do you expect from society and its government?" Tocqueville asked readers of *Democracy in America*. "Do you wish to raise mankind to an elevated and generous view of the things of this world? Do you want to inspire men with a certain scorn of material goods? Do you hope to engender deep convictions and prepare the arts to blossom? Do you desire poetry, renown, and glory? Do you set out to organize a nation so that it will have a powerful influence over all others? Do you expect it to attempt great enterprises and, whatever be the result of its efforts, to leave a great mark on history?"[11] If you find yourself assenting to these aspirations then you are likely to be a stranger in your own land, Tocqueville tells us, for these are the stuff of antiquity and aristocracy; they can't be met with via democratic government. Democratic government, by contrast, can promote well-being, tranquility, rationality. It can blunt the hand of fate, cultivate prosperity, provide civil protection. Grandeur or glory it cannot produce on its own.[12]

Tocqueville's convictions about society and politics pivot on the distinction between virtue and interest—on whether a regime founded on virtue or one predicated on interest is the more likely to advance the cause of liberty. As alternative springs of the civic participation that Tocqueville took to be the sine qua non of responsible government, virtue and interest represent the keystones of liberal politics. The ideal of virtue whose demise Tocqueville signals in *Democracy in America* derives from classical republicanism. Originating in the Athenian polis, or thereabouts, republicanism made its way to Tocqueville's generation via the Roman and Florentine republics and the political meditations of, among others, James Harrington, Montesquieu, and Rousseau. With so tortuous a provenance, republicanism eludes easy classification; nevertheless, two fundamental commitments have long characterized republican theory: a politics based on the principle of a balance of power among competing interests and a model of citizenship in which virtue is seen as its own reward. A belief in excellence as the object of life undergirded this conception of politics and virtue. Only by steadfastly pursuing an impersonal standard of excellence could individuals realize their fullest human potential. Striving toward excellence was necessarily a collective endeavor, dependent on constant political, athletic, and martial engagement. Republicans renounced luxury and vocational specialization, which, by luring individuals away from public obligations, cut them off from the contest—the clash of excellence—that constituted the good life.[13]

The aristocratic elite from which Tocqueville sprang left its mark on this ideal of virtue, notwithstanding the supposed tension between republicanism and feudalism. Aristocrats imbued virtue with a type of reciprocity based on the feudal ideal of chivalry, or noblesse oblige. In exchange for their subjects' fealty, feudal lords provided their dependents security of life and limb, first from the barbarian hordes who scoured Europe after the fall of the Roman Empire, then from rival knights and warlords who, while ostensibly exercising virtue, rewrote the book on avarice. Republicanism and feudalism make easy targets a century and a half after Tocqueville; sexist, racist, patriarchal, martial: virtue and its twin vehicles republicanism and feudalism were all these and more. But republicanism and feudalism were welcome if not indeed progressive expedients in their day. As Tocqueville and Edmund Burke remind us, they can be credited with conveying the ideals of republican government, democracy, equality, reciprocity, responsibility, and, above all, liberty and virtue to our era, thereby affording us the opportunity to rework them. And rework them we must, Tocqueville tells us. Do we want liberty? Justice? Grandeur? Excellence? Then we have to contemplate whether these can be won without social cohesion, and whether social cohesion is possible in an age where self-interest reigns and egoism runs rampant. This much Tocqueville and his friend Chabrol took for granted.

The two were skeptical, meanwhile, about the possibilities of interest—about the so-called virtues of liberalism. Liberalism emerged in European political discourse via the work of John Locke and Adam Smith, among others. From its inception, liberalism represented the ideals of a commercial bourgeoisie rather than republicanism's warrior-political elite. Thus liberalism heralded the empowering of individuals to pursue commercial interests secure from the interference of both government and unpropertied masses. In contrast to republicanism, liberalism described a model of citizenship in which self-interest was the means to the accumulation of private property, and politics the instrument for protecting property rights. Liberals clung to no impersonal standard of excellence publicly pursued as the object of life. Rather, making a virtue of necessity, liberals expected egoism to generate civic-mindedness: citizens would safeguard the government that safeguarded them. Liberal virtues were no less rigorous for being the product of self-interest. Success in the liberal political economy demanded self-discipline, sociability, imagination, honesty, and patience—the characteristics Adam Smith grouped in *The Theory of Moral Sentiments* under the mantle of sympathy and prudence.[14]

Now, having read Smith before he embarked for the New World, Tocqueville was familiar with the claim that man's propensity to truck, barter, and exchange could yield public-spiritedness. But the history of the French Revolution cast doubt on the generalizability of Smith's argument, in Tocqueville's mind, for beneath the Revolution's soaring rhetoric lay the conviction that society could be torn from its mooring in the hardpack of heredity, prejudice, and custom and reconstituted in the ephemera of reason and natural right. The point is not that Tocqueville was antiliberal; much in liberalism appealed to him. A self-proclaimed "liberal by reason and aristocrat by sympathy," Tocqueville endorsed natural rights philosophy, with its emphasis on individual autonomy and moral responsibility. But what was good for aristocrats and men of letters was not necessarily good for the ambitious middling or benighted lower ranks. As an observer of early-nineteenth-century French politics, Tocqueville recognized that autonomy was a potentially terrible burden to bear. To be autonomous, according to both classical and contemporary readings, meant to be free from temporal authority and coercion—free from landlords and lenders and, in Protestant variants, from the invidious influence of the pope. Independence of this sort required not only property, but a degree of leisure conducive to impartiality and reflection—conducive, that is, to the propensity to set aside personal interest the better to adjudicate the good of France.

Tocqueville doubted that ordinary Frenchmen could marshal the virtues requisite of liberalism. And by no means overnight. Hence the refrain that echoes through his qualified praise in *Democracy in America* for American institutions and mores: they were above all the product of *time*—of gradual, incremental development. Time made America's mistakes "retrievable," Tocqueville tells us, a luxury he calls "America's greatest privilege."[15] Conservative by nature, Americans had neither the need nor the presumption to elevate a hitherto dependent people to full citizenship overnight. In America, Tocqueville insists, democratic institutions developed in the company of democratic mores, thus in a climate of social order. Contrast France, where democratic ideology thrust headlong into a political and moral vacuum, and where French civil society disintegrated like matter into a black hole.

"There is a patriotism," Tocqueville writes in *Democracy in America,* "which mainly springs from the disinterested, undefinable, and unpondered feeling that ties a man's heart to the place where he was born." Thus Tocqueville introduces "instinctive patriotism," the love of the child for his father's house: a patriotism capable of eliciting obedience without coercion; one conducive to peace, and occasionally to great acts of selflessness, but not for extended periods of time. Instinctive patriotism prevailed in the times when kings reigned absolutely, when mores were simple and beliefs firm. This was the patriotism of the ancient order and the foremost casualty, in Tocqueville's mind, of modernity. In *Democracy in America,* this reading of ancient patriotism stands in for aristocracy as an ideal type. Juxtaposed to ancient or instinctive patriotism is a patriotism "more rational than that," Tocqueville continues; "less generous perhaps less ardent, but more creative and more lasting; it is engendered by enlightenment, grows by the aid of laws and the exercise of rights, and in the end becomes, in a sense, mingled with personal interest." Here we have democratic patriotism, another ideal type, this time the fruit of modernity—as seen in America—at its best.

It is these two more or less stable, more or less organic models of patriotic solidarity that Tocqueville contrasts to the void of civic cohesion consuming his native France:

> Sometimes there comes a time in the life of nations when old customs are changed, mores destroyed, beliefs shaken, and the prestige of memories vanished, but when nonetheless enlightenment has remained incomplete and political rights are ill-assured or restricted. Then men see their country only by a weak and doubtful light; their patriotism is not centered on the soil, which in their eyes is just inanimate earth, not on the customs of their ancestors, which they have been taught to regard as a yoke, nor on religion, which they doubt, nor on the laws, which they do not make, nor on the lawgiver, whom they fear and scorn. [In short], they find their country nowhere, recognizing neither its own nor any borrowed features and they retreat into a narrow and unenlightened egoism. Such men escape from prejudices without recognizing the rule of reason; they have neither the instinctive patriotism of a monarchy nor the reflective patriotism of a republic, but have come to a halt between the two amid confusion and misery.[16]

Witness the legacy of France's fateful encounter with modernity, on the one hand, and revolution, on the other. Caught between a rock and a hard place, she awaits her rescuer. Enter Tocqueville, aristocrat by heredity and sympathy yet liberal by conviction, who recognizes that retreat is out of the question—for "disinterested patriotism is fled beyond recall." Tocqueville identifies his raison d'etre in finding the mechanism that will inspire French citizens to take an interest in their country's fate. In his letter to Earnest de Chabrol, quoted above, Tocqueville tied the absence of roots and triumph of interest that he encountered in America to democracy's incapacity to promote grandeur and excellence. Long after he conceded that America had adequately, if *not* exaltedly, resolved the problem of social cohesion, Tocqueville clings to the conviction that modern existence pales in comparison to ancient existence: it's simply less meaningful. The charge derives from Tocqueville's criticism of French society. The French, mired in contests of unmitigated self-interest, have turned their backs on experience and transcendent ideals, ceding civic responsibility to others. In modern parlance, France has become a therapeutic culture: a centralized, bureaucratized regime lacking independent and creative individuals who might lead the nation toward enlightenment.

When the Abbé Sieyès, in his great pamphlet "What Is the Third Estate?" (1789), equated the lower order with the French nation, he did more than burst the bubble of a bloated nobility and clerisy. He underwrote, in effect, a modern, radical egoism in which history became foreshortened, and in which past commitments and future responsibilities appeared as hurdles in the way of individual aspiration. Though Tocqueville sympathized with the philosophes' critique of the old regime, the liberation Sieyès heralded came at the cost of the individual freedom the philosophes had sought to champion. Liberty of mind, Tocqueville had learned from experience, depended above all on intellectual engagement. A mind closed to all but itself did not constitute individuality and could not be called upon for judgment. Individuality derived from individuation, the cultivation of originality based on familiarity with accepted standards. And what was true of individuals was no less true of classes, courts, or countries. Tocqueville's great-grandfather, Lamoignon de Malesherbes, had promoted the French *Encyclopédie* and Tocqueville's father liberal reform precisely because they sensed that the court had lost contact with the outside world. Staleness would lead to sterility, sterility to revolution. Like the worst of contemporary identity-groups, the French of Tocqueville's generation had ceased to concern themselves with others' experiences and aspirations. France had lapsed into autobiography. Deprived of an impersonal standard of excellence, modern life had lost significance.

James, Roosevelt, and Wilson shared Tocqueville's concern about the effect of modernization on virtuous citizenship. Students of late-eighteenth-century America disagree about whether republicanism or liberalism exerted more influence on America's founding generation. But there can be little doubt that the U.S. Constitution inaugurated a liberal ascendancy in which Jefferson's concern about an ethical political economy yielded to liberal material interests. By the turn of the nineteenth century, the republican commitment to public duty had begun to lose its hold on what was becoming the nation's liberal imagination. To the extent that republicanism persisted, it endured primarily in the rhetoric of liberals themselves who appropriated republican terms like "autonomy" and "independence" to lend liberalism moral authority. By the mid—nineteenth century, in America as well as Britain, liberalism so dominated the political and cultural landscape that most Americans had come to associate "freedom with acquisition, liberty with property, and politics with strict non-intervention." Although there swirled undercurrents of republican discontent in sectors of the American political economy, the triumph of liberalism represented "the nearly unanimous desire to clear the field for capitalist expansion." [17]

Capitalist expansion proceeded apace in the aftermath of the Civil War, as Republican Party administrations exploited a combination of tariff, tax, and debt management policy to pin down Southern agricultural and Atlantic commercial interests, while promoting continental industrialization. The Republican economic policy spawned a second industrial revolution. Its financial rewards would not be realized until the last decade of the nineteenth century, when corporate consolidation and rationalization combined to create a climate favorable to moneymaking, but its effect on the autonomy and independence of wage earners became immediately apparent. The most obvious result of the new economic policy, and the one of greatest concern to working-class constituencies and to students of citizenship, was a redistribution of national income toward industrial capitalists and away from independent proprietors, small-scale entrepreneurs, and laborers. By concentrating wealth among capitalists, the second industrial revolution jeopardized social mobility, thereby imperiling republican politics and popular government alike.[18]

Evidence of the nation's social and economic maladjustment could be found in the inverse fortunes of capital and labor. Initially, during the period once known as the "great depression" (1873–1897), the concentration of income among industrialists in the Reconstruction era, along with commercial, transportation, and technological improvements, generated few dividends for business. Indeed, despite the erosion of workers' independence and autonomy, prices fell, real wages rose, and consumer goods proliferated, making the 1870s and 1880s a better time, relatively speaking, for labor than for capital. By the late 1890s, however, industrialists began to profit from their investment as marginalist economic theory whittled away America's commitment to entrepreneurial capitalism, thus clearing the path for the corporate consolidation of American business. Though the ensuing increase of mergers and rationalization of industry stabilized the American economy and promoted general economic prosperity, to the relief of owners and investors, its effect on industrial workers was less salutary, dictating "a set of standards antithetical to cherished values of voluntarism and independence."[19]

Had the corporate reconstruction of American capitalism been the only transformation in late-nineteenth-century American society, workers might have drawn on traditional religious and community affiliations to mitigate corporate capitalism's debilitating effects. But the reorganization of American industry and capital was part of a broader pattern of political, economic, and cultural centralization that splintered local community and religious affiliation. The centralization of American life occurred less as a result of conscious planning than as a reaction to a series of crises confronting mid—nineteenth-century Americans. The Civil War represented the most obvious cataclysm, inspiring an unprecedented degree of federal government intervention in the nation's economic and private life. Agricultural workers' abandonment of the family farm for urban living proved no less disruptive, contributing to the exploding urban population and promoting the further mechanization of agriculture and consequent escalation of costs that thrust farmers city-ward in the first place. Pushed off the land by the rising cost of farming and pulled toward the cities by purported opportunity, domestic migrants encountered there a similarly displaced immigrant population. A world of economic opportunity for some, this was a world of dislocation and disorientation for many, at once anonymous and interdependent. Although recent scholarship suggests that uprooted individuals quickly forged new communities to replace lost ones, the upheaval they experienced and the questions that upheaval raised about the future of American democracy cannot be discounted. The discrepancy between the republican shibboleths of autonomy and independence and the emergence of an industrial proletariat; the erosion of local forms of community and corresponding deterioration of a sense of a common good; increasing economic disparity; burgeoning ethnic heterogeneity: these and similar problems demanded national attention at the end of the nineteenth century.[20]

Seeking solutions to the crisis of modernization, James, Roosevelt, and Wilson turned their attention to American politics in the 1890s.[21] At the heart of the matter, they believed, lay the issue of individual moral development. Liberal theorists had argued that morality was the province of private life, virtue the product of market society. But in ways that theorists of liberal political economy could not have predicted, corporate capitalism interrupted the inculcation of liberal virtues by eroding local and religious communities and by barring entry to the market.[22] Emphasizing private and acquisitive virtues, liberal politics offered no solution to the dilemmas of capitalism, making it clear to James, Roosevelt, and Wilson alike that the answer to the problems of modernization lay beyond the scope of laissez-faire.[23]

Thus they adumbrated a politics more in line with civic humanism than with liberalism, a politics capable of promoting moral development and balancing private interest with the common good. Yet these commitments led them in different directions. James began to question the laissez-faire association of freedom with property, property with virtue, and government with the protection of property rights. By the time of the Philippine-American War, he had come to interpret an individual's right to property relative to the property rights of others and liberty as the freedom to participate intelligently in political decision making. Less solicitous than James of individuality as an end in itself, Roosevelt resolved to subsume Americans' allegedly excessive individualism into great national projects. He viewed capital maladjustment as a product rather than the cause of the crisis of national significance. Meanwhile, Wilson attributed the era's social upheaval to a collective lack of discipline. He expected U.S. participation in world events to both refocus citizens and restore efficiency to the nation's disheveled political and economic institutions. James's, Roosevelt's, and Wilson's common concern for the fate of American virtue makes their dispute over U.S. annexation of the Philippines all the more illuminating. Roosevelt and Wilson, among others, viewed imperialism as a natural step for an evolving nation-state; James regarded imperialism as evidence of Americans' eroding commitment to democracy.[24]

PRELUDE TO IMPERIALISM

By the time the United States annexed Puerto Rico, Hawaii, Guam, and the Philippines in February 1899, William James had been protesting America's global muscle flexing for three years. Temperamentally disinclined toward political activity, James was moved to political protest in late autumn 1895 when the United States and England came to the brink of war over a boundary dispute between British Guiana and Venezuela. In a speech to Congress, President Cleveland had petitioned the legislature for a commission to examine the border dispute, while simultaneously warning England that failure to abide by the commission's ruling would mean war. Cleveland's brinkmanship touched off a nationalist frenzy. James responded with a letter to his congressman, denouncing the president's coupling of the commission and threat of war as a "fearful blunder." Commissions appealed to reason, war to passion; what could be more "cynical," he wondered, "than to make of an incident where we pretend to urge on others the use of the humaner international methods the pretext and vehicle of a wanton and blustering provocation to war?"[25]

America's abrupt departure from a century of international conciliation appeared calamitous to James. The nation's international reputation had been damaged. The prospect for a "new and more civilized international order" had been set back. Where once the world had viewed the United States as the paragon of "humanity and civilization," in "three days of delirium" Americans proved themselves a people dangerous to world peace.[26] Bad for America's reputation, bad for the march of civilization, the Venezuelan crisis was also bad for American democracy. James's letters to his congressman, to the editor of the *Harvard Crimson,* and to various friends suggest that the speed with which Americans abandoned their principles bothered him as much as the act of abandonment itself. The nation's instantaneous and uncritical response to the president's threat of war revealed a people suffering from what Rudyard Kipling labeled "the curse of America—sheer, hopeless, well-ordered boredom"—and indifferent to the duties of citizenship. Where republican theorists had viewed work and politics as ennobling pursuits, late-nineteenth-century Americans did not associate them with heroism. When the prospect of war promised to lend their lives excitement, Americans arose in affirmation of Cleveland's bellicosity, unmindful of its consequences. If this was virtue, James remarked, virtue had run awry. Americans had become political consumers. From the top to the bottom of the political hierarchy, citizens failed to perform their democratic duty to deliberate.[27]

In opposing Cleveland's handling of the Venezuelan crisis James was not merely naive. Unlike many of his peers in the anti-imperialist movement of 1898–1900, he never advocated a policy of American isolation. He admitted that national greatness demanded a certain "obedience" from citizens. And he acknowledged that certain crises did not allow for lengthy deliberation. But the circumstances precipitating Cleveland's address did not represent such a crisis. On the contrary, the dispute in South America invited measured reflection about the role of developed nations in a world made increasingly interdependent by technological and commercial advances. The opportunity had been ripe for Americans to demonstrate their commitment to the principle of national self-determination and to international arbitration. Reason represented no impediment to action, from James's perspective. Reason led to effective action informed by consideration about its consequences. By contrast, passion led to impulsive action, uninformed about the past and unconcerned about the future.[28]

The nation's response to the Venezuelan crisis led James to conclude that the conditions of work and citizenship no longer afforded citizens an opportunity for exertion; a surplus of energy among the citizenry sought release. The uproar over Cleveland's address did "not necessarily show savagery, but only ignorance," James assured his friend, editor E. L. Godkin. "We are all ready to be savage in *some* cause. The difference between a good man and a bad one is the choice of the cause." James's distinction between good and bad causes separated him from idealists like Theodore Roosevelt and Oliver Wendell Holmes, who endorsed war and loyalty as ends in themselves. It also led James to resolve that "the only permanent safeguard against irrational explosions of the fighting instinct" was the permanent separation of "armament and opportunity." Hence he began to combat the effort of Roosevelt, Henry Cabot Lodge, and others to upgrade American armament. If James's cause seemed humble by comparison to the militarists', it was one that, by taking aim at the "internal enemies" of civilization, could take on an air of grandeur and heroism all its own.[29]

Once resolved that education would be the principal weapon in "this new war," James was dismayed to see Roosevelt equate James's criticism of the Cleveland administration with disloyalty in the pages of the *Harvard Crimson*. Addressed to future citizens of the United States, Roosevelt's conflation of loyalty with political obedience could not go unchallenged. The suggestion that citizens had no right to appeal to their representatives in the face of a president gone "mad" not only violated the American Constitution, it undercut democratic politics by transforming Americans into political spectators. James hoped that at least at Harvard University, "if no where else on the planet," citizens would "be patriotic enough *not* to remain passive whilst the destinies of our country are being settled by surprise." James warned the undergraduates not to be cowed by Roosevelt's saber rattling. "Let us consult our reason as to what is best," he exhorted, "and then exert ourselves as citizens with all our might."[30]

Roosevelt's attack on James's loyalty and James's indictment of Roosevelt's patriotism was the first salvo in what became a decade-long battle to reverse the cultural ennui identified by Kipling.[31] As we have seen, both James and Roosevelt viewed the advent of wage-labor, the emergence of a culture of consumption, and the erosion of local forms of social control as impediments to civic virtue; both sought to revitalize an enervated populace. Yet James's and Roosevelt's understanding of vitality could not have been more different. Theirs was above all a clash of psychological temperament: James was a skeptic, dedicated to the notion of contingent, socially derived truth; Roosevelt was an idealist, who believed that truth was what the people followed. James insisted that the nation's strength derived from the deliberations of an active citizenry; Roosevelt equated national power with military might. James believed that to reverse the nation's eroding capacity for "ardor, devotion, and joyous action" one had to identify its structural roots; a man of extraordinary energy, Roosevelt believed the problem could simply be willed away. Where James criticized corporate capitalism for undermining republican citizenship and thus weakening representative government, Roosevelt demanded unquestioning obedience to the state in order to counter the perceived erosion of Americans' loyalty. Viewed in the context of republicanism's emphasis on excellence as the end of citizen virtue, James could not countenance Roosevelt's divorce of virtue from democratic governance, while Roosevelt, exalting state power as the object of loyalty, could not suffer James's quibble about democracy in the face of cultural Armageddon.[32]

Not all Americans shared James's and Roosevelt's criticisms of America's corporate culture. Edward Bellamy, for one, believed that the rationalization introduced by industrial managers would promote greater economic efficiency and allow individuals to fulfill their lives outside the workplace. According to Bellamy, workers' freedom to choose from an ever-increasing array of consumer goods would compensate for the loss of economic autonomy. Bellamy conflated the liberty conferred on individuals by the freedom to consume with that vouchsafed by the freedom to work independently, unmindful of the political and moral significance the shift implied.[33]

But Americans, James and Roosevelt knew, could never be satisfied by mere plenty. It was no wonder, then, that in the face of what James called the "irremediable flatness" of late nineteenth-century life, Americans exhibited such a burning interest in war. Hoping to provide the antidote to flatness, James and Roosevelt summoned Americans to two very different kinds of war, one moral, the other martial. War seemed to occupy the minds of many late-nineteenth-century Americans; even Bellamy conceived of the routinization of work in the imagery of an industrial army. But it was not Bellamy or James or even Roosevelt who set the strain to war and heroism at the turn of the twentieth century. That credit belonged to James's lifelong friend, Oliver Wendell Holmes Jr., a veteran of the Civil War and the future justice of the U.S. Supreme Court. Six months before the eruption of the Venezuelan crisis, Holmes delivered a paean to war at the Harvard College commencement, titled "The Soldier's Faith," an address rivaling Pericles' "Funeral Oration" in its degree of moral abstraction. In good republican fashion, Holmes informed the graduates of a virus in their midst: "There are many, poor and rich, who think that love of country is an old wife's tale, to be replaced by interest in a labor union, or under the name of cosmopolitanism, by a rootless self-seeking search for a place where the most enjoyment may be had at the least cost." Like James, Holmes knew struggle to be humanity's lot. From battle mankind derived ideals to live by, foremost among them, honor. Holmes associated honor not just with war, but with "the senseless passion for knowledge out-reaching the flaming bounds of the possible" and "ideals the essence of which is that they can never be achieved." This far James could surely proceed with Holmes, whose notion of honor seemed a combination of James's own skepticism and unconventional religious faith. But further than that James could not go, as Holmes invoked an ideal of loyalty inimical to James's ideal of individual autonomy.

In an era of civil doubt—a "time of individualist negations, with its literature of French and American humor, revolting at discipline, loving flesh-pots, and denying that anything is worthy of reverence"—this future champion of legal pragmatism clung to the categorical imperative like a lifeline. "I do not know what is true," Holmes confessed, disguising his idealism; "I do not know the meaning of the universe. But in the midst of doubt, in the collapse of creeds, there is one thing I do not doubt . . . and that is [that] the faith is true and adorable which leads a soldier to throw away his life in obedience to a blindly accepted duty, in a cause which he little understands, in a plan of campaign of which he had no notion, under tactics of which he does not see the use." Anathema to James's politics and ethics, Holmes's celebration of obedience was likewise antithetical to the model of critical vigilance espoused by Eugene Debs, who would appeal to the Supreme Court in 1918 for the right to oppose America's participation in World War I, only to be informed by the Court—with Holmes himself writing for the majority—that the principle of free speech must yield to the imperative of loyalty.[34]

James's insistence that virtue accord with individual autonomy and social justice set him apart from Holmes and Roosevelt and other proponents of "the strenuous life." In contrast to their ideal of martial heroism, James invoked a civil or moral heroism that addressed concerns about mass society first articulated by such writers as Tocqueville and Carlyle. These thinkers had worried lest democracy stifle individual will and promote social and cultural conformity. Holmes and Roosevelt believed their ideal of heroism in war spoke to the very same concern, of course; but their heroism could last only as long as war itself. Rooted in instinct, it promoted a herd mentality averse to individual autonomy, creativity, and, hence, vital citizenship.

James's and Roosevelt's differing visions of the meaning of American identity had been implicit in U.S. politics since the nation's founding. The squabble between Jeffersonian Republicans and Federalists was an early phase of a transatlantic debate between Enlightenment proponents and romantic partisans about the proper foundation for civil society and the most reliable source of human inspiration. Opinion in this debate depended on societal position and philosophical temperament. Americans constrained by hierarchies of privilege were more likely to join Jeffersonian Democrats in welcoming a society based on reason and built on merit, just as those benefiting from privilege were more inclined to follow Federalists in fearing challenges to the established order. As a nation ostensibly cut from scratch and established by a political commitment, the United States promised to be a fertile ground for pro- and anti-Enlightenment debate. Scholars now take for granted that nations are in a sense cultural "fictions," as James had put it to his brother; nations are created by subcommunities that exploit myths of sovereignty to promote particular interests. Being fictitious, national identities are inevitably contested. As a cultural fiction masquerading as civic fact, the United States has endured recurrent "patriotic fevers" in which political and cultural membership is renegotiated.[35] The son of a liberal, Swedenborgian philosopher, William James regarded American citizenship inclusively. Historian Ralph Barton Perry long ago attributed James's anti-imperialism to his "individualistic internationalism," but that characterization slights James's abiding patriotism and ignores his awareness of the role of communities in promoting individual autonomy. Moreover, it confuses James's ecumenicalism with the abstract universalism ascendant in liberal circles at the turn of the twentieth century. I prefer to think of James's worldview in the rubric of cosmopolitanism, a label that acknowledges its progression outward from individual and local realms toward national and international affiliation.[36]

James's cosmopolitanism did not vitiate his love of country, as romantic critics assumed it would. Thin overseas, James's patriotism could be thick at home, but only as long as Americans abided by the principles of consensual government, equal opportunity, and equality before the law. At the same time that anthropologist Franz Boas and sociologist W. I. Thomas called into question the racist assumptions of Anglo-American social science, James defended the plurality of human affiliations. James relished such plurality. Thanking his brother Henry for one "heartbreakingly beautiful and loving letter," he confessed to living "as if a slave to family affections!" But "local affections I have too," he pointedly announced, "and patriotic ones," though the latter would have "bitter bread to eat" in the wake of the Philippines invasion. Indeed, the keenness of James's patriotism was very much a matter of context. In a letter about the Dreyfus affair, for example, he would at once castigate McKinley's handling of the Philippines and celebrate America's "innocence," all the while thanking God for blessing Americans with the world's most favored climate. Because James so obviously loved America and yet held it to the most exacting moral standard, his patriotism retained a critical edge. Critical engagement, James had argued during the Venezuelan crisis, was the essence of good citizenship. American intellectuals "must all work to keep our precious birthright of individualism and freedom" from corrupting institutions, he wrote his brother-in-law, William Salter, during the Dreyfus affair. He could not imagine that Americans might one day deem the critics of privilege and corruption enemies of the nation.[37]

But individuals less enamored than James of democratic politics had been spinning some national fictions of their own. McKinley's and Roosevelt's appeals to "national destiny" were merely the latest manifestations of an "organic" nationalism on the rise in America since before the Civil War. Derived from German romanticism, organic nationalism attributed to the state an independent moral will, championing war and other events that promoted national regeneration and extended state reach. Organic nationalists believed that individuals achieved self-realization through the nation, hence they elevated national imperatives over states' rights and individual liberties. The Civil War provided the boon for nation-state activism in America. From the outbreak of war to the end of the nineteenth century, there was scarcely an issue that could not be argued along nationalist lines. Union and Confederate governments appealed to organic nationalism to justify disregard for due process of the law; industrialists to promote favorable tariff, banking, note-redemption, and land distribution policies; Radical Republicans to vindicate Northern incursion into Southern states. Nor was organic nationalism simply the province of political and economic elites. Civil War veterans and homesteaders joined a chorus of civil service, agrarian, and industrial reformers to press their claims to justice in nationalist rhetoric. Invoked to support a disparate array of interests in the second half of the nineteenth century, the organic tradition's unifying potential remained largely inchoate in American society until the 1890s, when the mavericks of the corporate reconstruction of American capitalism exploited organic nationalism to consolidate economic and political power. During a period of economic depression and cultural disorientation, old-stock Americans hearkened to the new industrial and financial prophets who, by rationalizing finance and industry while simultaneously constricting the circle of Americanism, promised to restore order to American life.[38]

For those who had expected the cleavages in American society to suddenly fuse upon a handshake at Appomattox Courthouse in 1865, the postwar era must have seemed a disappointment. No sooner had rifles been cradled than Enlightenment proponents and their romanticist critics resharpened their quills and renewed their battle, this time to define the meaning of the war. Why had six hundred thousand Americans given their lives between 1861 and 1865? To address a narrow legal technicality about states' rights? To promote the natural rights of man? To settle once and for all the primacy of the federal government? Most Americans appeared to sympathize with the disciples of Edmund Burke, who, with the Jacobean excesses of the French Revolution but a generation or two behind them, resolved not to let the fall of Southern planters become the harbinger of radical reform.[39]

Orestes Brownson, Francis Lieber, and James Russell Lowell led the counterrevolutionary charge. These men viewed the war as a repudiation of the Enlightenment. On the one hand, they regarded the patriotism and obedience of Civil War soldiers as proof that the nation was not yet bereft of civic virtue; on the other hand, they argued that a nation less infatuated by natural rights would never have imperiled the Union in the first place. They had no truck with radical readings of the conflict. The purpose of the Civil War had been to achieve Hegel's "true state" in America, not to abolish slavery. Lincoln was a hardheaded nationalist and patriot, not a liberal reformer. "By making the very concept of 'revolution' or 'rebellion' anathema to many Northerners," historian George Fredrickson observed, the Civil War "widened the gulf that separated nineteenth century Americans from their revolutionary heritage." When Brownson and company celebrated the "crushing defeat" of Americans who had "sought to dissolve patriotism into a watery sentimentality called philanthropy," and when they hailed the "masculine emotions of patriotism and love and glory" for extinguishing the abolitionists' "feminine or humanitarian sentiments," they went a long way toward effecting the divorce of patriotism from principle described by William James.[40]

Like all ideology, organic nationalism masked parochial self-interest. What about disenfranchised groups and individuals? Perhaps because of his awareness of the contingent character of his own vision of American identity, James believed it to be all the more worth fighting for. He acknowledged that modernization posed hazards for morality, vitality, and democracy, but a chastened modernism was better, in his eyes, than a reactionary tradition that erected barriers of caste and privilege before the individual will. Some national fictions were more valid than others. When confronted by organic nationalists, James did not surrender his claim to the national idiom. Nationalism was not the problem, to his mind; he recognized that nationalism afforded individuals a sense of belonging in a disorienting world. The problem lay in the refusal of those like Brownson, Lieber, and Lowell to extend the rights of individual liberty and national belonging to cultural and economic strangers.[41]

THE PHILIPPINES TANGLE

The outbreak of the Spanish-American War in the summer of 1898 promised to test James's conviction about the compatibility of liberalism and nationalism. The circumstances of the "splendid little war" are well known.[42] Driven by some combination of idealism, jingoism, and manifest destiny, the United States declared war on Spain in the spring of 1898. Within four months, American forces had demolished the Spanish navy in Santiago and Manila harbors and established U.S. sovereignty over Cuba, Puerto Rico, Guam, and the Philippines. What had begun as a crusade undertaken "for humanity's sake," in the words of one Republican senator, had become a quest for empire. Cuba had been promised independence in the immediate wake of the American victory, but no such pledge constrained American dominion over Puerto Rico, Guam, and the Philippines. President McKinley found himself in the eye of a political storm: should the United States annex the "liberated" Spanish colonies? Should the colonies be merely occupied, or left entirely alone? "If old Dewey had just sailed away when he smashed the Spanish fleet," the president is said to have mumbled, "what a lot of trouble he would have saved us."[43]

Victory over Spain hung the United States on the horns of a vexing dilemma. Since ancient times, republican theorists have debated the compatibility of liberty and empire. Much of the debate has centered around the question of ultimate ends: was the end of the republic self-preservation, tranquility, or greatness? Machiavelli has confused students of republicanism into concluding that he held liberty and empire to be compatible.[44] After the classical historian, Sallus, Machiavelli insisted that republics should indeed pursue empire; yet, by doing so, they would invite evils corrosive of liberty. For Machiavelli, the end of citizenship was virtue, the end of republicanism was greatness; only by vying for empire could citizens and republics fulfill their promise.[45] Of course, Machiavelli was unburdened by contemporary faith in progress. From his perspective, every republic's days were numbered. The question was whether a republic would go out nobly or ignobly, as a lion or a lamb.[46]

The United States joined this old debate with the self-consciousness befitting a nation founded on the principle of popular sovereignty. And with considerable naiveté: "I have been criticized a good deal about the Philippines, but don't deserve it," President McKinley pleaded to a White House audience, in year one of the Philippine-American War. "The truth is I didn't want the Philippines, and when they came to us, as a gift from the gods, I did not know what to do with them."[47] With little warning, circumstances compelled Americans to choose between the country's commitment to self-rule, on the one hand, and its commercial and military interests and "manifest destiny," on the other. Imperialists appropriated republican rhetoric to justify annexation. Anti-imperialists insisted that republicanism did not lend itself to empire. "You can not govern a foreign territory, a foreign people, another people than your own," scolded George F. Hoar; imperialism violated republican tenets by nullifying popular checks on government policy, and by imposing an alien will on the colonized people. Despite initial misgivings, President McKinley justified empire by appealing to manifest destiny. The colonies "must be held," the president proclaimed, "if we are to fulfill our destinies as a nation" and provide the natives with "the benefits of a Christian civilization which has reached its highest development under our republican institutions."[48]

Thus were the terms of debate established: self-determination and consensual government versus American "national destiny" and "civilization." Once thought to be the source of virtue forged in the struggle between good and evil, Christianity and republican government had become gifts, in McKinley's rhetoric, bestowed upon fortunate natives by virtuous missionaries. Anti-imperialists viewed McKinley's conflation of republicanism with empire as evidence that America's civic republican tradition had been emptied of form and content by the end of the nineteenth century. The republic-become-nation-state could no longer countenance political deliberation. "Who will embarrass the government," the president challenged, "by sowing the seeds of dissatisfaction among the brave men who stand ready to serve and die, if need be, for their country? Who will darken the counsels of the republic in this hour, requiring the united wisdom of all?" The legacy of Tocqueville and Carlyle was plainly on retreat as the president demanded citizens to endorse a policy that suspended republican principles in the interest of "national destiny."[49]

Theodore Roosevelt and the Quest for National Greatness

Theodore Roosevelt, McKinley's vice president, regarded U.S. imperialism as ordained, not fortuitous—the natural course for an evolving nation-state. Victory over Spain revealed that America had completed its apprenticeship and was at long last poised to shoulder its burden of "the world's work." No sooner had McKinley announced his plans for the Philippines than Roosevelt sprang to the pulpit, embarking on a relentless publicity campaign. He was perfectly suited to the moment. The moral and political questions mooted by U.S. activity abroad exactly matched his own political and ideological commitments: the rudimentary state of American armament, the decline of American virtue, and the dialectical battle between civilization and savagery. And then there were lesser scourges with internal analogs: oriental despotism and the cloistered decadence of America's homegrown Sadducees; medieval tyranny and the avarice and rapacity of urban bosses. In confronting Spain and quashing the Filipino resistance, Roosevelt recognized the project that would redeem American virtue and restore significance to American life.[50]

Victory over Spain left the United States with a stark choice. It could leave the archipelago to its own devices, thereby exposing it to the predations of other European powers, or it could fulfill its duty to both the Filipinos and civilization itself by taking the islands as its ward. The situation there differed from circumstances in Puerto Rico and Cuba, Roosevelt averred, islands close at hand and with which he had some acquaintance. Puerto Rico was too small to defend itself from foreign powers; America would govern it "wisely and well, primarily in the interest of its people." Cuba was "entitled" ultimately to decide its own fate, though Americans would remain there temporarily to enforce order and stamp out "brigandage."[51]

The Philippines constituted a graver problem. No autonomy could be extended its population—"half caste and native Christian, war-like Moslems, and wild pagans." Filipinos were simply not fit for self-government (SL, 18–9). Two years' acquaintance with the country did not alter Roosevelt's opinion. In September 1901, he assured a Minnesota audience that the United States was promoting freedom and self-government in the Philippines. Such boons Filipinos never would have enjoyed had the United States "turned them loose to sink into a welter of blood and confusion, or to become the prey of some strong tyranny without or within." Having no "habit of orderly obedience to the law," Filipinos depended on the United States to free them "from their chains." No doubt this campaign entailed its share of injustice. But to make collateral injustice the excuse for American passivity would be to forfeit America's position at the advance guard of civilization. America in no way sought to "subjugate a people," Roosevelt insisted. It aimed only "to develop them and make them a law-abiding, industrious, and educated people . . . ultimately a self-governing people." Such policy was perfectly in keeping with "the true principles of [American] democracy."[52]

Roosevelt's understanding of the stakes in the Filipino-American conflict derived from prior acquaintance with "barbarity." His portrait of the Philippines recapitulates his depiction of American Indians in his four-volume

Winning of the West (1889–1896). No more than in the Philippines had war with native Americans been avoidable given the logic of civilization. On the frontier, American settlers confronted an indigenous population that had not owned the land and thus had no claims worthy of respect. The U.S. government could hardly have treated the Indians as individuals with attendant civil rights. Indians were "warlike and bloodthirsty." They were "jealous of each other and of other whites; they claimed land for their hunting grounds, but their claims all conflicted with one another; their knowledge of their own boundaries was so indefinite that they were always willing, for inadequate compensation, to sell land to which they had merely the vaguest title." In U.S.-Indian relations, injustice was inevitable though mistakes never "willful."[53] "Sentimentalists" could complain about treaties abrogated and promises reneged. But no treaty could satisfy the settlers or "serve the needs of humanity and civilization, unless it gave the land to the Americans as un-reservedly as any successful war." The American government had paid the Indians "many times what they were entitled to; many times what we would have paid any civilized people whose claims were as vague and shadowy as theirs." Indians lived lives "but a few degrees less meaningless, squalid, and ferocious than that of the wild beasts with whom they held joint ownership." In the face of such barbarity, the "rules of international morality" simply did not, could not apply (WW, 61–2).

Who would impeach "a course of conquest that has turned whole conti-nents into the seats of mighty and flourishing civilized nations"? Indian apol-ogists suffered from softheadedness born of indolence and comfort. Deca-dence prevented them from comprehending "the race-importance" of the work carried out by pioneers in "wild and distant lands." All Americans benefited from Western conquest, Roosevelt remarked, all were implicated in the violence. "The rude, fierce settler who drives the savage from the land lays all civilized mankind under a debt to him." American was to Indian as Boer to Zulu, Cossak to Tartar, New Zealander to Maori: in "each case the victor, horrible though many of his deed are, has laid deep the foundation for the future greatness of a mighty people" (WW, 62–3). Pacifists were blind to the blood on their own hands; the public had lost its appetite for work. "Freedom from effort in the present merely means that there has been stored up effort in the past. A man could be freed from the necessity of work only by the fact that he or his fathers before him have worked to good purpose" (SL, 2–3).

If, like the winning of the West, America's course in the Spanish- and Philippine-American Wars was ordained, as Roosevelt suggested, then there could be no reasonable basis for opposing it. Hence Roosevelt attributed opposition to annexation to a deficiency in American character. Indeed, he identified two sorts of deficiency: the first, materialist, inert, a product of passivity; the second, idealist, deliberate, and all the more pernicious. Roosevelt set out to vanquish both foes in "The Strenuous Life," an essay delivered at Chicago's Hamilton Club in April 1899. First he would rouse the complacent. "Soft" opposition to strenuousness abroad confirmed the existential clash besetting nations no less than individuals between immanence and agency. Most Americans did not cultivate passivity, Roosevelt admitted. Rather, after three centuries of nation making, they were prone to rest on past laurels, as if unaware that duties attended their hard-won rights, that rights unguarded could disappear at a moment's notice. The nation had "but little room among our people for the timid, the irresolute, the idle," he had warned the Minnesotans; there was "scant room in the world at large for the nation with mighty thews [muscles] that dares not to be great" (ND, 279–80). Problem was, Americans agreed, there was *but little room* remaining on the North American continent in which to exercise Roosevelt's ideal of virtue. Only a decade before, the 1890 census had declared the American frontier "closed."

And yet the world remained open. Opportunity for greatness abounded for nations with the proper mettle. Populating a continent and propagating republican institutions were but early stages in a perpetual crusade to civilize the world. Simply to revel in past accomplishments would be "to play the part of China, and be content to rot by inches in ignoble ease within our borders, taking no interest in what goes on beyond them, sunk in a scrambling commercialism, heedless of the higher life, the life of aspiration, of toil and risk, busying ourselves only with the wants of our bodies for the day." China had learned the hard way "that in this world the nation that has trained itself to a career of unwarlike and isolated ease is bound, in the end, to go down before the other nations which have not lost the manly and adventurous qualities" (SL, 6). Moreover, if it were material comfort Americans wanted, that could only be secured abroad. As communications made the world smaller, contact between nations increased. The country that hoped to "hold [its] own in the struggle for naval and commercial supremacy" would have to gird itself for battle (SL, 9).

But material comfort did not stoke Roosevelt's ardor. His passion was glory.[54] No sooner had Americans won the "right to struggle for a place among the peoples that shape the destiny of mankind," pacifists threatened to squander the chance (SL, 16). Hence Roosevelt trained his sites on this more insidious foe. Pacifists made a "pretense of humanitarianism to hide and cover their timidity"; they "cant about 'liberty' and the 'consent of the governed' in order to excuse themselves for their unwillingness to play the part of men" (SL, 18). To be a man, according to Roosevelt, meant to be a man of action; to be a great nation, similarly, meant to be a nation capable of world-historical acts. To the extent that America had demonstrated greatness, it was thanks to the existence of the American frontier. Nose to nose with the frontier, Americans had not the luxury of pacifism, which Roosevelt associated with cosmopolitan Europe. Pacifism derived from a propensity for imitativeness, increasingly common among America's cultural and commercial elite.[55] "Certain classes of our people still retain their spirit of colonial independence on, and exaggerated deference to, European opinion," he wrote in *Forum* magazine in 1894; "they fail to accomplish what they ought to." Roosevelt's poster boy for this "flaccid habit of mind which its possessors call cosmopolitanism" was novelist Henry James.[56]

In his yearning to have America stand among the great nations of the earth, Roosevelt looked both toward and beyond European exemplars. As long as England, Germany, and France remained America's principal rivals for global territory and resources, America would measure its power against theirs. But they, too, proved vulnerable to the decadence corroding American virtue. In an essay published in the journal *Independent* in December 1899, Roosevelt deliberately conflated anti-imperialism with pacifism, and pacifism with isolationism abroad. Opposition to the Philippines annexation constituted a willingness to "tamper with iniquity, to compromise with unrighteousness," to seek "peace at any price." Pacifism produced European complacency toward the Turkish genocide in Armenia. There, despite indescribable butchery, Euro-Turkish war was avoided and peace proclaimed. "But what a peace!" Roosevelt exclaimed. War was as likely as peace to promote justice. Witness Russia's victory over Turkey, which liberated Bulgaria and the Balkans. Had pacifists like Tolstoy won the day, Russia would have been subsumed by "Tartan barbarism" and Armenia's experience become the general rule.[57]

Selective in his historical examples and blind to subtleties of anti-imperialism, Roosevelt displayed an aficionado's eye for warfare. Wars with savages were the "most inhuman," wars between civilized countries the most "dreadful." Mercifully, the latter were becoming less frequent, thanks to protocols emanating from institutions like the Hague Peace Conference. But, lest pacifists misread the significance of the Hague developments, Roosevelt attributed America's moral influence at the Hague to its military might. Peace was a blessing of civilization. There could be no global peace so long as savagery persisted, for savagery constituted a relentless state of war (EP, 30–5). Nowhere was this plainer, according to Roosevelt, than in the Philippines. "The Arab wrecked the civilization of the Mediterranean coasts, the Turk wrecked the civilization of southeastern Europe, and the Tartar desolated from China to Russia and to Persia, setting back the progress of the world for centuries, solely because the civilized nations opposed to them had lost" the fighting virtues. It was up to the "mighty civilized races which have not lost the fighting instinct" to transport Western law, culture, and intelligence into the world's "red wastes where the barbarian peoples of the world hold sway" (EP, 38).

Woodrow Wilson and the Burden of Liberty

Less enamored of war than Roosevelt, Woodrow Wilson regarded the Philippine-American War as no less inevitable. Wilson issued his most explicit apology for America's Philippines policy in *The Atlantic Monthly* in December 1902.[58] Titled "The Ideals of America," the speech commemorated the one hundred twenty-fifth anniversary of the (Revolutionary War) Battle of Trenton and alerted Americans to the need for self-reflection. Wilson's burden in this address was to reconcile America's quashing of the Filipino revolution two years earlier with America's own declaration of independence over a century before. If the two events seemed incompatible, Wilson argued, Americans had forgotten the discipline that is liberty and the difficult problem of nation-state formation. Until December 1902, Wilson had uttered scarcely a word about American imperialism. When President McKinley announced his plans for the archipelago in January 1899, Wilson was at work completing his five-volume *History of the American People,* published in 1901.[59] Hence the American Revolution and the challenges of state-formation were fresh in the mind of the author who finally turned in the third year of the conflict to address the prospects of self-government among the loosely affiliated Filipino people.

"Those were indeed 'times that tried men's souls'!" Wilson wrote of the early days of the American Revolution. "It was no light matter to put the feeling as of a nation into those scattered settlements . . . Opinion was always making and to be made, and the campaign of the mind was as hard as that of arms" (IA, 722). History taught Wilson that *the campaign* to promote national feeling would never end. Wilson's writing from the period focuses on the challenges entailed in forging and maintaining national solidarity—challenges underappreciated, one thinks, a century after Wilson, amid a political climate that exalts the privileges of American citizenship without acknowledging the cooperation necessary to secure them.

Informing Wilson's writing on nationhood is a distinction between liberty and license. The Revolution "had not made a nation," Wilson pointedly remarked, "but only freed a group of colonies." In the aftermath of the Revolution, the nation found it "a grievous thing to be free, with no common power set over her to hold her to a settled course of life which should give her energy and bring her peace and honor and increase of wealth" (IA, 722, 725). License catapulted the confederation of states into social chaos, from which it barely emerged in 1789. License brought the nation to its knees in 1861. Though more unified now than ever before, the United States would confront the problem that had spawned the Civil War—the centrifugal tendency of national constituencies—so long as it persisted as a union. Union had to be cultivated assiduously. Such was the insight the historian gleaned from American history.

History informed Wilson's response to the Philippines controversy in two ways. First, he regarded America's victory over Spain and the acquisition of colonies abroad as evidence that America had attained maturity as a nation-state. "No previous years ever ran with so swift a change as the years since 1898," he remarked. "We have witnessed a new revolution. We have seen the transformation of America completed. That little group of states, which one hundred and twenty-five years ago cast the sovereignty of Britain off, is now grown into a mighty power" (IA, 726). Second, he insisted that no people could bear the burden of liberty that had not enjoyed America's long tutelage in self-government. Paraphrasing Edmund Burke, Wilson wondered how liberty in the Philippines had been combined with government. "Is there here a difficult thing, then? Are the two things not kindly disposed toward one another? Does it require any nice art and adjustment to unite and reconcile them? Is there here some cardinal test which those amiable persons have overlooked, who have dared to cheer the Filipino rebels on in their stubborn resistance to the very government they themselves live under and owe fealty to?" Wilson's choice of the word *fealty* gave the game away: "the fact is this," he wrote, "liberty is the privilege of maturity, of self-control, of self-mastery and a thoughtful care for righteous dealings,—that some people may have it, therefore, and others may not" (IA, 728).

Liberty was innately liable to neglect. Hence Wilson reminded his audience of the labor that was self-government. He began by transporting listeners back to the bitter winter of 1776, year one of the Revolution. Who could forget "the chill . . . the sleet at our backs . . . the sweeping fire of our guns . . . ?" America's victory over Britain merely cleared the ground for nation making. Even the Founding Fathers had left no nation in their wake. Their legacy was but "the outline, the formula, the broad and general program of our life." They left it to posterity to accrue "such rich store of achievement and sober experience as we should be able to gather in the days to come" (IA, 722–3). The adolescent nation acquired discipline and solidarity in the War of 1812. Only in its wake did Americans build a viable political system as they faced the task of continental expansion. Not the Civil War but the war with nature spawned the new race. "That endless accretion, that rolling, resistless tide, incalculable in its strength, infinite in its variety"—gave America its distinguishing characteristics. Here was "the real making of the nation"—"the logic of a tireless people" (IA, 725–6). Who could say where it should end?

Wilson's logic raised vexing questions about the fate of the Philippines. The *logic of a tireless people* had trampled the rights of indigenous Americans; were the Filipinos to be treated similarly—as a temporary impediment to American expansion? No, Wilson vowed. Filipinos would get self-government when they were "ready." But when, he demanded, would America's "work there be done, and how shall we know when they are ready?" To William James, this seemed a potentially intractable epistemological problem, as we shall see. Wilson regarded the question as narrowly political, and appealed once more to Burke. Wilson denounced critics of American annexation who saw in Aguinaldo, leader of Philippine independence, "a second Washington." No second Washington, Aguinaldo was a Filipino Robespierre. On one side, America: "a people busy with the tasks of mart and home, a group of commonwealths bound together by strong chords of their own weaving, institutions sealed and confirmed by debate and the suffrages of free men, but not by the pouring out of blood in civil strife." On the other side, the Philippines: "a nation frenzied, distempered, seeking it knew not what,—a nation which poured its best blood out in vain sacrifice, which cried of liberty and self-government until the heavens rang and yet ran straight and swift to anarchy, to give itself at last, with an almost glad relief, to the masterful tyranny of a soldier" (IA, 727).

Readers might justifiably wonder about Wilson's knowledge of the Philippines.[60] Like Roosevelt, he had encountered their analogs in U.S. history. Wilson's *History of the American People* is rife with references to "foreigners of the sort the Know Nothings had feared"—men who overran urban politics in the 1880s, having departed the old world "dissatisfied not merely with the governments they had lived under but with society itself, and who had come to America to speak treasons elsewhere forbidden" (HAP, 186). Discussing the immigration of the late-nineteenth century, Wilson noted the "alteration of stock which students of affairs marked with uneasiness." He evidently belonged among these students' ranks, so prone was he to deprecate the "multitudes of men of the lowest class from the south of Italy and men of the meaner sort out of Hungary and Poland, men out of the ranks where there was neither skill nor energy nor any initiative of quick intelligence." Wilson mustered none of the irony that redeemed Henry James's encounter with immigrants at Ellis Island in *The American Scene*. The new immigrants arrived in torrents, "as if the countries of the south of Europe were disburdening themselves of the more sordid and hapless elements of their population, the men whose standards of life and of work were such as American workmen had never dreamed hereto." In Wilson's racial and cultural hierarchy, these newcomers compared unfavorably to the reviled Chinese. Notwithstanding *their* "unsavory habits," their pluck and skill made them more desirable "as workmen if not as citizens, than most of the coarse crew that came crowding in every year at the eastern ports" (HAP, 212–3).

Anxious about American virtue, Wilson nevertheless trusted American citizens to discipline the newcomers. But what about the Filipinos? How could men living under masters achieve mastery of their own? There were degrees of self-government, Wilson explained in "The Ideals of America" (729). In the United States, as in England itself, popular sovereignty and national solidarity derived from common subjection to royal power. The American Revolution had succeeded where the French had failed, he argued, because Americans had enjoyed an apprenticeship under English kings accustomed to soliciting the opinion of the nation (IA, 729–30).[61] This begged the question why democracy had not developed in England. There, Wilson continued, Englishmen lacked the discipline conferred on Americans by the challenge of the American frontier. For it was the frontier that had cultivated Americans' "love for order, the poise of men self-commanded, the spirit of men who obey and yet speak their minds and are free, before they could be Americans." Thus had the experience of life lived under mastery combined with the discipline of an inexorably expanding people to yield "the blood of freedom." Could the Filipinos expect "quittance of the debt" Americans had paid? The Filipinos were but "children" where Americans were "men" in the "deep matters of government and justice" (IA, 731).

Moreover, the Filipinos lacked community of feeling. "You cannot call a miscellaneous people, unknit, scattered, diverse of race and speech and habit, a national community," Wilson argued. "No people can form a community or be wisely subjected to common forms of government who are as diverse and heterogeneous" as they. Filipinos comprised "many races"— "many stages of development, economically, socially, politically disintegrate, without community of feeling because without community of life, contrasted alike in experience and habit, having nothing in common except that they have lived for hundreds of years together under a government which held them always where they were when it arrested their development." Liberty was no guarantor of national solidarity, Wilson observed. America had its own problems in this regard. With one eye on America, he inquired whether a certain "equality of economic and social conditions" was not necessary to "breed full community of feeling" (IA, 732). In America, the recent war had given rise to "full self-consciousness as a nation." He hoped that contact with other powers would sustain "this centering of our thoughts." Isolationists and anti-imperialists had no need to fear the "expanding scene." America would hew to its old ideals and thereby vindicate its new "power in the world." It would "serve," not "subdue," the earth (IA, 734).

William James and the Burden of Blindness

William James delineated a different model of service. Determined not to let imperialists "crow all over our national barnyard," James arose to defend the ideals of individuality and consensual government. He picked up where he had left off during the Venezuelan crisis: imperialism contradicted America's democratic principles, leaving the world without its foremost symbol of freedom and fair play. But what had seemed to James merely a threat during the Venezuelan crisis had become fact three years later. By invading the Philippines and crushing the Filipino independence movement, America committed a grievous wrong. The nation had committed wrongs before, of course, but never so boldly, so hypocritically, or with so little dissent. By employing abstractions like "national destiny" and "civilization" to justify theft, imperialists inverted the rational order. On their lips, true became false and false true. "The worst of our imperialists," James wrote in the *Boston Evening Transcript*, "is that they do not themselves know where sincerity ends and insincerity begins. Their state of consciousness is so new, so mixed of primitively human passions and, in political circles, of calculations that are anything but primitively human; so at variance moreover, with their former mental habits; and so empty of data and contents; that they face various ways at once, and their portraits should be taken with a squint." Had American democracy remained robust at the turn of the twentieth century, citizens might have steered their wayward representatives back on course. But democracy proved no match for the expansionist mass politics and culture that characterized the modern age.[62]

James's account of the Philippine-American War may be read as allegory about the destruction of American democracy. The demon of the story is abstraction: "national destiny" and "bigness." The victim is "reality," "popular government," "plain moral sense." There are no heroes in this allegory, only a slumbering American public that enables the demon to devour the victim while evading responsibility. Writing in March 1899, one month after the American invasion, James claimed to be able to detect the first stirrings of dissent among an awakening citizenry. Whether to banish their slumber or bid his beloved principles good-bye, that spring he wrote several editorials whose "sober seriousness and definite English speech" aimed to expose the president's "precious proclamations," "moral platitudes," and "bland and evasive phraseology," suddenly so popular in America since the 1896 presidential campaign. From a contemporary perspective, James appears guilty of hyperbole and repetition of his own. But contemporary readers should guard against allowing our cynicism to impede our understanding of the transformation of American politics that James signaled. Although terms like "independence," "autonomy," and "self-government" were fast becoming shibboleths in James's day, some Americans still genuinely regretted the passing of republican virtue.[63]

Like history, allegory consists of irony. According to James, the "Philippines Tangle" featured irony aplenty. When America declared war on Spain in April 1898, even James believed that war "harnessed in a cause which promised to be freedom" might yet produce results "fairly safe." But virtue proved no match for war. Even when motivated by the most laudatory aims, war bred a "savage" and "piratical" passion that negated its justification. James resolved to "keep [war] chained for ever." For over a century, Americans had grasped this point innately; but suddenly they too had been "swept away by [war's] overmastering flood."[64] James's mixed metaphors, uncharacteristic in so lucid a writer, betray exasperation. From his perspective, passion did not excuse America's behavior. Once the "corrupting inwardness" of the Philippines invasion had become evident, McKinley should have called it to a halt. No "Soldiers Faith" could justify national "ignominy." Citizens' complacency in the face of blatant "piracy" astounded James. Skeptics who would not acknowledge the pernicious effect of corporate capitalism on civic virtue could now witness the erosion before their very eyes. The fate of Filipinos and American industrial workers and America's African-American minority were inextricably bound. By waging war on the Philippines, Americans "openly engaged in crushing out the sacredest thing in this great human world," he cried, "the attempt of a people long enslaved to attain to the possession of itself, to organize its laws and government, to be free to follow its internal destinies according to its own ideals."[65]

Once the president introduced the abstraction of "national destiny" into the Philippines context, it acquired its own momentum, justifying any and all abuses undertaken in its name. When the Filipinos did not yield in the face of the U.S. invasion, American journalists depicted their resistance as an impudent rejection of American authority. Every day the Filipinos held out against the American military afforded the "yellow journals" time to complete the divorce of rhetoric from reality, "to raise new monuments or capitals to the victories of Old Glory" and "extol the unrestrainable eagerness of our brave soldiers to rush into battles that remind them so much of rabbit hunts on Western plains." The calumny of the "yellow" press paled compared to the devastation wrecked by the mortars hurled from American gunboats into downtown Manila. "It is horrible," James protested, "simply horrible. Surely there cannot be many born and bred Americans who, when they look at the bare fact . . . do not blush with burning shame at the unspeakable meanness and ignominy of the trick."[66]

Shame derives from moral responsibility. Moral responsibility seemed to James the principal casualty of American modernization. Taking the measure of the American mind in 1899, James claimed to be unfazed by the sway of "war fever" and "pride," for these were "passions that interfere with the reasonable settlement of any affair." By this time, he was more interested in the abstract rhetoric of "national destiny"—so apparently "peculiar with our belief," he wrote, "and which for some inscrutable reason it has become infamous for us to disbelieve in or refuse." Having once seemed to all the world to be champions of self-determination, Americans were now "to be missionaries of civilization," James mocked, "and to bear the white man's burden, painful as it often is." Perhaps it was time to discard the very notion of civilization and its old association with freeing human will from coercive and stultifying provincialism. Indeed, James suggests that, by some perversion of logic, "civilization" had come to represent narrow self-interest and the Filipinos the universal striving for autonomy. "One Christian . . . one Buddhist or Mohammedan . . . one ethical reformer or philanthropist" could do more to promote the "inner realities" of the Filipinos, James sighed, than America's "whole army and navy . . . with our whole civilization at its back."[67]

Surely the Filipino independence movement had warranted America's support. What inspired the McKinley administration to treat Aguinaldo like a criminal? James blamed "the great Yankee business concern," whose commercial interest the administration concealed behind the rhetoric of Christian and republican missionizing: "We are here for your own good," James mocked McKinley and Roosevelt; "unconditionally surrender to our tender mercies, or we'll blow you into kingdom come."[68] No doubt market imperatives partly inspired American policy. But undergirding the Western market economy was a blindness toward non-Western civilizations and cultures that afflicted America's leaders. James's recognition that the Filipino "soul" possessed an "inner reality" beyond the ken of Western civilization made him a maverick among anti-imperialists, who generally condemned imperialism from an isolationist, and often racist, perspective. Even James's cosmopolitan peers did not demonstrate his sensitivity to the effect of colonialism on indigenous populations. Traditionally, republican theorists emphasized imperialism's cost to the republic itself: empire generated wealth, wealth spawned luxury, luxury promoted decadence, decadence invited conquest. America's Founding Fathers appended additional concerns: distance created ignorance, ignorance produced dependence, dependence bred indifference, indifference begat decay. James deployed both lines of criticism, but he also argued that distance impeded Americans' understanding of the Filipino people. Nations possessed their own "ideals which are a dead secret to other nations," he wrote; each "has to develop in its own way."[69] The United States had "treated the Filipinos as if they were a painted picture, an amount of mere matter in our way." American diplomats lacked the ability to understand the situation "psychologically." Even European nations would have tried to "ascertain the sentiments of the natives and the ideals they might be led by." Americans presumed to glean Filipino sentiments from afar. Blind to "the secrets of the Philippines soul," even the best-intentioned diplomats could only "work disaster," James concluded. The situation called for "different men."[70]

Different men bearing different ideals. James engaged the subject of difference in a collection of popular essays written throughout the 1890s and published as *Talks to Teachers on Psychology: and to Students on Some of Life's Ideals* in May 1899.[71] James wrote the preface to the book several months into the Philippine-American War. "I wish I were able to make [the essay] 'On a Certain Blindness in Human Beings' more impressive," he lamented. "It is more than the mere piece of sentimentalism which it may seem to some readers. It connects itself with a definite view of the world and of our moral relations to the same." Tenet number one of James's "pluralist philosophy" was that "the facts and worth of life need many cognizers to take them in." No individual or nation could boast a perspective "absolutely public and universal. Private and uncommunicable perceptions always remain over, and the worst of it is that those who look for them from the outside never know *where*." The essay recapitulates Mill's ideal of liberal tolerance, extending it from the individual to the group. James hoped that a socialized liberal philosophy might dissuade Americans from imposing their "own inner ideals and institutions *vi et armis* upon Orientals."[72]

Most of James's writing on the Philippine-American War rejects the distinction between civilization and savagery deployed by Roosevelt and Wilson. "On a Certain Blindness" reverses it. Behind Western myopia lay a vocational, or functional, narrowness that overwhelmed individuals confronting exigencies of modern life. Fixated on practical predicaments, individuals failed to comprehend the significance of others' lives. This point was brought home to James on an excursion through the American South. In the mountains of North Carolina, he encountered a method of settlement that offended his aesthetic taste. "Ugly indeed seemed the life of the squatter," he mused. "Talk about going back to Nature! I said to myself, oppressed by the dreariness, as I drove by. Talk of a country life for one's old age and for one's children! Never thus, with nothing but the bare ground and one's bare hands to fight the battle! Never, without the best spoils of culture woven in!" James queried his escort about the sort of people who could endure such a life. "All of us," replied the escort to James's amazement; "we ain't happy here unless we are getting one of these coves under cultivation." The scales fell from James's eyes. "I instantly felt that I had been losing the whole inward significance of the situation," he reported. "Because to me the clearings spoke of naught but denudation, I thought that to those whose sturdy arms and obedient axes had made them they could tell no other story. But when they looked on the hideous stumps, what they thought of was personal victory. The chips, the girdled trees and the vile split rails spoke of honest sweat, persistent toil and final reward." In short, "the clearing, which to me was a mere ugly picture on the retina, was to them a symbol redolent with moral memories and sang a very paean of duty, struggle, and success"

(OCB, 134). James came to refer to the significance he discovered in those Appalachian mountain coves as "eagerness." Such eagerness existed outside North Carolina, of course. It came in every shape and form and resided in every corner of the world. "Sometimes the eagerness is more knit up with the motor activities," he observed, "sometimes with the perceptions, sometimes with the imagination, sometimes with reflective thought. But wherever it is found, there is the zest, the tingle, the excitement, of reality; and there is 'importance' in the only real and positive sense in which importance ever anywhere can be" (OCB, 135).[73] Contrary to Roosevelt and Wilson, eagerness was not to be found merely in the West. Progress, James argued in "On a Certain Blindness," resided in the dawning recognition that eagerness, indeed, life itself, consisted of "fundamental static goods" as common among Filipinos as Americans (OCB, 147). Appalachian coves? *There is life,* James wrote. Filipino fields? *And there, a step away, is death.* "Savage" rites? *There is the only kind of beauty there ever was.* Harvard lecture halls? *There is the old human struggle and its fruits together.* Civilization? *There is the text and the sermon, the real and the ideal in one.* Barbarism? *But to the jaded and unquickened eye it is all dead and common, pure vulgarism, flatness and disgust* (OCB, 144).

It should be said that James was ambivalent about progress and the distinction between civilization and savagery that undergirded it. Notwithstanding his enthusiasm for "eternal truths," he welcomed what he called time's "stable gain"—the fact that "the world does get more human, and the religion of democracy tends toward permanent increase."[74] Like so many turn-of-the-century Americans, James viewed nationalism as a principal agent of democracy. He repudiated American imperialism partly because it revived "ancient tribal animosities" familiar to so-called savage epochs, and thereby impeded the march of history. James lamented America's arming of "Igorrote savages and Macabebe semi-savages" who, "too low to have a national consciousness," were exploited as mercenaries in the Philippine-American War.[75] "Any national life, however turbulent," James wrote in 1904, "should be respected which exhibits ferments of progress, human individualities, even small ones, struggling in the direction of enlightenment." Yet James knew that progress, like enlightenment, took a variety of forms. "Let them work out their own issues," he wrote in the next breath. "We Americans surely do not monopolize all the possible forms of goodness."[76]

Until men of broad sympathy emerged on the diplomatic stage bearing different ideals, James urged Americans who hoped that the country might yet repossess "its ancient soul" to exercise the rights of speech and pen. The all-or-nothing jingoism of turn-of-the-century America afforded citizens no other opportunity to demonstrate their citizenship. Although the odd salvo launched from the libraries of an aging anti-imperialist elite could scarcely halt the hail of jingoism pouring hourly off the yellow presses, James attributed the importance of anti-imperialist protest to its symbolism. As Tocqueville had predicted, it took a veritable act of heroism for individuals to dissent from the consensus of mass democratic politics by the end of the nineteenth century. By exhorting his readership to give their "representatives and senators in Washington a positive piece of mind," James did not expect to reverse American policy; rather, he aimed to keep the possibility of dissent alive. In this effort, he imagined himself laboring alongside *les intellectuels* of France (and other European nations) who, during the same summer and fall of 1899, were engaged in their own campaign against the "prestige of caste-opinion," only recently implicated in the French condemnation of Dreyfus. Watching the Dreyfus affair from a Germany retreat, James praised one critic as "a real *hero*—a precious possession of any country," inviting the parallel reference to his own coterie of anti-imperialists. The company of *les intellectuels* buoyed him. "If each of us does as well as he can in his own sphere at home," James wrote a friend, "he will do all he *can* do; that is why I hate to remain abroad so long."[77]

Throughout James's anti-imperialist writing courses the conviction that moral living is the highest end in life. In the face of a nation driven mad by war, what could be more patriotic than resisting the madness with all the moral and political force at one's command? Nowhere was the significance of James's "civic courage" clearer than in juxtaposition to Roosevelt's raw warrior ethic. Roosevelt recognized no form of "toil and effort, of labor and strife" that did not involve physical action. Of the many voices of abstraction in America at the turn of the twentieth century, James could tolerate Roosevelt's the least. From James's perspective, Roosevelt's martial ethos contained no moral compass. In Roosevelt's thought, "empty abstractions had unrestricted way. . . . To enslave a weak but heroic people, or to brazen out a blunder, is good enough cause, it appears, for Colonel Roosevelt. To us Massachusetts anti-imperialists, who have fought in better causes, it is not good enough."[78]

James had long recognized that idealism, and its baser form, abstraction, was a dubious foundation of politics, epistemology, and ethics. Americans' reaction to the Venezuelan incident and Philippines "tangle" confirmed his suspicion that virtue divorced from context would imperil the democratic principles and institutions on which American nationhood was based. Its behavior concerning the Philippines led James to the verge of rejecting war no matter what the circumstance. James could imagine a situation in which war might be defensible; but amid the current crisis of virtue, he feared that even the most justifiable war would devolve into a campaign waged for its own sake. James would eventually get round to addressing this crisis in "The

Moral Equivalent of War" (1910), but not until he had spent the immediate postwar years analyzing his historical data. "I think we have candidly to admit that in the manner of our Philippines conquest we . . . have failed to produce much immediate effect," James told the Anti-Imperialist League, in autumn 1903. " 'Duty and Destiny' have rolled over us like a Juggernaut car whose unwieldy bulk the majority of our countrymen were pushing and pulling forward." Anti-imperialists had been living a few illusions of their own, James confessed. "We used to believe then that we were of a different clay from other nations, that there was something deep in the American heart that answered to our happy birth, free from that hereditary burden which the nations of Europe bear, and which obliges them to grow by preying on their neighbors." As difficult as it was to witness the bastardization of American principles, the truth nonetheless braced this pragmatic philosopher. "Idle dream! pure Fourth of July fancy, scattered in five minutes by the first temptation. In every national soul there lie potentialities of the most barefaced piracy," James now knew; America's "soul is no exception to the rule." This had been a comforting dream, James acknowledged; but it was better "to rid ourselves of cant and humbug, and to know the truth about ourselves."[79]

The truth was that an appeal to the nation's conscience based on the principles enumerated in the American Declaration of Independence and Bill of Rights was out of date by 1903. "To the ordinary citizen, the word anti-imperialist suggests a thin-haired being just waked up from the day before yesterday, brandishing the Declaration of Independence excitedly, and shrieking after a railroad train thundering towards its destination to turn upon its tracks and come back." If James and his colleagues proposed to slow the imperialist juggernaut, they would have to chip away at its abstraction gradually. Nations were "masses with too enormous a momentum to reverse with a jerk," he observed. They could only "be brought round in a curve." But there would no reversing this juggernaut. Nor, try as he might, could James bring it round in a curve. By the turn of the twentieth century, his reading of American national identity was plainly on retreat, repelled by an abstract ideal of nationalism in which the so-called moral will of the nation eclipsed the old commitment to individual liberty, equal opportunity, and government by consent.[80] The question of America's role in the world was thereby sealed. Having "regurgitated" its founding Declaration, the United States had "deliberately pushed itself into the circle of international hatreds, and joined the common pack of wolves."[81]

In contrast to Roosevelt and Wilson, who envisioned the expansion of law across space, James promoted the evolution of law itself. Ideas that did not evolve with time could not keep up with exigency. It was not enough for James that Indians and Filipinos would one day be incorporated into civilization; he expected civilization—the storehouse of cultural wisdom and experience—to go equally far to meet them, as brother Henry had put it in *The American Scene*. James's cosmopolitanism leads to an interpretation of Burke very different from Wilson's. What was remarkable about Burke's response to the American Revolution, James might have said, was that Burke, against a backdrop of narrow national partisanship, was able to set national prejudice aside in the interest of international justice. Burke had indeed "struck a blow [for justice] for all the world," as Wilson wrote. But where Wilson would apply Burke's politics to the contemporary world, James would extend Burke's logic—he would play Burke to Wilson's Lord North. It was not that James believed Aguinaldo to be "a second Washington." James merely insisted that we lacked the information to conclude that Aguinaldo was *not*. Herein lay the cogency of James's anti-imperialism. The dialectical logic of the civilization/savagery opposition relieved Americans of the obligation to confront the Filipinos with an open mind. No familiarity with Philippines society was required to conclude that it was chaotic, lawless, bloodthirsty; Filipinos themselves could not possibly govern a society so disintegrate. Of course, Wilson and Roosevelt knew very little about Philippines culture. But they were all too familiar with savagery.

Of the many misconceptions promoted by the opposition of civilization to savagery, none seem more misleading than Roosevelt's and Wilson's portrayals of Filipino society as lawless and chaotic. Viewed as a form of projection, this characterization of the Philippines reveals more about the social chaos besetting American society and the anxiety of embattled elites. Nineteenth-century republican theorists had feared giving immigrants suffrage not because they were accustomed to anarchy and chaos but because they allegedly had no familiarity with liberty, so gripped were they by local strictures. Savage society, as portrayed by Roosevelt and Wilson, bears no resemblance to any society ever encountered: no local customs, no local ministry prevailed to stem disorder. More surprising, perhaps, savage society had no solidarity. Individuals simply preyed on one another in what amounted to endless, remorseless war.[82]

Roosevelt's and Wilson's assumptions about savage society led to logical inconsistencies in their thought. One might fairly wonder how the barbarian Turks and Tartars of Roosevelt's account marshaled the soldiers and equipment required to plunder Western civilization. What degree of order, hierarchy, organization, strategy did these "barbarian" campaigns demand? How were they funded? Were they too not carried out in the interest of glory and national greatness? By assuming that savages had no civilization of their own, and thus nothing that distinguished one savage group from another, Roosevelt and Wilson deprived them of memory. This engendered a simplistic account of the problems that might beset colonial rule. Once the Philippines insurrection was crushed, they supposed, Filipinos would accept the rule of masters. Having no memory, Filipinos could harbor no bitterness. Violence had no legacy. Brutality could serve the ends of peace.

Sure that economic imperatives spurred American imperialism, James looked to ideas to help bring productive forces into line. He did not expect to overturn the corporate-capitalist order, but he understood intuitively that individuals and peoples once given a face and granted a voice would be harder to exploit. Listen to Roosevelt applying James's logic to American society. America confronted a dire absence of social reciprocity at the time of the Philippine-American War. Citizens lacked a "spirit of brotherhood, of fellow-feeling and understanding between man and man, and the willingness to treat a man as a man, which are the essential factors in American democracy." The principal impediment to such an ethic, Roosevelt maintained, was ignorance. "Any healthy-minded American is bound to think well of his fellow Americans if he only gets to know them. The trouble is that he does not know them. If the banker and the farmer never meet, or meet only in the most perfunctory business way, if the banking is not done by men whom the farmer knows as his friends and associates, a spirit of mistrust is almost sure to spring up."[83] And again: "The average man, when he has no means of being brought into contact with another, or of gaining any insight into that other's ideas and aspirations, either ignores these ideas and aspirations completely, or feels toward them a more or less tepid dislike. The result is a complete and perhaps fatal misunderstanding, due primarily to the fact that the capacity for fellow-feeling is given no opportunity to flourish."[84] A fatal lack of fellow-feeling on the part of Americans like Roosevelt and Wilson doomed the Filipino revolution. But perhaps fellow-feeling for unknown peoples was too much to expect. Then "hands off," James replied; "neither the whole of truth nor the whole of good is revealed to any single observer. . . . It is enough to ask of each of us that he should be faithful to his own opportunities and make the most of his own blessings, without presuming to regulate the rest of the vast field."[85]

ROOM OF ONE'S OWN

There is a profound tension in the inclination of liberals like Roosevelt and Wilson to *regulate* the lives of others. Like Tocqueville and Mill, James attributed the tension to a conflict within the democratic psyche: so long as *equal* implies *same* then deviation from the norm will seem threatening. Popular sovereignty institutionalizes this tension, as democratic nation-states erect political and cultural boundaries to distinguish the sovereign community from "others." Filipinos were by no means the only "other" against whom Americans defined themselves at the end of the nineteenth century. All sorts of internal distinctions constituted the American people: not Indian, not African American, not female, not Catholic, not Jewish, not Asian, not southern or eastern European—the list goes on and on. Alleged to be inherently, permanently *different* from the white male Protestant majority, these people were thought to be, ipso facto, fundamentally unequal to it, hence unworthy of democratic citizenship.[1] The foremost aim of the cosmopolitan patriots was to end the invidious conflation of citizenship with cultural homogeneity at the heart of American nationalism.

Three of the cosmopolitan patriots grew up experiencing the exclusions of nationalism in person. As mature adults, Eugene V. Debs, Jane Addams, and W. E. B. Du Bois would work to make the so-called imaginings of the American national community more generous, more encompassing, a task made possible by the protean quality of national identity. As youths, they exploited fissures in America's self-definition to make their way in a world generally hostile to the aspirations of laborers, women, and African Americans. James's testimony suggests that there were fissures aplenty, notwithstanding the buoyant nationalism ascendant in the aftermath of the Civil War. Between the end of the Civil War and the turn of the twentieth century, America evolved from a primarily rural, agricultural, and demographically homogeneous society, with entrenched local and religious traditions, to an urban, industrial, and heterogeneous nation-state, increasingly mobile and interdependent. The demolition of the antebellum social order promoted a political and economic climate as fluid as it was uncertain.[2] One may chart the promise and portent of industrializing America in Debs's, Addams's, and Du Bois's young lives. They witnessed the unraveling of the proprietary capitalism and face-to-face community relations of their parents' generation, the emergence of interest-group politics and widespread political corruption, and redoubled racial and sexual prejudice. Yet they achieved things their parents could not have dreamed of. Debs's leadership of and victory in the Great Northern Railroad Strike, Addams's founding of Hull-House, Du Bois's founding of the National Association for the Advancement of Colored People (NAACP) were tokens of the opportunity awaiting exceptional individuals of their generation. These opportunities, no less than the economic and cultural hurdles impeding the aspirations of laborers, immigrants, African Americans, and women, described life in late-nineteenth-century America.

No homogeneous cultural standards constrained Debs, Addams, and Du Bois. Their young lives were marked by regional, racial, economic, and gender disparity; the vocations they pursued could not have been more different. The fleeting instances when their paths crossed do not provide evidence that they saw themselves engaged in common endeavor. Yet all confronted the difficulty of having to define their selfhood against both local and national cultural backgrounds hostile to individual autonomy.[3] Their cosmopolitan patriotism sprang in large part from early family and community dynamics rife with social and cultural as well as psychological and personal significance.

The process of self-definition is never easy and rarely fully successful. In his recent book, *The Human Stain,* novelist Philip Roth speaks suggestively to the challenge social ascription poses to modern subjectivity. Roth reminds us what communitarian critics of liberalism and nationalism sometimes forget: although an indispensable context for early self-definition, family and local communities often thwart the aspirations of emergent selfhood; they are no less prone to social ascription than cultural and political elites.[4] This insight constitutes an essential bulwark of cosmopolitan patriotism and is one of the most important lessons of Debs's, Addams's, and Du Bois's young lives.

Meet Coleman Silk, Roth's hero, born and raised in a black middle-class family outside Newark, New Jersey, in the 1930s. A brilliant and restless dreamer, Coleman resolves not to let his prospects be "unjustly limited by so arbitrary a designation as race."[5] In pursuit of an "actable self," Coleman adopts the identity of a cohort of young Greenwich Village intellectuals who had assumed "he was a Jew all along" (HS, 131–6). Coleman is not content to perform this charade merely among peers; he presents his new and indelible persona to his mother at her kitchen table, devastating her, of course, but once and for all freeing himself to pursue the American Dream—"the high drama that is upping and leaving—and the energy and cruelty that rapturous drive demands" (HS, 342).

Energy and cruelty are Roth's operative themes: cruelty, because exchanging identity entails sundering hearts; energy, because the agency such exchanging assumes proves elusive. Roth shows us that modern identity is dependent on recognition. Identities have to be ratified by others to be realized.[6] Thus, what appears to be a matter of individual caprice is fraught with social and moral ramifications. Ask Coleman's mother, who experiences Coleman's abandonment as "murder"; ask Coleman's brother, who interprets Coleman's apostasy as political "defection" (324–38). But the dynamic of recognition ensures that Coleman's family will not remain simply victims. They possess the recognizers' agency. By withholding recognition of Coleman's new identity, they exact psychological revenge. They know Coleman's secret. "Freedom," Roth remarks portentously, "is dangerous" (HS, 145).

Coleman is undone, ultimately, not by his family but by a fateful encounter with a larger community of recognizers that presumes to know his identity and, hence, his motivations. Coleman Silk: once a scrappy young black boxer from Jersey, now a respected Jewish classics professor, retirement age, at a small New England college, who inadvertently offends two African American students and is virtually run out of town. Coleman did something typical of *people like him*. Time is a bomb, Roth suggests, for the willful: "The man who decides to forge a distinct historical destiny, who sets out to spring the historical lock, and who does so, brilliantly succeeds at altering his personal lot, only to be ensnared by the history he hadn't quite counted on, the history that isn't yet history, the history that the clock is now ticking off" (HS, 342). Coleman sprang no lock; he merely exchanged one form of subjugation for another. Agency, like identity itself, turns on the problem of recognition—on what is really a matter of interpretation—and Roth, like William James before him, puts little stock in our interpretive acumen.[7]

Indeed, for Roth, the recognizer poses a well-nigh intractable challenge to modern subjectivity. Our attempts at self-making will collapse; it's only a matter of time. At least, so long as we remain overconfident in our capacity to know others. In Nathan Zuckerman, Roth's narrator, we encounter a ray of hope—a potentially saving ethic of uncertainty, a willingness to engage the unfamiliar without presuming to comprehend or appropriate it. Some such ethic, Roth implies, is required of successful self-making. *Our understanding of people must always be at best slightly wrong.*

FOUNDATIONS OF THE SELF

Eugene Victor Debs was born on November 5, 1855, in Terre Haute, Indiana, to Daniel and Marguerite Bettrich Debs. A native of Colmar, Alsace, Daniel emigrated to America in 1849, to be followed by Marguerite six months later. Both Daniel and Marguerite came from respectable families. Daniel, a bookish and romantic Protestant, in love with Marguerite, a Catholic, left home to escape religious and occupational constraints imposed on him by overbearing parents. The freedom he and Marguerite won by emigrating proved costly in the end, as both families disowned their children, repudiating their intermarriage. Eugene Debs remembers his father's and mother's enduring bitterness toward their parents at being disinherited. Debs's lasting enmity toward institutional religion likely stemmed from his parents' final banishment. Awed by his parents' devotion to their children, Eugene never second-guessed the impulsive flight from family that precipitated their fall from grace.[8]

If Daniel Debs had any illusions about making a life in America in the world of arts and letters, they vanished upon his arrival in New York City. His and Marguerite's first years in America were predictably difficult for two unconnected stowaways speaking little English and boasting no special skills. Between 1849 and 1854, Daniel shuttled from New York to Terre Haute, Indiana, and back, then returned to Terre Haute to stay, working long hours at odd jobs while siring two daughters, both of whom died in infancy. Despite the couple's eventual success, these five years of struggle together with their parents' condemnation lent their lives a tragic element in the eyes of their eldest son. Eugene appeared extraordinarily solicitous of his parents' welfare throughout his life, as if somehow holding himself responsible for the hardship that preceded him. A year before Eugene was born, misfortune getting the best of them, Daniel and Marguerite invested their last savings in a store of goods with the purpose of opening a little grocery. Through a proverbial combination of pluck and luck, the Debses' store flourished, and Daniel found himself the proud proprietor of a butcher shop virtually indistinguishable from the Alsatian butchery of his father.[9]

Jane Addams was born on September 6, 1860, in Cedarville, Illinois, to John and Sarah Weber Addams, a young couple more firmly rooted in America than Daniel and Marguerite Debs, but no less on the make. To be on the make in mid—nineteenth-century America often meant to be on the move, and like the Debses, John and Sarah Addams looked for their opportunity in the Midwest, departing their native Pennsylvania for the sparsely settled mill country of northwestern Illinois in the muddy summer of 1844. More than merely a conjugal alliance, the union of John's and Sarah's families was a meeting of business minds, an emblem of the commercial opportunity available to white, independent proprietors of antebellum America. Unlike the Debses, John and Sarah left home with their parents' blessing—indeed, in the company of Sarah's father, a miller with relatives recently relocated in Illinois, and a man who shared his son-in-law's sense of the profitability of the territory lying in the lee of the Midwest's greatest city. John's father, himself a miller, accompanied the newlyweds, too, at least symbolically, in the form of a four thousand dollar promissory note swelling John's pocket, to be invested in a mill of his own.[10]

Although Jane Addams scarcely mentions her mother, who died when Jane was two, it is reasonable to attribute the values that Jane and others ascribe to John Addams to him and Sarah both. John's career reads like a model of the proprietor-citizen. Tutored by his parents in the virtues of industry, honesty, and responsibility, John seems to have recognized no tension between the demands of self, family, community, and nation. Identifying life's significance in work and family, John struck out for the Midwest in order to ensure his family's autonomy and independence. Once settled in Cedarville, he established the mill of his family's dreams. Realizing that no mill could succeed without a neighboring market, John canvassed the county in a successful bid to raise money for a railway—becoming, in the words of one newspaper, "the best-known man in the district." John's diary suggests that a gnawing self-doubt accompanied his first foray into the world; but the railroad arrived, the mill flourished, the family grew, and, ten years after leaving Pennsylvania, John and Sarah Addams moved with Jane's three surviving elder siblings into a large, brand-new house that was the pride of Cedarville.

William Edward Burghardt Du Bois was born on February 23, 1868 in Great Barrington, Massachusetts, to Alfred and Mary Burghardt Du Bois. Alfred appears to have entered fleetingly into Mary's life a year before the birth of their son William and to have departed shortly thereafter. Like Daniel Debs and John Addams, the young Alfred pursued his dreams on the road. Unlike Daniel and John, however, this "illegitimate" son of a New Haven, Connecticut, merchant and his Haitian mistress never succeeded in establishing the economic foundation conducive to stable family life. In the thirty-odd years between his birth in the early 1830s and his desertion from the Union army at the end of the Civil War, Alfred drifted between upstate New York and the Caribbean basin. His restlessness appears to have stemmed as much from a faulty moral compass as from the economic and cultural discrimination visited upon even the lightest-skinned free blacks in antebellum America. Although the exact pattern of Alfred's roving remains the province of conjecture, there is no doubting the cool reception accorded him by Mary Burghardt's family upon his arrival in Great Barrington in 1867. Hailing from a long line of assiduous and conservative farmers and household servants, the Burghardts recognized Alfred for the rake that he was, opposing his overly expeditious betrothal to Mary. Thirty-seven years old and the mother of a child by a first cousin, Mary Burghardt must have seemed a likely catch to the already married Alfred. But quickly caught, Mary would be as cursorily dropped, as Alfred hit the road once more, permanently deserting his latest wife and child.[11]

There is a significant discrepancy between what W. E. B. Du Bois wrote about his parents' genealogy in his several autobiographies and what historians now know, a discrepancy complicated by inaccuracies that, as David L. Lewis observes, seem "surprising in an historian" and to border on willful distortion. Although it is probably anachronistic to trace the "double-consciousness" that W. E. B. Du Bois immortalized in *Souls of Black Folk* to lacunae in the Du Bois and Burghardt lineages, the mystery running through Alfred's and Mary's past both haunted their son and afforded him the artistic license to turn their secrets to advantage. Determined to win acceptance as a full and free American, Du Bois would stake his claim to American citizenship on the partially fabricated or whitewashed evidence of his family's bourgeois values and his forefathers' ready sacrifice in "every war of the Republic."[12]

The vicissitudes of Debs's, Addams's, and Du Bois's young parents shaped the cosmopolitan patriots' moral foundations. No less important was the influence of the communities in which the elder Debses, Addamses, and Du Boises exercised their early aspirations. William James's criticism of modernization stemmed from his conviction that capitalism imperiled community life. By luring individuals into an interdependent and impersonal mass marketplace, capitalism destroyed the face-to-face interaction on which community and religious affiliation and local democracy depended. James exaggerated the degree to which the "communities" of preindustrial America embraced the disparate individuals of any one place; by definition, communities exclude as well as include people. Moreover, James ignored the opportunities modernism allows individuals to form new, more variegated communities. Eugene Debs's idealization of the "beloved little community" of Terre Haute, "where all were neighbors and all friends," is a classic example of the sentimentality that often pervades the term. The multifaceted alliance that constituted Debs's Socialist Party would have been impossible to maintain without the modern networks of communication. For "community" to be a useful tool in historical analysis, it must be viewed with skepticism, as much a normative claim as an accurate depiction of historical reality.[13]

Much like Daniel and Marguerite Debs themselves, the Terre Haute, Indiana, into which they arrived at midcentury was a town struggling to make it. For the many Midwestern villages that sprung up in the wake of early-nineteenth-century settlers, making it as a town meant acquiring sufficient capital and labor to attract the institutions of economic development—railroads, banks, real estate agents—that would in turn lure more migrants and further swell the commodity and labor markets. Because the success of towns like Terre Haute depended on boosterism, these towns naturally developed their own social, political, and economic elite. Initially, membership among the elite seems to have been relatively open, determined more by good fortune and perseverance than by inherited position, although a comfortable birthright proved an undeniable advantage. Had Eugene Debs followed his father's footsteps into business, he almost certainly would have joined the ranks of Terre Haute's leading men—Daniel's and Marguerite's immigrant status proving no barrier to their son being accepted as a "native." Among Terre Haute's white families of Western European origin, the existence of "community" seems to have been taken for granted. In a town established on economic rather than religious commitment, the virtues associated with the Protestant work ethic provided the necessary social adhesive. But they could do so, as historian Salvatore observes, only as long as the opportunity for economic mobility persisted. In 1860, Terre Haute was Indiana's fourth largest town; its continued growth complicated early civic and cultural alliances, revealing the fragility of its entrepreneurial consensus.[14]

By contrast to Terre Haute, the Cedarville, Illinois, in which John and Sarah Addams arrived in 1844 had been settled for only ten years. The young Addamses were not so much immigrants into a preexisting town as they were a second wave of settlers. Still unincorporated, unsurveyed, and unnamed at the time of Jane's birth in 1860, Cedarville owed its sense of community to the self-conscious labor of John and Sarah Addams. Jane Addams's establishment of Hull-House in 1889 is a striking parallel to her parent's founding of Cedarville a generation earlier. To the business-minded Addamses, forging a community meant attracting economic and cultural institutions. John Addams's early campaign to bring the railroad to Cedarville was merely the first in a long line of civic duties undertaken by the town's leading man. Although populism would give railroaders, real estate speculators, lawyers, and bankers a bad name, John's career and the history of Cedarville's development suggest that these institutions were not the enemies of democracy that they would be made to seem. Besides investing his flour mill profits in real estate, railroad, and banking ventures, John helped organize a nearby bank, presided over a local life insurance company, founded the Cedarville public school, personally endowed the town library, established a church (while supporting others), served sixteen years in the Illinois senate, and raised a Civil War regiment labeled the "Addams Guards." It is no wonder that Jane Addams remembers as a girl being awed by her father. As a highly educated young woman pondering her future in the restrictive cultural climate of Victorian America, Jane would be daunted by her father's extraordinary civic achievements—all undertaken with preternatural humility and grace. Obviously the fruit of immense labor, John's success seemed to Jane to have come almost effortlessly.[15]

If there was money to be made and reputations to be won in the Great Barrington, Massachusetts, into which W. E. B. Du Bois was born, the Burghardt family would not have known of it. As residents of Great Barrington for over one hundred and fifty years, the Burghardts formed a veritable community of their own at midcentury, representing many of the town's roughly thirty black families out of a total population numbering around four thousand. Theirs was very much a community within a community, however, and all the privileges of membership they bestowed on one another could not have mitigated the fact of their second-class citizenship in Great Barrington. Most of the businesses owned by Great Barrington's African-American population were farms; those who had their minds on other work sold their labor to the white Protestant majority as domestic servants, barbers, stewards, or coachmen. Great Barrington's social relations became strained on the eve of the American Civil War, as neighboring mills attracted a new working-class population consisting of Irish Catholic and Czech immigrants. Initially, the unfamiliarity of the newcomers conferred a certain distinction on the town's African Americans, who, like the Burghardt clan, eschewed the degrading labor of the mills and clung to their Protestant beliefs as if to a badge of status. But the truth was that the Burghardts could not have found work in the mill even had they wanted to. Mill jobs were reserved for the burgeoning poor white population, whose numbers soon overwhelmed the demand for industrial labor, and who thus ended up competing for the household work once monopolized by Great Barrington's blacks. Always difficult, the struggle of the Burghardt yeomen intensified in the years surrounding W. E. B. Du Bois's birth. As the towns and cities of the Midwest flourished, the output of their harvests eroded the market share of Great Barrington's small farms, auguring a bleak future. Although Du Bois remembers relations between white and black Great Barrington to have been civil, they were barely so. Economic and political influence remained the province of white male Protestants, who bestowed their patronage upon an increasingly vulnerable black population.[16]

These were the "communities" in which Daniel and Marguerite Debs, John and Sarah Addams, and Alfred and Mary Du Bois brought forth their precocious progeny. These communities were linked to an outside world that contributed to their children's moral underpinning. In the wake of the American Civil War, local folkways became tied increasingly to a national politics and market, just as the nation itself became linked to an international arena through immigration, economic investment, and political expansion. Like many in their parents' generation, Eugene Debs, Jane Addams, and W. E. B. Du Bois would seek their opportunities away from home. For all the support and camaraderie community life afforded Eugene Debs and Jane Addams, they, like W. E. B. Du Bois, would turn to the outside world to escape parochial constraints.

Daniel and Marguerite Debses' geographic horizon stretched from the Alsace of their disenchantment to the New York of their misfortune to the Terre Haute of their prosperity. Although Daniel's unrelenting sourness toward his parents seems to have bred a corresponding enmity toward his native province, he remained fond of the French revolutionary and German romantic literature that had initially given wing to his wanderlust. Daniel's grandfather is reported to have been a representative in the French National Assembly; throughout his lifetime, Daniel evinced more loyalty to the Revolution's universal principles than to family or national affiliation. As a Terre Haute grocer and butcher, Daniel depended on the outside world and the Midwest's elaborate lines of exchange to buy and maintain the inventory for what had become a successful enterprise. Eugene Debs remembers having been early mesmerized by the coming and going of the trains in the Terre Haute rail yards. Those trains served as the vital link sustaining his father's dream of personal autonomy and economic independence.[17]

For Daniel and Marguerite Debs, who measured progress by the march of liberty, the United States must have seemed to be freedom's engine at the time of Eugene's birth in 1855. But not everybody in Terre Haute enjoyed the freedom or could partake of the equality and fraternity accorded the industrious young butcher from Alsace. American racism remained beyond Daniel's and Marguerite's moral purview, just as the rudimentary stirrings of the labor and suffrage movements eluded their sympathy. Although their son Eugene would boast of having been born into the veritable bosom of liberty, he came by his final commitment to race and gender equality—and even his socialism—in a roundabout way. If any of old grandfather Debs's revolutionary zeal still warmed the blood of his descendants, it remained latent in Daniel's veins in 1855.

When John Addams died in 1881 at the age of 59, he left behind him an estate worth a quarter of a million dollars. It is said that had he chosen a larger creek on which to establish his grist mill, its increased capacity combined with his business acumen could have made him a millionaire several times over. But like the office of the governor that had been his for the asking, a mill on such a scale would have impinged on his other vocations, restricting his world intolerably. This Cedarville Cincinnatus regarded his family business as merely one facet of the larger circle of opportunity and obligation constituting the life of the citizen. Present at the Ripon, Wisconsin, convention of 1854 that launched the Republican Party, John's political influence extended from Cedarville to Springfield and ultimately to Washington, D.C. Although John seemed to have lacked his friend Lincoln's enthusiasm for politics, he shared the latter's political moderation and commitment to free, proprietary capitalism. If John Addams's ties to corporate railroad, banking, and real estate ventures seem paradoxical in light of such commitments, they do so only in hindsight. By buying land on the Western frontier and connecting it to Eastern markets via the railway, John likely imagined himself to be promoting not only his family's interest but also the opportunity of like-minded entrepreneurs.[18]

John Addams resembled the sixteenth president of the United States in another way, sharing what political theorist John Schaar describes as Lincoln's "covenanted patriotism"—his sense of "America" as a "nation formed by a covenant, by a dedication to a set of principles and by an exchange of promises to uphold and advance certain commitments among ourselves and the world." Having ascended to political preeminence in a border state, it is difficult to say whether Lincoln would have one day incorporated African Americans within the mantle of his covenanted patriotism. By contrast, unburdened by state and national political aspiration, John Addams made plain his sympathy for racial equality. Moreover, this son of Pennsylvania Quakers would extend his principles overseas. Recalling her father's solemnity at the death of Mazzini, Jane remembers his "sense of the genuine relationship which may exist between men who share large hopes and like desires, even though they differ in nationality, language, and creed; that those things count for absolutely nothing between groups of men who are trying to abolish slavery in America or to throw off Hapsburg oppression in Italy."[19]

It would be left to W. E. B. Du Bois, among his family members, to trace back bloodlines to Europe and Africa, and to connect his aspirations to European and African literary and cultural traditions. The world of his parents was more circumscribed than the worlds of Daniel and Marguerite Debs and John and Sarah Addams—Alfred's by a debilitating anomie that combined with caste barriers to prevent him from establishing firm ties, Mary's by caste and family strictures that thwarted a sense of personal agency. Like Alfred, Mary seems to have spent the years of her early adulthood roving the Hudson River valley in an effort to realize ill-defined yearnings. As a single black woman obviously lacking the expertise and legacy that accompanied the young John Addamses into the world, Mary exercised one of the few forms of autonomy available to an individual of her rank: her sexuality. But the son produced by the first of her ill-fated unions only increased her dependence, catapulting her back into the lap of her deeply moralistic and undoubtedly disapproving family. Unable to find security and satisfaction as young adults, Alfred Du Bois and Mary Burghardt must have regarded the world as a disorienting if not dangerous place.[20]

BEGINNINGS

If Eugene Debs looked back on the Terre Haute of his youth with a certain wistfulness, he did so with reason. By the time he was five, his parents' store had taken hold and it occupied a large building in the heart of Terre Haute's commercial district. With the profits from their growing enterprise, the Debses erected a generous new home on two large lots in the center of town. Although the outbreak of Civil War nearly split Terre Haute, Indiana remained in the union, and the war proved a boon to Daniel's grocery. Before too long Daniel found Terre Haute's richest men walking through his doors, making him something of a celebrity in the eyes of an adoring son. Despite having abandoned his own father's butchery, Daniel seems to have expected Eugene to settle down at home in an enterprise similar to his own. Eugene accompanied his father to work, and his father exploited connections made over his counter to land his son jobs in the companies of Terre Haute's leading businessmen. The eldest of the Debs boys, Eugene was the obvious favorite. The sparkle that would make him popular among labor and socialist audiences emerged in childhood—as did his leadership and organizational ability, honed in the management of his siblings.[21]

Although comfortable in the public life of Terre Haute, the Debs family developed a reputation for clannishness, its six children and two adults constituting its own community. Eugene remembers enjoying Sunday evenings at home best, at which time the family would circle round to hear Daniel read excerpts from his beloved philosophes and German poets. How much of Eugene's future radicalism sprung from this early introduction to Rousseau, Voltaire, Dumas, Eugene Sue, Victor Hugo, and Goethe is difficult to know; but, as Nick Salvatore observes, there is no denying the potential clash between these writers' liberalism and idealism and the habits of deference and obedience inculcated in Terre Haute's youngsters by the city's civic and religious institutions. Daniel seems to have turned to these authors more to justify the course of his life than to preside over the explications de texte that the young John Stuart Mill endured at his father's knee. The paradox of pairing Rousseau and Voltaire or Goethe and Hugo evidently escaped the untutored butcher. Moreover, the life Daniel and Marguerite Debs *lived* was hardly radical. The lasting influence of these Sunday sessions is likely to have derived more from their confraternity than from their content, the children's early exposure to literature providing one cornerstone of their future autonomy: the freedom to read.[22]

In her autobiography, Jane Addams portrays her childhood as having consisted of a combination of youthful frolicking and gloomy meditation on the subject of death. Death she knew intimately, starting at age two when her mother Sarah unexpectedly fell ill and died. Her eldest sister died when Jane was six, her father when she was twenty-one. When Jane was eight her father remarried, further complicating an already disjointed life. Jane herself only narrowly eluded death from tuberculosis as a young child; she did not escape the ravages of scoliosis, however, which left her spine permanently hunched and her psyche vulnerable to episodes of pain-induced neurasthenic depression. Whether these more-than-usual vicissitudes inspired Jane's precocious interest in questions of ontology and metaphysics, we cannot be sure; but they seem cause enough. Her closest associate during childhood was her father, John, whose legendary magnanimity and self-possession awed her, but whose reticence could not have provided much solace for a daughter predisposed by fate and temperament to curiosity.[23]

The upheaval within her family notwithstanding, Jane's life eventually attained a degree of stability. John Addams's economic success and social connections created a safety net capable of cushioning the overt impact of his family's private woes. Jane's earliest memories describe her attempts to measure up to her father's achievements. Learning that he had worked his way through his town library as a boy, Jane essayed the same feat, reading the tomes of Western literature at a ludicrously young age. Aware of her father's reputation for unimpeachable honesty, Jane trembled with fear upon harboring even the most minuscule "lie" in her chest. As a young woman she displayed her father's reverence for literature and developed a reputation for straight talk of her own; mercifully, a playmate in the form of a stepbrother arrived before she had appropriated the whole of her father's gravity. In 1868, John Addams married a local widow, Anna Haldeman, whose two boys, opulent lifestyle, and sophisticated artistic and literary taste turned the Addams family upside down. After John's death and his daughter's founding of Hull-House, Jane and Anna's relationship soured so badly that Jane omitted all mention of Anna from her autobiography. But no evidence of early friction between them exists in the memoirs of Jane's siblings. Jane welcomed the companionship of her new brother, George Haldeman; and having an adult around to conduct domestic affairs freed Jane to romp like the child she was through the fields and streams on her father's property. Like the disparity between Jane's early pain and her present comfort, the discrepancy between her desire to live up to her father's reputation and her stepmother's traditional idea about women's roles would demand a reckoning, but one whose character was barely visible as Jane prepared herself for "college."[24]

In his several autobiographies, written over a span of some sixty years, W. E. B. Du Bois described his childhood as happy, making one wonder whether, by the turn of the twentieth century, a "happy childhood" had replaced the "log cabin" as the emblem of credibility in American politics and culture. Where Daniel and Marguerite Debs could have interpreted Eugene Debs's arrival on earth as a symbol of their increasing fortune, for Alfred and Mary Burghardt Du Bois, the significance of William's coming must have seemed opaque. Alfred's imminent departure dispelled any ambiguity, however: Mary would have to beseech her family for support at the very moment when the Burghardt farms were slipping toward the margin of subsistence. If William's early years were as benign as he remembered them, it is a testament to his mother's strength and success at sheltering him from her family's immiseration.[25]

The Union victory in the Civil War liberated four million slaves, but for the black Burghardts of Great Barrington, Massachusetts, the deflationary effect of the armistice together with the cheap produce arriving from out of state made the Reconstruction era anything but a time of celebration. Mary's father died insolvent when William was five, signaling a gradual decline in Burghardt family fortunes. A generation earlier, the Burghardts's private safety net might have incorporated Mary and her illegitimate sons, but by the mid-1870s that net had so unraveled that Mary found herself absorbing her increasingly dependent family. When her mother died, Mary and William's luck declined still further, pushing them to the brink of destitution and into a ramshackle apartment at the center of Great Barrington's saloon district. After a stroke left Mary partially paralyzed, William had no choice but to step up, and from the age of seven until he departed Great Barrington at age seventeen, he worked assiduously at odd jobs to help support the family. One wonders what William's future would have brought had the Burghardt fortunes been different during this era. Exigency demanded that William and his mother assert their threadbare autonomy. Although no amount of striving on William's part would likely have sprung him from the cycle of subsistence, his dogged work in town and at school impressed those white townsfolk with the penchant to notice, making him a candidate for their later assistance.[26]

Eugene Debs appears to have enjoyed as much prestige among his peers as among his siblings. When Eugene reached school age, his father registered him in the private school attended by the children of the city's elite, rather than enrolling him in Terre Haute's new public school, whose solvency Daniel distrusted. Having grown up in a literary household, Eugene proved an able and diligent pupil, popular with teachers and students alike. But at age fourteen, after one year of high school, Eugene withdrew himself from school against the protest of his parents. Tired of recounting by rote the actions of other men, he yearned for achievements of his own, and ended up pursuing his early dreams to a job on the railroad as a paint scraper. By leaving school prematurely, Eugene did not foreclose future economic opportunity. In the years just after the Civil War, the railroad offered a natural avenue for advancement. Railroad work paid well, commanded respect, and held out the opportunity for travel. If Daniel and Marguerite were disappointed by his son's decision, Eugene's friends knew his future to be full of promise. They expected Eugene to ascend to the top of Terre Haute's social hierarchy or even "step into a Master Mechanics job" on the railroad.[27]

Growing up in Terre Haute during the 1860s and 1870s, Eugene absorbed the city's entrepreneurial ethos, which imbued the ideals of manhood and community with a decidedly liberal bent. To be a "man" meant being financially independent and able to shoulder the responsibility of providing for one's family. To achieve and maintain financial independence, in turn, required developing the characteristics derived from work: industry, honesty, and respect for self and others. The shared commitment to these virtues fostered ideals of "citizenship" and "community" that nonetheless betrayed hierarchical assumptions. Citizens would defer to the authority of business and political leaders with the expectation that they might one day find themselves in leadership positions. Between the city's leaders and citizenry there was thought to exist a harmony of interests; mutually dependent on one another, citizens would eschew activity that compromised one another's autonomy. Designed to ensure stability and order, this ethos could serve paradoxically as a source of radical critique, as Salvatore observes. When corporate imperatives began to erode the living wages of American workers toward the end of the nineteenth century, Debs exploited the perceived connection between the community-based ideal of harmony and "American principles" to brush corporate magnates with the epithet of "treason."[28]

Had John Addams not died in 1881, his railroad, banking, and real-estate investments seem destined to have made him a robber baron from the perspective of Debsian socialism. But Jane Addams remembers the relationship between John and his workers and herself and her peers to have been one of fundamental equality. John labored alongside his mill hands; at school, Jane shared her books indiscriminately; in the Addams household, the servant girls participated in the nightly readings. Cedarville, Illinois, remains a small town to this day. In Jane's day, it was buffeted by few of the forces that upset the equilibrium of William's Great Barrington and would shatter the harmony of Eugene's Terre Haute. One has to look hard for evidence connecting Cedarville to Hull-House. Perhaps their connection lies in their extreme difference: rural, Protestant, comfortable, conservative, Cedarville offered no opposition to a young woman destined only to find happiness in public service.

Meanwhile, W. E. B. Du Bois scrambled for his life. In *Souls of Black Folk,* he reports having been unaware of the stigma of his Negro race until the age of ten. But, as Lewis suggests, it is unlikely that it took a classmate's "peremptory" refusal of a "visiting-card" to teach such a precocious youngster the lessons of caste. Those lessons were everywhere apparent in the Great Barrington of his early youth. Great Barrington looked upon William with amazement: a devoted child, William's tenderness to his mother was remarkable; an able student, his intellect appeared unusual; a tireless worker, his industry seemed outstanding. For a child who more than anything wanted simply to belong, there was hardly a way for him to do so. Nevertheless, with the Burghardt safety net in tatters, public attention would be William's ticket to a richer world than his mother and father ever knew. But in order for William to escape Great Barrington one day, Mary Burghardt believed that she would have to put some space between him and the commotion of the saloon district, a feat she accomplished by moving her family of two into more comfortable quarters adjacent to the Congregational Church and atop a hill overlooking the Housatonic—their board evidently subsidized by the benevolent landlord. More than an act of practicality, Mary's relocation of William proved to have been prophetic, his new vantage point affording him the amplitude his intellect demanded.[29]

For the first time with a room of his own, William set up a veritable office. He still spent daylight hours in school and working at odd jobs to help support the family, but the nights now were his own, and he made the most of them. Color was not the only thing that distinguished William from his peers; he could out-spell, out-calculate, and out-read them, and he later identified his intellectual capacity as the source of his self-esteem. At age thirteen, William entered Great Barrington High School. Before long he was the coeditor of the school paper and had attracted the attention of the school's principal, Frank Hosmer, a benevolent New England Congregationalist who recognized that education would be the key to Negro salvation, but that that salvation should come in the South. At Hosmer's suggestion, William entered the high school's college preparatory track; prodded by Hosmer, William found the "library" upon which his intellectual growth depended on the shelves of a kindly bookseller. He made the store a second home. Aware of the significance of her son's intellectual gift, Mary Burghardt promoted his education in the only way she could, permitting him to invest his precious earnings in books. His first purchase was Macaulay's five-volume *History of England.*[30]

With his formal education behind him, Eugene Debs began his work on the railroad in 1869. Before labor audiences, Debs recalled having handed over part of his railroad earnings to his mother, as if his departure from school had been motivated by financial need. His brother Theodore remembered things differently, however, testifying that the family's life during this period was perfectly secure. Evidently, Eugene had inherited some of his father's restlessness; as an adult, he would never appear comfortable at home. Several months of paint scraping and sign making preceded three heady years as a railroad fireman, after which Eugene became a casualty of the nationwide credit crunch of 1873. The following year saw him pursuing odd railway jobs, finally to East St. Louis, Illinois, where he allegedly encountered poverty for the first time. "It makes a person's heart ache to go along some of the main sts. in the city and see men, women and children begging to eat," Eugene wrote the family, warning his siblings not to take their good fortune for granted. Fifty years ago, biographer Ray Ginger attributed Debs's eventual repudiation of corporate capitalism to his response to the depression of 1873; Salvatore wisely urges caution here. There is no evidence to suggest that the nineteen-year-old recognized the connection between the imperatives of outside investment and local rate and wage tables. Throughout his late teens and twenties, Eugene evinced no discomfort with the liberal interpretation of manhood and community that he had absorbed in his youth. Furthermore, by the end of 1874, his tenure on the railroad was over. Having despaired of the likelihood of finding consistent railroad work in the midst of the depression, he heeded his mother's call to return home, accepting a position as a clerk in the offices of Herman Hulman, Terre Haute's largest wholesaler.[31]

Besides causing insecurity on the railroad, the depression of 1873 highlighted the need for accountability in all sectors of the American economy, particularly in the railway industry. The ensuing drive for efficiency resulted in the consolidation of rail lines under the aegis of large corporations whose subsequent belt-tightening measures would reverberate all along the line. In the early seventies, the fortunes of Terre Haute's Vandalia railroad became wed to that of the great Pennsylvania conglomerate, a development that tested the ideal of employee-employer harmony for the first time. Debs's retreat from the outside world proved a temporary reprieve; by the time that corporate cost-cutting measures ignited the nationwide railroad strikes of 1877, there was no denying that the world had followed him home.[32]

Paradoxically, Debs's career as a labor organizer on the railroad began just after he had taken up his white-collar clerkship at Hulman's. Still sympathetic to the firemen, Debs dropped in on the organizational meeting of what became the local chapter of the Brotherhood of Locomotive Firemen, a new trade union concerned primarily with insurance and death benefits, and committed to harmonious labor-management relations. Over the course of the next ten years, Debs helped build the fledgling organization into a national bastion of labor conservatism, ultimately becoming one of its principal officers and the editor-in-chief of its official journal. When a few ranking BLFM officials supported the striking railroad workers in 1877, Debs rebuked them publicly, arguing that strikes violated the principle of harmony. Debs's rise in the BLFM paralleled a brief stint in local and state politics, during which his celebration of individual responsibility and collective harmony won him the bipartisan support of Terre Haute's wealthiest men. Although a leader of the BLFM, Debs evidently identified with the men at the top of Terre Haute society, maintaining a belief in America as a land of universal opportunity and unlimited progress. This perspective, in turn, led him to blame interruptions of industrial harmony on worker intransigence and lack of discipline, rather than on a fundamental tension between corporate and "community" interests.[33]

Having completed high school at age sixteen in 1876, Jane Addams left home for the first time, hoping to find solutions to the questions that her father could or would not answer. What was the significance of this life so full of death? How might her psychological anxiety be reconciled with her material comfort? How could she live a life worthy of her father within the gender constraints imposed by Victorian America? Jane had hoped to pursue these questions at Smith College, one of the few academic institutions that offered women of her generation a formal bachelor's degree. Her father insisted, however, that she attend nearby Rockford Seminary, a school whose curriculum reflected the era's uneasy compromise between traditional Christian and modern liberal values. If John Addams had thought that Rockford's religious emphasis would steady Jane's perceptible spiritual restiveness or steer her toward a life of wifely service and motherhood—as it had her elder sisters—he underestimated his daughter's independence.[34]

Jane's matriculation at Rockford only heightened her sense of the tension between religion and liberalism, and between science and the liberal arts. Seeking relief from her spiritual craving, Jane turned to the classics of Western civilization. Finding few answers in the Western canon, she was drawn to the promise science held out for certainty. But it was literature, history, and philosophy that finally caught Jane's interest, not science, and least of all religion—that is, not the institutional religion propagated at Rockford. Although Jane resisted Rockford's proselytizing, she spent long hours contemplating her relationship to God. Her yearning for religious assurance evoked the passion and zeal of an earlier day: "I don't know, of course, whether I have the correct idea or not," Jane wrote her friend and fellow seeker Ellen Gates Starr, "but what I call it is this . . . Comprehending your deity and being in harmony with his plans is to be saved. If you realize Christ or not, that isn't the point. If God had become nearer to you, more of reality through him, then you are a Christian. Christ's mission to you has been fulfilled." One wonders what would have become of Jane's religious skepticism had she grown up during an era in which faith, rather than material condition and social behavior, had been the distinguishing sign of "grace."[35]

But few late-nineteenth-century Americans commanded the religious vocabulary that might have guided Jane on her quest. Even her friend Ellen Gates Starr came by her belief in God spontaneously and thus proved to be of limited help in the end. There remained an alternative to the complacent and constraining religion celebrated at Rockford, however: the new Social Gospel, an impulse every bit as worldly as the reigning paradigm, but one suspicious of its parochialism and commitment to the political and cultural status quo. Over the remainder of her lifetime, Jane professed to maintaining a satisfactory religious faith—a sign that her religious meditation had lost its intimacy and urgency. As she came to put increasing credence in the emerging enterprise of sociology, her religious belief took on a temporal and political aspect more characteristic of Walter Raushenbusch than William James.

Once inured to the constraining influence of Rockford religion, Jane blossomed as a student and leader of her peers. The writing of Carlyle, Emerson, and Schiller enforced her spirit of independence and buoyed her resolve to make something unusual of her life. Jane's independence of mind, in turn, attracted the admiration of her adolescent peers and even a few young teachers, whose emotional intimacy and generosity appeared likewise wondrous to this emotion-starved teenager. Rockford's all-female setting proved to be ideal for Jane, and she rose to top positions in the literary society, on the staff of the school newspaper, and, ultimately, to the presidency of her class. Although her family life had been and would remain gloomy, the "America" that she had come to know in Cedarville and at Rockford appeared democratic and buoying. But in her view, Cedarville and Rockford represented "America" only partially, and the more impetus they provided Jane to do something significant, the harder she would collide with the political and cultural barriers of her age. Jane had scarcely become radical, from a contemporary perspective; she clung to a belief in feminine intuition and distinct gender roles for women. What set her apart was her resolve that women's authority over certain public and private matters qualified women to enter the political milieu as autonomous agents.[36]

W. E. B. Du Bois did not have to leave Great Barrington to experience the outside world. Thirteen years Debs's junior, by the time William entered high school in the early 1880s, outside forces had already unsettled

Great Barrington's social and economic order, and the "community" that had once sustained Mary Burghardt's family eroded. But for an opportunistic and ambitious youth like William, change could bring hope as well as hardship, and the very transportation revolution that imported cheap produce and crippled the Burghardt farms also introduced black Great Barrington to T. T. Fortune's *New York Globe,* a newspaper of African-American affairs. By age fifteen, William had become the *Globe's* Great Barrington distributor, and over the course of the next several years he authored some twenty articles and stories covering a disparate range of events in the lives of western Massachusetts' blacks. Lewis reports that the young correspondent already demonstrated the mature author's penchant for cajoling and sometimes "scolding" commentary, as William peppered his pieces with remarks about the absence of a black literary society or the desultory participation of African Americans in town politics. Along with an occasional column in the more widely read *Springfield Republican,* William's contributions to the *Globe* connected him to a world whose fortunes did not rise or fall with local vicissitudes—a world that seemed interested in hearing what William had to say.[37]

William's first independent foray outside Great Barrington occurred the summer between his junior and senior years in high school when he accepted an invitation to visit his paternal grandfather in New Bedford, Massachusetts. Of the many sights and people he met along the way, none affected him like his first encounter with the reticent yet noble progenitor of his own mysterious father. Although William would learn very little about his father, Alfred Du Bois, on this trip, he would long remember the "ceremony" and "breeding" of grandfather Alexander's black New Bedford circle, which for the first time provided him with a yardstick by which to measure the somewhat homely bearing of the familiar Burghardt clan. Not surprisingly, William's family allegiance began to shift with this visit, as his imagination accompanied his father's lineage backward to the seventeenth-century Huguenot Chretian Du Bois, "and ultimately," writes Lewis, to "the primordial Geoffroi Du Bois who sailed with William the Conqueror." Impressed by the splendor that surrounded Alexander and his wife, William was similarly dazzled upon encountering "ten thousand Negroes of every hue and bearing" at a British Emancipation Day festival on his way home. A fitting capstone to this journey, his introduction to the "whole gorgeous gamut of the American Negro world; the swaggering men, the beautiful girls, the laughter and gaiety, the unhampered self-expression" sustained William throughout his two remaining years in Great Barrington. As he rose to the top of his high school class, William could be confident that he was bound for college. Whispers had him going to Williams, or to one of the new black institutions in the Reconstruction South; having seen something of the New

England seaboard, William wanted to go to Harvard, but there were limits to what his Congregationalist patrons could or would accomplish.[38]

CHOOSING THE CAUSE

As a young legislator in the Indiana State Assembly, Eugene Debs supported bills designed to give women the right to vote. But as a potential suitor in his mid-twenties just hitting his stride as a union organizer, Debs adhered to the gender norms of his era. Like many late-nineteenth-century Americans, Debs viewed gender roles in polar terms, juxtaposing the rough-and-tumble masculine arena of work and politics to the innocent and elevating feminine realm of hearth and home. Even at his most radical, Debs would insist that his socialism was designed to safeguard the integrity of American households. Family roles and chore distribution in his parents' home appear to have been entirely traditional, although there is a story, surely apocryphal, that Eugene's mother secured the family's fortune by single-handedly launching the family grocery in the hard days of 1854. When Eugene began to think seriously about a lifetime companion, he would have thought himself lucky to find a woman as devoted and enterprising as his own mother.[39]

As it turns out, by marrying Katherine Metzel in June 1885, Eugene got something more and something less. On the one hand, Debs married up, proving that America was still a land of opportunity. An acquaintance of one of Debs's sisters, Kate hailed from Terre Haute's "second level of prominence." Kate's stepfather, John Baur, owned (among other property) the city's biggest drug store, and Kate grew up hobnobbing with the city elite. After Kate's stepsister married the son of a leading banker, one can imagine her family's surprise when Kate chose Eugene for a mate, but the Baur's initial reluctance yielded to grudging assent, evidenced by Kate's brothers' recruiting their new in-law into the family business. If the union of Eugene and Kate was ever happy, it did not remain so for long. The couple's inability to have children combined with Eugene's dawning radicalism and frequent absences from home rendered their marriage formal and distant. Kate's persistent effort to make her home a showpiece despite her husband's meager income contrasted markedly with Eugene's family's increasing participation in and support of his labor work. Kate might have suited the Eugene of his twenties, so enamored had he been of appearance and social position; but on the cusp of thirty in June 1885, Eugene had begun to question his underlying paternalism, as the external forces preventing lowly workers from rising became increasingly hard to ignore.[40]

So cryptic was Jane Addams about her childhood that it is difficult to know what sparked her desire to go to Smith College at the end of her high school career. Was it merely Smith's promise of a formal liberal arts curriculum capped by a bachelor's degree? Or was she already developing a sense of the conflict between family claims and personal ambition that would characterize her twenties? By enrolling Jane at Rockford, John Addams kept his daughter close to home, but in a school conflicted about how to reconcile its liberal curriculum with its mandate to train missionaries and housewives. Jane's four years at Rockford exhilarated her at times but resolved nothing about her vocation, and Jane picked up at age twenty where she had left off at sixteen, hoping to spend the next year at Smith in order to earn the coveted degree. Home from Rockford in the summer of 1881, Jane suffered her first neurasthenic breakdown. Although the assassination in July of President James Garfield by the brother of one of her closest Rockford friends along with her father's unexpected death in August devastated her, those events appear to have exacerbated rather than caused her emotional collapse.[41]

Historian Allen Davis disputes Christopher Lasch's argument that Jane's guilt-ridden reaction to the "family claim" precipitated her illness and ultimately the founding of Hull-House, but the evidence supports Lasch. Once again, the senior Addamses opposed Jane's going to Smith; although a year at Smith would have merely postponed Jane's final reckoning with the conflict between her personal ambition and parental and cultural expectations, the promise of that year had nonetheless provided her with a sense of direction. Having lost her direction and her principal role model the same summer, Jane stood face to face with her stepmother, a woman toward whom she felt a sense of responsibility and even—as a child—a certain affection, but one whose cultivated, feminine lifestyle warred with Jane's early determination to do something "significant." After hurriedly and, one thinks, inadequately mourning the death of her father, Jane enrolled at the Women's Medical School of Philadelphia in the fall of 1881, where she performed passably for one semester before suffering another breakdown. A brief stay in a Philadelphia sanitarium did little to identify the roots of Jane's nervous disorder, but by April she was well enough to travel, whereupon she returned to Cedarville and into the lap of a family whose demands would nearly prove her undoing.[42]

W. E. B. Du Bois's mother died of a stroke in the spring of 1885, releasing him from all overt claims of family. Lewis observes that William's mother's death relieved him from having to make the unpleasant decision about whether to desert her or sacrifice the promise of a college education. After encountering his noble grandfather in New Bedford, William appears to have harbored some resentment toward his mother, as if holding her responsible for his father's abandonment of the family. But no evidence suggests that William, just turned seventeen, possessed the confidence or coldheartedness to walk out on Mary Burghardt. Later in life he would praise the Burghardt women's devotion to their men, recognizing that it entailed "the sacrifice of [their] intelligence and the chance to do their best work." Whatever were his feelings for his ailing mother, William remembered experiencing a "choking gladness and the solemn feel of wings" at the end of her suffering. "One more obstacle to Harvard College had fallen," Lewis remarks. "Finally, he was free to begin defining himself."[43]

As Eugene Debs entered his thirties in 1885, he began to rethink the meaning of labor-management harmony. Over the preceding eleven years he had witnessed the merger movement spread from the railroad to the banking, steel, and utility industries, eroding competition within the American economy and subjecting local workers to the will of distant corporate boards. Where once Debs ascribed to an ideal of "harmony" that compelled workers to defer to authorities entrusted to subserve a common good, by the late 1880s the notion of a "community of interests" had come to seem hollow. Talk of worker discipline and deference seemed out of place in an era of corporate absolutism, and with increasing frequency Debs invoked the more militant imagery of America's Protestant and Revolutionary past. This is not to say that Debs had become a radical overnight. He still believed that workers and owners could resolve their grievances; thus he remained wary of divisive measures like boycotts and strikes. But the more he imagined himself perpetuating America's Revolutionary tradition, the more Justice, Honesty, and Fair Play became his bywords, and the closer he came to conceding that some strikes were justifiable.[44]

An evolving sense of the conflict of interest between "the people" and "the corporations" did not lead Debs to renounce his old friends among the Terre Haute "community." His marriage to Katherine Metzel only increased his family's ties to the city's commercial and industrial elite, and throughout his socialist career Debs steadfastly invoked these friendships to deflect criticisms that he was anti-American. Naturally, he said less in public about his old associations after 1885, directing his concern about "harmony" to divisions within the labor movement itself. The issue of whether strikes and boycotts were an acceptable way to address workers' grievances was one of many questions confronting labor at the end of the nineteenth century. Should workers organize according to their trade, according to their industry, or according to their station as "laborers"? Should the goal of workers be merely to secure shorter hours, better wages, and safer working conditions, or should workers aim higher, and strive to ensure that the American economy remained fluid and the avenue for mobility out of the laboring class open? Should workers press their aims politically, and, if so, within the established parties or from a new political party of their own? When Debs joined the Brotherhood of Locomotive Firemen as a nineteen-year-old in 1874, the

BLFM was a paternalistic trade organization resolutely opposed to strikes and concerned primarily with providing firemen and their families with injury and death benefits. A decade later, as American workers became locked into permanent positions as wage laborers and corporate managers allied to government officials denied the right of workers to organize, Debs began to doubt whether coordinating workers by trade was the most effective way to counter the corporate juggernaut. Gradually, he recognized that the incorporation of industry demanded a similar consolidation of labor. Thus, over the next decade, he evolved from a conservative trade unionist to a proponent of a confederation of trade unions, then finally to an advocate of industrial unionism. Along the way, he stepped on many toes and made many enemies, thus demonstrating just how far the American labor movement was from constituting anything resembling a "community."[45]

Cedarville, Illinois, must not have seemed like much of a "community" to Jane Addams upon her arrival home from Philadelphia in the spring of 1882. Although seldom frivolous or jocular, John Addams had imbued his household with a palpable vitality that it could not sustain after his death. When the neighbors, townsfolk, and statesmen who had once courted John's counsel stopped calling at the Addams residence, Anna Haldeman Addams, Jane's stepmother, lost her raison d'être as elegant and cosmopolitan host, just as Jane herself had lost her rudder. To complicate matters, shortly after she returned to Cedarville, Jane's stepbrother and childhood playmate, George Haldeman, proposed to her. Jane's dismay at hurting one she loved so dearly was exacerbated by her stepmother's enduring bitterness at Jane's snubbing of her son. Paradoxically, it took the complete mental breakdown of Jane's brother, Weber, in the spring of 1883, to banish her lassitude. As she took control of the management of her father's estate, Jane's health recovered and her shame over her convalescence yielded to the fear that, by "becoming quite absorbed in business affairs," she would "lose all hold of the softer graces."[46]

By the fall of 1883, Jane's strength had improved sufficiently to allow her to accompany her stepmother and sister on a two-year grand tour of Europe. Best of all for Jane, two college friends along with her favorite college teacher swelled her party, allowing her to recover something of the sorority that had inspired her at Rockford and would one day energize her again. Although some enthusiasts claim to recognize the sources of Hull-House in Jane's encounter with Old World poverty on this trip, Allen Davis cautions that her letters and travelogue reflect more "curiosity than . . . indignation." Like other young women of her age and station, Jane viewed this journey as a supplement to her liberal arts education, abandoning herself to its living lessons with the enthusiasm of her college days. If at times throughout the tour Jane tired or lost interest, that seems natural considering the physical and emotional toll such travel exacts. In 1885, there was no Hull-House in the making.[47]

The year after W. E. B. Du Bois graduated from high school, he had worked to help raise money for his college tuition. His mother's death that March thrust him back into Great Barrington's black community for the last time. While living with his aunt Minerva, William met a worldly newcomer in town named J. Carlisle Dennis, the servant of a wealthy widow recently arrived from San Francisco. Perhaps because he recognized a bit of himself in William, J. Carlisle Dennis took a shining to the boy, trumpeting his intellect and industry in a letter to Fortune's *Globe* and landing him a lucrative job as a timekeeper on a local construction project. Dennis's attention buoyed William's spirit at a critical time, but for all the confidence William may have gleaned from their relationship, his final contact with Great Barrington's black community merely highlighted its limitations as a source of patronage. While "Willie Du Bois sat in a shed keeping time on the army of laborers at the 'fabulous wage' of a dollar a day," as David Lewis puts it, William's white patrons weighed whether to enroll him in a college in the North or South. Without Frank Hosmer and company, William might have remained a timekeeper for the rest of his life. Dependent on Hosmer for his ticket out of Great Barrington, William was disconcerted to learn that he had no say in the matter when Hosmer concluded that the best place for a Negro to be educated was where Negroes belonged. He was headed for Fisk University in Nashville, Tennessee. If disappointed, William did not let on; bidding his relatives adieu, he went off in search of life.[48]

As a young member of the Brotherhood of Locomotive Firemen, Eugene Debs believed that workers and employers shared a community of interests. The only thing distinguishing one from the other was a level of discipline, experience, and refinement. By 1885, having witnessed the corporate consolidation of the railroad industry, Debs began to doubt the existence of such a community, defending the plight of workers in increasingly strident terms. By 1890, Debs had grown wary of paternalism in all its forms, renouncing caste distinctions within the labor movement no less than in the economy at large. Spurred by corporate intransigence that denied recognition to even conservative labor voices and by internecine labor strife that impeded workers' efforts to defend themselves, Debs began to contemplate the potential of an industrial union. Such a union ideally suited his growing appreciation of America's Revolutionary heritage. The U.S. Constitution protected the right of workers to speak and associate freely, just as the Declaration of Independence legitimated their disaffection with labor organizations determined to keep them in their "place." By appropriating America's democratic tradition, Debs moved the issue of civic virtue to the foreground of "the labor question." Vital citizenship demanded independence; independence, in turn, required a living wage, a secure household, and the opportunity for mobility. By jeopardizing the independence, and thus the citizenship, of wage earners, corporate magnates proved themselves the enemies of American democracy. They were the real revolutionaries, Debs argued repeatedly; their boardroom machinations imperiled the republic.[49]

Armed with the rhetoric of the American Revolution, Debs summoned all railroad employees to the American Railway Union in the winter of 1893. He hoped that unanimity among railroad workers would induce corporations to recognize labor's right to bargain in good faith. Good faith was still very much Debs's objective at this time. His new emphasis on civic virtue had refocused rather than replaced his earlier interest in harmony. The ARU aimed to safeguard workers' "wages and their rights as employees," Debs explained. Once they received "fair wages" in exchange for "efficient service," he vowed, "harmonious relations" would abound "and the necessity for strike and lockout, boycott and blacklist" would vanish. Coming one year after the brutal labor strife at Homestead, Pennsylvania, and at Coeur d'Alene, Idaho, the emergence of the ARU could not have been more timely. Workers joined its ranks in numbers that surprised Debs and chagrined his rivals. But the rise of the ARU also coincided with yet another economic downturn, and as the depression of 1893 tightened its grip on the American economy, corporate and labor interests diverged once more. The ARU was barely a year old when wage reductions on the Union Pacific and Great Northern lines and at the Pullman company outside Chicago catapulted Debs and the ARU into national prominence in the spring and summer of 1894. As the newly consolidated railway workers squared off against the united General Managers Association during the Pullman strike, Debs's notion of "America" as the land of liberty and equality—of free speech and free association—came under close scrutiny. By the time the smoke cleared from Chicago streets in mid-July, Debs and his deputies in the ARU had been arrested, their vision of America soundly repudiated by a coalition of railroad owners and federal government officials who recognized no conflict between corporate and public interests.[50]

In the early days of the Pullman conflict, Jane Addams and fellow members of Chicago's Civic Federation had approached George Pullman with an offer to arbitrate the disagreement. Pullman's refusal to recognize the workers' right to protest their cut in pay inspired Addams to compare Pullman's intransigence toward his workforce to the stubbornness of Shakespeare's Lear. Addams's involvement in the Pullman strike contrasts sharply to her seeming indifference to the plight of workers in the 1880s before the founding of Hull-House. Shuttling back and forth to Europe between 1883 and 1888—

the period between trips spent caring for family or in solitary and frustrated study—she demonstrated no awareness of the upheaval gripping American industry. Though welcome distractions, her trips to Europe only exacerbated Addams's sense of "superfluity"; despite the excellent companionship of her first trip, she reported being unable to recover the sense of "necessity" that had characterized her Rockford days.[51]

Addams's family could make her feel needed, but their demands seemed cloying and did not elicit the sympathy that would animate her work at Hull-House. Home from her first European tour in the summer of 1885, she went to live with her older sister Mary, apparently repaying the nurturing that Mary had provided her when their mother died. A cloistered winter with her stepmother, now living in Baltimore, preceded a return to Mary's household the following spring, and with someone to lean on, Jane's family became increasingly dependent: Mary was pregnant, sister Alice was sick, snubbed stepbrother George Haldeman destined for an institution—all of which made Jane's stepmother, Anna Haldeman Addams, an increasingly unpleasant companion. But Jane's companion she remained, and as another winter in Baltimore followed another summer with Mary's family, Jane bobbed among alternating currents of responsibility, inadequacy, and guilt. How different were the responsibilities of the family claim from the social and political agency she had delineated in her commencement address at Rockford. A second tour of Europe interrupted the cycle of dependence, and sometime between departing for Europe in the fall of 1887 and arriving home a year later, she and Ellen Gates Starr hit upon the idea of founding a social settlement house in Chicago. Hull-House, as the settlement came to be named, proved to be the "ultimate solution" to Addams's two principal problems, forever freeing her from the family claim and providing her a "secular outlet . . . for energies essentially religious."[52]

In mid-June 1894, while Debs and Addams were embroiled in the Pullman controversy, W. E. B. Du Bois arrived home from two years' formal study abroad, completing what Lewis characterized as Du Bois's "ego learning decade." Ten years of education had rendered him one of the most learned African Americans in the land, and he returned to America with a newly inflated sense of the missionary zeal with which he had departed Great Barrington for Nashville in September 1885. Looking back on his arrival home from Europe many years later, Du Bois recalled that a certain foreboding accompanied his sense of optimism. The disenfranchisement, segregation, and lynching of Southern blacks that would make the 1890s notorious had already begun when Du Bois departed for Europe in the summer of 1892. No matter how vast his education, no matter how differently he viewed himself from the masses (black *and* white), white Americans would see only black when they saw Du Bois—a sharp contrast from the treatment to which he had grown accustomed during his two years abroad.[53]

In four years at Fisk University, Du Bois had left an indelible impression, his early shyness and wonder at black folkways having yielded to the public confidence and sense of personal destiny that characterized his adult life. Du Bois participated fully in the Fisk community, but, predictably, he made his mark there as a writer for the Fisk *Herald,* whose editorial page charged students to take seriously their role as elite representatives of a largely illiterate and outcast black population. In letters home, Du Bois reported relief at living among a black majority for the first time—one that did not "despise" his color—and he began to develop a zealous faith in his race. Du Bois embraced his black identity in an extraordinarily self-conscious and deliberate manner, as if it were a mantle that he could adopt or remove at will. E. Franklin Frazier believed that Du Bois's racial "ambivalence endowed him with a resilient superiority complex," one that "convinced [him] . . . that his lifelong espousal of the 'Darker World' was an optional commitment based above all upon principles and reason." This level of abstraction allowed Du Bois to identify with other "ego"-transformations, including that of Bismarck's Germany, which was the subject of Du Bois's valedictory address. Having forged a nation "out of bickering peoples," the Iron Chancellor won Du Bois's enduring admiration; he may very well have imagined himself playing a role similar to Bismarck's among fellow African Americans.[54]

In reward for finishing at the top of his class, Du Bois won a partial scholarship for graduate work at Harvard University. Three years of Harvard philosophy, history, and economics mellowed Du Bois's authoritarian leanings, but only a little. Although he proved vulnerable to the spell of William James, he demonstrated more intellectual affinity for the idealism of Josiah Royce and "social evangelicalism" of Francis Peabody, whose tenets he propounded among Boston's African-American population. Socially, Du Bois clung to affluent black Boston; white Harvard's genteel ostracism left him indignant and bitter. Though in retrospect access to James, Peabody, and company seemed adequate recompense for his isolation, Du Bois's tenure at Harvard stands in stark contrast to the sense of belonging he felt first in Nashville, and later in Berlin.[55]

DEMOCRACY AS ASSOCIATED LEARNING

In the laissez-faire world of late-nineteenth-century America, Debs, Addams, and Du Bois could have been excused for turning their personal gifts to private gain. But as young adults they proved incapable of separating their own experiences, their triumphs and tribulations, from the world around them. They were not saints. Their callings stoked their egos and slaked their appetites for public acclaim. No doubt the overlap between their immense ambitions and their sense of responsibility helps explain their remarkable careers. They made no pretense to selflessness, always acknowledging that they got at least as good as they gave.

This chapter explores the cosmopolitans' patriotic critique of American social and political conditions that the previous discussion saw just beginning to emerge. Their youthful encounters with the American Dream shaped the cosmopolitan patriots indelibly. Awed by his parents' immigrant experience, Debs committed his adult life to restoring conditions favorable to economic and social mobility, just as Jane Addams worked to extend the opportunity her parents enjoyed to groups and individuals marginalized by Victorian social and cultural constraints. W. E. B. Du Bois's upbringing bequeathed a different legacy but to similar effect: never having experienced genuine community or autonomy, Mary Burghardt welcomed her son's embrace of the life of the mind. In books, Du Bois discovered the "community" that his parents never knew—one that transcended caste proscription and provided welcome solace. With books as his armor, he set out to raze the edifice of caste.

The cosmopolitan patriots would prove their loyalty to American society by holding it to its highest ideals. Growing up, Debs, Addams, and Du

Bois discovered both the importance and fragility of the moral and material independence that the Founding Fathers knew to be the sine qua non of individual and collective well-being. At one extreme, urban masses surrendered their autonomy to industrial managers and city bosses in exchange for subsistence wages and personal favors; at the other extreme, industrial managers and government officials combined to bolster corporate profits and safeguard political power. In between, many Americans adopted the catch-as-catch-can mentality of mass consumer culture, navigating solitary paths to personal satisfaction. The result was an unmistakable erosion of civic consciousness and a corresponding constriction of the public sphere.[1] In pursuit of self-interest, citizens suspended their commitment to equal opportunity, equality before the law, and government by consent—the common principles that ostensibly bound the American people together.

In order to restore the independence of American citizens and thereby rescue the foundering republic, Debs, Addams, and Du Bois proposed to extend democracy from the political to the social realm. Laissez-faire liberals believed that political democracy and free-market capitalism were sufficient agents of liberty in a society of natural abundance. The cosmopolitan patriots learned firsthand that unfettered capitalism produced outcomes not always attributable to virtue. Freedom required positive as well as negative protection. But convincing American citizens to take positive steps to promote their fellows' liberty would prove difficult in a society nurtured on the tenets of individualism and stratified by distinctions of class, gender, and race. Debs, Addams, and Du Bois insisted that by socializing democracy they were merely completing the unfinished work of the American Revolution. Their many critics accused them of upsetting the natural order, emasculating citizenship, and fostering contempt for American institutions. Thus was joined a fight for what Du Bois characterized "the soul of American democracy," one whose outcome would influence not only local and national politics but American foreign policy as well.

In analyzing cosmopolitan patriotism at the local level, this chapter draws on John Dewey's *Democracy and Education* (1916) to provide an interpretive framework. The product of two decades' meditation on the problem of education for democratic citizenship, *Democracy and Education* reflects Dewey's bedrock assumption that the fate of the republic depended on the vitality of the nation's democratic institutions. From Dewey's perspective, democratic politics was not, ideally, a contest for influence, but an attempt to establish social solidarity and public consensus via open deliberation. A friend and colleague of Addams and an occasional associate of Du Bois, Dewey shared their conviction that the proper object of patriotic loyalty was not the American nation-state, but the ideal of democratic social reciprocity, for which the nation-state was a vehicle.[2]

Dewey's ideal of "democratic citizenship" contrasts markedly to three models of citizenship prevalent in his day: a "republican" ideal rooted in the work of Jean-Jacques Rousseau, a "pluralist" ideal articulated at the turn of the twentieth century by, among others, Horace Kallen, and an "organic" tradition derived from German romanticism. Both republican and pluralist theorists prized autonomy, self-discipline, flexibility, and compromise, but they applied these virtues toward different political ends. Where Rousseau believed that individual happiness and social and intellectual development derived from the citizen's participation in politics, Kallen argued that the private realm nourished the individual's deeper, truer self. Rousseau's citizen entered politics to promote a common good, Kallen's to safeguard the integrity of his or her particular community or cultural group. Sound in theory, both republicanism and pluralism proved problematic in practice: apotheosizing the common good, republicans persecuted cultural minorities and stifled individual dissent, while pluralists, exalting private over public interests, ignored the ways local communities inhibit individual autonomy.[3]

These republican and liberal paradigms vied for public favor with the "organic" tradition of citizenship repudiated by William James. In place of republican autonomy and liberal self-reliance, as we have seen, organic theorists celebrated obedience, loyalty, and self-sacrifice as primary virtues. Subordinating the individual will to the welfare of the state, they insisted that the individual realized his or her particular destiny only through the nation. Organic theorists rejected Locke's notion of contractual government, arguing that the state was not something one joined but an irrevocable allegiance into which one was born. Like late-nineteenth-century Anglo-Saxon nativism, organic nationalism appealed to men like Theodore Roosevelt and Henry Cabot Lodge, who feared both the dissolution of their once-proud Anglo-Saxon culture and the erosion of Americans' "capacity for loyalty," and who therefore embraced organic nationalism's abstract virtues to restore order to an increasingly disorienting world.[4]

These three models of citizenship provided the political backdrop against which the cosmopolitan patriots developed their own theories of democratic citizenship. I identify these traditions not to suggest that either republicanism or pluralism, much less organic nationalism, existed in "pure" form in America at the turn of the twentieth century. Rather, I use these distinctions because they help us decipher turn-of-the-century political discourse. Some historians argue that scholars exaggerate the prevalence of republican ideology in the workers' movements of the nineteenth century. Republicanism, the argument goes, is an instrument by which left-leaning academics smuggle communitarian principles into the American political tradition. We are told that the persistence of republican rhetoric does not necessarily denote the existence of republicanism; from time immemorial, individuals and organizations have cloaked private interest in public rhetoric. Insofar as this criticism promotes self-reflection among historians and acuity about the uses of rhetoric, its effect will have been bracing; but insofar as it blinds historians to counterliberal strains in the American political tradition, it will have performed a disservice. While it is true that language has the power to couch and conceal, it is no less true that people often mean what they say. Historians need to resist the temptation to view rhetoric merely as ideological cover.[5]

As the leading Socialist propagandist of his generation, Eugene Debs employed a Socialist rhetoric imbued at times with republicanism, pluralism, and organic nationalism—and sometimes with all three at once. In certain contexts, Jane Addams's and W. E. B. Du Bois's democratic rubric resembled Rousseau's; in other contexts, it more nearly recalled Horace Kallen's. Surely, upon occasion, the cosmopolitan patriots exploited the currency of republicanism for political gain; but just as assuredly, in other situations, their republican language reflected their own and their constituents' sincere desires. What's in a name? By labeling the cosmopolitan patriots' critiques of American democracy "republican," I want to highlight their emphasis on a common good, their commitment to communally derived, impersonal standards of achievement, and their appreciation that vitality lay not in pursuit of luxury and leisure, but in the open-ended pursuit of excellence and in safeguarding individual autonomy. I make no claim about the pervasiveness of republicanism at the turn of the twentieth century; on the contrary, I argue that Dewey, Debs, Addams, and Du Bois invoked a republican ethic to counter their era's rampant individualism. Theirs was not the martial, patriarchal republicanism of Machiavelli, nor the paternalist, Revolutionary-era republicanism of John Adams. Rather, theirs was a modern republicanism drawn from the old but at once representative and critical of its own age.

DEMOCRACY AND CITIZENSHIP

In *Democracy and Education,* John Dewey proposed two criteria by which any social group could be evaluated: "How numerous and varied are the interests which are consciously shared? How full and free is the interplay with other forms of association?" The more interests the members of a society shared, and the freer that society's association with other groups, the more nearly it approximated Dewey's democratic ideal. Dewey regarded democracy as more than a political system of governing institutions and procedures; democracy was "primarily a mode of associated living," as he put it, "of conjoint communicated experience." In order to highlight the importance of education in Dewey's democratic theory, it may be useful to amend his notion of democracy slightly—to think of "associated living" as associated *learning,* a constant and boundless exchange of experience and ideas.[6]

Dewey distinguished his vision of democracy from other forms of social organization by comparing the values of a criminal gang to the ethos of an ideal democratic family. Criminal gangs manifest "something of the praiseworthy qualities" that bind society together, Dewey admitted. "There is honor among thieves, and a band of robbers has a common interest as respects its members (DAE, 82)." But measured against the imperative of associated learning, life in a criminal band proved stultifying. The ties that "consciously hold the members together are few in number," Dewey averred, and are "reducible almost to a common interest in plunder"; moreover, a gang's predations naturally alienated "other groups with respect to give and take of the values of life." By clinging steadfastly to a unitary, or tribal, code of ethics, and thereby arbitrarily restricting its intercourse with the rest of society, Dewey's "criminal band"—like contemporary urban gangs and rural militias—foreclosed the opportunity for genuine individual and group development (DAE, 83).

Where the gang's parochialism impeded associated learning, a commitment to democracy propelled individuals and groups into a vast but organic web of instructive relationships. "If we take . . . the kind of family life which illustrates the standard [of associated learning]," Dewey wrote, "we find that there are material, intellectual, aesthetic interests in which all participate and that the progress of one member has worth for the experience of other members—it is readily communicable—and that the family is not an isolated whole but enters intimately into" civic, cultural, and economic relationships. The antithesis of gang morality, Dewey's democratic ideal also differed from Kallen's pluralism and the organic nationalism of Francis Lieber. Unlike Kallen's citizen, who *enters* politics deliberately and occasionally to defend private rights—to "protect his protection," as Hobbes put it—Dewey's democrat *resides* in a political realm consisting of overlapping affiliations. In Dewey's democracy, the individual's political participation promotes the welfare of society, and vice versa. Unlike Lieber's organic nationalist, who subordinates individual will to the national interest, Dewey's democrat views the nation as a means to the end of equal opportunity, equality before the law, and consensual government. From Dewey's perspective, organic nationalism betrayed the same limitation of the gang ethic: hiding behind their cultural bulwark, organic nationalists thwarted the exchange of ideas and experience that is the essence of education in a democracy (DAE, 83).[7]

Dewey's standard of democracy provides us with a tool for analyzing social developments. Insisting that the "progress" of one member of society must have "worth for the experience of other members," Dewey denounced the economic and social stratification of turn-of-the-century America. His concept of reciprocal worth would have consoled Tocqueville, who feared that America's emphasis on the equal value of individuals could too easily devolve into bland social conformity. Dewey argued that only if citizens valued one another equally regardless of social stature would they engage in the sort of transclass interaction that his "democracy" took for granted. Absent "a variety of shared interests," there could be no "free and equitable [social] intercourse," Dewey warned; "intellectual stimulation" could not help but become "unbalanced." By the turn of the twentieth century, the conditions for a truly catholic American discourse had disappeared. Despite the reluctance of early Puritans to associate wealth with grace, modern Americans had come to celebrate material accumulation as the measure of the good life. By exalting the rich, Americans could not help but stigmatize the poor, whose distinguishing characteristic became a lack of fortune. Although one could argue that the emerging gospel of wealth constituted a "shared interest," Dewey had in mind another sort of sharing. The problem lay in the new gospel's parsimony. Rather than encouraging Americans to accord equal value to every individual's contribution to society, it promoted the belief that to be American meant to subscribe to the tenets of materialism—just like everybody else (DAE, 84–5).

Contemporary politics treats rigid class distinctions primarily as a matter of economics: "liberals" would provide the poor an economic safety net, "conservatives" incentives for economic advancement. Dewey regarded turn-of-the-century America's economic and social stratification as a problem of culture: the greatest "gift" the wealthy could tender the poor would be to engage them in mutual discourse. It was not that Dewey failed to recognize the economic roots of social inequality; on the contrary, by highlighting the innate intellectual and cultural capacity of every individual, he hoped to make intellect and culture the measure of personhood, and thereby transcend America's invidious materialism. Dewey's vision exposed the cunning at the heart of the American Dream. He realized that everybody could not be rich, but he insisted that everybody be respected. Dewey believed that an appreciation for the different gifts of different classes would promote "balanced" and "diverse" intellectual stimulation, the "challenge of thought" that he knew to be the requisite of "novelty," or progress. Without such sympathy, there could be no progress. "The more activity is restricted to a few definite lines," he observed, "as it is when there are rigid class lines preventing adequate interplay of experiences—the more action tends to become routine on the part of the class at a disadvantage, and capricious, aimless, and explosive on the part of the class having the materially fortunate position" (DAE, 85).

Associating routinization with ignorance and ignorance with slavery, Dewey invoked Plato's definition of the slave—he who has ceded self-understanding to another—to expose the mind-numbing effect of industrial labor. With no understanding of the function of their work in the larger social organism, workers blindly followed the dictates of their employers, becoming little more than inanimate tools. Dewey called upon "science" to counter labor's immiseration. For Dewey "science" was not a process of mechanizing, or disciplining, industry, but rather a means to self-reflection, to providing workers with an awareness of their relation to industry as a whole in the expectation that such recognition would awaken their "intelligent interest." Dewey did not object to the division of labor or the rationalization of industry per se, only to the failure of self-styled efficiency experts to grasp the limitations of a "rationalized" labor force unable to think for itself. Although workers honed to "a very acute and intense intelligence in . . . narrow lines" might seem the embodiment of "efficiency," Dewey observed, in the long run, their "absence of mind" and the "corresponding distortion of emotional life" would incapacitate them as laborers and citizens alike (DAE, 85).

In pursuit of immediate profit, industrial managers sacrificed their own as well as their workers' long-term interests. Such was the fate of any group, Dewey maintained—whether nation, family, school, or class—whose egoism "shut it out from full interaction with other groups, so that its prevailing purpose is the protection of what it has got, instead of reorganization and progress through wider relationships." Arguing here for a transgroup discourse based on principles shared commonly, Dewey reiterated James's critique that America was becoming a nation characterized by interest-group politics. Though Dewey explicitly targeted the self-exile of the elite from the rest of society—with its ensuing "rigidity" and "institutionalizing of life"—his admonition applied equally to dispossessed individuals and groups striving to improve their social condition. "An alert and expanding mental life depends upon an enlarging range" of social contacts, he remarked. Though perhaps comforting from a psychological perspective, withdrawal into particularist enclaves seemed to Dewey a dubious strategy in an era characterized by inequalities of power and resources that threatened individual autonomy. To protect their wealth, the rich would have to share it; to attain their share, the poor would have to pursue it in a public discourse that all Americans could understand (DAE, 86).

Dewey recognized that democratic polities are bound to be particularly concerned about the education of their citizens. Traditionally, both republican and liberal theorists presumed the existence of an independent citizenry capable of promoting its enlightened self-interest. To be independent meant to possess both economic self-sufficiency and moral autonomy; only individuals unbeholden to others for wages or favors and possessing a spirit of voluntarism were deemed worthy of citizenship. Thus republicans and liberals prized industry, self-discipline, and thrift. But neither republicans nor liberals could adequately address the emerging class divisions and demographic upheaval of late-nineteenth-century America. Dewey's faith in progress and sense of mankind's "mutually interpenetrating" interests spawned virtues more attuned to the mounting diversity of turn-of-the-century America. Like traditional liberals and republicans, Dewey believed that the end of life was freedom, but he equated freedom with perpetual self-discovery, an open-ended ideal whose power lay in its pursuit (DAE, 87).

Dewey contended that democracy emerged historically not as the product of conscious human planning but as a result of "the command of science over natural energy." He warned that the dynamism that had initially pro-moted democracy would just as easily erode it if citizens could not respond efficiently to the constant social and technological change that democracy produced. Thus he delineated a philosophy of education designed to inculcate the virtues of "personal initiative and adaptability," and thereby prevent the "few" from preying on the "blind." History was rife with educational experi-ments, of course; in *Democracy and Education,* Dewey analyzed three histor-ical epochs whose recognition of the "social import of education" he found particularly instructive: Plato's Athens, Rousseau's France, and Hegel's Ger-many. These traditions served as the backdrop against which Dewey delin-eated his own model of a "democratic" education (DAE, 87–8).

From Plato, Dewey derived the conviction that justice depended on the ra-tional organization of a society in accordance with that society's end. Dewey applauded Plato's assertion that the business of education was to discover and promote the individual's natural aptitude. Like Dewey, Plato had ap-preciated that "social arrangements" exerted profound influence on edu-cation, and that education, in turn, could determine the future of the re-public. But Dewey criticized the ancient prejudice that led Plato to discount mankind's "incommensurability," or diversity, and thus reduce it to rigid cat-egories. And he rejected Plato's notion of transcendent principle, which, by denying the existence of evolutionary change—the good society would come by "happy accident" or not at all—rendered education virtually irrelevant (DAE, 88–91).

Although Rousseau's educational program seemed more palatable than Plato's to the democrat in Dewey, Rousseau's idealism violated the tenets of Dewey's pragmatism. On the one hand, Dewey sympathized with Rousseau's resolve to free individuals from constraints of rank and privilege; on the other hand, he resisted Rousseau's idealization of Nature as a realm distinct from everyday experience. Where the former promoted the idea of an autonomous individualism in tune with Dewey's commitment to cosmopolitanism and di-versity, the latter contradicted Dewey's fundamental belief in the social com-ponent of human existence. Like Plato's notion of ideal Truth, Rousseau's exaltation of Nature "negate[d] the very idea of education," according to Dewey. "Merely to leave everything to nature . . . was to trust to the acci-dents of circumstance. Not only was some method required but also some positive organ, some administrative agency for carrying on the process of instruction." Moreover, though putatively democratic, Rousseau's educational philosophy betrayed an elitism of its own; if Nature was distinct from daily life, then who got to define the aims of "Natural" education? (DAE, 106–7).

Germany first affixed the vision of "an enlightened and progressive humanity" to the "positive organ" of the state. Although the reactionary potential of national education was readily apparent by 1916, Dewey emphasized its liberal provenance in the response of the German princes to Napoleon: "The German states felt (and subsequent events demonstrate the correctness of the belief) that systematic attention to education was the best means of recovering and maintaining their political integrity and power." In the hostile world of nineteenth-century Europe, it did not take much to convince citizens that their freedom depended on their country's fate, and that their country's fate, conversely, required their own subordination. But as the good of the state began to eclipse personal development as the end of education, education became increasingly concerned with "social efficiency" and "disciplinary training" (DAE, 93–6). Where Kant had construed education as the gradual but infinite evolution of individual moral consciousness, and doubted the state's ability to promote a universal ideal, Fichte and Hegel regarded education as the method by which "egoistic" and "irrational" individuals subordinated their appetites to the nation (DAE, 96).

According to Dewey, then, Plato and Rousseau attenuated education by divorcing it from context, while Fichte and Hegel perverted it by reducing education to a handmaid of the state. Nowhere is the democratic implication of Dewey's pragmatism clearer than in his criticism of these historical educational philosophies. To be democratic, education had to be pragmatic; to be pragmatic, in turn, education had to reflect the input of society as a whole. Dewey argued that "the aim of education [wa]s to enable individuals to continue their education," an end that could only be realized in a society that prized "social reciprocity" and where every individual had a role in reconstructing the education curriculum. Dewey repudiated the notion of education as an instrument of social control. In his experience, curricula designed to effect some putative "higher" end outside the educational experience itself invariably belied inequitable social relations and served the "ulterior ends of others," rather than the interests of the students themselves (DAE, 100).

Notwithstanding their flaws, Plato's, Rousseau's, and Hegel's educational models underscored the tension between individual autonomy and technological advance that confronted would-be educators. On the one hand, science, commerce, and art propelled the universalist revolutions that dissolved aristocratic and monarchic privilege; on the other hand, they promoted new social distinctions that proved virtually as stifling. And while science, commerce, and art, like education, transcended national boundaries, they too depended on national sponsorship for their development. Was it possible, Dewey wondered, for education "to be conducted by a national state and yet the full social ends of the educative process not be restricted, constrained, or corrupted?" (DAE, 97).

Dewey believed that any educational theory that hoped to reconcile cosmopolitanism and nationalism would have to begin by establishing a clear notion "of the meaning of 'social' as a function and test of education." In a society in which economic disparity jeopardized the fundamental promise of equal opportunity, this meant that the state would have to do more than secure the negative safeguards that prevented "the exploitation of one class by another"; it would have to intercede positively on behalf of the less privileged by endowing good schools, providing financial support to the needy, and developing a curriculum relevant to modern industrial conditions. Only then could society expect students "to be masters of their own economic and social careers." It may be argued that Dewey's educational theory betrayed an idealism of its own. Its significance lies in Dewey's recognition that only a genuine democracy could promote its citizens' "natural aptitude." The state that pursued that objective, far from eroding the ideals of autonomy and self-reliance, perpetuated those virtues, thereby ensuring the vitality of democratic institutions (DAE, 97–8).

THE BREAKDOWN OF ASSOCIATED LEARNING

In sum, a genuine democracy promotes the self-realization of its constituents. The principle of self-realization mandates that nothing short of innate ability impede the individual's freedom to choose a path in life. Beside the customary "negative," or liberal, protections, freedom of choice requires "positive" safeguards to ensure that economic or social disparity does not thwart natural aptitude. Chief among these safeguards are schools dedicated to the proposition that the purpose of education is to enable individuals to continue their education, and a dynamic public sphere characterized by the reciprocal exchange of experience and ideas. Equating life with learning, a true democracy champions sharing and engagement as primary virtues, earning its citizens loyalty and devotion.

For committed democrats, the bane of democracy is a breakdown of the institution of reciprocal exchange, so that the influence of a single group or faction hinders the self-realization of others. Where Tocqueville, Mill, and Emerson feared the "dumbing down" of democratic society, Dewey and the cosmopolitans decried its numbing up—the development whereby the majority of Americans came to embrace commercial prosperity and consumption as the end of life. Dismay over turn-of-the-century America's materialism is a recurrent feature of the cosmopolitans' critique. And while it is true, of course, that anxiety about American "declension" has been and remains a pervasive characteristic of our cultural criticism, it would be a mistake to dismiss the cosmopolitans' concern as a mere political trope. Where late-twentieth-century cultural critics evince little awareness of the problem materialism poses for democracy, the cosmopolitans recognized, along with Dewey, that a culture that celebrates commercial prosperity as the end of life is unlikely to sustain the reciprocal exchange that constitutes associated learning.

According to Eugene Debs, the upheaval in Chicago during the summer of 1894 epitomized such a trend in social relations. Convicted of having violated a federal court injunction during the Pullman strike, Debs spent six months in jail the following year, during which he began to dabble in socialist and other radical literature. Pullman and its aftermath constituted a national coming out for Debs, and not just among workers disgruntled by the failure of conservative trade organizations to redress their underlying powerlessness and alienation. Coinciding with the rising tide of Populism, the emergence of Debs's radical industrial union (the American Railway Union) inspired consternation in the business and political community. In the several years after Pullman, Debs's speeches and writing resonated with republican rhetoric, though by about 1898, his republicanism became infused with the idiom of class consciousness. If class-conscious republicanism seems oxymoronic, it is not necessarily so. When the Progressive mayor of Toledo, Ohio, criticized the divisiveness of Debs's socialism, Debs rejoined that he too was all for harmony—but when confronted by a government "dominated by a class in its own selfish interest," he knew of no way to respond "except by party organization or violent revolution." In short, corporate capitalists had inaugurated class war; Debs would marshal the submerged classes to confront their oppressors in the interest of "all the people." [8]

By 1900, Debs had become a committed member of the new Socialist Party of America, serving as its presidential candidate in five of the next six federal elections. Throughout his tenure in socialism, Debs stuck to the role of propagandist, insisting that he was fitted neither by temperament nor taste for the office of the president. "If there were any chance of my election I wouldn't run," Debs quipped to journalist Lincoln Steffens. "The party wouldn't let me." Aware that socialism's success depended on workers developing "a common sense of common service, and a drilled-in capacity for mutual living and cooperative labor," Debs ran for president "to teach social consciousness and to ask men to sacrifice the present for the future." If orthodox party officials remained wary of Debs, their ambivalence likely stemmed from the fact that his thorough "Americanness" rendered him an imperfect Socialist at best. Salvatore's observation that Debsian socialism represented "the very fulfillment of the basic democratic promise of American life" is quite right, I think, and highlights the paradox of Debs serving as socialism's principal prophet. Whether in speeches or writing, when Debs hailed socialism as the consummation of America's democratic principles, he underscored that democracy rather than international socialism was to be the final arbiter of the nation's political institutions.[9]

Jane Addams viewed the corporate transformation of American capitalism with equal concern but different emphasis. Where Debs's sympathy for the downtrodden led him to accentuate corporate capitalism's debilitating effect on American workers, Addams insisted that the nation's economic polarization imperiled the nation as a whole. Once she recognized the link between her own situation—psychological turmoil and gender and generational constraints—and the social and economic polarization of Victorian America, Addams set out to address these problems collectively. If James and Dewey (along with Charles Sanders Peirce) were the founders of American pragmatism, Hull-House was pragmatism's first institution—the antidote to outworn Enlightenment ideals that circumscribed life in virtually every sector of American society. Addams always stressed the fundamental soundness of America's democratic principles, but she believed that they needed to be updated in order to retain their salience in twentieth-century life. In an attempt to reconcile democracy with the technological and commercial integration and social diversity that characterized the modern world, Addams exhorted young, educated, middle-class men and especially women to engage their learning in discovering and alleviating the causes of urban distress. Hull-House would serve as her laboratory, welcoming all seekers after truth; its only criterion of admission was a readiness to engage in associated learning.

In the summer of 1892, Addams regaled a convocation of the Ethical and Cultural Societies meeting in Plymouth, Massachusetts, with a description of the circumstances and vision that led to the establishment of Hull-House three years before. Describing Hull-House, Addams might well have been characterizing herself. In the understated prose that would become her signature, she remarked that Hull-House represented less an "association" than a meeting ground "opened by two women, backed by many friends, in the belief that the mere foothold of a house, easily accessible, ample in space, hospitable and tolerant in spirit, situated in the midst of the large foreign colonies which so easily isolate themselves in American cities, would be in itself a serviceable thing for Chicago." In language that anticipated *Democracy and Education* by twenty-five years, she emphasized that " Hull-House endeavors to make social intercourse express the growing sense of the economic unity of society. It is an effort to add the social function to democracy. It was opened on the theory that the dependence of classes on each other is reciprocal; and that as the social relation is essentially a reciprocal relation, it gave a form of expression that has particular value." Dewey could not have described democracy any better.[10]

As a highly educated but unemployed African American set ashore amid a climate of mounting racism, W. E. B. Du Bois experienced America's lack of reciprocity from the underside. Arriving home in the summer of 1894 from his studies in Germany, Du Bois evinced little awareness of the upheaval in which Debs, and to a lesser extent Addams, was embroiled. Self-preservation dictated that he land himself a job. In the fall of 1894, he joined the classics department of all-black Wilberforce University in Ohio. Though Du Bois's duties at Wilberforce kept him busy, he became increasingly bitter about his exclusion from the faculties of the nation's premier white colleges and universities. Nor did Wilberforce's petty political intrigue and patronizing cultural and intellectual climate endear Du Bois to his new surroundings; within a few months, he began to inquire about opportunities elsewhere. In the summer of 1896, Du Bois moved with his new wife, Nina Gomer Du Bois, to Philadelphia, accepting the unofficial and unadvertised position as staff sociologist at the University of Pennsylvania, where he would produce his magisterial analysis of black Philadelphia, *The Philadelphia Negro*. If Du Bois's sojourn at Wilberforce had accomplished anything besides affording him a meager living, it was in elevating his demand for political equality and social reciprocity to a fever pitch.[11]

Although Du Bois would one day despair over America's lack of racial reciprocity, at this point he clung to the notion that the fate of America was linked to the future of African Americans, and that the future of African Americans, in turn, would determine the destiny of the Negro race. He delivered this message in two early and cogent essays, "The Conservation of Races" and "Strivings of the Negro People." Both appeared in 1897, but only the latter, when reissued in 1903 as chapter 1 of *The Souls of Black Folk*, garnered widespread attention. These two essays are lucid statements of Du Bois's cosmopolitan patriotism. "Strivings" introduced Du Bois's potent imagery of the Veil and expressed his yearning "to be a co-worker in the kingdom of culture, to escape both death and isolation, and to husband and use his best powers." Meanwhile "Conservation" posed the "dilemma" that underlay that aspiration, and which has confronted members of every non-Anglo ethnic group who have had to weigh the cultural cost of pledging allegiance to American institutions: "What, after all am I?" Du Bois demanded. "Am I an American or am I a Negro? Can I be both? Or is it my duty to cease to be a Negro as soon as possible and be an American?" According to American principles and Dewey's tenet of reciprocal exchange, there could be but one answer to this query: race was irrelevant as a function of citizenship; cultural diversity was essential to national vitality.[12]

From his cell in Woodstock (Illinois) prison in the fall of 1895, Eugene Debs warned readers of the journal *Arena* that materialism robbed American principles of their promise. Where once America appeared before the world as the beacon of democracy, by the turn of the twentieth century, "love of money" had become the nation's distinguishing characteristic. Egoism and economic disparity yielded a population in which individuals viewed one another as impediments to personal prosperity. These alienated citizens could not help but remain ignorant of one another's motivations.

Such was the indelible lesson that Debs had learned at Pullman. Here was a company boasting an annual surplus of $25,000,000, according to its own published figures, but which had instituted three wage reductions in the year before the strike. Here was an industrialist who harbored a vision of a factory town that would meet all the needs of his employees while returning their wages to the company coffers. Here was a workforce that had witnessed its wages decline inexorably while rents remained steady, and that had petitioned its employer for redress only to be accused of disloyalty. Here, Debs declared, was despotism, a model of "benevolent feudalism" entirely out of touch with the ideals of liberty and justice. Deadening to the human will, such industrial relations imperiled the republic. "If multiplied thousands of working men are ground and crushed to an extent that they cannot educate their children," Debs warned, "what a change a few generations will produce."[13]

Debs could already detect the deterioration of the practice of reciprocal social exchange. When delegates of the Pullman employees approached company management with grievances in the late spring of 1894, no common bond existed between the two sides through which a settlement could be worked out. "Have I not been a father to you?" was the best George Pullman could muster, before firing the representatives for insubordination. At fault here, Debs recognized, was a social ethic that allowed so-called philanthropists to *love* their fellow citizens from on high without actually knowing them. Had George Pullman known his workers' plight firsthand, Debs suggested, the entire upheaval might have been avoided. But rather than investigating his employee's complaints, much less submitting them to "the American principle of arbitration," Pullman turned for support to an alliance of Chicago railway owners whose business and political influence extended to Washington, D.C. Violating his oath to preserve the public interest, the attorney general intervened in the dispute on behalf of railway friends and former colleagues, enjoining Debs from orchestrating the strike, while dispatching federal troops to Chicago over the protest of local government officials.[14]

Debs contended that the federal intervention represented private interest masquerading as public law. Law by injunction was law made by a single judge, responsible to no jury, and checked by no right of appeal to the U.S. Constitution. To Debs's mind, industry's appropriation of antitrust legislation symbolized the auctioning off of legal equality. While cracking down on restive workers and petty thieves, local, state, and federal authorities allowed white-collar criminals to buy their way to freedom. Like Du Bois, Debs worried that such a perversion of the law would sow contempt for the very idea of justice and thereby foreclose the possibility of institutional reform. Alarmed by the increasing convergence of public and private power, Debs embraced socialism not to divide Americans from one another, as his critics charged, but to combat the nation's political and economic polarization and to vindicate equality before the law.

Like James, Debs understood that dependent workers made passive democrats, and that political passivity, in turn, fostered a social dynamic in which knowledge became the province of an economic, political, and intellectual elite. In such an intellectual climate there could be no associated learning. Debs confronted this problem every time he encountered a public audience. On the hustings, he spent much of his energy trying to persuade listeners of his and their commonality. In the aftermath of Pullman, he beseeched audiences to ignore the caricature of him in the mainstream press and give him "the benefit of a fair and impartial hearing." Where newspaper accounts had portrayed the striking Pullman workers as anarchists and opportunists, Debs asked his audience to look sympathetically upon those who, "in striking for their rights, did only as you would have done, had you been similarly oppressed." At Pullman, a man's wages did not enable him to "provide for his wife [or] rear his children as becomes an American citizen." Although Debs confessed to generally opposing strikes, he insisted that there come times "now and then when you have got to choose between a strike and degradation." He had intervened in the controversy out of a sense of "duty" toward desperate "brothers and sisters"; given the circumstances, it would have been "cowardly" to have done otherwise.[15]

By portraying striking workers as anarchic and self-interested, Debs's critics discredited agitation as a form of democratic expression. Agitation was the source of progress, Debs insisted; agitators were "misrepresented by those who cannot conceive of a pure, disinterested motive." Although Debs blamed "public opinion" for America's mounting cynicism, the evidence he marshaled suggests that it was less public opinion than elite manipulation of the public that was to blame. Capitalizing on people's ignorance, business and political magnates exploited popular fears to bolster support for the status quo. Debs argued that the solution to this crisis lay in teaching the "common people . . . to think for themselves," and that the first step must be to arouse their curiosity. Alert for signs of progress, he appeared heartened that workers once "satisfied to do their thinking by proxy" had begun "to ask why it is that they must press their rags still closer lest they jostle against the silken garment which their fingers have made; why . . . they must walk weary and shelterless in the shadow of homes that they have erected, but may not enter." [16]

Where corporate and political leaders exploited public ignorance and amnesia to divide Americans, Debs turned to history to accentuate their commonality. Though strikes were now anathema in the reactionary political climate, Debs reminded his audience that they lived under a government founded by agitators and predicated on the right to strike. In his telling, the American Revolution was a "continuous succession of strikes for liberty and independence," and the Revolutionaries men but for whose "magnificent courage and patriotism . . . we would have been British subjects tonight instead of sovereign American citizens." More than their heroism on the battlefield, it was the Revolutionaries' forbearance in the face of withering public scorn that endeared them to the speaker. The longevity of the republic depended on the fortitude of individuals whose allegiance to principle trumped their inclination to "leave well enough alone." [17]

Where Debs attributed virtually all social ills to corporate capitalism, Jane Addams numbered corporate capitalism as merely one of the many unfortunate effects of outdated Enlightenment idealism on democracy. Picking up where Debs left off, Addams spelled out the cultural dimension that remained largely latent in his critique. From Addams's point of view, the problem with industrial America was not merely that it pushed workers to the margin of subsistence—with all that that implied for individual autonomy and cultural integrity—but that the ensuing class divisions cut off the cultural exchange that was the lifeblood of her cosmopolitan ideal. At the root of the problem lay a curious paradox that characterized the first century of American history: in the fields of technology and commerce, Americans had demonstrated tremendous ingenuity, yet in political matters, they had proven themselves uncharacteristically reluctant to change. The result was an advanced industrial system unsupported by modern political institutions, and which consequently produced severe social and economic maladjustment. By "add[ing] the social function to democracy," Addams hoped to restore balance to the industrial and political equation, and thereby realize the liberty and equality at the heart of the American dream. [18]

Addams began by scrutinizing the work of her predecessors. In a speech delivered at the St. Louis Exposition of 1904, she told an audience convened to honor the genius of Thomas Jefferson that failure in American municipal administration derived from "weakness inherent in the historic and doctrinaire method" of the Founding Fathers. Heirs to the "seventeenth-century Puritans," the Founders represented what Addams labeled "the first type of humanitarian": devoted to "pure principle" and "afraid of experience," they "love[d] the people without really knowing them." Although Addams herself acknowledged the appeal of the notion of universal love, she protested that it had led the Founders to disregard local models of self-government and to establish America's legal system on an outdated English prototype. Rooted in the dynamic between "sovereign and subject," and concerned primarily with safeguarding prerogative and property, American law evolved as a narrow and "mechanical method of civil control." Designed to check the predations of the vicious, law, like politics, ignored the needs and interests of the "dutiful majority."

In modern parlance, Addams accused the Founding Fathers of thinking globally and *acting* globally, thus violating the tenets of representative democracy. It is one thing for representatives to promote the interests of their constituents "thinly"; it is quite another for elected or appointed officials to presume to know their constituents' interests without consulting them. This was James's criticism of American policy in the Philippines. Addams suggested that a combination of universal sympathy and strong local commitment compelled educated young men and women of her generation toward settlement-house work in this, "the second phase of democracy." Like their Enlightenment predecessors, Hull-House residents quickened "to the notion of human brotherhood," but unencumbered by their forefathers' idealism, they pursued this end amid the maelstrom of daily urban life.[19]

Had America remained a nation of farmers and artisans, Addams observed, family, community, and artisanal ties might have bridged the chasm between the popular will and the nation's political and legal institutions. Rapid urbanization foreclosed that possibility. It gave rise to a population of dislocated immigrant and industrial workers eager to participate in democratic politics, but whose civic enthusiasm was quashed by archaic city charters. Predictably, such a system produced two classes of individuals: the "indifferent citizen," who withdrew from politics because of its authoritarian focus, and the "professional politician," who filled the political void. Christopher Lasch once described Addams's work as "an exercise in anthropology." To a population suspicious of the aspirations of women and African Americans and unfamiliar with urban and immigrant culture, Addams served as an interpreter. She and other young women revolted against the claims of their families not out of disrespect, but to apply years of theoretical preparation to obvious social needs. Middle-class Americans quit politics not out of egoism, but because a coercive government left them disaffected. Working people struggling to make good in urban America wanted not charity but "only that the means of attaining [their aspirations] be put at their disposal."

Machine politicians were undeniably self-interested, but their avarice had to be weighed against the real services they provided their constituents in a dysfunctional democracy.[20]

Of Addams's many interpretive claims, the last two may have been her most significant. Where many old-stock Americans derided the primitive quid pro quo of machine politics, Addams insisted that the social ethics of the political machine were no baser than those of civil-service reformers and aristocrats who exploited their social position for personal gain. As always, her standard was "social democracy": did the individual act mindless of his effect on fellow citizens? However corrupt it might be, the patron-client relationship of machine politics at least recognized mankind's interdependence. In *Democracy and Social Ethics* (1902), Addams wondered "what headway [could] the notion of civic purity, of honesty of administration" make against the political machine's "big manifestation of human friendliness, this stalking survival of village kindness?" The machine politician "understands what the people want and ministers just as truly to a great human need as the musician or the artist." By contrast, the methods of the civil servant were largely "negative." Too often civil servants posed as problem solvers in order to stake "a claim upon the public gratitude"; "dramatically" exposing the "easy partnership between vice and administrative government," they ignored "all the human kindnesses upon which [political corruption] has grown." Worse, from Addams's perspective, were the cloistered elite. Addams anticipated the day when the urban politician would "not be considered more base in his code of morals, more hardened in his practice, than the woman who constantly invites to her receptions those alone who bring her an equal social return, who shares her beautiful surroundings only with those who minister to a liking she has for successful social events." Was such a woman any less "unmindful of the common weal," any less "unscrupulous in her use of power" than the "city 'boss' who consults only the interests of his 'ring'?"[21]

The problems of municipal corruption called for a little sympathy. If Americans would only view the matter from the perspective of the "humbler people," they might discover, after Addams, that political "evils" were not "always hideous," and that individuals "sin often through weakness and passion, but seldom through hardness of heart." But lest the George Washington Plunkitts of the world mistake Addams's sympathetic understanding of machine politics for an endorsement, she emphasized that they, no less than civil servants and aristocrats, failed the test of her democracy. Rather than providing their constituents with the means of self-realization, they purposefully cultivated their constituents' dependence. By reducing human interaction to the level of subsistence and ridiculing book-learning and public discussion, they fostered a climate of ignorance that foreclosed the possibility of reciprocal exchange.[22]

Democracy, Addams reminded her listeners, meant the rule of the people—not the rule of a few over them; only those who had a voice in defining the subject and scope of politics could rightly be regarded "democrats." Refusing to let a century of unparalleled economic development obscure the glaring absence in America of "civic machinery for simple democratic expression," Addams insisted that enfranchising the people's "social needs and ideals" would release the "vital forces" requisite for self-realization, thus guaranteeing to the state the fealty of an intelligent citizenry. Following Tocqueville, Addams appreciated democracy's crucial educative and nurturing potential; along with James and Dewey, she warned that a state that circumscribed its citizens' political participation deprived itself of the "untold capacity, talent, and even genius" of its people.[23]

Like Addams, W. E. B. Du Bois viewed democracy as the solution to America's many problems. In chapter 2 of *The Souls of Black Folk* (1903), Du Bois made the often-quoted remark that "the problem of the twentieth century is the problem of the color-line." But in a lesser-known speech delivered in Des Moines, Iowa, the year after *Souls* appeared, he insisted that "the Negro problem" was merely part of "a deeper national problem" that "would remain to be settled . . . were there not a single black man in the land." The deeper problem, Du Bois announced, was "caste," and its recrudescence in a nation "founded on the bed-rock of eternal opposition to class privileges" jeopardized far more than the fate of the nation's ten million blacks; a society riven by caste distinctions could never sustain the intellectual debate that was the lifeblood of democracy. Du Bois's concern for a matter in which the plight of African Americans figured only partially was perfectly in keeping with his sense of himself as an American citizen. In numerous speeches and essays written before the end of World War I, he emphasized that plural allegiances were compatible when undergirded by a commitment to individual and social justice. Of course, this did not make them easy to maintain. As democracy's primary exponent, America occupied a position of privilege in Du Bois's hierarchy. The nation was flawed, of course, and badly; but if "the child of emancipation" was ever to "be himself, and not another," Du Bois vowed in "Strivings of the Negro People," his vindication would come on account of, and not despite, "the greater ideals of the American republic."[24]

Expanding Eugene Debs's critique of corporate America, Du Bois tutored Des Moines listeners on the distinction between class and caste. He remarked that the classification of individuals and groups was only to be expected in a young and burgeoning nation, whose citizens differed from one another in terms of "gifts and appearances, in likes and dislikes." Trouble arose when prejudice intervened to reify differences and stamp the downtrodden as deficient. Those who succumbed to a caste perspective ignored the fallibility of the privileged and the capacity of the oppressed for improvement, "enthron[ing] over the destinies of the nation that particular form of immorality most prevalent among the ruling classes of the land." Stealing was America's immorality of the moment. In industry, the "earnings of thrift, efficiency, and genius" fell prey to the "strong, the crafty, and the impudent"; in the media, a lax moral code permitted the "theft of truth and the flaunting of bare-face lies"; in society at large, avarice spawned apathy about the deterioration of America's social and political institutions. As a result, Du Bois declared, in rhetoric redolent of Addams's, "we are aware throughout the land of growing respect for snobbery. We are discreetly silent, or even mildly effusive over an open traffic in gilded maidens and foreign titles; we see greater and greater disinclination to remember humble parentage and the dirty finger nails of our grandfathers and even our great and growing efforts at charity and reform are developing tendencies which make them quite as often agencies of social separation as means of class obliteration."[25]

Just as Dewey and Addams protested that materialism blinded Americans to the virtues of the middle and lower classes, Du Bois argued that caste encouraged people to judge "good and evil" from the perspective of the privileged. Nowhere was this more apparent than in the matter of education. Where once Americans had committed themselves to train "the children of servants" and "mechanics" to be "men," by the turn of the twentieth century, a yearning for "better servants" and "better houses" had led Americans to discredit education as an avenue for individual advancement. This made sense, Du Bois announced, "if house service and houses are the objects of national life; but are they?" On the contrary, the end of life was the realization of one's humanity, and the purpose of education was to teach students that life's "vast possibilities" could be realized through "human toil and aspiration." Du Bois acknowledged that as long as African Americans remained the primary victims, Americans would conveniently point to black indigence and immorality as the cause of prejudice rather than its consequence. They would do so at their peril. By the turn of the new century, Du Bois saw evidence that the pattern "initiated in the South" was tightening its grip on the nation as a whole. "There is growing a feeling that certain classes of white children do not need high schools," he reported; "that good birth ought to bestow certain privileges by a sort of divine right, and that the man who wrote the Declaration of Independence was a fool."[26]

The pernicious effects of caste were particularly apparent in the South. In chapter 9 of *The Souls of Black Folk,* Du Bois escorted readers on a tour of Southern social, economic, and political institutions, highlighting the many ways in which caste violated the tenets of "nature." Domestically, custom prohibited black and white elites from sharing the same neighborhood, ensuring that the races saw only "the worst of each other." Socially, Southern life proceeded as if divided into "two great streams," which occasionally commingled but ultimately ran off in separate directions. Intellectually, no "point of transference" existed by which black and white professionals could share ideas and compare experience. The result was the near total absence of social reciprocity between the races. The meager interaction that did occur took place in the halls of the criminal justice system or the almshouse—institutions that only underscored the pathology of Southern race relations, and in which blacks and whites never met as equals.[27]

Industrially, circumstances were no better. In the aftermath of the Civil War, ignorance bred from prejudice led white Americans to underestimate the ravages of slavery on the newly freed black population. Clinging to free-market ideology, Southern entrepreneurs had expected merely a little technical training and capital to equip African Americans for industrial competition, later regarding their predictable failure as evidence of inferiority. Du Bois attributed the South's social and economic maladjustment to this fundamental misconception. A people trained "for centuries as slaves" should not have been expected to develop overnight the virtues of the modern "democratic laborer," he averred. Black workers needed the guidance and sympathy "of men with hearts in their bosoms, to train them to foresight, carefulness, and honesty." Just whose responsibility that had been—whether the ex-master's, the Northern philanthropist's, the federal government's—Du Bois would not say; he did protest that it had been *someone's* duty "to see that these workingmen were not left alone and unguided, without capital, without land, without skill, without economic organization, without even the bald protection of law, order, and decency." Like Dewey, Du Bois believed that the system of free enterprise depended on reciprocal social relations as well as equal opportunity. Far from eroding self-reliance and individual initiative, timely intervention on behalf of African Americans during Reconstruction would have restored integrity to a social and economic system that had come to symbolize the thwarting of excellence and the exaltation of mediocrity.[28]

Du Bois acknowledged that there was little chance racist America would provide "that close sympathetic and self-sacrificing leadership" that the situation demanded. In a society devoid of reciprocal exchange, African Americans would have to develop their own leaders—a perfectly salutary imperative, Du Bois believed, but one difficult if not impossible to achieve in the face of political and cultural disenfranchisement. Booker T. Washington argued that African Americans' civil rights could await black economic independence and moral self-discipline. By contrast, along with Dewey, Du Bois viewed political participation as a requisite of individual and group self-realization, and self-realization, in turn, as the sine qua non of social, economic, and moral development. From Dewey's and Du Bois's perspective, the public arena served as a kind of advanced intellectual training for political leaders; contending with their peers and presenting their platforms to the people, politicians honed their analytic and oratorical skills, all the while staying abreast of the latest legal, economic, and cultural developments. For political followers, politics afforded a rare opportunity to participate in a genuine public discussion; weighing the issues of tariff and taxation and choosing their representatives, the electorate reaffirmed its stake in the nation. A people cut off from political participation was a people stripped of personal autonomy and robbed of the opportunity for group advancement—a plight made all the more untenable in a constantly changing technological environment in which political empowerment was all that separated American workers from industrial exploitation.[29]

Was it any wonder that in a society based on the principle of consensual government a disenfranchised people would prove difficult to govern? Owing nothing to government, naturally African Americans showed government no loyalty. Barred from establishing and maintaining the law, African Americans ignored laws that violated principles of justice. Deserving but not garnering recognition for their many accomplishments, African Americans scorned a system of hierarchy based on caste. Only grant us a modicum of sympathy and access to America's democratic institutions, Du Bois cried, then you might hold us accountable for our behavior. The prerequisite of social reciprocity was mutual responsibility: "It is not enough for the Negroes to declare that color-prejudice is the sole cause of their social condition," he remarked, "nor for the South to reply that their social condition is the main cause of prejudice. . . . Both must change, or neither can improve to any great extent. . . . Only by a union of intelligence and sympathy across the color-line in this critical period of the Republic shall justice and right triumph, 'That mind and soul according well, / May make one music as before, / But vaster.' "[30]

The cosmopolitan patriots were not the only ones, of course, to criticize the state of American democracy. In early January 1916, Louis Brandeis, future associate justice of the U.S. Supreme Court, looked back on two generations of industrial development and enumerated a litany of "new dangers to liberty." Speaking before the Chicago Bar Association, Brandeis attributed many of these perils to the failure of America's legal system to keep pace with social, economic, and political developments. Aiming to wrest the legal profession from complacency, Brandeis indicted a cross-section of America's social, economic, and political elite. The speech reiterated much of Debs's, Addams's, and Du Bois's criticism and suggested the impediments to realizing Dewey's democratic ideal. Brandeis began by engaging the yearning among social activists to replace the old notion of "legal justice" with an updated commitment to "social justice"—in part a response to Americans' palpable diminishing respect for the law. By legal justice, Brandeis meant the philosophy and system of law designed to safeguard individuals from predations of the powerful; by social justice, he meant a system intended to protect collectivities—workers, for example—from potent individuals and combinations. Aloof from the evolving sentiment such yearning expressed, law appeared destined to forfeit citizens' loyalty, at once the bulwark of law and the foundation of the nation.[31] The next chapter depicts the cosmopolitan patriot's attempt to resolve the problems besetting American democracy by redefining American identity itself.

EX UNO PLURA

One cold, clammy morning in spring 1905 a steamship pulled alongside a dock at Ellis Island in New York harbor and discharged its human cargo. Among the crowd that shuffled down the gangway that day was a writer, less a newcomer to the United States than a *re-comer,* a cultural apostate absent from home some twenty-nine years. The writer had boarded the ship that remained idling nearby not in some distant port but just over the bay in Lower Manhattan, his quarantine elective, his visit merely a local stop on a proverbial grand tour. As tourist and celebrity, Henry James strode unimpeded through gates that parted for immigrants, as he noted in *The American Scene,* "only with a hundred forms and ceremonies, grindings and grumblings of the key."[1] James's first impression of Ellis Island was one of extraordinary discipline. He gazed in awe at immigrants "marshaled, herded, divided, subdivided, sorted, sifted, searched, [and] fumigated" by the decidedly "scientific" machinery of the U.S. customs service. Here was a drama that proceeded without "pause, day by day and year by year, this visible act of ingurgitation on the part of our body politic and social, and constituting really an appeal to amazement" beyond the circus. James returned to Manhattan indelibly transformed, like the "questionably privileged person who has . . . seen a ghost in his supposedly safe old house." Long after his visit, the question of America's civic fate lingered on his mind. He who has gazed upon Ellis Island, James remarked, "has eaten of the tree of knowledge, and the taste will be forever in his mouth."[2]

James's candor, so jarring to contemporary ears, provides an opportunity for students of American history to examine the social and political dilemmas facing the United States in an era of cultural upheaval. Scholarship of late has been more apt to heed immigrant experiences than the testimony of men like James. Scholars who attend to "old-stock" Americans focus on their "nativism," as if James's apprehension was somehow unnatural, as if nothing but self-interest was at stake in his response to demographic upheaval.[3] We acknowledge *that* James recoiled from the scene at Ellis Island, but we are disinclined to ask *why*. Or, rather, we presume to know his motivation: James recoiled from Ellis Island because he lacked our cultural sensitivity and open-mindedness. And yet, while there is no denying James's snobbery, surely more was at play in his reaction than mere prejudice.[4]

Indeed, James's fall from grace precipitated an extraordinary meditation on America's cultural composition. Irretrievably lost that morning in New York harbor was James's grip on what he called his "supreme relation" to kin and country. It was not that he had once presumed exclusive claim to national belonging—he long recognized, in theory at least, that it was "his American fate to share the sanctity of his American consciousness, the intimacy of his American patriotism, with the inconceivable alien"—but "the truth had never come home to him with any such force." For over a century it had been possible for Americans of James's heritage to deny the universal logic of the nation's founding principles. To be sure, America's demographic composition had never been homogenous or stable, but political, economic, and cultural hegemony had enabled James's cohort to perpetuate the "fond tradition," as he put it, that the nation comprised a mirror image of itself.[5] No more. In the face of Ellis Island, that fond tradition underwent "profane overhauling." By a dizzying inversion old-stock Americans had become alien. Were they "to recover confidence and regain lost ground," James exhorted, they themselves and not the immigrants "must make the surrender and accept the orientation"—"must go, in other words, *more* than half-way to meet them." James's epiphany left him at once intrigued (ever the insatiable ethnographer) and envious of "the luxury of some such close and sweet and *whole* national consciousness as that of the Switzer and the Scot."

At Ellis Island James admitted being repelled by the odor and appearance of the new arrivals, but throughout his grand tour the cultural trappings of the newcomers were as apt to excite as to estrange him.[6] What troubled him most was the potentially stultifying social and political cost of cultural diversity—the inability of old and new to communicate, with all that that entailed for the affective bonds of solidarity and the spontaneity of civil and political life. This problem was brought home to James one day when, traipsing the grounds of a New Jersey estate, he encountered a group of workers with whom communication was impossible. "To pause before them for interest in their labor," James recounted, "was, and would have been everywhere, instinctive; but what came home to me on the spot was that whatever more would have been anywhere else involved had here inevitably to lapse." Total dumbness descended, "as if contact were out of the question and the sterility of the passage between us recorded, with due dryness, in our staring silence." Again James conjured up denizens of the Old World for whom the principal character "of any rural excursion, of the rural in particular, had been . . . the easy sense . . . of a social relation with any encountered type, from whichever end of the scale proceeding. Had that not ever been, exactly, a part of the vague warmth, the intrinsic colour, of any honest man's rural walk in his England, or his Italy, his Germany or his France, and was not the effect of its so suddenly dropping out, in the land of universal brotherhood—for he was to find it drop out again and again—rather a chill, straightway, for the heart, and rather a puzzle, not less, for the head?"[7]

This chapter addresses the cosmopolitan patriots' responses of heart and head to America's mounting diversity and increasing inequality. The fin de siècle America in which Eugene V. Debs, Jane Addams, and W. E. B. Du Bois began to propound their models of democratic citizenship differed markedly from the nation into which they were born at midcentury. To describe mid—nineteenth-century America as a "nation" at all raises the question of what constitutes nationhood and invites debate about whether the forces that separated the states and regions from one another were not stronger than the cords that bound them. The Civil War proved the tenuousness of political ties in the face of economic and cultural differences. The Union victory, along with the Thirteenth, Fourteenth, and Fifteenth Amendments, established the constitutional foundation of national consciousness, but it was the economic consolidation spawned by the war that first compelled citizens of the United States into a national marketplace of commerce and ideas. By the turn of the twentieth century, the country could boast of a continental communications network, a centrally driven economy, an indigenous mass culture, and a battle-tested navy. The resolutely federated American republic had acquired many of the hallmarks of a modern nation-state.[8]

But the very developments that promised to bring the United States together unleashed countervailing forces that threatened to drive its people apart. The technological and managerial innovations that propelled America's second industrial revolution outstripped moral and civic adjustment, giving rise to a system of corporate capitalism that impeded competition and eroded concern for the common good. The resulting alienation of labor combined with a surge of immigration and civil rights and feminist agitation to make America appear anything but "united." Of course, the coincidence of centripetal and centrifugal forces in late—nineteenth-century America is not paradoxical. It underscores a fundamental characteristic of nationalization—namely, that nationalist movements, despite appealing to popular sovereignty, mask the particularistic cultural, economic, and/or political interests of self-conscious and powerful minorities.[9]

Several self-conscious and powerful minorities vied to define American identity at the end of the nineteenth century. The economic and social change that exposed old Anglo-American caste and cultural boundaries to assault in the aftermath of war inspired an intellectual effervescence from which new ideas emerged and by which old concepts were given new meaning. The harvest of this flowering of ideas was not solely, or even largely, liberating. For every William James declaring America to be liberty's last best hope on earth, there was a Francis Lieber, a Henry Cabot Lodge, an Oliver Wendell Holmes Jr. erecting models of citizen loyalty designed specifically to quash dissent and bolster the faltering Anglo-American order. Moreover, the truths declared in this new age of reason were not everywhere empowering. The naturalism current in popular culture resembled less the pluralist vision of Darwin, James, and Dewey than the conservative temperament of the British social scientist Herbert Spencer and his American counterpart William Graham Sumner. Women, African Americans, Asians, Jews, and southern and eastern Europeans suffered the brunt of this reaction; hitherto assumed to be inferior to white Anglo-Saxon men—and therefore unequipped to participate in republican government—they were allegedly proved so by the "scientific" practitioners of phrenology and eugenics.[10]

The dubiousness of these proofs together with their authors' parochialism inspired a reaction among a group of liberal intellectuals and social scientists determined to rescue American democracy from retrograde race theorists. None garnered more acclaim than the philosopher Horace Kallen. In the winter of 1915, Kallen published a two-part essay in *The Nation* titled "Democracy *Versus* the Melting Pot" in which he repudiated the Anglo-American cultural conservatism of the American sociologist E. A. Ross. Along with Ross, Kallen subscribed to the romantic notion that cultures possessed essential natures that it was the business of the American state to affirm and protect. Like Ross's essentialism, Kallen's predisposed him to emphasize the importance of preserving cultural legacies. But Kallen broke with Ross by interpreting America as a work in progress rather than a nation in the grip of cultural decline. Where Ross regarded the United States as the province of an Anglo-American cultural majority, Kallen advanced an ideal of cultural diversity. Where Ross delineated a program for cultural renewal that combined immigration restriction with assimilation to Anglo-American norms, Kallen discarded the metaphor of America-as-melting-pot in favor of the symbol of orchestral harmony.[11]

A cogent defense of cultural pluralism, "Democracy *Versus* the Melting Pot" was a rhetorical tour de force, and it served as a wake-up call for a generation of democrats slow to respond to mounting cultural reaction. The timing of Kallen's essay had much to do with its reception. World War I made American intellectuals particularly self-conscious about the hazards of national identity based on geographic, linguistic, and ancestral ties. Was it possible to cultivate the community-forming aspects of national affiliation thought to be essential for individual and cultural realization without promoting the chauvinism that too often accompanied them? Kallen, along with Randolph Bourne, Jane Addams, John Dewey, and Louis Brandeis, among others, believed that the same principle that regulated individual behavior in a democracy—Tocqueville's self-interest rightly understood—might also safeguard the integrity of groups. In a heterogeneous nation, no less than in an increasingly interconnected world, the way to protect the interests of one's own community was to defend the community rights of all. [12]

Aligned against Ross's cultural conservatism, Kallen, Bourne, Brandeis, Dewey, and Addams may be said to have constituted a liberal front. But this liberal front concealed fissures about the cultural requirements of a functioning democracy, and about the salience of gender, class, and race for national identity. Some liberals echoed the conservative's concern about America's cultural disintegration. Playwright Israel Zangwill and philosopher Morris Cohen, for example, feared pluralism would undercut the universal principles underlying the American republic. As "universalists," Zangwill and Cohen viewed the world in terms of individuals rather than groups and exalted public participation over private right. Where Kallen drew his commitment to cultural integrity from romanticism, Zangwill and Cohen derived their suspicion of cultural boundaries from the Enlightenment. Heirs to America's Enlightenment tradition, early-twentieth-century universalists deplored boundaries of all sorts—economic, racial, and sexual, as well as cultural or "ethnic." Like cultural conservatives, universalists defended assimilation. In contrast to conservatives, however, the universalists' melting pot was home to no dominant stock: ethnic groups of all varieties would be welcomed into the cauldron but expected to surrender their uniqueness in the name of an undifferentiated "American" ideal.

The cosmopolitan patriots described a mediating ethos: a world in which individuals might affiliate themselves with any number of overlapping voluntary or cultural groups. This voluntarism distinguished cosmopolitanism from pluralism. Where Kallen regarded cultural identity as indelible, Bourne, Brandeis, Dewey, and Addams shared Zangwill's and Cohen's conviction that culture, like church or club membership, could be exchanged, discarded, or left to lapse. But Bourne, Brandeis, Dewey, and Addams broke with Zangwill and Cohen by insisting that individuals remain attached, electively, to culture, synagogue, church, or club—institutions thought to provide the reciprocal human interaction that made life meaningful. Finally, though cosmopolitanism and conservatism would appear to have had very little in common, the cosmopolitans' interest in "social control" and cultivation of the "talented tenth" left them open to charges of elitism. These charges are misplaced, a symptom of scholarly failure to distinguish Ross's cultural commitments from the attempt of Dewey and company to construct an educational curriculum and civic ideal that would prepare individuals for a lifetime of social reciprocity and democratic deliberation.[13]

The paradox of American conservatives defending democracy by denying its extension to others was not lost on universalists, pluralists, and cosmopolitans. Liberals of the Progressive era relished exposing conservative illiberalism. But universalism, pluralism, and cosmopolitanism betrayed tensions of their own. Where conservatives may have underestimated human potential, universalists seem to have exaggerated it. In their desire to free individuals from constraints of caste and privilege, universalists cut them loose from all geographical, cultural, and linguistic moorings. Where universalists did not reckon the function of cultural boundaries, pluralists made too much of them. Both within and among cultures, power is seldom distributed evenly. For oppressed individuals and communities, culture does not necessarily afford the surest footing on which to stake claims to political rights. Finally, where pluralists did not acknowledge the tension between cultural and individual rights, cosmopolitans may have overestimated the possibilities of multiple affiliations. Although cosmopolitans could point to Progressive-Era industrial reforms as evidence of effective coalition building, the long-term evisceration of workers' living standards together with enduring racial inequality suggests the limitations of loose affiliation in the face of consolidated economic and political power.[14]

The disparity between conservatives and liberals about the nature of American identity derived from contrasting notions of "culture" and "nationhood." When Robert and Helen Lynd published *Middletown,* their path-breaking sociological analysis of Muncie, Indiana, in 1929, they subtitled the book "A Study in Modern American Culture." Unremarkable from a late-twentieth-century perspective, the Lynds's use of the word culture to signify categories of work, family life, education, leisure, religion, and politics represented an etymological break from nineteenth-century tradition. In 1890, "culture" typically connoted the intellectual and artistic sophistication and excellence associated with British critic Matthew Arnold. At that time, a visitor to Muncie, having absorbed the workaday routines of the local inhabitants, would have been hard-pressed to identify any such culture at all. Insofar as the particular customs and traditions of a community like Muncie attracted the attention of outside observers in 1890, they did so as minor variations on putative "national" traits. Not until the influence of the anthropologist Franz Boas and his students began to infiltrate the social science literature in the first two decades of the twentieth century did local folkways and traditions receive scholarly recognition as "culture."[15]

Kallen's "Democracy *Versus* the Melting Pot" confirms this transformation. In 1915 Kallen used "culture" interchangeably with "ethnicity" to refer to the sense of community established by a people's shared behavior, institutions, and ideals. Kallen associated artistic and literary production—culture in Arnold's sense—with the word "civilization," a stage of development within the reach of any community or nation possessing a requisite self-consciousness. The transformation of the word culture influenced the meanings of "nation" and "race," in effect freeing them to take on new significance. Early-nineteenth-century Americans used nation and race to describe the collective attributes of peoplehood, but with this difference: they invoked the word race to make qualitative comparisons and uphold cultural assumptions.[16] Thus, Anglo-Saxon propagandists declared their culture superior to the Gallic, the Gallic superior to the Iberian, the Iberian to the Slavic, and so on. The triumph of European nationalism and, not coincidentally, imperialism in the second half of the nineteenth century exaggerated this subtle distinction—with nation connoting the aspiration for political recognition of a particular people in a particular place, and race signifying the involuntary and presumably indelible markings of the genetic code. Putative genetic, or racial, distinctions could now justify Western imperialism.[17]

As a liberal and a Jew, Kallen renounced claims based on biological determinism; those not guilty of special pleading ignored the nearly universal evidence of racial miscegenation. But as a democrat and a Zionist, Kallen embraced the culture-affirming potential of national affiliation; a people organized to defend and promote its interests was more likely to attain the group consciousness from which genius derived. Nationhood, in the sense of political identity, did not necessarily confer statehood. Kallen hoped that America might become a nation of discrete nationalisms, each underwritten by an impartial, democratic state. But to an extent that Kallen did not acknowledge, nation-states are not impartial. At the turn of the twentieth century, the American state was governed by men more interested in defending outworn Anglo-American norms than in promoting an atmosphere conducive to cultural realization.[18]

The acknowledgment that people of all races and nations possessed "cultures" of their own influenced the discussion about American identity in several ways. For individuals who regarded ethnic differences not as the product of an alleged racial hierarchy but rather as a function of a people's adaptation to its environment, culture acquired a value hitherto denied. Suddenly America's mounting ethnic diversity, so threatening from an Anglo-Saxon perspective, became a national asset: American civilization had the potential to be richer than its European counterparts because it was woven from more variegated thread. The tendency to view culture as the totality of socially transmitted behaviors from which individuals derived meaning influenced discussion about what Americans owed one another. If this new understanding of "culture," like the old, was a requisite of self-realization, what were the requisites of "culture"? According to some liberals, the answer was economic independence and civil rights; according to others, the answer was territory; to still others, the answer was social and intellectual exchange. Most liberals believed that individual and cultural realization lay in some combination of these ingredients. The extent to which certain thinkers elevated some of these elements over others marks them universalist, pluralist, or cosmopolitan in the ensuing discussion.

The enthusiasm with which turn-of-the-century liberals embraced the nation-state as a vehicle for progressive reform distinguishes them from their liberal counterparts of the post-Vietnam era for whom national identity appears suspect, if not pernicious. With a few exceptions, the contemporary Left has ceded the rhetorical terrain of the nation to cultural and political conservatives.[19] Nation-states, the conventional wisdom goes, are ineluctably coercive; ethnic and cultural groups, meanwhile, are the source of empowerment and self-esteem. The democratic nationalists who came of age with Dewey, Debs, Addams, and Du Bois rejected this reductionism. They recognized that communities of every sort had the potential to be both coercive and empowering, often at the same time. To them coercion was a trade-off: were the restraints inevitably enacted by society ultimately conducive or inimical to individual self-realization? They greeted evidence of an emerging national consciousness at the end of the nineteenth century as an opportunity to generate the mutual obligation required of social and political reform.

CLASS-CONSCIOUS
COSMOPOLITANISM

Eugene V. Debs's discovery of the extent of America's economic and political consolidation inspired his conversion to socialism in the wake of the Pullman strike. Business had organized politically in the interest of class, Debs discovered; workers had no choice but to respond in kind. And because industrial exploitation, like commerce itself, was becoming increasingly international at the turn of the twentieth century, Debs exhorted workers to adopt a universal rather than an ethnic, racial, or national perspective.[20] For Debs, culture was irrelevant in the face of consolidated capital and politics; workers driven to the margin of subsistence could barely feed and clothe their families let alone sustain anything resembling community. Nor did Debs have any use for nations and their so-called patriotisms. These were products of a corporate capitalist imagination designed to keep the world's workers in their place.

Yet even Debs knew that the socialist revolution must proceed country by country, one nation at a time. Indeed, Debs's universalist rhetoric belies a history of engagement with both the fact and idea of the nation. Though a product of the Second International, the Socialist Party of America was, after all, a national political organization intent on capturing control of the nation's government. It held national conventions, delineated a national platform, and selected national officers to take part in nationwide elections. It exploited America's vast transportation and communications network to propagate its good news, all the while insisting that socialism was merely the fulfillment of American democracy. Debs himself appeared perfectly at home in the United States. Over the course of his lifetime, he seldom left the country, and then only once or twice to Canada and Bermuda. Debs's progressive reading of U.S. history inspired his socialist career. Regarding himself as an heir to Washington, Lincoln, and John Brown, he charged Americans to uphold the nation's legacy. So adamant was Debs's patriotism that it may have mitigated his socialist critique. Every time he insisted that international socialism was only the fulfillment of America's principles, he reminded audiences of what made the American nation great.[21]

Debs's class-conscious Americanism highlights tensions within pluralist and cosmopolitan theory. To pluralists, Debs offered the lesson that there could be no culture, let alone pluralism, for those without the means of subsistence. Pluralism was both an aspiration and a luxury of the arrived. Among cultures, pluralism assumed a degree of equality unattainable in practice. Within cultures, pluralism ignored imbalances of power that privileged some and hindered others. In a corporate capitalist world, Debs asserted, man might be moral but society not; culture and community offered individuals no harbor from fellow members on the make. To cosmopolitans, meanwhile, Debs protested that poverty was incompatible with choice. Free agency depended on autonomy and independence, the principal casualties of an industrial system that robbed individuals of initiative and deprived them of the product of their labor. Class-conscious unity, not pluralism, working-class loyalty, not fickle ecumenicalism—these, according to Debs, were the means to a just and egalitarian society, a society compatible with cosmopolitanism, as we shall see, but one that had to precede it.[22]

Of course, for all Debs's talk of unity, the history of the Socialist Party under his leadership was one of shrill discord. Conflicts between party elites and the rank and file, conservatives and radicals, purists and pragmatists, easterners and westerners, proponents of craft unionism and partisans of industrial organization, integrationists and irreconcilables were legion. The history of Debs's role in most of these disputes has been well documented; but the record of Debs's opinion on the issue of race has been misconstrued. Rather than trivializing the problem of race in turn-of-the-century America, as scholars have concluded, Debs's essays on the relationship between the class struggle and the fight for African-American civil rights explain the stubborn salience of race in American society despite evidence of miscegenation and social mixing. These essays represent a bold defense of universalism in the face of particularist claims. But in them Debs goes beyond universalism, suggesting that, once economic justice had been attained, individuals would possess the intellectual and moral autonomy conducive to voluntarism. For Debs, then, socialism represented the means to cosmopolitan affiliation.[23]

The cosmopolitan feel of Debs's "universalism" emerges in comparison with the universalist ideology of the English Zionist Israel Zangwill. In 1908 Zangwill's play *The Melting Pot* introduced British and American audiences to what has become the standard metaphor for cultural hybridization. In *The Melting Pot* itself and in an apology tacked onto the 1914 edition, Zangwill dismissed the conservatives' jeremiad as the product of Europhilia: "afflicted by all the old European diseases," conservatives had not yet caught the spirit of the "crucible of love." Ironically, Zangwill shared the conservatives' antipathy to cultural diversity. *The Melting Pot* was Zangwill's repudiation of the world after Babel—one that impeded understanding and sundered hearts. Its hero, David, was the survivor of a Russian pogrom, for whom the promise of a yet unfolding America offered both escape from a horrendous past and relief from the cultural confusion inside his humble New York home, where three generations of Jews had all but lost the ability to communicate. Its heroine, Vera, was the daughter of the Russian aristocrat who had commanded the pogrom that left young David homeless; for Vera, a settlement-house worker, union with David—unthinkable outside America—offered an opportunity to exorcise her family's guilt. The play's climax turned on David's orchestration at Vera's settlement house of a symphony he composed celebrating America as the triumph of reason over culture. Its historical significance derives not from any artistic or literary value, to be sure, but from its extraordinary popular appeal. Not only had *The Melting Pot* "contribute[d] its title to current thought," Zangwill boasted in his apology, but Jane Addams herself had praised it for "reminding us of the high hopes of the founders of the Republic" (216).[24]

A busy woman, Addams either did not read or view the play critically or did not read or view the play at all. *The Melting Pot* is simply not about remembering. On the contrary, Zangwill implies, history does not matter in a postmillennial age. Convinced that he could not "mend" the past, Zangwill's hero resolves to "forget" it by extending his "hands with prayer and music toward the Republic of Man and the Kingdom of God!"(TMP, 97). At one point, when David cannot believe that his troubles have really "melted away," Vera reminds him that he immigrated to America precisely "to end the tragic history; to throw off the coils of centuries." Thanking Vera for helping him retrieve his "sunnier self," David resolves to remain "a pioneer on the lost road of happiness. To-day," he announces, "shall be all joy, all lyric ecstasy" (TMP, 148). Here Zangwill does to universalism what scholars have accused Horace Kallen of doing to pluralism: he ignores the problem of how social inequality will influence relations inside the cauldron. Thinkers as diverse as Eugene Debs, W. E. B. Du Bois, Louis Brandeis, and the sociologist W. I. Thomas knew that inequality was an obstacle to assimilation. They recognized that victims of oppression do not have the luxury of forgetting American history—a chronicle of the putative triumph of liberty over privilege. Zangwill's declaration of the end of history may have sounded sweet to audiences at Bryn Mawr, Radcliffe, and Mt. Holyoke Colleges, as he maintained, but to individuals and cultures still striving to make it in America, the end of history had come too soon.

Zangwill's failure to identify the indigenous roots of America's cultural conservatism caused him to miss the connection between the nation's racism and xenophobia and its liberal institutions. This, in turn, prevented him from contributing more substantively to the debate about American civic identity. The conservatives' hyperbole, special pleading, and scapegoating was undeniably noxious, but at least conservatives took the problem of self-government seriously.[25] As John Dewey insisted, self-government demands consensus—if not about specific ends, then about the means by which group interests may be defined. And about minority rights. Zangwill assumed that consensus would reign in the melting pot. To Zangwill, consensus and democracy were not products of humans striving, but bequests from God (TMP, 32–3).

At one point in Eugene Debs's life, Zangwill's celebration of forgetting might well have seemed appealing. Debs's rise to national prominence as the Socialist candidate for president in 1900 marked the end of a youthful odyssey that took him from cultural conservatism through a period of buoyant universalism, ultimately to socialism in 1896. As a young man coming of age in Terre Haute, Indiana, Debs possessed few attributes of the dissident-to-be. Midwestern prejudice neutralized the lesson of his parents' early hardship and his father's weekly readings, instilling in him a deep suspicion of unfamiliar cultures and races. Like many second-generation Americans, Debs wasted no time in shrugging off the residue of his parents' foreign heritage. Growing up under the wing of Terre Haute's Republican majority, Debs appropriated its reverence for American democracy and Christian justice—one that was egalitarian but hardly ecumenical. Beneath Debs's youthful rhetoric of harmony lay many qualifying assumptions about just who was and was not to be included. Quick with dialect jokes and anti-immigrant innuendo, Debs painted immigrants as ignorant dupes of capitalist plutocrats and their agents. No less often, he vilified the new arrivals themselves, decrying their avarice, dirtiness, and lack of sophistication. African Americans fared little better at Debs's hands. Although his name appears in support of a bill to abolish racial segregation in Indiana in the 1880s, convention steered him in the opposite direction. Until his turn toward industrial organization in the early 1890s, Debs remained unsympathetic to attempts to integrate Southern railway unions.[26]

Debs's early racism and xenophobia have combined with his stolid refusal to admit cultural claims into his blossoming class analysis to render him irrelevant in the minds of students of American identity. Following the lead of his contemporary, W. E. B. Du Bois, scholars have extracted a few lines from several of Debs's essays to conclude that he was "naive" or "blind" on the subject of race as a factor in social inequality. The offending passages derive from a series of remarks Debs made in protest to his party's adoption of a Negro resolution at its annual convention in the summer of 1903. Due to "their long training in slavery and but recent emancipation therefrom," the Socialist plank announced, African Americans occupied a "peculiar position in the working class and in society at large." Debs was an adamant opponent of what we have come to call interest-group politics. In the wake of the Pullman strike, he accused corporate capitalists and their political and legal allies of usurping public privileges and protections for private gain. Debs believed that a Socialist platform that included resolutions in the name of particular constituencies would split the party into competing interest groups and hence thwart preparations for a final showdown between The Usurpers and The People. In the *American Labor Journal* that July, Debs remarked indelicately that "the Negro is not one whit worse off than the thousands of white slaves who throng the same labor market to sell their labor power to the same industrial masters."[27]

Debs's combativeness prevented him from saying that the way to fight capitalism was not to adopt the capitalists' methods—the divisiveness of which he aptly demonstrated by engaging in debates about victimization—but to emphasize workers' community of interest. This he was given an opportunity to say later that year, when the *International Socialist Review* commissioned his response to the subject of "The Negro in the Class Struggle." Here Debs reiterated his conviction that there was "no Negro question outside of the labor question." But this time he carefully elucidated it, arguing that, by accentuating African Americans' peculiar grievances, Socialists played into capitalists' hands. "In capitalism," Debs wrote, "the Negro problem is a grave one and will grow more threatening as the contradictions and complications of capitalist society multiply." Socialism would expose the bankruptcy of the racialist edifice by identifying the real source of labor's oppression.[28]

In short, Debs objected to the party's Negro resolution because he believed that racial identity shrouded workers' depravity in a veil of self-esteem. This point was driven home to him in the fall of 1903 when, on a swing through the American South, he encountered a group of indolent white men whose color constituted their sole badge of distinction. How such a "savory bouquet of white superiority" could deem themselves superior to anybody, Debs could not imagine. "One glance," he remarked, "was sufficient to satisfy me that they represented all there is of justification for the implacable hatred of the Negro race." To one who equated humanity with moral agency, the brutishness of these loafers was all too plain. Bereft of moral and intellectual autonomy, they had adopted the perspective of white elites. At the time Debs wrote, the reigning shibboleth in the South concerned the black man's assault on white womanhood. In "The Negro in the Class Struggle," Debs exposed the "fraudulence" of this uproar, insisting that "the real issue" was not "social equality, but economic freedom." After all, he wondered, what had white workers' alleged social parity with the planters gotten them?[29]

The extent to which this argument represented Debs's own opinion rather than the view of Socialists generally was revealed by an anonymous letter warning Debs that his endorsement of black political equality would jeopardize Party interests. Political equality would lead inevitably to social equality, the writer cautioned; and once "you get social and political equality for the Negro, then let him come and ask the hand of your daughter in marriage." Did not Debs recognize that "just a little sour dough will spoil the whole batch of bread"? Urging him to consult Thomas Dixon's "The Leopard's Spots" if he retained doubts about the matter, the writer signed off, declaring himself "a staunch member of the Socialist Party." Debs knew better than to debate anonymous authors. But in this case, the writer's inclination to "shoot from ambush," as Debs put it, illustrated his point about the inadequacy of racial identity as a substitute for manhood. Like the emperor whose hubris exaggerated his nakedness, so this writer's self-described "staunchness" deflated "his foolish and fanatical criticism."[30]

The writer had shot himself in the foot. In a follow-up essay the next January, Debs thought to permanently disarm him. To the assertion that political equality would result, ultimately, in miscegenation and the adulteration of the Anglo-Saxon race, Debs responded: what Anglo-Saxon race? In the South, the keenest defenders of racial purity were liable to have been the "white" (Debs's quotation marks) offspring of slaveholders who had so recently made sport of defiling their female slaves. Indeed, in light of past and present evidence of the forced and voluntary sexual and social congress between the races, white Southerners' concern for racial purity appeared ironic to say the least. With some exaggeration Debs concluded that racial differences—already hard to distinguish in the workplace—were becoming undetectable in the laboratory. To the extent that race still mattered in American society, its salience reflected the success of white elites in fomenting racial animosity in order to degrade black and white workers alike.[31]

Debs argued, in effect, that social affiliation had to be voluntary to be real. As he explained it, the Socialist Party was mute on the issue of "social equality" because, in capitalism, the notion of equality was plainly counterfeit. Maldistribution of resources ensured that "equality" among white Southerners was barely skin deep. By distributing resources more equitably, Debs promised, socialism would promote the conditions of free agency. In postmillennial society, social relations—"like religion"—would be a function of individual choice. No doubt some individuals would continue to cling to race as the foundation of their identity, just as others would be content to live their lives within the contours of class. Our "Negro-hater," Debs wrote, could "consider himself just as 'superior' as he chooses, confine his social attentions exclusively to white folks, and enjoy his leisure time in hunting down the black specter who is bent on asking his daughter's hand in marriage." Socialism appealed to Debs precisely because it paved the way toward more vital affiliative possibilities. Class consciousness was but the means to a casteless, classless society.[32]

BEYOND RACE-CONSCIOUSNESS

W. E. B. Du Bois shared Eugene Debs's conviction that poverty and ignorance were incompatible with freedom. In chapter 9 of *The Souls of Black Folk,* Du Bois protested that releasing four million slaves into a competitive marketplace—"alone and unguided, without capital, without land, without skill, without economic organization, without even the bald protection of law, order, and decency"—had been irresponsible, not to mention foolish. Liberty required more than the mere loosening of bonds, he scolded; liberty demanded positive action undertaken on the victims' behalf. Although Du Bois sympathized with Debs's class analysis, experience taught him that the Socialist Party's "welcome" of 1903 reflected the sentiment of a small minority. Until America's virulent racism abated, Du Bois would look warily upon Debs's universalist pretensions. Indeed, from Du Bois's perspective, Debs's universalism seemed incomplete. A truly universal order required not merely an equitable distribution of economic, cultural, and intellectual resources, but the mutual respect of individuals and cultures for one another. Mutual respect, in turn, could only follow self-respect, a quality beaten out of African Americans by centuries of servitude. Debs might have improved on Zangwill's paean to the melting pot by demonstrating the social construction of racial animosity, but from Du Bois's vantage point, Debs's failure to consider how the residue of racism would influence mutuality and democracy in postmillennial society rendered his solution chimerical.[33]

Individual and collective self-respect, Du Bois insisted, were prerequisites of black participation in American cultural and political life. By coupling the concept of "race pride" with a commitment to integration—by linking the private to the public—Du Bois distinguished himself from the two most influential late-nineteenth-century African Americans, Booker T. Washington and Frederick Douglass. Unlike Douglass, Du Bois did not view race pride and integration as mutually exclusive. As a young man, Douglass had defended race pride, suggesting that African Americans would have to maintain "institutions of a complexional character" as the surest means to achieve "human brotherhood"; individual and group independence, Douglass then believed, was the "essential condition of respectability." But the aging, intermarried Douglass came to regard pride of race and human brotherhood as anathema. In an 1889 address commemorating the twenty-seventh anniversary of the abolition of slavery in the District of Columbia, Douglass anticipated Debs's remarks about the hollowness of identity based on inherited physical attributes. He argued that to regard skin color as the source of self-esteem and to prize race loyalty above principle was to adopt the mindset of the oppressor. Blacks should commend achievement among their fellows not because they were black but because they were men. Douglass also declared the uproar over miscegenation moot. Evidence everywhere around him suggested that Negroes and Caucasians had long since been mixed.[34]

If these convictions betray a certain self-consciousness about Douglass's intermarriage and integrationist agenda, they nevertheless present a compelling critique of interest-group politics. Historically, minorities tended to benefit from political unity, Douglass admitted; but the history of African Americans in the United States was anything but typical. The "ice" under African Americans was simply too thin, he believed, to sustain group concentration. Racial union would only exacerbate their social isolation and retard their entry into civilized society. "When we thus isolate ourselves," Douglass warned, "we say to those around us: 'we have nothing in common with you,' and, very naturally, the reply of our neighbors is in the same tone and to the same effect; for when a people care for nobody, nobody will care for them." Douglass exhorted African Americans to distribute themselves throughout white society and thereby hitch their fortunes to those of their white neighbors. "Common dangers," he concluded, "create common safeguards."[35]

Viewed charitably, one might interpret Douglass's integrationism as evidence of self-respect. Even so, from Booker T. Washington's point of view, one success story did not justify a general policy. In contrast to Douglass,

Washington believed that the time was not yet ripe for integration. In his notorious Atlanta Exposition Address of 1895, Washington assured an audience of white sponsors that their contribution to his campaign for black economic self-sufficiency would not underwrite the release into white society of untutored and undisciplined blacks. Socially, he averred, whites and blacks could remain "as separate as the fingers" on the hand, and "yet one in all things essential to mutual progress." Washington warned that responsible black leaders would not advocate a platform of social equality; black civil and political rights could only come after a period of intense "preparation"— a remark with which Du Bois himself might have concurred had Washington only subjected whites and blacks to the same criteria. Superficially, Washington's notion of "preparation" for citizenship jibed with Du Bois's sense of himself as a member of an African-American and Western cultural and intellectual vanguard. For who was more prepared than he? But Du Bois's confidence in his unimpeachable qualifications made Washington's gradualism and segregationism abhorrent. With increasing forcefulness at the turn of the twentieth century, Du Bois demanded that African Americans possessing the requisite moral and intellectual autonomy and economic independence be accorded the rights and immunities of American citizenship immediately; those wanting in this regard should be granted civil and political privileges just as soon as they were ready. The same, of course, should apply to whites.[36]

In autumn 1904, Du Bois proved that he had transcended the terms of the Douglass-Washington debate. That October he published a cryptic manifesto in the journal *Independent*, titled "Credo." After professing faith "in God who made of one blood all races that dwell on the earth" and which differed in "no essential particular," Du Bois testified to a special belief in the Negro race—with its "beauty . . . sweetness . . . and meekness"—and to a "pride of race so chivalrous as neither to offer bastardy to the weak nor beg wedlock of the strong." Du Bois also believed in Liberty, he announced, and in sacrifice and service. Evidently intended to dispel uncertainty among a mostly white audience (*The Souls of Black Folk* had appeared the previous year), "Credo" left a few questions unresolved in the mind of one young reader who interrogated the author about the relationship between black and white ideals. Should not African Americans live according to "absolute" rather than white standards? Was not this the way to "self-dependence and self-respect," and thus, ultimately, to the respect of white society? We can only imagine Du Bois's assent. Yet tensions remained amid his starkly professed beliefs. The object of life was to advance the march of principle, yet access to the realm of principle could come only through pride of race. All men deserved the liberty to live, associate, and reason freely, yet freedom could only follow the elevation of the entire group. Races differed in "no essential particular," yet the Negro race possessed a "genius," "soul," and "strength" all its own.[37] The ambiguity of these positions served Du Bois well over the years by leaving him room to maneuver.[38]

In order to appreciate Du Bois's ideas about the contingency of race and racial affiliation, we can compare them to Kallen's pluralism. On the face of it, Kallen and Du Bois had much in common. Both were members of historically persecuted minorities for whom culture represented the means to self-esteem. Both had been influenced by a Germany under the spell of Fichte, Hegel, and, especially, Herder, whose notions about the intrinsic qualities of peoplehood informed cultural conservatism and pluralism alike. Members of an educated elite, both Kallen and Du Bois shuddered at the cultural desiccation they saw in America around them. Both embraced culture—artistic and literary production—as the path to a new "American" ideal. Finally, both recognized a tension running through American democracy between liberty and equality, individualism and conformity, creativity and imitation. It was in their responses to this tension that Du Bois and Kallen differed, with Kallen evincing a serenity that Du Bois could never muster. Surely, Kallen's composure derived in part from the comparatively stable position of Jews in turn-of-the-century American life. Where Du Bois viewed culture and democracy as matters of life and death—as the foundation of African America's self-defense in the face of an outbreak of lynching, Kallen regarded pluralism as the means to consolidate and enrich gains already won.

"Democracy *Versus* the Melting Pot" is both a defense of cultural diversity and a saga of cultural decline. Kallen began by dismissing the contention of E. A. Ross that the so-called new immigrants imperiled American political and cultural institutions. Economically bereft, Ross's argument went, the newcomers could not help but lack the political virtues undergirding republican government. Kallen turned Ross's analysis on its head. Mere observation suggested that, far from jeopardizing American institutions, new immigrants numbered among the few constituencies that held American institutions to their highest standard. American government and immigrant cultures themselves acquired vitality from their mutual contact.[39] Kallen suspected that what bothered old-stock Americans like Ross was less a concern for social inequality than an aversion to cultural difference. For the first time since the nation's inception, old-stock Americans confronted in earnest the democratic logic of the founding documents that presaged not just geographic and administrative federation but cultural federation besides (DVM, 107–8; 81–2).

Conservatives like Ross misconstrued the stakes in the debate over the new immigration. Nurtured on principles of laissez-faire, they viewed economic and political independence not as the means to a higher end but as ends in themselves. Even if one granted conservatives the best intentions in decrying the destitution and industrial exploitation of the new arrivals, Kallen observed, their critique touched only the "conditions of life" in the United States, "not the kind of life," which conservatives assumed to be unitary and unchanging (DVM, 109; 115–6). In short, Americans confronted a profound choice at the turn of the twentieth century. They could realize the promise of democracy by extending it to the realm of culture, or throttle democracy by restricting it to an Anglo-American political, economic, and cultural elite. Meanwhile the world would be watching, its peace disturbed, its surface littered by past and present attempts to eradicate cultural difference in the interest of national "unison" (DVM, 110).

Kallen attributed the anxiety of American elites to cultural drift. The American colonies, especially New England, had once constituted a self-conscious and homogeneous civilization characterized by a prevailing "like-mindedness" and "ethnic and cultural unity." Cultural homogeneity combined with abundant resources to create rough social parity along with a spirit of freedom; equality and freedom, in turn, yielded an orderly and articulate "common life" capable of sustaining New England's wholesome dissenting tradition. As long as the colonies retained their cultural integrity, New England's sharp minds and biting wits stood a fair chance of mitigating the egoism and avarice endemic in American liberalism. But the twin shocks of industrialism and immigration combined with the triumph of laissez-faire to overwhelm Americans' traditional iconoclasm. As wealth came to represent its own end and the rich emerged as arbiters of what it meant to be "American," decay set in: imitation of Anglo-Americans on the part of immigrants, boosterism of Anglo-American civilization on the part of writers like Emerson. Kallen recognized signs of decline everywhere—in the transformation of New England literature from the "agonized" to the "optimistic"; in the bastardization of America's numerous subcultures, whose numbers staggered back and forth between New and Old Worlds as members of neither.[40]

To combat the "wastefulness" of American public life, Kallen vowed to make cultural "units" out of what had become social "aggregations." Joining Herder to John Locke, Kallen delineated a model of a "federal state" consisting of ethnic and cultural groups that compacted with one another to safeguard cultural integrity (DVM, 116). But where Locke had expected nongovernmental institutions like the market to provide the restraining and civilizing influences that made private life worth living, Kallen simply denied that anything meaningful derived from common life. "City life," he wrote, was "external, inarticulate, and incidental"; by contrast, the "inalienable" in life, its "intrinsic positive quality," derived from the "psycho-physical inheritance" of one's ancestors (DVM, 78). But how to convince America's disparate cultures, especially the dominant Anglo-Saxons, to join this confederation? Here Kallen's exuberance impeded rigorous analysis. Who could oppose an instrument that would release one's psycho-physical inheritance?

(DVM, 81). In contrast to Debs, Kallen assumed that mankind's will to ancestral connectedness trumped other kinds of affiliative desire. Pointing to the war in Europe as proof that "the poor of two different peoples tend to be less like-minded than the poor and the rich of the same peoples," Kallen ignored the war's evidence of the peril of compacts struck between cultural, or national, rivals. Following Locke, Kallen stressed the importance of self-restraint, equating "patriotism" with the recognition "that democracy means self-realization through self-control" and "self-discipline" (DVM, 121). But Kallen leaves readers wondering how member cultures were to develop these virtues. So thin is his conception of public life that is seems unlikely to have cultivated the necessary discipline. If his unstated assumption was that commercial intercourse would act as a restraining influence, then that raises the more vexing question of whether ethnic groups contending in the economy could retain cultural integrity. Furthermore, as the lament of E. A. Ross suggests, political and economic institutions are hardly culturally neutral. In short, "Democracy *Versus* the Melting Pot" presents an ahistorical model of culture that denies the inevitable overlap between public and private and ignores hierarchies of power both within and among cultures. It is not obvious, as Kallen claimed, that the poor and rich of a single culture have more in common than the poor of different cultures. If World War I proved anything decisively, it was the inescapability of historical context: in certain circumstances, culture and nation *will* trump other commitments, but on other occasions, class consciousness, for example, can overwhelm the influence of nation or culture. Egoism knows no cultural boundaries.[41]

Although Kallen ignored African Americans in "Democracy *Versus* the Melting Pot," his vision, applied to them, would have permanently inscribed inherited physical attributes as the badge of African-American identity. By contrast, W. E. B. Du Bois insisted that culture figured more prominently in determining racial identity than genes. Du Bois first articulated this belief in "The Conservation of Races," an address delivered at the inaugural meeting of the American Negro Academy in early March 1897 in Washington, D.C. The inspiration of the neo-Hegelian critic Alexander Crummell, the American Negro Academy repudiated Booker T. Washington's policy of subordinating higher education and civil rights to industrial training. If African Americans were ever to take their place among the world's great races, the academicians vowed, they would have to develop minds as well as muscle, cultivate race-consciousness, and stand up unabashedly for civil, legal, political rights. After reading "The Conservation of Races," it becomes clear that Du Bois proscribed African Americans from "beg[ging] wedlock of the strong," as he put it in "Credo," not because intermarriage would contaminate bloodlines—the races were already mixed—but because intermarriage without genuine social exchange would ensure the extinction of African-American civilization, one that had "much to teach the world." At the turn of the twentieth century, the prospects for genuine social exchange between the races were dwindling. The founding of the American Negro Academy coincided with mounting incidents of lynching, the near-total disenfranchisement of Southern blacks, and the one-year anniversary of *Plessy v. Ferguson*. In the face of physical, economic, and psychological oppression, it was natural for African Americans to want to de-emphasize race distinctions, Du Bois acknowledged, but such a response defied the laws of nature and history and invited further scorn.[42]

Du Bois began his Academy address by challenging the "scientific" conception of race. The multiplicity of world cultures far exceeded the three (Huxley and Raetzel) or five (Blumenbach) racial groupings posited by biologists. For race to retain its salience as a criteria of historical and sociological analysis, it would have to account for the earth's cultural diversity. "What, then, is a race?" Du Bois asked, with this in mind. "It is a vast family of human beings, *generally* of common blood and language, *always* of common history, traditions and impulses, who are voluntarily or involuntarily striving together for the accomplishment of certain more or less vividly conceived ideals of life" (emphasis mine). Du Bois identified eight such races extant in the world whose "spiritual, psychical, differences" were "more important" than "common blood" in determining their "cohesiveness and continuity." These "historical" races emerged in the modern era as a result of the teleological development by which families coalesced into cities and cities into nations. In this process, cultural differentiation *increased* among the nations as physical differences *diminished*. By the nineteenth century, culture combined with ancestry in the hereditary nation-state, which came to be seen as the repository for and guarantor of a people's unique ideals. As examples, Du Bois pointed to England and Germany, among others, each of which had come to represent a hallmark of Western civilization. Meanwhile, other race groups were "striving, each in its own way, to develop for civilization its particular message, its particular ideal, which shall help to guide the world nearer and nearer that perfection of human life for which we all long" (COR, 7–9).

On the face of it, "The Conservation of Races" seems to advance a theory of cultural identity consistent with Kallen's pluralism, or essentialism. The idea that each race, or culture, possessed a particular message and ideal might have come from Kallen himself. But by emphasizing the role of history in racial and cultural development, Du Bois delineated a cosmopolitan perspective that was more pragmatic than Kallen's and allowed for greater individual agency.[43] Where Kallen had expected individuals to perpetuate rather than shape culture—and hence reduced democracy to a set of procedures—Du Bois expected individuals to participate in an unfolding historical process that would result in cultural *and* individual realization. Where Kallen feared that all but the most rudimentary political contact would erode cultural integrity, Du Bois insisted that a people of mixed blood could nevertheless develop its own identity. Indeed, Du Bois implied that racial identity depended on cultural contact, which by throwing ideas into contest and comparison promoted excellence at the same time that it encouraged differentiation. Finally, where Kallen viewed the public realm as an instrument for private fulfillment, Du Bois regarded cultural realization as a preparation for the participation that would, in turn, deepen culture. As an end rather than an instrument, Du Bois's "public" far exceeded the scope of Kallen's. Once a people had secured its place in history, it must act the part of the talented tenth among races elsewhere, promoting self-expression and democracy throughout the world.[44]

Du Bois believed that the primary impediment to African-American cultural expression was self-doubt. Three centuries of persecution had convinced many African Americans that the way to avoid trouble was to de-emphasize racial distinctiveness. According to Du Bois, this fueled more persecution, as a people willing to cede its individuality would never garner public respect. But from Du Bois's perspective, race-consciousness was perfectly compatible with loyalty to the United States. In a passage in "The Conservation of Races" typically construed as essentialist, Du Bois underscored African Americans' overlapping affiliation: "We are Americans not only by birth and by citizenship," he maintained, "but by our political ideals, our language, our religion. Farther than that, our Americanism does not go. At that point, we are Negroes, members of a vast historic race that from the very dawn of creation has slept, but [is] half awakening in the dark forests of its African fatherland." Surely this was *far enough*. A still-fettered African-American culture had lent the nation "its only touch of pathos and humor amid its mad money-getting plutocracy," Du Bois observed; one more fully realized could not only "soften the whiteness of the Teutonic to-day," but would promote "that broader humanity which freely recognizes differences in men, but sternly deprecates inequality in their opportunities of development" (COR, 11–2).[45]

With their local "mission" complete and "the ideal of human brotherhood" established, African Americans would be free to affiliate with whom they chose. But Du Bois warned constituents not to seek their freedom in culture- or color-blindness. Freedom consisted in "social equilibrium"—a "due and just consideration to culture, ability, and moral worth." In order to achieve social equilibrium, blacks would have to cultivate moral discipline, while whites would have to uphold the nation's liberal principles by judging individuals on the basis of merit rather than race (COR, 15). Instead of using slavery to apologize for black degradation, Du Bois bound the fate of blacks and whites together. As long as prejudice and social condition were "reciprocal," he remarked in *The Souls of Black Folk,* only "a union of intelligence and sympathy across the color-line" could ensure the ascendancy of "justice and right."[46]

"HALLELUJAH CHORUS"

Like W. E. B. Du Bois, Jane Addams hoped that America might develop "music" representative of the nation's cultural and ethnic diversity. But where Du Bois focused primarily on the contribution of African Americans, Addams addressed the product of the nation as a whole. In "The Subjective Necessity for Social Settlements" (1892), she likened the role of Hull-House amid the maelstrom of late-nineteenth-century urban life to that of a choral conductor. "If you have heard a thousand voices singing in the Hallelujah Chorus in Handel's 'Messiah,'" she remarked, "you have found that the leading voices could still be distinguished, but that the differences of training and cultivation between them and the voices of the chorus were lost in the unity of purpose and the fact that they were all human voices lifted by a high motive. This is a weak illustration of what a settlement attempts to do." Actually, hers was a striking metaphor—so appropriate to the cultural atmosphere of turn-of-the-century America that Horace Kallen would return to it twenty-three years later. To both Addams and Kallen, the relationship among members of a chorus, or symphony, seemed ideally democratic: all were given individual voice, but individuality was subordinated to total effect; all understood the impact of their actions on the entire ensemble; all enjoyed the opportunity to advance, limited only by industry and natural ability. But who would write the symphony? Who conduct it? Where Kallen ignored how the distribution of resources would influence power relations in his orchestra, Addams spent her first three decades at Hull-House trying to establish the moral and practical foundation for a genuine democratic order.[47]

By the turn of the twentieth century, commercial and technological advances had altered the economic foundation of American citizenship at the same time that immigration rendered America's cultural homogeneity obsolete. Addams believed that if American democracy were to meet these global economic and demographic developments, it would have to be torn from its scholastic and paternalist moorings and set down among the people. To Addams this meant identifying a common interest capable of galvanizing the nation's different cultural groups without alienating its Anglo-American majority. Her experience at Hull-House convinced her that intimacy was the route to commonality. Where civil-service reformers thought to preserve their distance from the masses in order to legislate in their interest, Addams took up residency among the downtrodden to better identify the integrating force. She would found her social democracy on fundamental human compulsions.[48]

By the time World War I erupted, Jane Addams had been forging an ideal of "cosmopolitanism" for years. But it was Randolph Bourne who popularized the term among liberals with the publication of his essay "Trans-National America" in the *Atlantic Monthly* in summer 1916.[49] Bourne's transnationalism owed a great debt to Horace Kallen. Like Kallen, Bourne marveled at the irony of "hyphenated English-Americans" lamenting the provincialism of America's immigrant groups (TA, 251). Far from promoting immigrant assimilation to a single cultural norm, Anglo-American chauvinism had the paradoxical effect of encouraging cultural particularism, a development that Bourne viewed not as evidence of a failure of American democracy but as a sign of its enduring strength. The unintended consequences of Anglo-American chauvinism inspired Bourne to contemplate "what Americanism may rightly mean." Here was opportunity, he remarked, "to ask ourselves whether our ideal has been broad or narrow—whether perhaps the time has not come to assert a higher ideal than the 'melting pot' " (TA, 248–9). Like William James, Bourne viewed America as a "wandering star in a sky dominated by two colossal constellations of states." Could she not, he wondered, "work out some position of her own, some life of being in, yet not quite of, this seething and embroiled European world" (TA, 263)?

Like all the intellectuals of this study, Bourne regarded nationalism as a potentially saving grace. The point was not to jettison nationalism, from his perspective, but to redeem nationalism from nativism by challenging the Anglo-American monopoly on true "Americanism." In America, all citizens were foreign-born, all arrived seeking liberty and opportunity, all proved equally reluctant to surrender Old-World traditions. To insist, as Woodrow Wilson had during the Philippine-American War, that Anglo-Saxons possessed a unique predilection to democracy and liberty was to misinterpret both the nature of mankind and the significance of the saga unfolding on the American frontier. For it was the frontier, in Bourne's argument, not Anglo-Saxon political inheritance, that rendered America exceptional. Inanimate and inert, all potential and devoid of prejudice, the frontier functioned in Bourne's analysis as a universal public square. On the frontier, national cultures combined with nature to produce "a democratic cooperation in determining ideals and purposes and industrial and social conditions." Skeptics need only compare the "the great 'alien' states of Wisconsin and Minnesota" to the American South—that most Anglo-Saxon of regions—to comprehend the frontier's transforming force. "Let the Anglo-Saxon ask himself," Bourne charged, "whether he would really like to see the foreign hordes Americanized" along Southern lines. "Let him ask himself how much more wisdom, intelligence, industry and social leadership has come out of these alien states than out of all the truly American ones" (TA, 253). "Just in so far as our American genius has expressed the pioneer spirit, the adventurous, forward-looking drive of a colonial empire, is it representative of that whole America of the many races and peoples, and not of any partial or traditional enthusiasm" (TA, 256). By unfettering America from Anglo-American parochialism, Bourne aimed to demolish the "chief obstacle to the nation's social advance" (TA, 250).

Like Kallen, Du Bois, and even Debs, Bourne hoped America might become "a real nation, with a tenacious, richly woven fabric of native culture"—a vision that required replacing Americans' negative conception of freedom with a positive ideal. "If freedom means the right to do pretty much as one pleases, so long as one does not interfere with others, the immigrant has found freedom, and the ruling element has been singularly liberal in its treatment of the invading hordes," Bourne announced. "But if freedom means a democratic cooperation in determining the ideals and purposes and industrial and social institutions of a country, then the immigrant has not been free, and the Anglo-Saxon element is guilty of just what every dominant race is guilty of in every European country: the imposition of its own culture upon the minority peoples" (TA, 252). Here Bourne diverged from Kallen toward the cosmopolitans Dewey and Addams, and, to a certain extent, Du Bois. Where Kallen propounded an ideal of cultural democracy designed to maintain group integrity and mediate group interaction, Bourne expected cultural exchange to yield the integrating ideal itself.[50] For cosmopolitans, contact was the principal requisite of democracy and the means to both cultural development and national solidarity. Notwithstanding the conservatives' best effort, Bourne observed, America was the arena of a "thrilling and bloodless battle of Kulturs." In states like Wisconsin and Minnesota, Scandinavian, Polish, and German culture had found peculiarly hospitable soil. The result was a liberating "cross-fertilization" in which politics and society had attained "new potency." Far from succumbing to a numbing assimilation, these communities "remained distinct but cooperating to the greater glory and benefit, not only of themselves but of all the native 'Americanism' around them" (TA, 253). Quite by accident, America had developed into "a cosmopolitan federation of national colonies" living peaceably side by side. If citizens would cultivate this "world-federation in miniature," Bourne suggested, America might lead the way out of the world's devastating cycle of nationalist wars (TA, 258). This required elevating America's inchoate cosmopolitanism to full national consciousness, no mean feat in a "loose, free country" in which "no constraining national purpose, no tenacious folk-tradition and folk-style hold the people to a line" (TA, 255).

To this point, Bourne's defense of cultural democracy against Anglo-America's domestic imperialism, together with his notion that cultural interaction offered the only sane basis for national solidarity, perfectly jibed with Dewey's and Addams's cosmopolitanism. But Bourne's cosmopolitanism had its limits. James, Dewey, Addams, and Du Bois sought not to overcome nationalism, in the manner of traditional cosmopolitans, but to maintain nationalism and liberalism in dynamic equilibrium. Their cosmopolitanism, aside from being compatible with nationalism, was less elitist and more democratic than its Enlightenment predecessor; it came closer than other theoretical formulations to describing everyday life. Naturally, it was not tension-free. Cosmopolitanism presented my subjects with a host of political and moral dilemmas, none more vexing than the question of the relationship of leaders to followers and the problem of America's role in the world— dilemmas on full display in "Trans-National America."

At the core of "Trans-National America" lay a yearning that America might develop an indigenous aesthetic tradition capable of garnering the respect of American and European cultural arbiters.[51] This yearning posed a dilemma similar to that confronting James, Wilson, and Roosevelt as described in chapter 1: to whom should Americans of Bourne's generation turn for cultural recognition? Would the United States abide by conventional standards of aesthetic achievement? Or would the United States point the way toward new forms of cultural creativity based on its own history and environment? Committed to the principal of cultural originality, Bourne unwittingly promoted imitation by excluding from cultural participation legions of Americans who did not conform to his narrow ideal of what constituted cultural authenticity. According to Bourne, the hope for a vital national culture resided in the nuclei of America's disparate national groups. It was these rich stores of cultural expression that he vowed to protect from Anglo-American intolerance. But when Bourne turned from celebrating the cultural keenness of the core to denigrating those he described as "cultural half-breeds," he exposed the boundary of his cosmopolitan ideal. Blasting the "fringe" elements of America's cultural groups, he neglected both what James recognized as the hidden reservoirs of "eagerness" that constitute individuality and the social and political forces that thrust individuals toward the cultural margins in the first place—forces unlikely to submit to his and Kallen's reified notion of cultural integrity. Bourne imagined himself an advocate of dispossessed Americans, but his writing betrays condescension not unlike that which Addams detected among civil-service bureaucrats (TNA, 254). "Just so surely as we tend to disintegrate these nuclei of nationalistic culture do we tend to create hordes of men and women without a spiritual country, cultural outlaws, without taste, without standards but those of the mob," Bourne wrote. "The influences at the fringe . . . are centrifugal, anarchical. They make for detached fragments of peoples. Those who came to find liberty achieve only license. They become the flotsam and jetsam of American life, the downward undertow of our civilization with its leering cheapness and falseness of taste and spiritual outlook, the absence of mind and sincere feeling which we see in our slovenly towns, our vapid motion pictures, our popular novels, and in the vacuous faces of the crowds on the city street" (TA, 254–5).[52] Addams's experience in the neighborhoods surrounding Hull-House refuted Bourne's characterization of the cultural fringe. Adopting her perspective, we might ask whether Bourne's half-breeds appeared so derelict and, by contrast, his cultural clashes so bloodless, because he restricted his gaze to philosophical rivalries played out amid the open air of Midwestern pastures and the nation's universities. Just how his "intellectual internationalism" would influence relations in the nation's urban cauldrons—which Addams, despite her own pastoral bias, knew to be the testing ground of any democratic theory—we are left to guess (TNA, 259).[53]

Bourne's condescension invites us to distinguish not only pluralism from cosmopolitanism, but also democracy from elitism. Dewey's call for leadership, Addams's desire for a choral conductor, and Du Bois's celebration of the talented tenth should not be mistaken as evidence of underlying paternalism. Leadership is compatible with democracy. Democracy promises not that there will be no leaders and led, but that all will have the opportunity to rise to positions of authority limited only by the combination of ambition and innate ability. James, Dewey, Debs, Addams, and Du Bois expected the able-minded to help create conditions favorable to universal self-realization. To confuse their ideal of public service with elitism is to ignore their warning that it is not talent and expertise that pose a threat to democracy, but injustice.

Lapsed Bohemians, Germans, and Jews were not the only ones excluded from Bourne's beloved cosmopolitan community. By maintaining nationalism and liberalism in dynamic equilibrium, the cosmopolitans ensured that the two would come into conflict. Addams and Debs met such dilemmas by elevating universal over national interests, as we shall see. When nationalist push came to universalist shove, Bourne, Dewey, Du Bois, and James stood staunchly by the nation. Bourne's nationalism manifested itself ironically. In "The State," a manuscript left unfinished at his death in 1919, Bourne remarked on the deep strain of mythology informing Americans' understanding of U.S. history. Interpreting the founding era as a contest between democracy and privilege, Bourne observed that "the somewhat shockingly undemocratic origins of the American State have been almost completely glossed over and the unveiling is bitterly resented, by none so bitterly as the significant classes who have been most industrious in cultivating patriotic myth and legend."[54] A distinction between "country" and "state" informs this argument. The state, in Bourne's analysis, represents the entrenched power of a political and economic minority. Elevated to power by the U.S. Constitution, this elite maintained its position by manipulating state symbols (flag, anthem, holidays) and by propagating civic mythology. By contrast, the "country," which Bourne defined as the "inescapable group into which we are born, and which makes us its particular kind of a citizen of the world," was innately free of coercion.[55] It was the country, not the state, which loosed its energy on the American frontier. "The history of America as a country is quite different from that of America as a State," Bourne maintained. "In one case it is the drama of the pioneering conquest of the land, of the growth of wealth and the ways in which it was used, of the enterprise in education, and the carrying out of spiritual ideals, of the struggle of economic classes." By contrast, "as a State, its history is that of playing a part in the world, making war, obstructing international trade, preventing itself from being split to pieces, punishing those citizens whom society agrees are offensive, and collecting money to pay for all" (TS, 358). Bourne's rendering of westward expansion as free of coercion is notable for discounting the extensive role of the state in vanquishing the American frontier, for ignoring the violence befalling Native Americans and settlers alike, and for revealing the imperialist logic undergirding his cosmopolitanism. Read in conjunction with "The State," Bourne's enthusiasm in "Trans-National America" for "the forward-looking drive of a colonial empire" takes on an ominous character more consistent with Wilson's and Roosevelt's imperialism than with James's epistemological humility.

In an era of increasing sensitivity to cultural distinctions, Bourne's avowed cosmopolitanism lagged. Where James had cautioned Americans against judging foreign cultures on the basis of local norms, Bourne did not waver when describing the salutary potential of his transnational ideal on "the laggard peoples" of southeastern Europe. Anglo-Americans need not fear for the loyalty of America's migratory immigrants, Bourne observed; while it was undeniable that they often took their earnings back to the old country, they inevitably returned with a critical appreciation of "the superiority of American organization to the primitive living around them" (TNA, 262). To James, such appreciation would have seemed unfortunate. The cosmopolitan James hoped that America might export a democratic spirit, not a specific model of democratic organization, much less a cultural or commercial type. James would have recognized great irony in Bourne defending cultural pluralism at home while simultaneously celebrating the process by which all of Europe was becoming America.[56]

Comparing Dewey, Addams, and Du Bois to Bourne and Kallen, one senses that cosmopolitans believed that social democracy would result in putting the nation's resources at the disposal of all the people, while pluralists hoped that cultural democracy would make America safe for high cultural production. Viewed from this perspective, Bourne's "beloved community" betrays a certain clubbiness. Though there is much that draws one to his conviction that America's "idealisms must be those of future social goals in which all can participate," by this time he has given us ample reason to wonder about the precondition of admission to his *all* (TNA, 264).

Like Bourne and Kallen, John Dewey entered the debate about American identity not to refute the arguments of fellow liberals, but to challenge conservative programs for Americanization. As an educator Dewey opposed the campaign of Theodore Roosevelt and others to introduce military drill in public schools as a means to inculcate national loyalty. Imitative and atavistic, such proposals did not address America's modern predicament. "When Mr. Roosevelt writes with as much vehemence about national aid to vocational education," Dewey wrote in 1916, "national aid to wipe out illiteracy, and national aid for evening and continuation schools for our immigrants, as he now writes in behalf of military service, I for one shall take him more seriously as an authority on the educational advantages of setting-up exercises, firing guns and living in the camp."[57] Yet, for all his palpable frustration with Roosevelt and company, Dewey welcomed America's "awakening to the presence in our country of large immigrant masses who may remain as much aliens as if they never entered our gateways."[58] In a series of essays published in *The New Republic, Journal of Education,* and *Menorah Journal* between 1916 and 1918, Dewey described a vision of American civic identity that tried to reconcile enthusiasm for cultural diversity with the imperatives of individual autonomy and national cohesion.

As we saw in chapter 1, James, Wilson, and Roosevelt regarded the passing of the American frontier as a problem for national solidarity. In the face of nature's gripping challenges, the argument went, Americans lost their egoism and laid the foundation for a genuine national culture. Dewey addressed the same concern. But where James, Wilson, and Roosevelt eschewed industry as an arena of virtue and culture, Dewey saw industry as the source and site of America's cultural development. Herein lay his contribution to the civic identity debate: visions of politics and culture aloof from material environment were irrelevant and doomed to failure. "Any democracy which is more than an imitation of some archaic republican government must issue from the womb of our chaotic industrialism," he wrote. American society comprised an industrial base, a diverse population, and a political constitution that separated nationality (race and ethnicity) from citizenship—conditions with the potential to yield a mass "community of directed thought and emotion." Dewey was not naive about the odds for success. The very material, political, and demographic resources that he marshaled for his cultural project were rife with conflict and inequality. But better to meet conflict and inequality head-on than to fly in its face. And far better to have tried and failed than to endorse the "puny irrelevancy that measures our strivings with yardsticks handed down from class cultures of the past."[59] Not by fealty to the forefathers would the world's great nations be judged, but by their "contribution to art and science."

As with Du Bois, Dewey's originality emerges in comparison with Horace Kallen. Besides coining the term "cultural pluralism," Kallen is known for having likened cultural pluralism to orchestral harmony.[60] Once politics and economics were brought to heel and construed as means rather than ends, Kallen maintained, they would underwrite "the realization of the distinctive individuality of each *natio* that composes it and of the pooling of these in a harmony above them all." Like the instruments of an orchestra, America's different cultures would contribute distinct themes and melodies to the "symphony of civilization." Thus far, Kallen's metaphor accords with Addams's likening of Hull-House to Handel's "Hallelujah Chorus." In the "Hallelujah Chorus," Addams suggested, individual voices, performing the same score and under expert direction, combine to create soaring harmony. Kallen pressed the metaphor further, dispensing with both score and direction. Where conventional symphonies were prearranged, he explained, "in the symphony of civilization the playing is the writing, so that there is nothing so fixed and inevitable about its progressions as in music, so that within the limits set by nature they may vary at will, and the range and variety may become wider and richer and more beautiful."[61] Undeniably arresting, Kallen's vision borders on anarchy. "I quite agree with your orchestra idea," wrote Dewey, "but upon condition we really get a symphony and not a lot of different instruments playing simultaneously."[62] Kallen, of course, could provide no such guarantee. Indeed, he seems to have fixed on a metaphor that outpaced even his own enthusiasm for improvisation, which, in the economic and political spheres, had been the principal target of his larger critique. When republishing the essay in 1924, he appended the mitigating phrase "or the reverse" to the end of a peroration anticipating "richer and more beautiful harmonies." Evidently inserted to refute charges of naiveté, the caveat seems more likely to have substantiated skeptics' original fears—for who could endorse a civic ideal conducive to bedlam?[63]

Not Dewey. Dewey assented to Kallen's posing of the social and cultural dilemmas confronting America. He shared Kallen's aversion to laissez-faire economics and the political passivity it bred. And he concurred with Kallen's conviction that the spirit of America was yet "inarticulate." But Dewey disagreed with Kallen about the end cultural diversity would serve. Their difference stemmed from contrasting views of culture itself. Where Kallen prized culture for ennobling the private realm, Dewey viewed it as a source of public enrichment and a requisite of political mobilization. Where Kallen aimed to safeguard cultural integrity for oppressed national groups, Dewey hoped to promote cultural assimilation. His was an essentially Hegelian vision, but with the unity coming from the bottom up. "I never did care for the melting pot metaphor," he wrote Kallen, "but genuine assimilation *to one another*—not to Anglo-Saxondom—seems to be essential to an America. That each cultural section should maintain its distinctive literary and artistic traditions seems to me most desirable, but in order that it might have the more to contribute to others."[64] Kallen's "cultural revivals," as Dewey called them, appeared too "reminiscent and literary" to provide sustenance to an industrializing nation. They merely perpetuated in group form America's "legalistic individualism," a social philosophy as hostile as militarism to genuine civic-mindedness but no less derivative. Worse, Dewey suggested in the *Journal of Education,* by emphasizing self-preservation and recapitulation, cultural revivalism threatened to spawn the sort of self-serving, invidious cultural valorizations that inspired Kallen's critique in the first place (205).[65]

To be fair, Kallen's principal rhetorical burden in "Democracy *Versus* the Melting Pot" was not to promote an ideal of national culture, but to make the country safe for ethnic diversity. It was nativists' counterfeit claim to be speaking for the nation, after all, that justified the oppression of cultural minorities undertaken in the nation's name. Kallen's ideal inevitably implicated him in the civic national aspect of Dewey's larger cultural project—for the same reason that had implicated Du Bois. To unhinge American civic identity from skin color or national origin required attaching it to a shared political culture. Kallen was moved to clarify his thoughts on the relationship of pluralism to nationalism in the spring of 1919, when the philosopher Morris Cohen attacked Zionism in the *New Republic.* Cohen accused Zionists of sacrificing Enlightenment rationality ("impartial truth") to group loyalty. Rooted in "nationalist philosophy," Cohen contended, Zionism constituted an implacable "challenge to all those who still believe in liberalism." Zionism opposed assimilation, "the slow movement known as enlightenment" that bound Jews and gentiles in common fate. Zionism was outdated, recalling days when group solidarity constituted a reasonable response to group suffering. Modern communication and interdependence rendered that response obsolete, Cohen averred, a point missed by ambitious academics who stoked reaction against "the old faith in the power of cosmopolitan reason and enlightenment" in order to clear the few remaining hurdles. Blinded by ambition and dead to irony, Zionists adapted the racist ideology of their oppressors, merely turning it on its head. Jews now became the superior race, Judaism the chosen religion. "All sorts of virtues," mocked Cohen, "love of family, idealism, etc., are the characteristic qualities of its spirit. Only in Palestine can this spirit find root and only in the Hebrew language its adequate expression."[66]

Cohen drew on emerging scientific evidence to repudiate Zionism's putative racialist premise as "false and profoundly inimical to humanistic civilization." Biologically, racial purity would promote degeneracy; culturally, it would result in stagnation. Hybridism was the stuff of cultural distinction. "No great civilization was ever achieved," Cohen wrote, "except by a mixed people freely borrowing from others in religion, language, laws and manners." Jews themselves had made their notable contributions to humanity only after departing Palestine (ZTL, 182). Ideologically misguided and culturally bereft, Zionism contradicted American principles, particularly the commitment to individuality. Cohen contrasted Zionism's emphasis on group autonomy and tribal loyalty to the freedom of conscience and association individuals enjoyed on American soil. Freedom of conscience and association sparked the creativity that propelled civilization, leading Cohen to conclude that Palestine offered Jews no "single opportunity . . . not open, to a larger extent, here." In sum, Cohen accused Zionists of trying to evade the principal burden of early-twentieth-century life and the ultimate test of the Enlightenment: enabling different cultures to dwell harmoniously in a shrinking world. Zionism proved the inevitability of cultural contact in this era, if only inadvertently. For what about the fate of Palestinians? Zionists appeared only too willing "to ignore the rights of the vast majority of the non-Jewish population of Palestine, quite like the Teutonic idealists with their superior kultur." Nor were Palestinians the only analogue that came to mind. The presumption that a Palestinian homeland would somehow inspire and uplift American Judaism seemed to Cohen as dubious as "the argument that an independent Liberia will elevate the position of the American Negro." The Enlightenment would be measured against contemporary states resolving, not evading, the Jewish, Negro, and, indeed, Palestinian problems. Their persistence suggested not that the Enlightenment had somehow failed, but merely that work remained to be done. "The stress of recent events calls out loudly the need for a refreshing faith in individual freedom and enlightenment" (ZTL, 183).

Though his target was Zionism, Cohen's vindication of the Enlightenment can be read as an indictment of pluralism itself. Kallen's response to Cohen, also in the *New Republic,* suggests that there were two Kallens at work in the 1915 *Nation* essay: the sworn enemy of nativism and the colleague and admirer of Dewey. The enemy of nativism was conventionally pluralist. In repudiating Ross, Kallen drew on a strain of German romanticism emanating from Herder and averse to cultural mixing. By contrast, the author of the beleaguered orchestra metaphor was both more open than Herder to the prospect of cultural exchange and, necessarily, more attuned to the imperative of political solidarity.[67] The ideal of federation Kallen articulated in "Democracy *Versus* the Melting Pot" tacitly traded on Enlightenment ideals, as Kallen wed Herder to socialized versions of Locke and Mill to ensure a political climate conducive to cultural tolerance. In meeting Cohen's attack on Zionism, Kallen made plain his commitment to the Enlightenment. In the process, a more cosmopolitan, if still culturally elitist, Kallen emerged than has been generally recognized by Kallen scholars.[68] At the heart of his rebuttal lay the premise that Zionism and liberalism, far from being anathema, were part of a modern Enlightenment project whose prophet was Mazzini.

Kallen began his rejoinder to Cohen determined to retrieve nationalism from the historical wasteland to which Cohen had consigned it. Far from atavistic, Kallen argued, nationalism was a natural and enduring sentiment no less universal than the individual's vaunted capacity for reason. Particularly keen among oppressed peoples, it uttered "a state of mind and feeling basic to established as well as aspiring nationalities." Kallen acknowledged that nationalism, "like other philosophies," rested "upon premises in nature and in human experience and aspiration which can be used to establish conclusions that are paranoia and fantasy." The same was true of liberalism. Kallen resented Cohen's associating Zionism with the pathological fulminations of a few zealots. Mainstream Zionism rested on the "normal nationalist philosophy" common to Poles, Greeks, Italians, and so on. Far from contradicting liberalism, Zionism extended the tenets of liberalism "from the individual to the group." Indeed, Kallen suggested, the liberalism imbedded in Zionism and other religions had antedated by a millennium the political liberalism that Spinoza, for example, anticipated would one day resolve the Jewish problem. To decry Zionism for being anti-assimilationist in the face of the ongoing cultural persecution sponsored by Pan-Germanic and Pan-Slavic reactionaries—with "their echoes in America"—was to join league with the historical Inquisition. After all, democracy itself was anti-assimilationist, Kallen observed, now with a nod to Dewey's and Addams's insistence on the need for cultural leadership. "It stands for the acknowledgment, the harmony and organization of group diversities in cooperative expansion of the common life." It was just this ideal—really the essence of democracy—that had been denied Jews on account of creed and nationality (ZDP, 311).[69]

Cohen's account of the Enlightenment was parsimonious. It offered Jews individual liberty only on condition that they ceased to be Jews. By contrast, Kallen's Zionism would extend "the principle of enlightenment by requiring for the Jew complete individual liberty not only as an abstract 'human being' of ambiguous nationality, but also as a Jew" (ZDP, 312). Like Du Bois, the Kallen of 1919 regarded group liberty as a prerequisite of individual autonomy: only individuals possessing the choice of whether to affiliate with their inherited culture could accurately be described as free. If, as Cohen maintained, nationality no longer posed a problem for French, Polish, and Italian Americans, that was because majorities of them dwelled in states recognized as homelands. Their status was not ambiguous. A Jewish homeland would similarly resolve the problem of Jewish ambiguity (ZDP, 312–3). Kallen concurred with Cohen's conclusion that any contribution American

Jews might make to civilization they would make *as Americans*. But Kallen was not satisfied with that. He found it "a curious sort of liberalism" that would celebrate the cultural distinctiveness of, say, the Spanish and French all the while denying such distinctiveness to Jews. "The French or English or Italian contributions to civilization come from France and England and Italy, not from America," he wrote. "For obvious reasons each is more purely and essentially that and nothing else in the home country which is a living individuality of its particular kind, absorbing and assimilating influences from the whole world and making them over into the substance of its own flesh and spirit" (ZDP, 313). Absorbing and assimilating aspects of other cultures, yet honing these influences into a distinctive community of flesh and spirit—here was a cosmopolitan take on Enlightenment: "a democratic cooperative organization of nationalities, no less than of other forms of the association of men, in the endeavor after life, liberty and happiness" (ZDP, 313).

In the years leading up to his appointment to the Supreme Court in 1916, Louis Brandeis defended Zionism in similar terms—as true Americanism, a model of the civic vitality bequeathed the nation by cultural diversity. A Deweyan democrat no less averse than James to "bigness" and as fiercely solicitous as Debs of the rights of labor, Brandeis brought together many of the different strains of civic identity described in this chapter. Like so many Progressive-Era intellectuals, Brandeis did not include African Americans, Native Americans, or Chinese and Japanese immigrants in his analysis, but there is nothing in his logic that precludes its extension to these and other ethnoracial groups. His writing about the plight of Palestinians lacked such amplitude, by contrast. Brandeis simply expected Palestinians to submit to Jewish rule, as if his observations about the universal will to nationhood and the reciprocal relationship between freedom and choice did not apply to them.[70] In Brandeis we encounter one of the fullest accounts of early-twentieth-century American cosmopolitanism while coming face to face with its limits.

Brandeis did not come to Zionism by inheritance. Born in 1856 in Louisville, Kentucky, to a largely assimilated family, he was educated in Germany and at Harvard University and rose to prominence in Boston's legal community in the 1880s and 1890s. Much of his business and most of his writing up to 1916 addressed the social and economic upheaval attending the rise of American industrialism. Increasingly, he exploited ethical principles in the Jewish prophetic tradition and professional contacts among Boston Jewish society to promote social and industrial reform, so that by the early 1910s he had begun to identify himself as a Jew. Historian Allon Gal has described the process by which Brandeis's "Judaization" yielded to "Zionization," once he resolved that the way to preserve Judaism's ethical ideals and cultural riches was to establish a homeland in Palestine. The record of early Jewish settlement in Palestine enchanted him. There he found, in Gal's words, a salutary "balance between the enhancement of individual potential and the imperatives of social responsibility. The accomplishments of small, democratic Jewish Palestine were for him a cherished model and antidote to the stifling monopolization and the oppressive bigness he bitterly fought against in America."[71] Through the end of World War I, Brandeis regarded Zionism not as a means to escape local problems, but as a paragon of industrial and social democracy thoroughly in keeping with American ideals.

Progressive-era historiography regards Americanization as inherently coercive.[72] For the cosmopolitan patriots, Americanization *became* coercive in the hands of nativists. Brandeis was no more adverse to the notion of Americanization, per se, than Bourne, Dewey, or Addams. Like theirs, his reading of Americanization was unconventional, as critical of American injustice as it was demanding of old stock and immigrant alike. Wilson, Roosevelt, and Bourne believed self-discipline tracked along cultural lines; they feared liberty would become license in the hands of peoples untutored in self-government. Brandeis had more faith in individuals and more confidence in the binding power of freedom. On Independence Day 1915, he delivered a speech titled "True Americanism" to a gathering at Boston's Faneuil Hall. Amid mounting agitation about national disintegration that summer, President Wilson had urged Americans to make the July 4 holiday "Americanization Day." Brandeis was only too happy to comply. "What is Americanization?" he demanded. Superficially, it meant immigrants adopting American clothes, customs, and manners. Significantly, it entailed immigrants learning and using English "as the common medium of speech." Yet language itself was nothing compared to the more fundamental shift of allegiance Americanization implied. "Immigrants must be brought into complete harmony with our ideals and aspirations and cooperate with us for their attainment," Brandeis declared; only then could they be said to "possess the national consciousness of an American."[73] Thus far, little distinguished Brandeis on Americanization from Wilson or Roosevelt. But Brandeis acknowledged something they ignored. Despite their strange customs and lack of English, many immigrants arrived in the new world "already truly American" by the standard he delineated. If their allegiance eroded upon arrival, fault lay not with the newcomers but with Americans' failure to abide by the principles of equal opportunity and equality before the law (TA, 4–5).

Brandeis insisted that industrial dependence, not strangeness itself, constituted the principal threat to immigrants' and workers' virtue. Hence Americans would have to revise their programs for Americanization. Liberal theory expects individuals once freed from fetters to make their happy way in the world. Brandeis argued that the egalitarian marketplace that liberalism

assumes did not exist in early-twentieth-century America. It therefore de-
volved upon the state to maintain conditions conducive to open competition
and hence virtue—the better "to fit its rulers for their task" (TA, 5). As we
saw in the writing of Randolph Bourne, it is easy to decry the state as a font
of coercion. Like Debs, Brandeis regarded state coercion not as proof of the
state's innate evil, but as evidence that an ideally public institution had been
overrun by private interests. If the state waxed monstrous at the turn of the
twentieth century, as Henry James suggested, this was due to its hijacking by
a corporate elite. And to Americans' failure to identify genuine threats to the
national welfare. Like Dewey and Addams, Brandeis argued that a state less
obsessed with sorting, sifting, and fumigating immigrants at Ellis Island and
more committed to ensuring the viability of "the American standard of living" would have no reason to fear its citizens' loyalty. By curbing "capitalis-
tic combination," upholding the workers' right to organize, and introducing
"some system of social insurance," the state could secure workers' health,
education, and leisure—minimal requirements of an independent, and loyal,
citizenry (TA, 5–7).

Brandeis acknowledged that other European nations outpaced America in
providing some of these safeguards. Many were no less committed than the
United States to individuality, liberty, and democracy. What distinguished
America from other nations, he observed, was its extension of democracy
from individuals to cultural minorities. America recognized "racial equality
as an essential of full human liberty and true brotherhood, and that racial
equality is the complement of democracy." America believed "that we must
not only give to the immigrant the best we have, but must preserve for America the good that is in the immigrant and develop in him the best of which
he is capable." And it placed democracy and humility before aristocracy and
arrogance, rejecting the claim that "strong nationalities . . . possessed the divine right to subject other peoples to their sway" (TA, 9–10). In retrospect,
of course, Brandeis's vision appears foreshortened. How could he trumpet
America's racial tolerance while turning a blind eye on the plight of, say,
African Americans? His vantage point was comparative, or horizontal: by
contrast to cultural persecution around the world, America's record seemed
noteworthy.

Brandeis was closer to Kallen than to Dewey in delineating an ideal of
national solidarity based on politics rather than culture. For Brandeis, virtue
was a means to political participation, for Dewey the means to cultural creativity and self-expression. But Brandeis was more like Dewey and Addams
in expecting immigrants to ultimately relinquish their peculiar cultural gifts
into what Dewey called the nation's "common fund" (NE, 203). Hence the
importance to Brandeis of immigrants being able to reach back to homelands
from which to draw the sustenance requisite of cultural renewal. Zionism,

as he saw it, not only maintained communities requisite to individual autonomy, it simultaneously ensured the perpetuity of these communities in both
pure (Old World) and mongrel (New World) form. So long as immigrants
had homelands and the nation's borders remained porous, American society at large and immigrant communities in particular would be revitalized
by new arrivals. In "Democracy *Versus* the Melting Pot," Kallen advanced
an ideal of cultural perpetuation. Brandeis described a model of generational
reciprocity reminiscent of Du Bois. Individuals should resist assimilation and
enlist in the Zionist cause, thereby promoting the ultimate end of freedom.
Zionism was "not a movement to remove all the Jews of the world com-
pulsorily to Palestine," he cautioned. Nor was it "a movement to compel
anyone to go to Palestine." Zionism aimed, simply, to enable Jews "to live
at their option either in the land of their fathers or in some other country"
altogether—"a right which members of small nations as well as large, which
Irish, Greek, Bulgarian, Serbian, or Belgian, may now exercise as fully as
Germans or English."[74] In drafting Jewish men and women into Zionism,
Brandeis was no less mindful than Du Bois of the importance of autonomy
and creativity to a functioning democracy. Brandeis recognized that as a mere
program for cultural preservation, Zionism would fade into what Dewey
called "puny irrelevancy." Where Kallen wed Herder to Locke and Mill to
protect ethnoracial diversity, Brandeis joined Mazzini to Zionist sage Ahad
Ha'am to secure individual autonomy and community integrity at the same
time. "I live for the sake of the perpetuation and happiness of the community of which I am a member," Ha'am had written. "I die to make room for
new individuals, who will mould the community afresh and not allow it to
stagnate and remain forever in one position." Such give and take, Du Bois
had argued, constituted what he and Brandeis knew to be the "very essence"
of democracy.[75]

Brandeis had once shared Roosevelt's and Wilson's suspicion of "hype-
nates."[76] By 1915 he had come to regard Old-World attachment as compatible with American citizenship. Zionism, like other forms of national allegiance, did not conflict with patriotism, he told a convocation of New York
City rabbis the previous June. As we have seen, he believed that the chief
impediment to national loyalty derived not from competing forms of attachment, but from the incapacity for loyalty of any kind among workers and
immigrants pushed to the margin of subsistence, a sentiment he shared with
philosophers James and Royce.[77] "Multiple loyalties are objectionable," he
remarked, "only if they are inconsistent. A man is a better citizen of the
United States for being also a loyal citizen of his state, and of his city; for
being loyal to his family, and to his profession or trade; for being loyal to his
college or his lodge." Hence, just as "every Irish American who contributed
towards advancing home rule was a better man and a better American for

the sacrifice he made," so "every American Jew who aids in advancing the Jewish settlement in Palestine, though he feels that neither he nor his descendants will ever live there, will likewise be a better man and a better American for doing so." Struggle made for excellence. Zionist exertion and discipline would simultaneously ennoble Jews and brace American society (JP, 28). Moreover, Jews brought to citizenship something other immigrants did not. Theorist Rogers Smith has described the arguments that Anglo-American nativists deployed over the course of the nineteenth century to bar unwanted immigration. Refugees from southern and eastern European autocracies allegedly made poor citizen material for having had no prior experience with self-rule.[78] Brandeis turned this argument back on nativists. Not only did many immigrants arrive already American, as we have seen, but Jews particularly came "not as to a strange land, but as to a home." Witness Russian Jews' ready adjustment to American society. This was due not to some peculiar Jewish proclivity, but to "the fact that the twentieth century ideals of America have been the ideals of the Jew for more than twenty centuries." For American Jews, "democracy was not an ideal merely. It was a practice . . . made possible by the existence among them of certain conditions essential to democracy": a sense of duty, high intellectual attainment, submission to leadership ("as distinguished from authority"), and a sense of community (CEJ, 63). "The Jewish spirit," Brandeis proclaimed, was "essentially modern and essentially American. . . . America's fundamental law seeks to make real the brotherhood of man. That brotherhood became the Jewish fundamental law more than twenty-five hundred years ago." Like Du Bois on slavery, Brandeis put a positive gloss on centuries of Jewish persecution. Their "affliction as well as their religion has prepared the Jews for effective democracy. Persecution broadened their sympathies" and "trained them in patient endurance, in self-control, and in sacrifice." In short, "it deepened the passion for righteousness" (JP, 29). Compared to this record, nativists were but neophytes in the tradition of self-government.[79]

Read in light of Dewey's unifying project, Kallen's and Brandeis's Enlightenment-based defense of Zionism suggests that cosmopolitanism can sustain a range of ideas about national culture. To the extent that Kallen and Brandeis described a national culture at all, it was born of commitment to a set of political safeguards designed to promote cultural diversity. Though negative in theoretical terms, this ideal need not be hollow. By enumerating the political practices Zionist Americanism entailed, Brandeis redeemed the abstraction of Kallen's orchestra metaphor. Whether Brandeis met Du Bois's objections to Kallen is less clear. Du Bois, as we have seen, found Kallen's pluralism insufficiently sensitive to the requisites of modern subjectivity forged in the crucible of public cultural exchange. Du Bois's aspiration to *sit with Shakespeare* required more than a negative commitment to liberty and tolerance.[80] It demanded citizens consciously engaging with one another in political, economic, and high cultural projects despite real or imagined ethnoracial and cultural differences. For Kallen, political culture safeguarded America's ethnic groups from one another; for Du Bois, as well as for Bourne, culture allied these groups in common endeavors. This did not go far enough for Dewey. From Dewey's perspective, a genuine national culture needed the backdrop not of common endeavors, but of a singular endeavor—an inanimate "other" (nature or industry) whose taming would inspire citizens to new levels of solidarity, initiative, and excellence. As critic Lewis Menand suggests, this is the lesson Florence Kelley taught Jane Addams. No amount of goodwill could create among settlement-house workers and their neighbors the solidarity forged by joining together to root out municipal corruption. In words that might have come from Dewey, Kelley warned colleagues against retreat in the face of the modern industrial juggernaut. "We must learn to trust our democracy, giant-like and threatening as it may appear in its uncouth strength and untried applications," she wrote. And later: "We have learned to say that the good must be extended to all of society before it can be held secure by any one person or any one class; but we have not yet learned to add to that statement, that unless all men and all classes contribute to a good, we cannot even be sure that it is worth having."[81] By this standard Brandeis seems to have been closer to Kelley, Debs, Addams, and Dewey than to Kallen and Bourne, whose visions of national enterprise did not seem to connect with the aspirations of ordinary citizens.

Dewey argued that a culture rooted in industry (and therefore "science") could reflect the input of every citizen. Heretofore, even the most vital of the world's cultures did not reflect the contribution of their entire populations. Rather, national elites—buoyed by "the accidents of a learned education, the possession of leisure and a reasonably apt memory for some phrases, and a facile pen for others"—produced cultural artifacts that they later adorned with the national seal. By contrast, science made democracy possible, Dewey wrote, by relieving society of its dependence on "massed human labor," by substituting "inanimate forces for human muscular energy," and by releasing "resources for excess production and easy distribution."[82] In Europe, the liberating potential of science was thwarted by enduring class divisions and cultural particularism; by contrast, in the United States, no such legacy—and indeed no entrenched cultural inheritance—existed to impede the creation of the world's first universal culture. But only if America resisted the European inclination to equate unity with cultural homogeneity. The "peculiarity of *our* nationalism," Dewey wrote in the *Journal of Education* in 1916, "is its internationalism"; America's "national spirit" comprised "a common fund of wisdom and experience" drawn from peoples the world over (NE, 204–6).

Who could say what new forms of "thought and sentiment" a culture rooted in industry and crisscrossed by all classes and peoples would spawn? Dewey only knew that "effecting the transfiguration of the mechanics of modern life into sentiment and imagination" constituted an enterprise of "heroic dimensions."[83]

If Dewey's writing on national culture seems to pay too much attention to getting along and not enough to specific structural changes implied by his ideal, surely it is due partly to the kinds of questions he was asked, as an educator, to address: "What has the American public school done toward subordinating a local, provincial, sectarian, and partisan spirit of mind to aims and interests which are common to all the men and women of the country—to what extent has it taught men to think and feel in ideas broad enough to be inclusive of the purposes and happiness of all sections and classes" (NE, 203)? Dewey took for granted that schools would teach reading, writing, arithmetic, science, history, and geography, among other topics. But he thought schools could do more. They could promote individual autonomy and communal solidarity and thereby check racial and industrial "feudalism." Here was a source of national solidarity, an educational curriculum designed to promote not workers' docility, but "industrial intelligence": "knowledge of the conditions and processes of present manufacturing, transportation and commerce—so that the individual may be able to make his own choices and his own adjustments, and be master, so far as in him lies, of his own economic fate."[84] By bringing "the light of science and the power of work to the aid of every soul that it may discover its quality," such a curriculum would enable every individual to "realize distinction. For the first time in history, culture would be seen as an individual achievement and not a class possession" (AEC, 200). As we noted, Kallen hesitated endorsing any sort of social leadership in the United States. Dewey harbored no such compunctions. His problem was not leadership per se, but caste and condescension. Hence Dewey expected government to play the leading role in the work of Americanization—a role at once "paternal and scientific."[85] Dewey took seriously the plight of newcomers to the United States, many of them destitute upon arrival and alienated both by America's anonymous mass culture and by corporate industrialism. Reasonably, he concluded that immigrants would have an easier time finding work and pressing claims in America if they spoke English. Judging from their behavior, immigrants concurred with him.[86] Government would demand something of immigrants; they should speak English, for example, and work and obey the laws. But Dewey put the major onus of Americanization on government itself, in a way perhaps surprising to many scholars. "If every foreign illiterate had compulsory educational service to perform," Dewey wrote in the *New Republic,* "if he had not only the opportunity but the obligation to learn the English language, if he found conditions of labor safeguarded in the interest of his health and his integrity as an economic agent, and if he learned to associate these things in whatever part of the country he found himself with the United States and not with the district, township or state, it would not be long before compulsory military service, if it had to be discussed at all, would be discussed as a military proposition and not as an educational one." [87] A genuine democracy had no need to fear its citizens' loyalty. *E Pluribus Unum* meet *Quid Pro Quo*.

Like Dewey and Brandeis, Jane Addams equated America not with some Anglo-Saxon inheritance, but with self-government. Where Kallen viewed the private, or cultural, realm as the route to self-realization, Addams insisted that self-expression was a function of public engagement—of political, social, and cultural exchange. Addams regarded self-discipline as one component of self-government; but, from her perspective, self-government demanded more than the "negative" ability to keep one's ego in check: it required a "positive" commitment among its citizenry to promote universal self-expression. Addams saw the debates about immigration restriction and military drill not as a momentary aberration but as an inevitable consequence of Americans' failure to adjust the nation's democratic institutions to a century of demographic and economic change. In her St. Louis Exposition address of 1904, and in her subsequent book, *Newer Ideals of Peace,* Addams evinced no surprise that a government that had not concerned itself with the lives of ordinary people soon found itself alienated from its constituents and searching vainly for some mechanism by which to inculcate popular loyalty. A self-described "patriot," Addams confessed to being "jealous" of the American labor movement for receiving immigrants' "comradeship and fine *esprit de corps*" when it ought to have accrued to government. But it had been the union and not the government, she regretted, that "had concerned itself with real life, shelter, a chance to work, and bread for [immigrant] children"; it had been the union and not the government that had approached immigrants "in a language they could understand"; it had been the union and not the government that had given immigrants their "first chance to express themselves through a democratic vote, to register by a ballot their real opinion upon a very important matter." [88]

Resolved to make America's democratic institutions reflect the diversity of her age, Addams struck out in search of a "national ideality"—a "method by which to discover men, to spiritualize, to understand, to hold intercourse with aliens and to receive of what they bring." Although she admired the Socialist Party's determination to make politics bear on industry, she recoiled instinctively from its divide-and-conquer strategy. Addams viewed group morality as the product of reciprocal group relations; unless means jibed with ends, there would be no end to social resentment and economic oppression (NIP, 127). Moreover, Addams accused Socialists of reinscribing the conservatives' "imperialism of virtue" (NIP, 112). Erecting "two substitutes for human nature"—proletariat and capitalist—Socialists ignored humankind's "imperfect" and "incalculable" character, thereby inadvertently circumscribing self-expression, and, ultimately, self-government (NIP, 86). There had been a time when individuals had met in local public counsel to address the problems of industry, Addams observed. She urged the so-called advanced men of her own era to investigate "those early organizations of village communities, folk motes, and mirs, those primary cells of both industrial and political organizations, where the people knew no difference between the two, but, quite simply, met to consider in common discussion all that concerned their common life" (NIP, 121–2).

If medieval guilds did not provide exact models for modern municipal government, they did at least refute the conservative inference that immigrants and industrial workers made bad democratic material. Thus in *Newer Ideals of Peace*, Addams turned the conservative argument on its head, insisting that, far from constituting a grave threat to the American republic, the urban working class possessed the moral and cultural resources necessary to realize the ideal of self-government for the first time. Among isolated communities, Addams explained, ethics typically divided along lines of private compassion and public morality. But the proximity of life in a "cosmopolitan city," as she put it, demolished the private/public dichotomy, yielding a synthesis— "a higher moral line" (NIP, 11). Repudiating both Debs's assertion about the impossibility of culture and morality amid poverty and the rough-and-tumble Darwinism of Herbert Spencer, Addams asserted that the residue of hardship was not viciousness but a sense of pity, charity, and justice. While elsewhere in America it was becoming hard to separate philanthropy from egoism, the poor and immigrant quarters revealed virtues unassociated with material "success" (NIP, 15). But hardship bred more than pity. It inspired an emotional toughness and mental perceptiveness increasingly rare amid a comfort-loving culture. "Democratic government has ever been the result of spiritual travail and moral effort," Addams maintained (NIP, 75). By tapping the moral urgency and associative inclination of urban dwellers "unlike each other in all save the universal characteristics of man," she hoped to inaugurate a "new history of government" (NIP, 15).

Cosmopolitan patriots believed that political, material, and cultural rights would never be secure until they were distributed universally, notwithstanding the challenge of that. They insisted that local rights have regional, national, and international repercussions that are both imprudent and immoral to ignore. In *Democracy and Social Ethics*, Addams provided an account of the interplay between local politics and universal sympathy while simultaneously describing how cosmopolitan patriotism is born.

Democracy and Social Ethics recounted the challenge of trying to unseat a corrupt Chicago alderman in a ward comprising "fifty thousand people, representing a score of nationalities" having "little in common save the basic experiences which come to men in all countries and under all conditions." How might this mass of people, "so heterogeneous in nationality, religion, and customs," converge on a course of action? The solution, Addams discovered, lay in appealing to the "universal" self-interest of individual ward members. Such was the wisdom of urban bosses, who recognized the futility of invoking abstract "civic virtue" in an urban environment characterized by social and political alienation.[89] Unlike the urban bosses, Addams did not renounce the goal of cultivating civic virtue. She recognized that civic virtue would have to be reconstituted from scratch. This entailed building on the "foundation" of machine politics: civic virtue was self-interest "socialized and enlarged." "If we believe the individual struggle for life may widen into a struggle for the lives of all," she wrote, "surely the demand of an individual for decency and comfort, for a chance to work and obtain the fullness of life may be widened until it gradually embraces all the members of the community, and rises into a sense of the common weal."[90]

Addams's celebration of the universalism latent in American cities did not reflect a desire to minimize cultural distinctions. On the contrary, at Hull-House she established programs designed specifically to showcase cultural differences, on the premise that a people's respect for its own culture would promote mutual cultural recognition.[91] Like Bourne, Addams expected cultural contact to result in dynamism rather than stasis or decline. She sought "a certain balance and concord of opposing and contending forces"; not universalism itself, but "a gravitation toward the universal."[92] But where Kallen and Bourne viewed cultural differences as primary and fundamental, Addams insisted that "the things that make men alike are stronger and more primitive than the things that separate them" (NIP, 17). Coming from a universalist, such a statement could be dismissed as hollow. But coming from Addams, it warrants consideration insofar as it advances a brand of civic interaction that promised the kind of fellowship typically found in private. Crush or be crushed might well have been the mantra of those whom social alienation had reduced to the level of brutes. But to Addams—for whom citizenship meant dissolving " 'humanity' into its component parts" and serving its "humblest needs with an enthusiasm . . . sustained only by daily knowledge and constant companionship"—public life seemed exhilarating because it afforded democrats an opportunity to become intimate with the world (NIP, 30).

TO MAKE DEMOCRACY SAFE FOR THE WORLD

If not exactly intimate with the world, turn-of-the-century Americans were becoming increasingly familiar with it. Of the many developments contributing to Americans' heightened national consciousness, none exerted more influence than America's emergence as a global power. Nothing makes for national cohesion like foreign competition. In an era in which international contact seemed to lead inevitably to conflict, once-dreaded foreign entanglements became the fulcrum around which political coalitions mobilized. Amid the messianism of the late-Victorian era, few Americans denied that the United States had some role to play in international affairs. Liberal Protestants and social Darwinists hoped to convert and civilize heathens. Captains of commerce and industry wanted to secure resources and open markets. Critics of cultural desiccation sought new arenas for virtue. Ardent expansionists vowed to repel the advances of European rivals. As economic, political, and ideological imperatives anathema to individual autonomy and consensual government impelled Americans abroad, American foreign policy came under close scrutiny. Time and time again between 1895 and 1919, citizens arose to defend America's honor, elevating national interest over liberal and democratic principles.

This chapter traces the cosmopolitan patriot's response to American foreign policy between the early 1890s and the outbreak of World War I. They took for granted America's "going out into the world," as Addams put it, but they sought to export a democratic ethos rather than a specific form of democratic government.[1] Adhering to the ideal of self-government, they aimed not to impose order and efficiency on foreign peoples, but to promote political, social, and economic institutions conducive to political and moral autonomy. The cosmopolitan patriots argued that as long as one people believed it could solve another people's problems, there could never be lasting peace. Peace required not a balance of Western power but a vision of democracy that balanced the ideal of universal self-government with respect for local government and tradition.

Realists deride foreign policy predicated on democratic commitments. Undue devotion to fairness and self-government, the argument goes, entails constant intervention and open-ended commitments.[2] On the contrary, the cosmopolitan patriots protested, the abstract and elastic idea of "national interest" is more likely than democratic ideals to embroil the United States in international conflict and erode citizen loyalty. A true democracy does not intervene impulsively into another state's affairs. Democrats might sympathize with the plight of another people, but the principles of autonomy and self-government mandate deliberation: Has the aggrieved nation invited intervention? Has the American citizenry weighed the merits of the case? Do the preconditions of democracy exist among the aggrieved people? How will American intervention influence democratic institutions at home and abroad? The cosmopolitan patriots maintained that, far from promoting hypocrisy or cynicism, a foreign policy based on such deliberation—on national interest rightly understood—would garner popular approval by limiting U.S. intervention abroad to actions Americans could be proud of.

NATIONAL INTEREST RIGHTLY UNDERSTOOD

We can grasp the stakes of the cosmopolitans' dissent from American foreign policy by examining the "realism" of Herbert Croly. Croly would write sympathetically about popular government in *Progressive Democracy* (1914); in *The Promise of American Life* (1909), he attempted to reconcile American liberalism with an expansionist, corporate capitalist economy. Croly's realism informed both Roosevelt Progressivism and the foreign policy of the two Wilson administrations. Its hallmark was a frank, if inadvertent, acknowledgment of the tension between national and global democracy—one that throws critical light on the cosmopolitans' universalist pretensions.[3]

Ostensibly, the Croly of 1909 and the cosmopolitan patriots had much in common. Like the cosmopolitans, Croly worried that a combination of egoism and complacency had vitiated the democratic commitments thought to undergird the American republic. Nature had blessed Americans with abundant resources and opportunities for so long, he observed, that they had come to take for granted their standard of living rather than acknowledging that it had to be protected.[4] Consequently, Americans appeared hamstrung in the face of changing social and industrial conditions. On the one hand, they sensed something awry in the nation's yawning economic disparity; on the other hand, they seemed to have lost their political initiative and sense of fairness. Unbridled self-interest had given rise to "a morally and socially undesirable distribution of wealth," Croly wrote. It was time for citizens to subordinate self-interest to the "fulfillment of a national purpose," to transform American democracy itself from a set of political procedures into a rigorous moral and social ideal. Where nineteenth-century Americans had regarded the so-called promise of American life as a guarantee of personal prosperity, Croly interpreted this promise as a covenant struck between citizens and the nation-state to solve "the social problem" (PAL, 22–4).

Croly's commitment to moral and social democracy faltered on his vision of a citizenry subordinate to a ruling elite. The cosmopolitan patriots expected national solidarity to emerge from political practices and common civil endeavors. Croly described a top-down process by which citizens embraced an ideal of solidarity whose formulation they had little to do with, as if their complacency stemmed from the lack of a galvanizing national vision rather than from a political system in hock to private interests. Like Roosevelt and Holmes, who embraced war as the means to civic virtue, Croly invoked an abstract notion of solidarity divorced from democratic practices to rekindle democracy itself. He confronted Americans with the mere negative duty of curbing their personal appetites. Only to the few did he assign a more positive task: once having "conquered" a "following," American politicians would face the challenge of retaining citizens' "loyalty."

In *Democracy in America,* Tocqueville described two scourges besetting popular government: majority tyranny and democratic despotism. In majority tyranny, citizens cowed by peers forfeit their individuality and conform to the herd; in democratic despotism, citizens transfixed by private interests cede their autonomy to elected officials. Tocqueville never made clear the precise connection between majority tyranny and democratic despotism, the former of which he associated with America, the latter with his native France.[5] Like Kallen and Bourne, Croly regarded complacency as a product of conformity, hence he hoped to elevate to power a cohort of leaders whose originality and iconoclasm would inspire their compatriots to exchange "cheap forms and standards" for "better forms and methods of social intercourse" (PAL, 450). Where the cosmopolitan patriots looked to local and national political alliances to empower citizens and encourage social interaction, Croly expected politics to effect a distribution of income conducive to high cultural appreciation. From Croly's perspective, America's representative institutions were essentially sound (PAL, 24–5). If Croly's consciousness of the material requisites of culture seemed to accord with Debs's critique of corporate capitalism, it did so only superficially. Debs sought for workers the material security required of voluntarism.

Croly's ideas about international affairs recapitulated his materialism.

"What the American people of the present and the future have really been promised by our patriotic prophesies," Croly remarked, is "comfort, prosperity, and the opportunity for self-improvement" (PAL, 24). What he did not explain until later was that fulfilling this promise at home entailed violating the tenets of democracy abroad. With its frontier disappearing and its population doubling every generation, America would be forced to look outside its borders for the resources and markets on which prosperity relied. Croly took for granted "the validity of colonial expansion even for a democracy"—as long as "the people whose independence is thereby diminished are incapable of efficient national organization" (PAL, 308).

Croly's foreign policy turned on this notion of efficiency—on what he construed to be a proper balance between American national interests and the nation's democratic ideals. Applying this criterion backward through U.S. history, he criticized Thomas Jefferson for erecting foreign policy on the "treacherous sands of international democratic propaganda," while faulting his idol Alexander Hamilton for failing "to identify [the national interest] with any positive democratic purpose" (PAL, 289–90). The key to successful diplomacy, Croly maintained, was to unite ends with practicable means. In a volatile world, overextension of either principle or interest would invite an "unrighteous war." Croly's standard of righteousness applied only to the West. He denounced the Monroe Doctrine and its subsequent corollaries not because it smothered the countries of Central and South America in American hegemony, but because in an epoch of colonial expansion the Monroe Doctrine threw European and American interests into conflict. Similarly, his concern about unrighteous war reflected no reservation about democrats forcing their way into foreign markets, but anxiety lest America impede a "legitimate interest" of like-minded Europeans. To protect their investments, Croly announced, the nations of Europe had as "justifiable [a] right under the law of nations to interfere" in the Western Hemisphere as the United States (PAL, 293–4).

In order to avoid the sort of clash of national interests that had brought the United States and England to the brink of war over Venezuela in 1895, while simultaneously maintaining America's regional hegemony, Croly proposed to replace the Monroe Doctrine with an "American system." The way to keep European armies out the Western Hemisphere was not for the United States to arm itself in anticipation of conflict but for it to establish stability within the nations of Central and South America. By maintaining hemispheric stability, the United States would "testify to its sincere democracy both by its negative attitude towards a militant European system and by its positive promotion of a peaceful international system in the two Americas" (PAL, 299). Here again, Croly's rhetoric appears consistent with cosmopolitan ends. But in Croly's lexicon, "peace" serves as code for a state of order and tranquility not necessarily conducive to democracy. To the many Latin

American revolutionaries striving to rid their nations of autocracy, Croly's *Pax Americana* must have seemed a mixed blessing at best. In the case of Mexico, by Croly's logic, the people's struggle for self-government would take a backseat to American national interests. Any recrudescence of revolution there would thwart America's attempt to win the cooperation of "Mexican statesmen"—autocrats whose sympathy constituted the sine qua non of the new "American system" (PAL, 302–3).

When the United States invaded the Philippines in 1899, Croly was completing an extended tenure at Harvard College lasting over a decade. There is no evidence he paid much attention to the debate in the *Harvard Crimson* between his mentor William James and his future champion Theodore Roosevelt about the merits of the Philippines annexation. Looking back on the events of 1899 in *The Promise of American Life,* Croly allowed that in contrast to U.S. policy in Cuba and Puerto Rico, America's seizure of the Philippines raised "a series of much more doubtful questions." These questions reduced to the matter of efficiency: did the benefits of annexation outweigh the costs? Surely not, he concluded. "They have already cost an amount of money far beyond any chance of compensation, and an amount of American and Filipino blood, the shedding of which constitutes a grave responsibility." Croly viewed the matter of American "responsibility" from the perspective of a global balance of power. Its "gravity" stemmed not from any inherent tension between American and Filipino interests, but from America's sudden stand-off with expansionist Japan (PAL, 308–9).

For all his elitism, Croly gives proponents of universal democracy reason to pause. From time immemorial, secular theorists have regarded economic independence as a prerequisite of moral and political empowerment. Like Frederick Jackson Turner before him, Croly understood that by promising to extend economic independence to greater and greater numbers of people, democracy overtaxed the nation's natural resources. To sustain democracy, Americans would have to inaugurate an imperial policy or submit to a decline in living standards. Croly's analysis mocks the notion of "universal democracy": earth could ill-sustain the harvest of resources necessary to provide its inhabitants economic independence. Unless, that is, Americans construed independence in moral as well as material terms and curbed their gratuitous consumption.[6]

According to historian Nick Salvatore, Eugene Debs assented to America's annexation of Hawaii in 1898 on grounds that accorded with Croly's realism. Debs viewed the absorption of Hawaii as "entirely proper and in perfect keeping with the constitution of the United States. In the first place," he wrote, "it was the desire of the natives of Hawaii to become citizens of the United States through annexation. They are composed in a degree of Caucasians, and they already have a government established. Then Honolulu is a coaling station for the United States, and this government must need protect itself in this regard."[7] If Debs's remarks convey a realist's privileging of national interests over democratic principles, they nonetheless reflect his evolving commitment to democracy: foreign no less than domestic policy is beholden to the Constitution; annexation requires colonial consent. Moreover, while there can be no denying Debs's residual prejudice, his perspective on the annexation of Hawaii does not reduce to racism. As early as 1895, Debs had made plain his empathy for Cuba's Hispanic revolutionaries. Released from Woodstock, Illinois, prison in the fall of 1895, Debs bid a group of well-wishers to look "across the Florida channel" where "a gallant band of native Cubans are fighting for liberty and independence." The Cuban revolutionaries appealed "to the United States for recognition as belligerents that they may have all the rights and privileges guaranteed by the laws of nations," Debs proclaimed. American workers must make the plight of the Cuban patriots their own; "anything less would be un-American and a national shame."[8]

By 1909—the year Croly published *The Promise of American Life*—Debs had come to equate national interest with the ideals of equal opportunity, equality before the law, and consensual government. Late that winter, he championed the cause of five Mexican dissidents languishing in a Texas jail for having violated U.S. neutrality in the Mexican Revolution. Could Americans remain "neutral" in this clash between liberty and despotism? Debs asked Senator Robert La Follette in a letter. Neutrality was a hoax contrived by American capitalists and their puppet Diaz to thwart the Mexican crusade for social justice. Debs urged La Follette to sponsor a resolution calling for an investigation into the Mexicans' cases. The revolution in Mexico was merely the latest outbreak in the immemorial struggle between liberty and despotism. "Diaz is a devil in human form," Debs wrote. "He is getting his full share of the plunder that is being wrung from the peon slaves by American capitalists." By contrast, Mexican dissidents were "patriots in the loftiest sense of the term": "cultured, high-minded" individuals who loved their "fellow men too well to allow the present flood of tyranny to exist without protest." These dissidents "sacrificed their material interests, their liberty, and have repeatedly risked their lives in the cause of freedom." Was it not "the concern of the American people that such men are allowed to lie in our jails for two years without being granted a trial?" If Americans only knew of "the atrocities that are being perpetrated at this very hour," Debs maintained, "they would rise in revolt across the land."[9]

As the Socialist Party's chief propagandist, Debs aimed to awaken America's conscience to the cost of predatory corporate capitalism. He had neither the time nor inclination to explore the details of the emerging global political economy. But his question haunted Jane Addams: was it, indeed, America's concern that patriots in Cuba, Mexico, the Philippines, or elsewhere were locked in battle against despotism? Addams believed so, but she would have difficulty convincing her peers. Like Debs, Addams repudiated Croly's realism. But where Debs ignored realism's cautionary tenet, Addams propounded a pluralist ideal of self-government potentially compatible with global democratization. Debs viewed American imperialism as evidence of hypocrisy. Addams regarded imperialism as the product of a failure of nerve. Speaking before Chicago's Central Anti-Imperialist League in the winter of 1899, Addams charged her listeners to come clean on their commitment to democracy. "None of us who have been reared and nurtured in America can be wholly without the democratic instinct," Addams asserted. "It is not a question with any of us of having it or not having it; it is merely a question of trusting it or not trusting it." America's sudden absorption of Puerto Rico, Hawaii, Guam, and the Philippines brought the issue to a head. "Do we mean to democratize the situation," Addams demanded, "or are we going to weakly imitate the policy of other governments, which have never claimed a democratic basis?"[10]

Addams delighted in the prospect of Americans venturing forth into the world. "The question," as she put it, is "how shall we go out? Shall we go out with the narrow notion of national life, which would claim democracy for itself alone, or shall we be really and truly inter-national in that we throw our energy into other lands, mingling in an absolute equality and only knowing that progress belongs to us together?"[11] Conscious of the tensions within industrial society, Addams believed that Western technology chastened by a spirit of democracy could promote material prosperity conducive to universal individual and cultural realization. While there is no denying that this faith led to a certain presumption on her part—what was good for America was good for the world—her imperialism was remarkable for sustaining a commitment to reciprocity: what was good for the world was also good for America. By regarding U.S. policy in the Philippines as a test of American democracy, Addams invited the Filipinos to participate in the open-ended process of perfecting democratic institutions. In an era of contact between different peoples, democracy would be measured not solely by its domestic, material accomplishments, but by its success or failure in effecting global moral and political autonomy (DM, 35).

A contemporary foreign policy could not abide Croly's paternalism. If government were to keep pace with mankind's moral development, it could not consist of privileged individuals administering to the needs of others. "Ideal government," Addams informed her listeners, "is merely an adjustment between men concerning the mutual relations toward those general matters which concern them all." By contrast, "the office of an outside and alien people must always be to collect taxes and to hold a negative law and order." In the process of imposing order, the outside interest typically destroyed the rudiments of local government, forcing the conquered people to establish working relations with their conquerors but without "the more virile and initiative forces" among them. Addams's coupling of virility and initiative calls to mind Debs's equation of manhood with moral integrity and exposes the contradiction of Croly's suggestion that pacification could pave the way for democracy. If democracy meant the existence of docile citizens endorsing the edicts of an externally appointed elite, then pacification accorded with democracy. But if, as Addams and Dewey contended, democracy presumed the existence of an engaged citizenry inspiring one another to ever higher levels of human attainment, then pacification and democracy were mutually exclusive (DM, 38).

Five years later, in an address delivered at the Universal Peace Conference in Boston, Addams elucidated the implications of the "new morality" for American democracy. Juxtaposing the soldier to the democrat, she reiterated her concern that the former, in his readiness to force "the blessings" of civilization and self-government upon non-Western peoples, extinguished "the most precious germs of some new exotic contribution to the science of human government." By contrast, the democrat—"the believer in the creative energy of mankind"—recognized that progress sprang from local roots. Cautious and patient by nature, the democrat was as inclined to observe as to act, to nourish self-government as to impose a set of "old and possibly worn out ideas" on a distant people. The democrat arrived not seeking wealth, but bearing the "new riches of human interest." Like the soldier, the democrat was committed to development; but where the soldier expected ultimately to harvest material resources, the democrat hoped to foster what Addams labeled "the most wonderful thing in the world"—"a new combination of people coming together in the line of self-government." [12]

In *Twenty Years at Hull-House*, Addams recalled being awed by her father's marshalling of a Civil War regiment, the so-called Addams Guard. Her repudiation of America's annexation of the Philippines did not necessarily entail renunciation of the Spanish-American War, which liberated Cuba and Puerto Rico, at least, from Spanish tyranny. Hull-House relied on the philanthropy of American capitalists, which often influenced Addams's public remarks on economics and politics, and one suspects that her "soldier" stood in for the capitalist in her Peace Conference address. It was *these* soldiers of fortune whom Addams blamed for perpetuating war. The soldier and the democrat espoused incompatible ideas of "civilization," she observed. Where the soldier clung to civilization as a yardstick by which to measure a people's progress, the democrat knew that civilization advanced not by "metes and bounds" but "along devious paths" (RDW, 121). In the controversy that swirled around the U.S. invasion of the Philippines, Americans had come to confuse civilization with "the opening of gold mines, the establishment of garrisons, the controlling of weaker men by brute force." In February 1900, Addams lamented that an America imbued with militarism had forgotten that "civilization is an idea, a method of living, an attitude of respect toward all men." [13] In blaming materialism for perverting American foreign policy, Addams did not absolve American civilians from complicity in U.S. imperialism. On the contrary, she told the Sunset Club the following winter, the soldier is "us." Thus Addams connected America's aggression overseas to her critique of domestic politics. Americans had come to regard success as a function of material prosperity, hardship as evidence of moral and cultural inferiority. This bred condescension toward the poor, eroding the nation's faith in the sanctity of every individual. As a result, Americans naturally fell in with their European counterparts, ostracizing indigents and immigrants at home while trampling the rights of strangers around the world. [14]

W. E. B. Du Bois had a phrase that captured Addams's ideal for American foreign policy: "moral hegemony." If the pairing of morality with a word connoting dominion seems ironic to twenty-first-century ears, it nonetheless conveys the cosmopolitans' faith in the compatibility of national interest and democratic principles. Moreover, it highlights their sense of the need for moral engagement in foreign policy. Writing in the *American Journal of Sociology* in May 1908, Du Bois repeated what was becoming an increasingly common refrain: for the United States to take its place among the great nations of the world, "she has got right here in her own land to find out how to live in peace and prosperity with her own black citizens." Resolution of the race problem at home, Du Bois promised, would catapult the United States into its rightful position of global leadership, a development "simply inestimable [for] the new commerce and . . . humanity." [15]

But the new commerce and humanity were all but stillborn at the turn of the twentieth century, as Du Bois well knew. In a lecture commemorating the late Frederick Douglass at Wilberforce University in March 1895, Du Bois contrasted the unswerving moral rectitude of Douglass's ambassadorship to Haiti to the blatant hypocrisy of Western imperialism. "It is strange," he remarked, "that modern civilization still sanctions a code of morals between nations which if used between men would bring the severest condemnation; to steal a book is theft, but to steal an island is missionary enterprise; to tell a neighbor an untruth is to lie, but to tell a neighboring country a whole portfolio full is to be diplomatic." Along with William James, Du Bois greeted American imperialism as a pivotal development. Like James, Du Bois associated modernism with the unleashing of human creativity and reciprocal social relations. It was not that Du Bois disparaged technological and industrial advance; on the contrary, to the extent that technology promoted leisure and leisure fostered autonomy, he was as materialistic as the next. But imperialism robbed modernism of its liberating potential by inverting the relationship of freedom to leisure and by turning public contact into private gain.[16]

Echoing James, Du Bois denounced imperialism as a moral masquerade. Writing in the journal *The East and The West* in January 1904, Du Bois conceded that America's imperialist transgressions typically emerged from noble aspirations. Americans first penetrated Hawaii as emissaries of God; they first embarked for the Philippines to vanquish Spanish oppression. To err, of course, was human, but to adorn avarice in the rhetoric of philanthropy inverted the rational order and invited the wrath of God. "Making all due allowances for different ways of interpreting facts," Du Bois wrote, "it must be confessed by all honest men that a theory of civilization which stands sponsor for the enormities committed by European civilization on native races is an outrage and a lie." Du Bois interpreted the West's refusal to admit its error, let alone atone for its behavior, as evidence of moral degeneracy. A civilization true to the ideal of autonomy would have steered clear of imperialism in the first place. Not only was "the man of true learning and breadth of view . . . less sanguine of the overmastering completeness of our present culture," Du Bois wrote, but "he sees its strengths and weaknesses, and above all else he realizes that the one conspicuous triumph of modern culture—namely, the diffusion of its benefits among the lower strata of society—is an accomplishment which is, logically, a flat contradiction to the theory of the natural aristocracy of the races."[17]

By appropriating for themselves putative universal rights and by mocking common sense, Western imperialists propelled mankind into an egoistic world devoid of knowledge of good and evil and bereft of human responsibility. Egoism was worse than tribalism, from Du Bois's perspective. Tribes might plead ignorance of human potential. Egoists had glimpsed the world in its variety and abundance and resolved to privatize its blessings. There could be but one fate for such parsimony, Du Bois warned, pointing to the history of China: "that marvelous internal decay that overcomes the nation that trifles with Truth and Right and Justice, and makes force and fraud and dishonesty and caste distinction the rule of its life and government." Yet there remained an antidote to modern disintegration: "Unity." Not a difference-denying unity, but one that recognized that the promise of modernity resided in a celebration of diverse forms of human expression. In exhorting African Americans to "make common cause with the oppressed of all races and peoples; with our kindred of South Africa and West Indies; with our fellows in Mexico, India and Russia and with the cause of working classes everywhere," Du Bois, in effect, challenged them to accept responsibility for the fate of Western civilization. A huge onus, theirs was the opportunity of a millennium: "On us," Du Bois wrote in the journal *Horizon*, "rests to no little degree the burden of the cause of individual Freedom, Human Brotherhood, and Universal Peace in a day when America is forgetting her promise and destiny."[18]

Like Jane Addams and William James, Du Bois regarded sympathy as an essential ingredient of an up-to-date foreign policy. Although Du Bois regretted the circumstances by which Western nations typically accumulated their colonial holdings, once accumulated, he insisted, colonies must be governed democratically—for the good of all, rather than for the benefit of the colonial power. Du Bois's attitude toward the "undeveloped world," as he put it, was much like Addams's insofar as he associated civilization with human contact, and human contact with the proliferation of Western institutions— particularly self-government. In their critique of American realism, it apparently never occurred to either Du Bois or Addams that certain peoples and cultures might wish to be left alone. Though chastened by genuine curiosity, their presumption left them as close, in practical effect, to Croly as to James. Once having made contact with non-Western peoples, Western nations would find it excruciatingly difficult, in James's parlance, to maintain a policy of "hands off."

In January 1907, Du Bois founded the journal *The Horizon* to propagate his conviction that American race relations had to be viewed in an international context. *The Horizon* of February 1908 contained an editorial praising England's Colonial Office for undertaking a systematic investigation into "the customs and folk-lore" of its African subjects. "The fountain of all intelligent government by aliens must be a knowledge of the habits, customs, laws, traditions, and modes of the people governed," *The Horizon* announced. Britain's administration of its colonists had hitherto "lacked the gift of sympathy," been "too cast-iron" in its prejudices, "too scornful" of what had appeared to be "mere antediluvianism and superstition, too apt to destroy by the very unimaginative regularity of [its] rule much of what is romantic and worth preserving in the political and social economy of [its] subjects." Commitments such as Britain's to improve its colonial administration compelled Du Bois to uphold distinctions between benign and evil imperialisms. Herein lay *his* realism, which, in contrast to Croly's, did not apologize for Western hubris. Taking Western hubris as a starting point, Du Bois demanded whether the "Force and Fear" characterizing "the white attitude toward darker races" would persist indefinitely or yield eventually to "Freedom and Friendship."[19]

Where Croly had not questioned Americans' conflation of democracy and consumption, Du Bois shared Addams's sense of democracy as a moral endeavor. In England's self-criticism and in the growing colonial restiveness around the world, Du Bois recognized the rudiments of "a new standard of national efficiency." Its cardinal characteristic, he informed readers of the *American Journal of Sociology,* would be a spirit of neighborliness—that moral mutuality that "men" accorded "men." In a letter to Woodrow Wilson in the summer of 1915, Du Bois listed four conditions for a successful Haitian policy. First, Americans must be sensitive to Haitian-American history with all its symbolism and suspicion. Second, Haitians must be treated like partners in a reciprocal relationship; to "rescue [Haiti] from her worst self," America would have to elicit *Haiti's* best self, a feat impossible without "the cordial support" of Haitians themselves. Third, American policy must reflect the counsel of the American people; the nation's mission there could only win approbation if the "ten million American citizens of Negro descent are made to feel that we have no designs on the political independence of the island and no desire to exploit it ruthlessly for the sake of selfish business interests here." Finally, America must effect there "not mere grudging justice," Du Bois remarked, quoting Wilson himself, "but justice executed with liberality and cordial good feeling."[20]

THE MORAL EQUIVALENT OF WAR

Those who interpreted American imperialism as evidence of faltering faith in democracy were left to ponder why democracy ceased to stir the nation's imagination at the turn of the twentieth century. The cosmopolitan patriots contended that democracy had become devalued as liberalism became associated with material prosperity rather than political and moral autonomy. Yet notwithstanding the valorization of wealth, the mass of Americans seemed to recognize intuitively what William James discovered at Chautauqua, New York, in 1892: wealth and leisure were insufficient to make "life significant."[21] This perception did not inspire Americans to repudiate prosperity as the end of life, to be sure. Rather, it left them vulnerable to diversions that promised to relieve their boredom without attacking its roots. And no diversion more consumed Americans of this era than war. When not actually fighting, as in 1898 and 1917, Americans kept war current by glorifying the recent battle between the states. Whether casting the Civil War as a struggle between liberty and tyranny, as the subordination of self to state authority, or as simple heroism, turn-of-the-century Americans tried to conceal their egoism by cloaking it in the mantle of their forefathers.[22] Amid such a climate, the cosmopolitans believed that the way to slake Americans' yearning for meaning was not to deny the virtues spawned by war but to enlist citizens' untapped energy in a campaign for social justice. Exploiting a regrettable byproduct of nineteenth-century liberalism, they would strike at the heart of laissez-faire.

It was William James himself who, in his quest for "A Moral Equivalent of War," linked Americans' romance of war to a moral crisis in the nation's liberal political economy. James's argument complicates Addams's portrait of the military as atavistic. James began his quest for the moral equivalent of war by identifying the springs of hardihood, valor, and self-forgetfulness in mankind's natural self. At the turn of the twentieth century only the military succeeded in tapping these reserves, hence the military was America's sole agent of innovation. "Nothing is more striking," James wrote, "than to compare the progress of civil conveniences which has been left to the trader, to the progress in military apparatus during the last few decades." Where "the household appliances of to-day . . . are little better than they were fifty years ago," the "rifle or battleship of fifty years ago was beyond all comparison inferior to those we possess." [23]

The point was not to militarize civilian life, à la Roosevelt, but to infuse civil society with the spirit of civic consciousness. Know thy enemy, James counseled delegates to the Boston Peace Congress of 1904: human nature was essentially bellicose; people wanted war; the possibility of war relieved the tedium of daily life. Pacifists should not hope to transform human nature; they should work to "cheat" or "circumvent" it. In one crucial respect, James observed, war was like love. Both left mankind with "intervals of rest" during which "life goes on perfectly well without them, though the imagination still dallies with their possibility." Just as "old maids and bachelors" attained their status by "sliding on from year to year with no sufficient provocation," so nations ripened in the face of war without being actually at one another's throats. James urged pacifists to "let the general possibility of war be left open . . . for the imagination to deal with." Soldiers must be free to "dream of killing, as the old maids dream of marrying." Meanwhile, proponents of peace should "organize in every conceivable way the practical machinery for making each successive chance of war abortive." This entailed not only promoting arbitration and elevating pacifists to positions of political power, but fostering "rival excitements" and identifying "new outlets for heroic energy." [24]

Six years later, having heeded his own counsel, James broadcasted his results. As before, he was most cogent when penetrating the minds of his opponents. War made for unity, not to mention union; war's horrors made the thrill; the moral benefit of war outweighed its human cost; war was life at its most extreme (MEW, 6–10). But this time, James's articulation of mankind's essential bellicosity and praise of martial virtues as the "enduring cement" of the state contended with his pragmatism to undermine his argument. On the one hand, he criticized as "nonsense" the "fatalistic" notion that war alone could inspire self-sacrifice and heroism; on the other hand, he praised these virtues as "absolute and permanent human goods," as if ignoring pragmatism's cardinal rule that ends must necessarily evolve as means themselves are readjusted (MEW, 11–2). James's lapsed pragmatism resulted in a vision at once sentimental and undemocratic. In the first place, working inductively, he embarked on a futile search for the means capable of realizing his prescribed end. Compared to the urgency of battle, his "immemorial human warfare against nature"—with its mining and fishing, its dishwashing and clothes-washing, its road-building and railroading—sounded overblown and uncompelling. In the second place, as Randolph Bourne would later note, the absolute goods to which James adhered did not reflect the contribution of women and individuals unfit, as Bourne himself was, for physical labor. Where Debs and Du Bois used the term "manhood" to distinguish (moral) man from (amoral) brute, James, like his nemesis Roosevelt, associated manliness with masculinity, a counterforce to the perceived softening influence of women. Indeed, a certain hostility toward women lurks beneath the surface of "A Moral Equivalent of War." All that was noble in Nature James ascribed to men, all that was problematic James attributed to women (MEW, 13–4).[25]

James's inconsistency becomes manifest when we compare his "moral equivalent" to Jane Addams's "moral substitute." From the outset, James and Addams pursued this quarry together. Both were motivated by a commitment to self-government and moved to action by the American invasion of the Philippines. They shared the dais at the Universal Peace Congress in Boston in 1904. And they maintained a cordial friendship through the mail. Yet despite praising Addams privately for her book *Newer Ideals of Peace* (1907), James did not publicly acknowledge his indebtedness to her in "A Moral Equivalent of War."[26] And there can be no denying his debt. In 1904, James dismissed the suggestion that war might be a "transitory phenomenon," as he would later call it, and admonished pacifists to banish their dreams of permanent peace. In 1910, having read Addams's book, James reversed himself, intimating that permanent peace might derive from the contending "sciences" of destruction and production. But come time to identify the source of mankind's productive passion, James's juxtaposition of Nature to Reason afforded him no explanation of how human aggression could be channeled toward industry. The only thing James could offer his readers was hope. "Constructive interests may some day seem no less imperative" than war, he wrote, "and impose on the individual a hardly lighter burden" (MEW, 13).

By contrast, in *Newer Ideals of Peace*, Addams rejected James's juxtaposition of nature to reason in favor of an ideal of Nature that encompassed compassion as well as aggression—that counterbalanced James's masculine will to power with a feminine, nurturing instinct. According to Addams, the struggle to perpetuate life called forth virtues no less virile than war. But Addams's moral substitute did not merely uphold traditional gender stereotypes. Consistent with politics and physical exertion, her moral substitute presented an alternative moral paradigm, juxtaposing militarism to industry, flexibility to stubbornness, "dogmatism" to "humanism," and tribalism to cosmopolitanism.[27]

Newer Ideals of Peace opens with the claim that the means existed by which to banish war *naturally*, a contention compelling Addams to demonstrate the artificiality of both "the older dovelike ideal" of peace and the traditional apology for war. Historically, Addams explained, peace advocates had argued along two lines: one group, exemplified by Tolstoy, appealed to mankind's "imaginative pity," portraying war's tedium and brutality from the perspective of the peasant. Meanwhile, a second group, typified by the Russian economist Jean de Bloch, exposed war's improvidence and inefficiency. Although Addams admitted that these protests had, over the years, expanded mankind's moral horizon, she repudiated them for being rooted in "the appeal of dogma." Reducible to "a command to cease from evil," they represented no adjustment of morals to contemporary social and material conditions. Addams noted that pacifists' failure to respond to current political conditions resulted in such spectacles as the International Hague Tribunal threatening to penalize aggressor nations whose foreign ministers had "nothing to do with accumulating the treasure they vote to expend" (NIP, 3–7).[28]

Addams attributed war's hold on the modern imagination as evidence of America's moral escapism and intellectual immaturity. To cling to militarism as a source of heroism and sacrifice, she complained, was "to borrow our virtues from a former age." Concluding that America's "humanitarianism has been too soft and literary," Addams did not so much declare war on the life of the mind, as Christopher Lasch has suggested, as unleash the mind on pressing human problems.[29] It was not a Jefferson or an Emerson or a Lincoln whom the nation needed, but individuals of their bearing capable of adapting "our morality and courage to our present social and industrial developments" (NIP, 27). Here the democratic implications of Addams's pragmatism are plain. Those who would apply old answers to contemporary problems alienated the democratic public from whom genuine solutions must come. Nostalgia not only bred intellectual complacency, it relieved the electorate of its obligation to strike what Addams called "a nice balance between continuity and change"—in effect robbing citizens of political agency (NIP, 209–12).

Once embarked on a search for a moral foundation for peace, Addams did not have to venture far. The basis of peace, like the bulwark of virtue, lay at the heart of the cosmopolitan city. With people having come from all over the world, America's urban cauldrons constituted what Addams labeled an "American tribunal," in which inhabitants' practical concerns overwhelmed Old-World jealousies (NIP, 235–6). In the modern metropolis, exigency demanded that neighbors regard one another sympathetically; mutual dependence, in turn, bred an irrepressible "power of association" at odds with "the old and negative bonds of discipline and coercion" (NIP, 9–14). Was Addams naive in expecting peace to emanate from "the 'quarrelsome mob' turned into kindly citizens of the world through the pressure of the cosmopolitan neighborhood"? She harbored no illusions that peace was foremost in the minds of urban denizens. On the contrary, she acknowledged, if city folk clamored for anything, it was for war. But peace they inadvertently promoted by "attaining cosmopolitan relations through daily experience." Indeed, she observed, immigrants "will probably believe for a long time that war is noble and necessary both to engender and cherish patriotism; and yet all of the time, below their shouting, they are living in the kingdom of human kindness. They are laying the simple and inevitable foundations for an international order" (NIP, 18).

To erect an edifice of peace on the foundation of cosmopolitanism, Addams summoned "philosophers"—men and women capable of integrating "the spiritual efforts of the common man into the internationalism of good will." Like St. Francis, these architects of peace would reveal "hitherto unsuspected . . . possibilities of the human soul"; like the "Gothic cathedrals," this edifice would be "glorious beyond the dreams of artists," notwithstanding that it was constructed "by unknown men, or rather by so many men that it was a matter of indifference to record their names" (NIP, 22). Like Dewey, Addams believed that the fate of democracy and the peace movement rested on the philosophers' ability to elevate industrial amelioration to the level of national defense. This, in turn, required exposing "those forms of governmental machinery and social organization which are the historic outgrowth of conquest and repression" (NIP, 28). Only then might Americans recognize the "subordination of sensation to sentiment in [the] hundreds of careers which are not military"; only then might they appreciate the "bodily pain and peril" endured by American workers as a moral equivalent of war (NIP, 218–9).[30]

Like James, Addams was at her best when critiquing the methods of her allies, rather than in delineating the path to permanent peace. It seems Addams, no less than James, had mistaken a part of human instinct for the whole. Despite her claim to have accounted for war's psychological allure, her moral substitute denied the endurance of evil, just as James's juxtaposition of Nature to Reason disregarded mankind's innate propensity for good. James had been more right in 1904 than either he or Addams would be thereafter: pacifists should not hope to banish war; they could only strive to postpone war indefinitely. In the intervals, loyalty might be inculcated by national service, but heroism would inhere in the dissident's struggle to maintain open avenues of reconciliation. And in the perpetual campaign for political and economic justice. Comparing James's and Addams's dissent during the Philippine controversy to their prophesies of peace, one is tempted to concede the argument to war's apologists: whereas James's and Addams's critiques of imperialism were shot through with acuity and verve, their pacifist prophecy betrayed an abstract, disembodied quality uncharacteristic of their pragmatism.

In contrast to James and Addams, Eugene Debs sought not to identify a moral equivalent of war but to distinguish between wars moral and immoral. In contrast to Herbert Croly, Debs would base this distinction on principles of universal justice, rather than on an ideal of fairness applicable only among the nations of the West. Debs shared Addams's conviction that war repudiated the premise of Western civilization. And he grasped her point about violence breeding resentment. But Debs's sense of himself at the vanguard of a submerged proletariat compelled him to reject Addams's claim that the reign of peace could somehow precede the rule of justice. Moreover, though Debs and Addams both equated civilization with the advance of liberal and democratic principles, Debs's patriotism harbored an element of masculinity missing from Addams's—one that thrilled to the prospect of a fight. Thus Debs not only enjoined Americans from preying upon the weak, he charged embattled workers to arm themselves to resist corporate lawlessness and defend their homes and loved ones. Of course, Addams never denied the right to self-defense, she simply did not associate self-defense with militarism. Taking the long view, she aimed to de-legitimize the capitalist exploitation of the world that made war inevitable.[31]

The philosopher could afford to ponder the future; the politician remained anchored in the present. Not only was politics an arena of confrontation, as Addams knew, but war spurred political mobilization. In the plight of the imprisoned Mexican dissidents, Debs identified a moral war. They inspired a rhapsody of the soldier's strenuous life. "These heroes have fought and suffered a thousand times more than any of us," Debs wrote the editor of the *Appeal to Reason* in February 1910. "I am ashamed of my paltry record when I think of these grand souls and their transcendent heroism, rotting in our prisons. . . . When I read of this I become almost wild. I feel disgraced that this should be so and I submitting to it. By God," Debs thundered, "I feel at this very moment like issuing a call to arms to rescue these patriots and humanitarians, and if this be treason, the God damned scoundrels can make the most of it." With a national election on the horizon, Debs maintained that the *Appeal*'s championing of the Mexicans' plight would benefit the Socialist campaign. But more than Socialism was at stake here. American virtue hung in the balance: "If the American people are not dead as mummies this can be made to arouse them as they have never been aroused before." Here was a cause "to make us forget all about ourselves," Debs exclaimed, one for which he would happily "be shot full of holes." Vowing to be "what La Fayette was to Washington," Debs would marshal a regiment of volunteers and place himself at their head.[32]

But war was no foundation from which to launch a moral crusade. Not only did war elude rational control, it quickly expended the emotional energy on which it depended. By July 1910, Debs had withdrawn himself from the fray. Chronically exhausted by his grueling itinerary, Debs retreated to Minnesota for surgery. By the time the Mexican dissidents were released from federal prison in early August, the international crisis had abated and Debs's "patriotic" ardor vanished without a trace. When Debs resumed stumping for Socialist candidates in the fall of 1910, his letters and speeches no longer mentioned the Mexican Revolution.

W. E. B. Du Bois was well versed in the paradox of war. Du Bois knew that wars typically eluded control and mocked their declared ends. As an African American, he realized that participation in America's wars had provided African Americans one of their few avenues to freedom. Du Bois's sense of the precariousness of his freedom disinclined him from using incendiary rhetoric like Debs's to motivate his constituents, except in dire circumstances. Like Addams, Du Bois maintained the legitimacy of self-defense, but he was determined to deprive racists of any "excuse" for further violence. More self-consciously than Debs, Du Bois identified his civil rights campaign as a moral equivalent of war: this was war insofar as it involved bombardment; this war was moral in that Du Bois pummeled the enemy not with threats or innuendo but with the demand for liberty and justice.[33]

Du Bois's ambivalence about war reflected the changing nature of America's global involvement at the turn of the twentieth century. Proud of his forefathers' military service, Du Bois was relieved by his family's innocence in the Philippines invasion. His forebears had "fought in every single war the United States has waged," he boasted in autumn 1907, "except, thank God, the last."[34] America's aggression in the Philippines impelled Du Bois to renounce war categorically in his "Credo" of 1904. "War is Murder," he proclaimed, and "armies and navies are at bottom the tinsel and braggadocio of oppression and wrong." Du Bois sustained this conviction until 1914, when the sinister character of German militarism elicited finer distinctions. In the meantime, he decried the West's refusal to recognize its "lust for land and slaves in Africa, Asia, and the South Seas" as "the greatest and almost the only cause of war between the so-called civilized peoples." Along with Addams, Du Bois insisted that peace required democratizing international relations. Absent a universal commitment to individual autonomy and consensual government, he chided, the peace movement would remain an "aristocratic refuge."[35]

Linking the prospect for peace among Western nations to the global struggle for self-determination, Du Bois summoned African Americans to the "Last Crusade": the battle "to deliver from the Heathen the Sacred Truth of Human Equality and Brotherhood." The ammunition in this campaign must not be "knocks and blows," Du Bois had cautioned a decade earlier, but "moral mastery over the minds of men—true desert, unquestioned ability, thorough work and purity of purpose." In this effort, short-term means would be matched with long-term ends. Fighting for Truth, conscripts would develop the discipline and cooperation capable of halting America's decline from a culture of "excellence" to a culture of "notoriety."[36] Where Debs's crusade perpetuated a militant rhetoric anathema to Addams, Du Bois subordinated masculinity to moral autonomy, thus inviting the participation of women. Du Bois viewed the problem of the color line in the context of a cosmopolitan impulse to expand humanity's moral compass. "Who are men?" he demanded in the *Christian Register* in autumn 1905. "Who compose the group, the nation, or the race whose common experiences are like to mine, who stand bound to me in common aspiration and sympathy, in common ideal?" Surely, "capitalists" possessed no monopoly on the claim; nor did "laborers"—nor even males themselves. No: "men's mothers and daughters" must be welcomed into the moral confraternity, and anybody else, regardless of race, who aspired "to life's higher ideal."

No mere brawn or simple bravery could revitalize the moral and political commitments once thought to undergird "civilization." This required new virtues: an ability to maintain one's poise in the face of discrimination and "cold contempt"; a willingness to dissent from public opinion; a genius for self-criticism; and a capacity to remain "hopeful in the face of hopeless meanness." Where Eugene Debs promised his recruits abundance, Du Bois assured his crusaders only that the fighting would be hard. Debs relished the thought of war. Du Bois quickened to the moral battle itself.[37]

COSMIC PATRIOTISM

Debs's letters and papers suggest that the meaning of patriotism, like the nature of war, was changing in America at the turn of the twentieth century. In the aftermath of the Pullman strike, as Debs converted to Socialism, he referred to patriotism matter-of-factly as a liberating, revolutionary, and noble sentiment. In the wake of the Spanish-American War, Debs's references to patriotism became comparative, always invoking a *good* patriotism in opposition to a *bad*. Patriots had apparently become despots. As the world entered a twenty-year period of seemingly constant battle, Debs's revolutionary patriotism came under siege. He continued to associate patriotism with the defense of liberty and democracy, but other Americans had begun to imbue patriotism with a different set of values.

In March 1895, writing in the *Railway Times,* Debs recalled the events of the previous July that had led to his arrest for complicity in the Pullman strike. Debs argued that the court injunction precipitating the intervention of federal troops in the strike augured the return of despotism to America. "Only a semblance of liberty remains, when courts and the military put forth their unrestrained power," Debs had warned his readers. The collusion of public officials and railway owners highlighted the need for "a new party to take the reigns of government and bring it back to pristine purity." Just as their forefathers had done before them, Debs urged "all who are animated by the spirit of patriotic devotion to liberty to unify to perpetuate the liberties of the people." Confident that patriotism denoted a devotion to freedom, Debs did not qualify the term as he would come to do, nor did he acknowledge contest over its meaning. Indeed, in a speech that same month, Debs swaddled Pullman strikers in the American flag, as yet unperturbed by the flag "fetishism" he would eventually denounce. The Stars and Stripes "tell of strikes for liberty and independence," Debs remarked in an attempt to legitimate his role at Pullman; the American Revolutionaries themselves had been "strikers and boycotters."[38]

Independence Day 1895 found Debs ruminating about the state of American liberty in a cell in Woodstock, Illinois, prison, as fireworks shook the countryside around him. Why celebrate the nation's birthday, Debs wondered, "when Liberty itself lies cold and stiff and dead, stabbed to death" by a federal injunction? Anxious about the future, Debs gazed back wistfully to liberty's past—to "the dead, who, when living, in the spirit of heroism expanded to the full stature of patriots and dared all things, battles, wounds, imprisonment, confiscation, and death, to secure liberty for themselves and their posterity." A year later, on Labor Day, perceiving the further erosion of freedom, Debs remarked, "again, I ask celebrate what?" Once more he found solace in the "the patriots" of the American Revolution who, "fired by the immortal declaration of Patrick Henry, . . . wrested from the British crown the jewel of Political Independence." If the American worker would only wield his ballot like the patriots of old, Debs observed, Labor Day might become "a second Fourth of July—a day when Americans may repeat the language of the Declaration of Independence." Debs's indictment of corporate America had sharpened, but he retained faith in patriotism based on equal opportunity, equality before the law, and consensual government— patriotism that compelled critical vigilance. Daring all and fearing nothing, the American Revolutionaries had proved their devotion to a cause larger than themselves. A little such patriotism, Debs believed, would go a long way toward beating back the egotism rampant in fin de siècle America.[39]

Two years later, as President McKinley committed American ground troops to the Philippines, Debs began to qualify his references to patriotism. "We [socialists] are not afflicted with the kind of patriotism which makes the slaves of our nation itch to murder the slaves of another nation in the interest of a plutocracy that wields the same lash over them all," Debs announced in the *Social Democrat*. "It seems not a little singular that thousands are so patriotic (!) in a country in which the only interest they have is six feet in a potter's field." Detecting corporate capitalism's influence in stoking Americans' jingoism, Debs urged American workers not to let "the booming of cannon" silence their agitation. Beneath the uproar waged "the real warfare for humanity." The following year saw Debs's bitterness mounting. Alarmed by America's annexation of the Philippines, Debs declared the American "patriot" to be "the biggest humbug on earth. Under the pretense of loving his country, he struts and swaggers, prates about the 'flag' and the 'glories of war' and makes a spectacle of himself generally." This new "patriotism"—hereafter, he would allude to it in quotation marks—masked the self-interest of a plutocratic elite; emanating from "sumptuous banquet halls," it reflected the interests not of the soldiers who would be expected to surrender their lives, but of investors keen to open distant mines and markets. Debs would side with partisans of liberty against proponents of empire. He was "for the Filipinos," hoping beyond hope that they might "yet repel the invaders and achieve their independence."[40]

The symbolic meaning of the American flag was changing too, according to Debs. Once thought to represent the principles underlying the American republic, the flag had become the emblem of the new patriotism itself. Like the new patriotism, the flag "fetish worship" demanded blind loyalty to state policy. On Independence Day, 1899, Debs scored the hypocrisy and braggadocio of those like Roosevelt, who elevated loyalty to the flag above defense of the nation's democratic institutions. "Thousands of orators all over this broad land will glorify the institutions under which we live," Debs observed. "In pride they will point to Old Glory and declare that it is a flag that waves over a free country." He would abstain from such celebration, having no respect for a flag symbolizing "capitalist class rule and wage slavery."[41]

Debs was not alone in protesting the conformist thrust of the new patriotism. In the spring of 1900, the philosopher William Everett called the attention of the Phi Beta Kappa Society of Harvard College to patriotism's curious transformation from "a generous and laudable emotion" to "a paramount and overwhelming duty to which everything else which men have called duties must give way."[42] Everett called on the "philosophers" before him to defend American principles from vicissitudes of "interest" and "passion." The field of linguistics constituted a crucial arena in this contest. Linguistically, Americans surrendered the enduring meaning of concepts like patriotism to fickle convention, rendering them "worthless when we come to some great public or private crisis" (PAT, 5). To Everett's mind, the industrial and cultural upheaval confronting his generation constituted one such crisis, and the apotheosizing of patriotism as obedience and soldiering illustrated the rule. Did philosophy have anything to teach patriotism, Everett asked, or could patriotism defy philosophy "as she claims the submission of every other human interest?" (PAT, 8).

The role of philosophy was to uphold standards of Truth and Right. The new patriotism undermined Truth and Right by valorizing a bankrupt ideal of virtue. Everett regarded virtue as both the sum and standard of citizens' joint enterprise. A virtuous citizenry did not hew to the dictates of corporate capitalist and government elites, but delineated its ideals collectively. It loved Truth and Right, not some flag or physical territory. Land could fall under evil proprietorship, so too a government and even a country: "a whole people may be wrong and deserve, at best, the pity of a real patriot rather than his active love." The point was not that standards of Truth and Right remained unchanged. Rather, the patriot defended a reading of Truth and Right that consisted of the sum total of past, present, and future experience—one that transcended his or her immediate perspective. To Everett, "America" constituted "something more than the single procession which passes across its borders in one generation: it means the land with all its people in all their periods; the ancestors whose exertions made us what we are, and whose memory is precious to us; the posterity to whom we are to transmit what we prize, unstained, as we receive it." Thus the real patriot acted and spoke "not for the present generation alone, but for all that rightly live, every event in whose history is inseparable from every other." What, then, should the patriot do? Anything that would promote his or her country's "perfection," though here too perfection was less something to be attained than a goal for which to strive. "What our country chiefly calls on us for is not mighty exertions and sacrifices," Everett insisted, "but those particular ones, small or great, which shall do her real good, and not harm." Like Debs's patriot, Everett's was a vigilant, engaged citizen quick with both criticism and praise, as ready to act locally as internationally, as concerned about others' liberty as he was about his own (PAT, 15–6).[43]

If it was the philosopher's job to demystify patriotism, it was the publicist's burden to inculcate it. But how should nations promote patriotism, E. L. Godkin asked in the summer of 1906 in the pages of *The Nation*?

Although Godkin professed to be weary of the recent spate of legally mandated school programs designed to instill patriotism in students by rote, he
admitted the legitimacy of the problem of loyalty in a nation founded on
political commitments and composed of diverse peoples. In place of America's "idiotic flag-fetishism," Godkin offered the counsel of Edmund Burke.
From Burke's perspective, loyalty was the stuff not of forced oaths but of
like privileges and equal protection. Rising before Parliament in 1755, Burke
urged his peers to "let the [American] colonies always keep the idea of their
civil rights associated with your government." Only then will they "cling
and grapple to you, and no force under heaven will be of the power to tear
them from their allegiance." After Burke, Godkin believed that reciprocity
was the solution to the problem of loyalty: just as the citizen had to earn his
or her rights, so the nation had to deserve its citizens' loyalty. Like Dewey,
Godkin believed this quid pro quo to be essential in promoting an engaged
and loyal citizenry. "The truth," wrote Godkin, "is that love of country, in
the high and proper sense, cannot be taught. It is commanded by the country
that deserves it. . . . Give men justice freedom, and equal treatment before
the laws, and you do more than all possible schools and schoolmasters to
intensify their national love for land and kin. Try to stimulate this by hot-
house methods, and you make patriotism artificial and false, an idle name;
you stifle the noble kinds of love of country, now exemplified in Russia—the
readiness to overthrow duly constituted authorities who betray the public
trust." [44]

In the labor strife that marked the era, the "old" and "new" patriotisms
locked horns. Just as Debs urged workers to adopt the patriotism of the
American revolutionary heroes and "strike for liberty" against corporate
capitalism, so the captains of industry bid "loyal" workers to defend the
American system against the alien influence of socialist agitators. When, in
1902, Debs's Americanism was impugned by capitalist detractors, he told a
Boulder, Colorado, audience that "in the capitalist system" he was indeed
"a rebel and not a patriot." But Debs's confident dismissal of "capitalist
patriotism" belied a deeper problem. His principal rhetorical strategy for
motivating workers to convert to socialism was being appropriated by his
adversaries to ensure workers' loyalty to state capitalism—and it seemed to
be working. In the summer of 1903, Debs noted the paradoxical effect of the
new patriotism on his ideal of manhood. Responding to an announcement
that the U.S. Postmaster General planned to commission railroad conductors
as employees of the U.S. Postal Service—and thereby invoke the Sherman Act
to derail a strike—Debs mourned that "this will make a scab, a patriotic scab,
of every railroad man engaged in train service." [45]

Debs viewed the global nationalist conflicts of the early twentieth century as a conspiracy among capitalists throughout the world to thwart the progress of international justice. "The chief significance of national boundaries, and of the so-called patriotisms which the ruling class of each nation is seeking to revive," he wrote in the *Independent,* "is the power which these give to capitalism to keep the workers of the world from uniting, and to throw them against each other in the struggles of contending capitalist interests for the control of the yet unexploited markets of the world." If Debs's conspiracy theory ignores the extent to which Western consumers—as well as capitalists—benefited from imperialism, it nonetheless highlights the connection between capitalism, imperialism, and the rise of the nation-state. All were implicated in the new patriotism. Writing in *Miner's Magazine* in 1902, Debs attributed America's aggression in the Philippines to industrial overproduction. Private ownership of the means of production combined with economic disparity to ensure that workers and capitalists consumed only a fraction of the nation's industrial surplus. Hence the need for American soldiers to secure foreign markets; hence, as Croly had implied, it was "patriotic for man to murder man."[46]

No doubt there was an element of self-interest and hypocrisy behind the new patriotic fervor, but surely there was more to it than that. Why were Americans drawn to a brand of nationalism that ostensibly benefited only their "masters"? By depicting the new patriotism as the work of a corrupt minority, Debs robbed American citizens of agency, unwittingly reinforcing corporate America's elitism. By contrast, Jane Addams held the people no less than their leaders responsible for the dysfunctions of society and government. From Addams's perspective, if American citizens embraced "capitalist patriotism," then that patriotism must be meeting an important human need. It followed that the way to vanquish the new patriotism was not to denounce the relatively few capitalists themselves, but to address the underlying circumstances that left Americans in need of patriotic catharsis.

This Addams attempted to do in a series of essays begun around the time of the Spanish-American War and that culminated in the publication of *Newer Ideals of Peace* in 1907. Like Debs, Godkin, and Everett, Addams professed frustration at the "abstract" and "institutionalized" patriotism taught increasingly in the public schools—so "remote from actual living." Writing in the journal *Unity* in December 1898, she worried lest this artificial patriotism, together with "our made-up philanthropy," dispossess schoolchildren of their appreciation for "the natural democratic relation." Viewing patriotism as a "great leveler and promoter of right relations," Addams hoped that it could be kept "normal and vital." Toward this end, she suggested that students be held accountable for the condition of their schools and playgrounds—a burden she thought would inculcate in them a more general sense of responsibility "in regard to the public streets and community duties."[47]

Three years later, as her "normal" patriotism receded before the clamor for empire, Addams challenged the members of Chicago's Sunset Club to account for war's remarkable allure. Where Debs viewed America's jingoism as a symptom of materialism, Addams, like James, attributed it to a spiritual crisis emanating from a breakdown in the institutions of self-government. The uproar over expansion provided Americans with a necessary "outlet for their beliefs," Addams observed; it gave them "a consciousness of nationality, the sense of being in the sweep of the world's activities." By contrast, the reform movement tapped none of the citizenry's latent altruism or craving for belonging. Orchestrated from on high, reform movements presuppose that the people are "paralyzed morally and have no share in pushing forward social reforms for themselves."[48]

Addams was tempted to cede patriotism to jingoists, so rabid had it become by the turn of the century. Her ambivalence is captured in a speech titled "Newer Ideals of Peace," from which her later book would get its title. A new peace required "a new type of patriotism," Addams announced, though, with its disregard for national borders, her new ideal was hardly patriotism at all. This she seemed to recognize, imagining "the time when the feeling shall grow perhaps not into international patriotism but a certain sense of duty which shall soak up the old one of national patriotism." Here Addams missed the truth that she would later champion—that patriotism and international fair play were not only compatible, but in America must be indistinguishable; that, however well-meaning, it was fatuous to insist that American citizens were equally beholden to "an Italian living in the United States [and] one living in Italy."[49]

Nations *had* a role to play in promoting universal justice. The point was not to obliterate nations, she later recognized, but to impress upon national communities that their own rights and privileges could never be secure if they came at the expense of others. Could not American patriotism both "hold up a standard of life for its people" and demand "that [the nation] shall compete on the highest possible planes"?[50] This, Addams believed, is what patriotism had meant to America's Founding Fathers. This was a "wise patriotism" useful at home and abroad, capable of enacting and enforcing laws to resolve the era's social problems, aware "that if the meanest man in the republic is deprived of his rights, then every man in the republic is deprived of his rights." This, Addams insisted, was "the only patriotism by which public-spirited men and women, with a thoroughly aroused conscience, can worthily serve this republic."[51]

Any ambivalence Addams harbored about patriotism vanished with *Newer Ideals of Peace*. A compilation of essays written over the course of a decade, this book provided the fullest statement of Addams's cosmopolitan patriotism. World peace, Addams believed, depended on the outward extension of cosmopolitanism from urban neighborhoods to municipal, state, and national governments, and ultimately to the institutions of international commerce and law. Addams's cosmopolitan patriotism consisted above all of sympathy, the compassion derived from common political and social activities. By personalizing the public, sympathy eradicated outworn stereotypes and age-old animosities. By contrast, official or state patriotism spawned an indoctrination campaign inimical to the social and cultural institutions of women and cultural minorities and incompatible with democratic principles. Ideally, according to Dewey and Du Bois, the business of the school was to promote reciprocity. Addams lamented not only that educators treated pupils as empty receptacles of nationalist pabulum, but, in the case of immigrant children, tried to banish the cultural traditions that accompanied immigrants to the new world. Such policy alienated pupils, bred resentment, and thwarted the "natural foundation of patriotism"—"genuine sacrifice for the nation's law" (NIP, 74–7). The result was a juvenile contest of one-upmanship, as common among adults as among children. Let me tell you about my ancestors, Addams overheard a young boy say to a friend. Let me tell you about mine, the friend replied. "Mine could beat yours out" (NIP, 77).

The cosmopolitan patriots met their match in World War I. At its best, cosmopolitan patriotism refused to separate local economic, political, and moral practices and commitments from national and global developments. War imperiled cosmopolitan patriotism by eroding the sympathy and reciprocity that sustained awareness of these interconnections. Rooted in a commitment to civic vigilance, cosmopolitan patriotism withered in a political atmosphere impatient with civil liberty and democratic deliberation. Increasingly on the political defensive, Debs, Addams, and Du Bois resorted to bald pronouncements and bland prophesizing. Cosmopolitan patriotism lost its dynamism.

As a committed pacifist, Jane Addams had no choice but to oppose the disintegration of Western civilization into armed nationalist camps. But for a pragmatist, the evidence emanating from Europe had to be disconcerting. War proved her pacifism to be less social science than wishful thinking, as the local, national, and international developments that she turned to as evidence of war's atavism were subsumed by the tumult. Plainly, in its first, great practical trial, *the newer ideals of peace* had failed to slow the militarist juggernaut. For Eugene Debs, the war proved equally confounding. Theoretically, socialists could not be partisans in "a capitalist war." Yet many socialists viewed Germany as a threat to the democratic principles undergirding the American republic and supposedly renewed in the Bolshevik revolution. Despite his international rhetoric, Debs had always betrayed intense national devotion. That devotion made him nearsighted during World War I. The closer America moved toward mobilization, the more alienated Debs became from the local and national scene. As he began to discount the need to root international socialism in local and national political mobilization, his rhetoric took an abstract and idealistic quality reminiscent of Addams's. For W. E. B. Du Bois, the challenge lay in retaining skepticism of President Wilson's idealist notion of a war to end all war. Du Bois's conviction that the Negro race had much to gain from participation in the Allied cause led him to downplay war's impact on democratic institutions around the world. In the face of war, Du Bois compromised his commitment to fairness and free expression. The more confident he became in his own position, the less inclined was he to entertain dissent.

THE COSMOPOLITAN MOMENT

The collapse of American progressivism in the face of World War I caught many American intellectuals off guard. Nativism and the excesses of corporate capitalism appeared to be on retreat in the opening decade and a half of the twentieth century. In November 1912 Americans selected as their next president a man whose first four years in office would make him look for all the world like a cosmopolitan. In November 1916, Americans returned that president to power, little reckoning how war could transform a practical and charismatic leader into an sullen and solitary ideologue. The latter Woodrow Wilson lay dormant in the former, suggesting the tenuousness of cosmopolitan ideals when unrooted in local political practices. The more Germany and its allies seemed to imperil American democracy, the more Wilson adopted policies contradictory to democracy to vanquish the German threat. Of the cosmopolitan patriots and their allies only Debs, Addams, and Randolph Bourne resisted war's siren call. But their fortitude proved cold comfort in the end, as war bred a popular fury inimical to their pragmatism—one that equated skepticism with dissent, and dissent, in turn, with treason.[1]

Wilson's cosmopolitanism was as much a product of historical circumstance as of ideological commitment. The legislative achievements of his first term reflected national resolve, mounting over the previous two decades, to correct the blatant indignities of corporate industrialism. This was an epoch unprecedented in American history, Wilson announced in his Second Inaugural. Never before had the nation as a whole been so eager to "set our house in order, correct the grosser errors and abuses of our industrial life, liberate and quicken the processes of our national genius and energy, and lift our politics to a broader view of the people's essential interest." Progressives such as Addams shared the president's enthusiasm. Campaigning for Wilson in the fall of 1916, Addams praised his administration for protecting workers' rights, promoting the general welfare, and furthering the cause of international peace. In foreign affairs, Addams marveled, Wilson's "consistent concern for the man at the bottom" inspired the remarkable conviction "that the Mexicans should have an opportunity to work out their own political institutions" free from outside coercion.[2]

Historian Garry Wills cautions against viewing political utterances as mere "rhetoric." On the lips of gifted orators, Wills observes, words can move audiences and alter the course of nations. Wilson's war oratory of 1917–1918 illustrates the point. In the face of the president's idealism, pragmatists forgot their skepticism and socialists their internationalism as Americans arose in near unison to vanquish evil. Wilson oratory was so compelling one wonders what its impact might have been had America remained unembroiled in World War I. Whether defining the meaning of patriotism or describing his global vision, Wilson evinced a worldview strikingly similar to the cosmopolitan patriots' own.[3]

In May 1914, Wilson performed a eulogy for American soldiers killed at the recent battle of Vera Cruz. He equated American "blood" not with a single race or culture, nor with a people circumscribed by a national boundary, but with a universal "spirit" compounded of "all the best elements of the whole globe." In an era rife with anti-immigrant harangue, the president defended immigration for keeping American society vibrant. "A nation that is not constantly renewed out of new sources is apt to have the narrowness and prejudice of a family," he told a group of naturalized Americans. "My urgent advice to you would be, not only always to think first of America, but always, also, to think first of humanity . . . for America was created to unite mankind by those passions which lift and not by the passions which separate and debase." To be American, the president maintained, meant to elevate "the ideals of men, to make them see finer things than they had seen before, to get rid of the things that divide and to make sure of the things that unite."[4]

Like the cosmopolitan patriots, Wilson viewed political cynicism and the disempowerment of immigrant minorities as the principal impediments to national well-being. With them, he regarded sympathy and mutual obligation as essential civic virtues. On Independence Day, 1916, he associated a multitude of flags arrayed before him with Americans' obligation to take an interest in one another. "Every one of those flags," the president chided, "ought to have suggested to every one of us that we have not yet fulfilled the full conscientious duty of America in understanding each other and, through comprehension of each other, understanding and serving the world." Familiarity was essential to democratic coalition building. Where authoritarian regimes demanded only their subjects' fealty, democratic rule depended on citizens' readiness to work cooperatively. Speaking on the subject of citizenship in the summer of 1916, Wilson echoed Addams in blaming the shortcomings of Progressive reform on a breakdown of democracy: "a law cannot work," the president warned, "until it expresses the spirit of the community for which it is enacted."⁵

By this point in his career, Wilson had come to view the American national community inclusively. In spring 1914, he confessed his desire for "orderly and righteous" government in Mexico. But order would have to benefit the Mexican people rather than outside investors or the "old-time regime." Wilson was not averse to Americans doing business there, so long as they sought "to develop rather than exploit" Mexico's resources. Convinced that the resolution of the Mexican conflict depended on an equitable distribution of land, Wilson pledged to promote land reform and thereby establish a "new order" founded "on human liberty and human rights." This platform implied a repudiation of America's annexation of the Philippines. Careful not to dishonor fallen soldiers, the president vowed a year later that the United States would "never again take another foot of territory by conquest" or "make an independent people subject to our dominion." America stood for nothing if not for "the right of every people to choose their own allegiance and be free of masters altogether."⁶

The surge of European nationalism in 1914 provoked in Wilson a cosmopolitan commitment to universal self-government. In October 1915 he admonished a meeting of the Daughters of the American Revolution that patriotism inhered in "active conduct" rather than in "mere sentiment." It was "born into the world not to please it, but to regenerate it," the president remarked. Like patriots elsewhere, Americans would remain quick to defend their nation's honor, but for them honor entailed elevating democratic principles above national interest. It would take moral as well as physical courage to vindicate this ideal, Wilson had told Philadelphia and Washington, D.C., audiences the previous year. "The most patriotic man is sometimes the man who goes in the direction that he thinks is right even when half the world is against him." The toll exacted on such a patriot was no less real than the suffering endured by the soldier. "When they shoot at you," he declared, "they can only take your natural life; when they sneer at you, they can wound your living heart, and men who are brave enough, steadfast enough, steady in their principles enough, to go about their duty with regard to their fellow men, no matter whether there are hisses or cheers . . . are men for a nation to be proud of."⁷

On point after point, the president's rhetoric seemed to accord with the tenets of cosmopolitan patriotism. And yet there was a portentous quality to Wilson's words. As long as calm prevailed, Americans might uphold his association of honor with honesty, patriotism with candor, and nationalism with individual autonomy. But calm proved elusive in a nation composed of representatives of Europe's warring parties. German naval aggression polarized

American opinion in the second year of the war. Wilson's thinking betrayed a conformist impulse; his calls for unity conveyed a certain volkishness. Lately a champion of democracy and dissent, Wilson grew hostile to dissent on the eve of his second term.

Historian Thomas Knock has portrayed the author of the Fourteen Points as the pivot of a spectrum of Progressive and radical Democrats extending from Croly and Dewey and Addams to Max Eastman, Mother Jones, and Debs. But no matter how much Debs and Addams may have sympathized with Wilson's vision of a League of Nations, long before 1918 they had become skeptical of his commitment to democracy. By the time the United States declared war on Germany in April 1917, Wilson had all but throttled free speech. To be sure, war also compromised cosmopolitan patriotism; but, no matter what their professed opinion of the war, the cosmopolitan patriots remained skeptical of the idealist fallacy that one could suspend democracy in democracy's name without wreaking inestimable havoc.[8]

NEUTRALITY AS SELF-MASTERY

In April 1915, President Wilson warned that the word "neutrality" did not adequately describe America's perspective toward the combatants. As the custodian of "justice and righteousness and human liberty," America could never watch indifferently or self-interestedly—as neutrality seemed to imply—while modern civilization went down in ruin. "We are compounded of the nations of the world," Wilson told the Associated Press; "we mediate their blood, we mediate their traditions, we mediate their sentiments, their tastes, their passions." Thus America was uniquely equipped to comprehend the nations, Wilson maintained, not individually but collectively. With its eye on the big picture, the Unites States could straddle the scales of justice, interpreting the warring parties to one another, arbitrating differences, paving the path to peace. But only as long as Americans withstood war's centripetal force, an imperative that called forth virtues never before realized, according to the president—"absolute self-control and self-mastery."[9]

The imperative of self-mastery occupied the mind of Eugene Debs. With the collapse of European socialism in 1914, American socialism took on the mantle of internationalism's last best hope on earth. To Debs, the outbreak of war seemed both tragic and exhilarating. On the one hand, the capitulation of European socialists suggested that much teaching remained to be done. On the other hand, war exposed the twin evils of capitalism and nationalism as no publicity campaign could. Debs was loath to admit any "good" emanating from what he regarded essentially as a clash of workers; but in

1915 he told the Scripps news syndicate that if war resulted in the razing of capitalism and the erection of an edifice for international peace, it would be worth the carnage. [10]

Like Wilson, Debs expected Americans to remain poised "to help in every way in their power to terminate this unholy massacre and bring peace to the world." Convinced that "capitalist patriotism" had precipitated the collapse of European socialism, Debs resolved to make patriotism itself the battleground of his neutrality campaign. This entailed awakening Americans to "the narrow, mean and contemptible 'patriotism' surreptitiously inculcated in the minds of unsophisticated workers by their crafty and unscrupulous masters." In a series of essays in the socialist journal *National Rip-Saw* in the fall and winter of 1914–1915, Debs tried to distinguish "genuine" patriotism from its "fraudulent" cousin. Where fraudulent patriotism betrayed an artificial, or "bureaucratic," character, genuine patriotism sprang naturally from citizens' affection for a nation devoted to equal opportunity, equality before the law, and consensual government. Where false patriotism was quick to take offense and identify scapegoats, true patriotism was deliberate, self-critical, and above all wary of trying to resolve problems elsewhere when there was so much work left to be done at home. As a socialist, Debs did not advocate isolation; he acknowledged the impact of local decisions on global politics. But he found it ironic that it in a nation so steeped in patriotism "so many of the 'patriots' [we]re gravitating toward pauperism. 'Patriotism' and 'pauperism,' " he concluded, "flourish side by side." [11]

War highlighted differences among socialists, no less than between socialists and capitalists. One issue dividing the Socialist Party concerned socialism's relationship to organized pacifism. In the spring of 1915, Debs exchanged letters with Allan L. Benson, the man who would lead the Socialist ticket in 1916 while Debs ran for Congress. Where Benson embraced the call of conventional pacifists for popular referenda and arbitration, Debs argued that the way to halt war was to end capitalism, which he knew to be "the breeder of war." Whether the Socialist Party could tolerate dissension in its ranks became another dividing point. Benson equated opposition and uncertainty with disloyalty. By contrast, Debs appeared more tolerant of disagreement, at least for the time being. "It would be not only strange but a miracle," he wrote Benson, "if you and I were in perfect agreement on this great question [of war and peace] upon which scarcely two can be found who hold identical views." Debs no more than Benson would excuse "treason" to the party, but there were times, he wrote another friend, "when moral weakness"—much less uncertainty—was "not a crime." [12]

Like Wilson and Debs, Jane Addams recognized the need for mastery. In early January 1915, Addams delivered her first explicit statement about the war to the inaugural meeting of the Woman's Peace Party in Washington, D.C. Although Addams seems in retrospect the natural person to preside at the founding of this organization, her participation in the conference was by no means foreordained. When war erupted the previous summer, Addams worked resolutely to keep true to her pragmatism amid a climate of rhetorical hyperbole. Her correspondence that fall with colleagues in the settlement-house movement chronicles the anticipation and yet caution with which she prepared to put her cosmopolitanism to the test. She would align herself warily. Had her reputation been humbler and the demands on her time less prodigious, Addams might have delineated the deliberate, perspicacious response she knew that war demanded. But her prestige among American moral reformers propelled her to the forefront of international pacifism quite against her will. Resolved to make the best of a delicate situation, Addams took the helm of the Women's Peace Party in the winter of 1915, attempting to guide its precious cargo between the Scylla of reactionary jingoism and the Charybdis of the militant left.[13]

With great trepidation Addams mounted the podium of the Women's Peace Party Conference in early January 1915. The eyes fastened upon her from the audience represented a mere fraction of the attention that would be accorded her remarks across the country and around the world. What could a conference of pacifist women presume to offer a world torn apart by war? Declaring that war jeopardized causes in which "women, as women, have held a vested interest," Addams moved at once to unify and justify the meeting. Women had long labored to foster an ideal of patriotism in which creativity played as crucial a role as destruction. For centuries they had struggled to advance a cosmopolitan consciousness of the sanctity of human life. This record of duty met in response to a natural obligation had earned women the civil right to protest anything that imperiled their work. When war summoned men to battle under the aegis of a "tribal" patriotism, women had no choice but to resist it. "A state founded upon such a tribal ideal of patriotism, has no place for women within its councils," Addams declared prophetically, just as "a world put back upon a basis of brute force [is] a world in which [women] can play no part."[14]

If Addams's decision to stake women's civil claim on a right grounded in nature and exercised in a separate sphere seems a dubious stratagem, it should be remembered that she viewed gender as only one of many overlapping affiliations. Her earlier correspondence with settlement-house peers shows her weighing the merits of affiliating with pacifist men, women, and suffragists. Typically with Addams, it was a personal appeal made by two women from the belligerent countries that compelled her to attend the women's conference. Furthermore, she would insist, a whole generation of young men now shared women's traditional revulsion of war. Still, there can be no denying the parallel between Addams's gendered rhetoric and that of one detractor who exhorted her—"splendid in your womanhood"—to hew to her "special field of work."[15]

In May 1915 Addams's work sped her to the Hague, head of a Women's Peace Party delegation to the International Congress of Women. The Hague Congress, in turn, authorized a committee, again led by Addams, to canvass Europe's civil authorities about interest in a conference of neutral nations. This whirlwind tour exposed Addams to war's civic and martial tribulations, an experience that formed the basis of her peace protest in the years preceding American intervention. In the keynote address at the Hague, Addams underscored the compatibility of patriotism and internationalism. "These two great affections should never have been set one against the other," Addams remarked, picking up where she had left off in 1907; "it is too late in the day for war." Whether it was really too late for war depended, as Debs observed, on one's political and economic perspective. Addams's conviction about the compatibility of national allegiance and internationalism reflected her belief that internationalism fulfilled patriotism in the same way that community completed the individual.

Addams attributed the war, with its clashing patriotism and internationalism, to a political coup d'état on the part of senior European politicians ignorant of the *newer ideals of peace*. In her report to the Women's Peace Party, Addams maintained that "the enthusiasm for war was not as universal among the young men who were doing the fighting as it was among the elderly men established in the high places of church and state." Where those in power entertained no alternative to war as a means of settling international disputes, their constituents had begun to view war as outdated. Where the older generation clung to a rhetoric of moral abstraction, the young expressed a pragmatism born of increasing commercial and cultural contact. It was not that Europe's youth disdained love of country, Addams was quick to observe; but they fought with tragic hearts. Tragedy, she had discovered from personal experience, involved no mere clash between good and evil, but conflict between competing goods, "so that the mind of the victims is torn as to which he ought to follow."[16]

An abstract ideal of peace accompanied the older generation's atavistic view of nationhood. Where the old believed that "the world would be federated when wise men from many nations get together and accomplish it," the young inhabited a world "where common experience has in fact become largely internationalized." They had developed the friendships and political alliances, hence, the understanding from which genuine peace might emerge. Again, Addams took pains to explain the younger generation's cosmopolitanism. The young aimed not to substitute cosmopolitanism for love of country, but to maintain the two in equilibrium. Of course, they "continue to salute the flag," Addams remarked pointedly, but they regarded the flag "as a symbol and realize that it has the danger of all abstractions—that a wrong content may be substituted for the right one, and that men in a nation, an army, a crowd may do horrible things as well as heroic that they could never do alone."[17]

The leaders of England and America portrayed the war as a struggle between militarism and democracy. Juxtaposing age and youth, idealism and pragmatism, parochialism and internationalism, Addams attributed war to the very same struggle but located it within each nation rather than between the separate belligerents. A coterie of old men in high places, out of touch with their epoch and uninformed by their constituents, had propelled Europe irrevocably down the road to war. War stifled social and political reciprocity. Within the warring nations, Addams reported, "a good patriot of differing opinion finds it almost impossible to reach his fellow countrymen with that opinion." If that patriot be a woman, dissent itself constituted a veritable "act of heroism." But then, Addams observed, "even to differ from those she loves in the hour of their afflictions has ever been the supreme test of a woman's conscience."[18]

Addams would confront this test herself sooner than she imagined. Having returned from Europe in the summer 1915, she embarked on a speaking tour of the United States. Except in the eyes of a few loyal friends, the tour ended the day it began at New York's Carnegie Hall, in early July. While describing her experience as a peace delegate in Europe, Addams made a four-sentence remark about the warring nations having to intoxicate their soldiers to prepare them for the bayonet charge. A minor part of her address, "the bayonet charge," as it became known, unleashed a torrent of protest, both at home and abroad, affording Addams a firsthand lesson of the treatment awaiting those whose self-mastery lapsed. From the vice-consul of France came a letter deploring Addams's "horrible calumny." Where she would emasculate France's soldiers, they thought only of protecting their womenfolk.[19] From the *New York Times* came two objections castigating Addams's trespass into the affairs of men. Knowing war as only a man could, one writer resented "this insult, flung by a complacent and self-satisfied woman at men who gave their lives for men." Meanwhile another thought Addams betrayed a "pitiful ignorance of human nature." She failed to comprehend the "joys of combat." Notwithstanding Addams's attempt to distance herself from peace militants, her obloquy bore the suffragist signature. "No fable is too gross for them to swallow," the critic wrote, "if it reflects on the tyrant man."[20]

By diverting attention from Addams's cosmopolitanism to an impolitic aside, Addams's detractors accomplished their goal of silencing her. Over the ensuing weeks, Addams spent as much time defending herself from petty charges as she did describing conditions in Europe. Concerned not to provide adversaries with more fodder for criticism, she demonstrated how the will to self-mastery could jeopardize individual expression.[21]

The imperative for self-mastery was nothing new to African Americans. By 1914 they had been waging a struggle for liberty lasting 300 years. Particularly for Southern blacks, the United States resembled an armed camp; the merest lapse of self-discipline could result in a lynching. In November 1914 W. E. B. Du Bois responded to events in Europe in an editorial published in *The Crisis*. Founded in autumn 1910 as the organ of the new NAACP, *The Crisis* remained Du Bois's principal social and political platform for the next twenty-five years—though the racial politics of the NAACP itself constrained his independence. Du Bois's tenure at *The Crisis* would severely test his commitment to institutional integration. In his response to World War I, he veered back and forth between trying to please the mostly white conservatives on the NAACP board and the more militant African Americans who composed the bulk of his constituency.[22]

In *The Crisis* of November 1914, Du Bois admonished "colored persons, and persons interested in them" not to let the conflagration abroad distract them from their own battle against racism at home. The two were rooted in the same "imperial expansion" with its rationale of racial superiority. The explosion in the Balkans was a mere sideshow to the real conflict in the war: Europe's scramble for African colonies. Covetous of the earth's resources, Europe warred not in the name of noble principle, but for the right to "confiscate land, work the natives at low wages, make large profits, and open wide markets for cheap European manufactures." Only America's own monopoly on the jewels of the Western Hemisphere spared it from the conflict. But how long America could remain aloof from war Du Bois could not say. Unless white folk quit their exploitation of the darker world, he warned, it would arise in revolution.[23]

As both a product and apostle of Western civilization, Du Bois took no satisfaction from his prediction. Even as he damned German militarism and autocracy he confessed to *Crisis* readers a sincere love of the German people. It had been the Germans, after all, who had enabled him to recognize "the essential humanity of white folk." Moreover, in England's "ability to learn from her mistakes" and in France's "personal relations with colored folk," Du Bois identified signs of progress. Du Bois never considered neutrality an option for African Americans. He would sink or swim with Western culture. Thus from the beginning of the war and over the protest of the president, he threw his support to England and France as the nations most likely to keep that culture afloat. Despite their uneven record on race prejudice, France and England had "at least begun to realize its cost and evil, while Germany exalts it." Not only did colored Americans have a special stake in an Allied victory, but colored races generally promised to benefit from participation in the war. In a preview of arguments to come, Du Bois speculated that the contribution of "black Africans and brown Indians and yellow Japanese" on behalf of the Allies would promote "new ideas of the essential equality of man."[24]

Six months later in May 1915 the *Atlantic Monthly* published what proved to be Du Bois's most trenchant wartime essay. In "The African Roots of War" Du Bois exposed the tension at the heart of Western democracy, denounced the hollowness of the international peace movement, and outlined his vision of a truly democratic world. He also unveiled the paradox at the core of his identity as an African-American intellectual struggling to make it in Western civilization. For those who missed his initial statement, Du Bois reiterated his warning that Western nations should quit their rape of "colored" races or brace for a battle whose violence would exceed "any war this world has yet seen." Du Bois repeated this augury to counter the notion that America's mandate was solely to end European hostilities. Calls for reconciliation among the belligerents would do nothing to avert looming racial conflagration, Du Bois declared, if reconciliation implied a "satisfaction with, or acquiescence in, a given division of the spoils of world dominion." Nor would mere peace talk prevent "renewed jealousy" from igniting future European wars, or address the revolutionary discontent of Europe's industrial masses who shouldered the burden of the arms race. If Western nations earnestly hoped to allay these threefold threats, they would have to acknowledge the African roots of war.[25]

Du Bois surely surprised *Atlantic* readers by announcing that democracy, not militarism, was the principal root of war. The quintessential development of the modern age, democracy harbored an internal paradox: the franchisement of the many entailed the alienation of many more. As "divine right" yielded inexorably to democracy over the course of the previous three centuries, there had occurred "the dipping of more and grimier hands into the wealth-bag of the nation." Lest the booty of powerful merchants and trading monopolies shrink to naught before the onslaught of the masses, the national purse would have to be expanded. Thus Western capitalists and workers forged a "new democratic nation"—a bond of "wealth, power, and luxury for all [white] classes on a scale the world never saw before." Thus Western nations inaugurated a "new democratic despotism" beyond the ken of Tocqueville, a paradox allowing "the most rapid advance of democracy to go hand in hand in its very centers with increased aristocracy and hatred toward darker races."

To be sure, the new predatory democracies could accommodate inequality among members of the privileged race. White labor's "investment" in color prejudice may have offered it a pathetic variety of self-esteem; it did little to strengthen labor's hand in relation to management. By purposefully

promoting racial animosity among workers, management deflected the grievances of white labor away from themselves to black workers. It was no wonder, Du Bois observed, that all over the world people believed that "if white
men do not throttle colored men, then China, India, and Africa will do to
Europe what Europe had done and seeks to do to them."

Individuals committed to breaking this cycle of exploitation and oppression had much to learn from the failure of international pacifism. Du Bois
criticized pacifists who argued along economic or humanist lines. As long as
the reward of imperial conquest exceeded the cost of military engagement,
economic exceptions to war would remain ineffectual. No less quixotic were
moral appeals to nations whose mercantilist policy expressly denied black
humanity. But Du Bois's response to Western imperialism revealed contradictions of its own. Having described the nexus between democracy and
oppression, he nevertheless insisted that to achieve "real peace and lasting
culture," Western nations would have to "extend the democratic ideal to the
yellow, brown and black peoples." Similarly, to make "modern men" out of
"docile beasts of burden," the West would have to provide colonized people
an "honest" and "effective" education in "modern civilization." This merely
begged the question he himself had raised of how more Western civilization
could remedy Western-induced ills. Moreover, if one person's freedom entailed another person's servitude, then on whom fell the burden of the world's
salvation? Mooting these dilemmas, Du Bois exhorted white folk to quit their
racial slander in the name of a "steadfast faith in humanity," sounding much
like the pacifists whose "platitudes" he decried.[26]

Du Bois's faith in Western progress did not prevent him from playing an
occasional race card to trump the hands of racist demagogues. Until German
intransigence made American entry into the war inevitable in the spring of
1917, Du Bois periodically flirted with separatism in the pages of *The Crisis*,
as if trying to convince himself that in the event Western civilization went
down with the *Lusitania* he would have a place to stand. From Du Bois's
perspective, the *Lusitania* incident unmasked the mendacity of Christian civilization. For centuries the West had pillaged the darker world for selfish
gain, all the while broadcasting the virtues of law and order. As long as
their victims remained colored, whites implicitly justified these attacks as the
treatment naturally accorded savages. But by making the "brutality and inhumanity" of European civilization manifest, the war cast African and African-
American culture in an entirely different light. "It is a great privilege," Du
Bois proclaimed, "in the midst of this frightful catastrophe to belong to a
race that can stand before Heaven with clean hands and say: we have not
oppressed, we have been oppressed; we are not thieves, we are victims; we
are not murderers, we are lynched!"[27] The following year Du Bois escalated
his indictment of Western civilization, with its "gloss of culture and wealth

and religion," behind which "lurk[ed] the world-old lust for bloodshed and power gained at the cost of honor." The unraveling of Western civilization presaged a return to "old ideals," and Du Bois encouraged blacks to celebrate African conceptions of honor, law, beauty, and art. Not "blue-eyed, white-skinned types" should be their model, but rather "rich, brown and black men and women with glowing dark eyes and crinkling hair." The Orient had long since demonstrated its inability to redeem the world; war proved the Occident similarly barren. Might the world not look toward colored Africa? "Let ours be the civilization of no *man,* but of *all men,*" Du Bois announced. "This is the truth that sets us free."[28]

Du Bois's anguished cry suggests that he was hardly free of Europe's grip. Moreover, his ambivalence about war lent his writing ambiguity. No sooner had he repudiated Western civilization on account of its war than he reasserted his initial conviction that war would effect "the greater emancipation of European women, the downfall of monarchies, the gradual but certain dissolution of caste and the advance of a true Socialism"—in short, all the causes to which he had committed himself. A rich and regal African civilization could not promise him all that. Indeed, Du Bois never delineated exactly what black Americans would gain by exalting Africa. Nor is it clear how African civilization would redeem the Western world. Here Du Bois appears to have been torn between his multiple allegiances—now American, now African American, now European, now African—and the disparate obligations that accompanied them. Difficult to reconcile in 1916, these commitments proved doubly so once America joined the war.

DRIFTING FROM MASTERY

When Woodrow Wilson described the challenges confronting a neutral nation to the Associated Press in April 1915, he stressed the need to elevate truth above innuendo. Truth, the president suggested, tended to be a stabilizing force, whereas innuendo fueled flights of fancy incompatible with mastery. Wills traces Wilson's descent from mastery to the sinking of the *Lusitania* the month after the president's call on the Associated Press. Though "truth" had the *Lusitania* passengers sailing on a ship loaded with contraband, exigency demanded bending the truth "to put the whole note," in Wilson's words, "on very high grounds." By demonizing the submarine as he would later execrate pacifism, Wilson lent his imprimatur to Americans' forfeiture of critical vigilance to blind loyalty. In the interest of permanently exorcising evil, who could oppose a temporary abridgment of civil rights? By the time Wilson embarked on his preparedness campaign the next fall, his latent idealism had pushed its way to the fore. "I love peace," Wilson told an audience in Pittsburgh, "but I know that peace costs something" and is dependent on "respect." I loathe might, he assured his listeners, but America's was the "might of righteous purpose and of a sincere love for the freedom of mankind." Where liberty and justice had once been Wilson's watchwords, by 1916 "honor" and "flag" had become his operative terms. "I am very much stirred by every sight that I get of the flag of the United States," Wilson remarked in tones akin to those Addams encountered in Europe. "I did not use to have the sentiment as poignantly as I have it now, but if you stood in my place, ladies and gentlemen, and felt that in some peculiar and unusual degree the honour of that flag were entrusted to your keeping, how would you feel?"[29]

That would depend, as Debs had told Roosevelt back in 1902, on what the flag signified. By the time Wilson addressed the Associated Press, Debs believed the American flag had come to symbolize blind loyalty. In August 1916 Debs confronted the Socialist mayor of Milwaukee about his alleged capitulation to capitalist patriotism. "The press dispatches reported some time ago that you headed a military preparedness parade at Milwaukee," Debs wrote Daniel W. Hoan. "I simply cannot believe anything of the kind." In reply, Hoan explained that although local newspapers had declared the march a preparedness parade, he had considered it a "Patriotic Demonstration." To have refused to march in the parade, Hoan maintained, would have been "to deny any national feeling whatsoever, and probably cripple the party for years." Besides, Hoan observed, socialists possessed "a genuine patriotic spirit" and were devoting their "lives to make this nation a better place in which the men who toil may live, as well as in displaying an international patriotism." "Rather than scoff at the word patriotism," Hoan suggested, socialists should "seize upon it and make it a word to express our ideas and popularize our thought."[30]

Debs rejected Hoan's apology, pinning responsibility for his parading on Victor Berger and fellow Milwaukee socialists, whom Debs had long accused of selling out principles for influence. Hoan's participation left him in a position vis-à-vis the ruling class analogous to that of the poor whites Debs had encountered on his swing through the American South in 1903. Milwaukee's capitalist elite undoubtedly appreciated the Socialists' show of support, Debs remarked bitterly; "the capitalist politicians were just a little too shrewd for the socialist politicians of Milwaukee and their press was not slow to spread the news over the country that the socialist mayor of Milwaukee had marched at the head of a preparedness parade." Hoan's willingness to invoke an ideal of "patriotism" divorced from content contributed to the erosion of American liberty. Appealing to the advantage of "the party," Hoan elevated national interest above democratic principles—something Debs adamantly refused to do. Although Milwaukee socialists may have thought their "perversion of principle" to be "good vote-catching politics," Debs scolded, they had insulted "militant socialism." Debs vowed that when socialists had to march in "capitalist parades" to prove their patriotism, he would "quit the party" and deny his socialism altogether.[31]

The only kind of national preparedness Debs would endorse was preparation for peace. In November 1915, the *New York Sun* solicited his opinion on the issue of American armament. Socialist Charles Edward Russell had just declared American participation in the war inevitable and had come out in favor of a military buildup. What was Debs's response? Notwithstanding Russell's "high standing" in the Socialist Party, he had forfeited socialist principles, Debs insisted. America might still avoid being drawn into the war, but not by arming itself. Europe proved "a flaming example" of what preparedness meant for civilization. A state organized around a large standing army was a throwback to the medieval era, as anathema to the ideal of democracy as it was inimical to the interests of American workers. America had an opportunity to strike the note of global harmony. What a contrast it would make if in the face of the European slaughter the U.S. government issued "a proclamation of peace" and set "an example of disarmament to the nations of the world." Not only would such a model of preparedness accord with the nation's "vaunted principles," but it would constitute "a thousandfold greater guarantee to the respect of its neighbors and to its own security and peace than if it were loaded down with all the implements of death and destruction on earth." America's exploited workers had "no country to fight for," Debs would later tell Upton Sinclair. Their only credible threat emanated from within.[32]

What had seemed in peacetime to be dynamic equilibrium between Debs's socialism and the new cosmopolitanism came to resemble in war nothing so much as logical inconsistency. America's *vaunted principles,* Debs had once argued, no matter how imperfectly applied, constituted the birthright of American workers. How could claimants to such a birthright have *no country to fight for?* The closer Americans moved to war, the more desperate Debs's rhetoric became, as the dynamism of the moment overwhelmed his equilibrium.

Jane Addams shared Debs's conviction that preparedness amounted to a capitulation of American principles to Old-World practices. In January 1916 Addams told the Pan-American Scientific Congress that talk of armament ignored evidence of the developing cosmopolitanism emanating from America's urban laboratories. Once abstract and disembodied, internationalism had become empirical and practical as it became bound to innovations in commerce and communications. Its practitioners' commitment to human inquiry lent the new internationalism a sense of humility and hope conducive to mediating and adjusting international differences. "We have an opportunity such as never faced the world before," Addams exhorted her fellow scientists. "[If we do not] found human internationalism from experience and understanding, rather than the formal thing which comes from philosophy, and gets results, then it seems to me that we will have lost the one opportunity, the great opportunity which has been put into our hands."[33]

A few days later, Addams reiterated this sentiment with slightly different emphasis in the U.S. Congress. Testifying before the House Committee on Military Affairs, she urged her hosts to prepare for disarmament rather than war. She also took pains to defend America's cultural diversity from partisans of cultural conservatism, newly emboldened by the clamor for 100 percent Americanism. Far from imperiling American institutions and precipitating conflict, Addams assured her audience, Chicago's immigrants represented the vanguard of a dawning "international understanding." During the Balkan Wars, for example, the familiarity of Balkan emigrants with one another bred a sympathy in stark contrast to the enmity unfolding on the continent. If anything, Addams continued, the immigrants' firsthand experience of Old-World enmities made them less likely to be seduced by war's allure. Whether they came for economic or political reasons, immigrants clung to the faith "that in America the government rests upon the consent of the governed and does not have to be backed up by military force."[34]

How much of Addams's testimony got through to her listeners, one cannot be sure. One representative thought to make Addams pay for her late support of Theodore Roosevelt's presidential candidacy. Could Roosevelt have been so right about the need for industrial reform in 1912 and so wrong about the importance of armament now? Others focused on inconsistencies in Addams's remarks—hasty analogies, slips of tongue—which, like her comment on the bayonet, were really beside the point. A more sympathetic audience might have discovered what had become by now Addams's consistent refrain: powerful nations must be wary about intervening in other nations' affairs; military training in the schools was anathema to education; preparedness did not prevent war; war's virtues could be got by other means.[35]

The representatives' subterfuge confirmed what Addams dreaded most about war: it cut short the communication on which peace as well as democracy depended. Throughout autumn and winter 1915–16, Addams campaigned for the convening of a conference of neutral nations to establish a platform for discussion of peace, all talk of which had become virtually impossible within the warring nations themselves. In the *Survey* of January 1916, Addams observed that the stifling of pacifism in Europe had resulted in a monopoly of information on the part of belligerent governments. Nations engaged in war did not quibble about the issues of free expression and citizen consent. Intimidated publics colluded with government officials to enforce national unity. Hence, inevitably, the fate of peace no less than the plan of war was left in the hands of individuals least inclined to consult popular opinion or negotiate, creating a potentially explosive political climate. If the pattern persists, Addams warned, "the people will know nothing of the terms of peace until these are practically ratified; and the only way popular opposition could then express itself would partake of the character of revolution." [36]

At the end of 1916, Addams returned to Congress to reiterate the relationship between war and public ignorance. Not Germany alone, but Japan too now constituted a threat to American security in the eyes of American lawmakers. What had pacifists to offer such a situation? Dispassion, Addams replied, along with a dose of pragmatism. The way to diffuse a perceived clash of interests was not to "go on in the dark about it," but to "find out what the matter is, and, in an intelligent way, try to straighten out the difficulty and have it explained to the people of both countries." Surely there were people in America and Japan more "versed in the [practical] difficulties and the tasks of international affairs and international relations" than America's representatives of state. To ignore the counsel of individuals actually engaged in international commerce and communications would be to proceed "in the same stupid way that all these nations have gone on in for the last few centuries." By putting these matters before a public tribunal, America could take a "step forward" in the matter of international conciliation. Sounding much like William James during the Philippines conflict, Addams suggested that the situation demanded a "fresh set of citizens to take up the matter in an active way"—to "open it up *de novo.*" [37]

From W. E. B. Du Bois's perspective, war highlighted the need for new thinking among African Americans, as well. As Debs and Addams discussed preparedness in the winter of 1915–16, African Americans debated what they owed a nation that denied them civil rights. Few African Americans openly opposed black participation in the war. African Americans disagreed, however, about how forcefully their own agenda should be pursued amid the national crisis. Partisanship in the debate divided along lines of ideology and even temperament: integrationists and optimists generally committed themselves to America's preparedness campaign; separatists and pessimists counseled a conditional approach.

This fault line first appeared on the opinion page of *The Crisis* in July 1915 when Du Bois published a sample of editorials culled from black journals. In the *Southern Workman,* one writer had predicted that colored troops would strike "a shattering blow to race prejudice," closely mirroring Du Bois's own sentiment. Referring to "hints" in the French and British papers about improving racial conditions overseas, the writer announced matter-of-factly that race relations could "never be the same"; African Americans' destiny was simply "bound to be reshaped." The *New York Evening Mail* countered with sober reflection acknowledging African America's valiant record in past wars but maintaining that they had "achieved no equal position with all their fighting." It was easier to review the past than read the future. History betrayed the optimists' naiveté. Though black soldiers had "saved the day at Las Guasisinas, in the Spanish War, and fought at San Juan Hill and El Caney with heroism unsurpassed by any white organization," there was no evidence that their "record of intrepidity has socially or politically advantaged the race."[38]

Germany's renewal of unrestricted submarine warfare lent this debate cogency in the late winter of 1917. Anticipating that war would introduce the conscription of black soldiers, Du Bois asked what sort of army black conscripts would enter and under whose command they would serve. At the urging of his NAACP colleague Joel Spingarn, Du Bois petitioned the General Staff of the U.S. Army to establish a segregated training camp to commission black officers. Du Bois would have preferred to have had black officers trained in white camps, of course, but his appeal for integration in the armed service had met intractable resistance. The editor's apparent capitulation to segregation provoked an outcry among some black leaders, whose criticism reverberated through the pages of *The Crisis*.

Segregated training camps confronted African Americans with yet another episode in what Du Bois called African America's "Perpetual Dilemma." They had always to "choose between insult and injury: no schools or separate schools; no travel or 'Jim Crow' travel; homes with disdainful neighbors or homes in slums." According to Du Bois, theirs was a painful but nonetheless obvious choice: separate was better than none, when none implied the stifling of human aspiration. Self-realization depended on individuals having the opportunity to rise to positions of leadership in classrooms, communities, and jobs. Du Bois acceded to "the insult of the separate camp" only to forestall the "irreparable injury" of reinforcing current strictures against elevating African Americans to positions of leadership. Where power and authority were at stake, the choice was "clear as noonday." Moreover, Du Bois argued, opposition to the training of black officers within the army and throughout the South justified the policy. Few Americans anywhere wanted to see blacks in positions of authority; Southerners, particularly, trembled at the thought of a well-organized black soldiery.

Du Bois's interpretation of the issue of the separate camp exposed a point of tension in his thought that would divide African Americans once America joined the war. At the core of his cosmopolitanism resided the conviction that segregation impeded self-realization. A life without full civil rights, Du Bois had insisted, was a life devoid of reciprocity—was in fact a kind of death itself. Accordingly, civil rights functioned both as a means of self-defense and as a foundation of national patriotism, a point Du Bois had pressed repeatedly throughout the *Souls of Black Folk*. There he invoked "patriotism and loyalty" in repudiating Booker T. Washington's capitulation to the South on the issues of segregation and disenfranchisement. Individuals who submitted to Washington's program, Du Bois warned, shirked a "heavy responsibility" to all "whose future depends so largely on this American experiment, but especially, a responsibility to this nation,—this common Fatherland." For undergirding America, Du Bois made plain, was no shifting boundary, changing tongue, or fickle sense of peoplehood, but an immortal set of principles: "We hold these truths to be self-evident . . ." Similarly, in chapter 9 of *Souls*, Du Bois admonished readers that the "perpetuity of American institutions" depended on Americans getting their house in order—on elevating voting "to the plane of a solemn duty which a patriotic citizen neglects to his peril and to the peril of his children's' children." [39]

Du Bois's championing of the separate camp signaled a compromise with bitter reality. Convinced that the World War offered African Americans an unprecedented opportunity to gain citizenship, Du Bois began to discourage dissent. A declaration of war would make the debate about segregation in the military "entirely academic," he wrote. African Americans who believed they might choose between enlistment or abstention were naive. Theirs was the choice "between conscription and rebellion." [40]

WAR

A month before America formally entered World War I, President Wilson proved war's peril to cosmopolitan patriotism. Though there was work left to be done at home, Wilson announced in his Second Inaugural, Americans knew "that the greatest things that remain to be done must be done with the whole world for our stage and in cooperation with the wide and universal forces of mankind, and we are making our spirits ready for those things." Where term-one Wilson had regarded America's foreign and domestic initiatives as part of a single, simultaneous, and open-ended enterprise, term-two Wilson distinguished between work done at home and abroad, thereby clearing the way for persecuting individuals who remained as concerned about local liberty as they were about the nation's international agenda. Persecution was not long in coming. On Flag Day 1917, the president accused all who disagreed with his war platform of sympathizing with Germany. "The facts are patent to all the world," he proclaimed, "this is a People's War, a war for freedom and justice and self-government amongst all the nations of the world." For America there could be "but one choice," the president maintained. "Woe be to the man or group of men that seeks to stand in the way in this day of high resolution when every principle we hold dearest is to be vindicated and made secure for the salvation of the nations." [41]

With due solemnity, Eugene Debs took up Wilson's gauntlet. "Conscription, enforced military service, a rigid censorship, espionage, military training in public schools, the guarding of industrial plants by federal troops, compulsory arbitration, the penalizing of strikes"—in short, all the evils to which socialism was opposed—were about to be loosed upon the land, Debs wrote the Socialist Party secretary, Adolph Germer, five days after America entered the war. Socialists were "morally bound" to repudiate "this arch-conspiracy of capitalist preparedness" until "every jail in the land is choked with rebels and revolutionaries." It would take fourteen months for Debs to utter the calumny that ushered him to jail. Ray Ginger, Debs's biographer, claimed Debs floundered throughout 1917 and 1918, unable to respond to Wilson's evolving idea of a war to end war. Ginger suggested that Debs's ill health or his wife's or brother's moderation caused him to lose his militant voice. More likely, the issues confronting socialists simply stymied him. No one who knew Debs ever accused him of hesitancy, but America's declaration of war gave him reason to pause. [42]

America's entry into World War I occasioned the divorce of stalwart socialists from the party. Accompanying these shocks were private appeals to Debs's Americanism on the part of proven friends. In June 1917, Debs received two letters from the son of his old Terre Haute boss, beseeching him to maintain an open mind. "Your wonderful power will be for naught unless you 'get in tune' with the world," wrote Herman Hulman Jr. "Your wonderful power will be unleashed for the good of the mankind if you 'get in tune' now." Though America had "not yet perfected democracy," Hulman acknowledged, the nations at war with Germany were at least "laboratories in which the problem may be solved, workshops in which the several parts of a better social structure may be fashioned." [43] By suggesting that Debs floundered in the face of World War I, Ginger ignores the strain of his predicament. Floundering suggests confusion—a lack of clarity, a loss for words. Debs remained lucid throughout the war. His difficulty lay not in finding something to say, but in saying something that could be heard in a climate inimical to nuance. In the first year of American participation, Debs shaped his remarks to particular constituencies. To socialists drifting toward embracing the war, he emphasized America's own lack of liberty and democracy. "Autocracy is autocracy," he wrote one colleague, "and there are others besides that which bears the German brand, and we do not have to go three thousand miles away from home to fight it." Though Debs would not discount "the utter infamy" of German militarism, "when it goes down it will be because it has been put down by the German people and not because it has been destroyed by the no less autocratic powers and personalities represented by such servile tools and arch-enemies of the people as Elihu Root." To comrades blind to developments in Europe, Debs stressed the need for perspective and flexibility. The Russian Revolution and Germany's atrocious invasion of Russia "has created a tremendous change of sentiment throughout the world," Debs wrote Secretary Germer in April 1918; it was time to convene a meeting of Socialists "to re-state the attitude of the party toward the war and its policy and purpose when the war is over." [44]

By May 1918, Debs had wearied of beating back and forth against shifting winds. "This is a trying ordeal for us all," he sighed to his friend Stephen M. Reynolds. "We have simply to be true to the light within and all will come well in the end." [45] Thenceforth Debs would be true to his cosmopolitanism. Maintaining the compatibility of patriotism and internationalism, he made his way toward jail. Debs's Canton speech and appeal to his Cleveland jurors offered little new. The distillation of two decades of thought, they are remarkable for their candor and unflagging idealism. At their heart lay the conviction that "manhood" resided in the individual's ability to think autonomously and express him- or herself openly. Arrayed against autonomy were any number of evils, from stifling inequality of wealth, to the privatization of the public domain, to the withering inertia of public opinion. In both speeches Debs's avowed purpose was to "educate" audiences about proper objects of affection. Still convinced that "America" inhered in a set of liberal principles, he treated his listeners to a chronicle of American heroes who had elevated the principle of liberty over national interest. [46]

Colonial America functioned in Debs's allegory as a trope—a veritable paradise in which self-reliant men and women pursued their interests on small farms and in humble shops while living harmoniously among their neighbors. Avarice was alien, stolen into colonial society by an egocentric foreign ministry cut loose by a grasping king. Fate forced the colonists to choose between submitting to tyranny and standing on principle, a dilemma that served as the leitmotif of Debs's story. Tory submission to British authority reflected something akin to Tocqueville's self-interest wrongly understood. Constrained by no impersonal code of ethics, the self-absorbed Tories could not discriminate between the reward and price of loyalty. By contrast, the Patriots possessed the material and moral autonomy necessary to endure public opprobrium and personal privation in the name of liberty. Beneath the surface of Debs's allegory lay a crucial conviction about the meaning of American national identity: the American Revolutionaries broke with England only after they became convinced that divorce offered the means to vindicate democracy. Fighting for democracy, the Revolutionaries founded a nation; nation came second to liberty in their eyes, an order and emphasis crucial to Debs's reconciliation of patriotism and cosmopolitanism (SCAJ, 9–10).

But for all its universal implication, the American Revolution represented a local uprising. It was one thing to promote democratic principles among one's peers, Debs suggested; it was another thing to extend those principles to others. No sooner had the Founding Fathers vanquished the threat of political despotism than national expansion thrust the paradox of American slavery irrevocably onto the national consciousness. Obviously, the institution of slavery contradicted the premise of democracy, yet slavery appeared particularly vexing for having robbed its victims of agency. Where the majority of American citizens justified support for the status quo on the grounds of the slaves' purported inhumanity, a few visionaries resolved to make slavery the test case of American democracy. Abraham Lincoln, William Lloyd Garrison, Wendell Phillips, Elijah Lovejoy, and, especially, John Brown won Debs's admiration for perceiving that freedom denied anywhere imperiled freedom everywhere. Here was a generation that had lived up to its progenitors by *surpassing* their conception of democracy. Brown, Debs had written earlier, "set an example of moral courage and of single-hearted devotion to an ideal for all men and for all ages. . . . So God-like was his unconquerable soul that he dared to face the world alone" (SCAJ, 11).[47]

Still, empathy was a far cry from reciprocity. As the era of small proprietorship yielded to the age of industry, wage slavery emerged in American society to further test the nation's democratic faith. Though free from the caste distinctions that branded African-Americans slaves *ad perpetuam*, wage slavery was equally confounding for having arisen allegedly as a natural consequence of market capitalism. Consequently, the problem of wage slavery did not lend itself to the bald moral testament undertaken by Brown at Harper's Ferry. In order to understand, much less alleviate, the causes and consequences of industrial servitude, one had to know them intimately. Where John Brown had "dared to face the world alone," as Debs put it, turn-of-the-century Americans serious about abolishing wage slavery would have to work collectively to ensure that economic and political liberty did not result in social injustice.

Circumstances demanded that Debs compress his chronicle in Cleveland federal court. Elsewhere he evoked Abraham Lincoln to link the abolitionists' empathy to the sympathy he would champion as "social democracy." Back in 1895, Debs had celebrated Lincoln for having recognized in the Civil War's centralization of industry the harbinger of Gilded Age corporatism and corruption. Where Debs's contemporaries threatened to transform Lincoln into a philosopher of abstract nationalism, Debs fought throughout his career to keep Lincoln an abolitionist—not just of slaves, but of workers. Debs identified with the many figures who constituted his chronicle, but particularly with Lincoln, whose humble origin and rudimentary education Debs likened to his own. In Debs's allegory, Lincoln appears the model democrat who shared Debs's taste for common ribaldry; who suffered, as Debs suffered, from nervous exhaustion; and who, as Debs would, died before his time.[48]

If Lincoln's Gettysburg Address "remade America," as Garry Wills has argued, it remained for Americans of Debs's generation to realize Lincoln's promise of a "new birth of freedom." That would require a new kind of citizenship, Debs told his Cleveland jurors, one based on sympathy rather than philanthropy, intimacy rather than abstraction, humility rather than expertise. In their occasional speeches at the end of the nineteenth century, Oliver Wendell Holmes Jr. and Theodore Roosevelt endorsed a model of martial strenuousness to revitalize the emasculated selves of a generation of displaced northeastern cultural elites. Identifying a symptom of their diminished influence for its cause, Holmes and Roosevelt demonstrated little awareness that vital selfhood would depend on coming to grips with America's cultural diversity. By contrast, Debs's early experience on the railroad convinced him of the futility of disassociating personal well-being from the commonweal. Like Holmes and Roosevelt, Debs prized self-forgetting action, but only if directed toward a self-transcending end (SCAJ, 11–4).

Twenty-first-century populists and communitarians deride liberals' "watery" universalism; liberals and social democrats, for their part, respond by urging their constituents to "think globally and act locally." Debs would have been mystified by these formulations. Having derived his universalism pragmatically, via local labor politics, Debs insisted that one served Liberty by confronting the forces of reaction wherever they appeared. To Debs the notion of *local* engagement would have seemed redundant. Beyond his universalist and utopian rhetoric lay a conviction that excellence derived from fighting for the good, side by side with ones' comrades. Debs lectured his jurors on the compatibility of love of country and love of man. In his lexicon love was one element of a constellation of virtues centered on the concept of "manhood," a term that discriminated between the volunteerism and self-consciousness of human beings and the instinct and egoism of brutes. Debs repudiated corporate capitalism because, by eroding labor's autonomy and blinding owners to the plight of their workers, it turned labor and management into beasts. For Debs, "love" functioned as an element of manhood by enabling individuals to remain conscious of what was at stake when a fellow human being was driven to the margin of subsistence (SCAJ, 5, 18).

As Eugene Debs underwent his public ordeal, Jane Addams was enduring personal tribulation. In mid-May 1917, Addams delivered an address before the City Club of Chicago, titled "Patriots and Pacifists in Wartime," in which she broadcast her "newer ideals of peace." Her speech inspired great controversy. Letters inundated Hull-House castigating her trespass into the affairs of men and impugning her loyalty. Not only did her pacifism abet the enemy, according to one critic, but it exposed the elitism undergirding Addams's democratic ideal. The United States was her country. Did she claim "a larger vision of the real and crystallizing methods of civilizations, than the great mass of men and women who must bear the burdens of the real work?" "Let me beg of you to seal your lips," enjoined another, "lest you add to the dangers which are thickening around everything that we have stood for as a Nation." Germany knew but one language. The time had come for the United States to counter German militarism with uncompromising force.[49]

These reproaches cut to the heart of Addams's cosmopolitanism, pragmatism, and commitment to reciprocal exchange. If she could not convince her genteel admirers of the merits of pacifism, its fate was sealed. Ostensibly, Addams and her detractors had much in common, including an antipathy to war and a commitment to progressive social and economic reform. Their frank and familiar tone suggests that they hailed from backgrounds similar to hers and had been reared in the same discursive tradition. They betrayed no reluctance to engage Addams, a woman, in debate, and one even hinted that she might emerge from the war as a great national leader if she would only fall discreetly into line. Yet beneath their professions of friendship swirled an undercurrent of social control. Pacifism was naive and un-American, soldiering was the apotheosis of citizenship, democracy meant obeying the will of the majority, critical thinking was dangerous and elitist. With charge after charge, Addams's critics laid claim to the meaning of the war, as if the terms "American," "citizenship," and "democracy" had never been the subject of debate.[50]

In contrast to Eugene Debs, Jane Addams mounted only the leanest defense of her Chicago speech. When initial attempts to clarify her position inspired renewed criticism, she resigned herself to the fact that pacifism would never obtain an open hearing amid war. Despite being "profoundly discouraged," Addams remembered having continued to speak out against the war. The historical record suggests otherwise. The career author of over five hundred books and articles produced a meager twenty-eight pages of text in the remaining seventeen months of war, none of them controversial. As if abiding by one correspondent's demand to "confine your activities to philanthropic affairs," Addams withdrew from the male arena of politics and diplomacy to the "female" realm of food relief.[51]

Addams's retreat in the face of public opprobrium says as much about America's political climate and her own philosophical temperament as it does about the weakness in her cosmopolitan patriotism. Her retreat to the world of food relief did not contradict her cosmopolitanism; it circumscribed her activity intolerably. Feminine affiliation represented one of the many different affiliations Addams's cosmopolitanism had held in equilibrium. With the conditions of cosmopolitanism banished, it was inevitable, perhaps, given the context of war, that Addams fall back on an affiliation that had always been a great, if ambiguous, comfort to her. But she did so at considerable cost. The unraveling of cosmopolitanism in the face of war does not suggest any intractable weakness with cosmopolitanism per se, any more than does the erosion of democratic deliberation during wartime point to a problem with the idea of democratic deliberation. There can be no denying that America's jingoism bowled her over. But surely jingoism is not the more valid for being more powerful. Addams, Debs, and the early Du Bois anticipated the problems of the Versailles Treaty practically to the letter. Indeed, several years after the armistice, Addams finally got round to answering her critics' charges, defending her antiwar protest as the most up-to-date Americanism. In "Patriots and Pacifists in Wartime," she had merely enjoined Americans to promote their country's mission, she explained. America's democratic institutions and cosmopolitan citizenry ideally suited the country to lead "the world into a wider life of coordinated political activity." Moreover, as demonstrated by their rush to enlist in the war, American citizens had never appeared so eager for "self-forgetting" action. If only they would "refuse to follow the beaten paths of upholding the rights of a separate nationalism by war," Addams declared, "American patriotism might rise to a supreme effort." Finally, Addams denied that her pacifism rendered *her* antidemocratic. On the contrary, as she had argued in 1915, it was Europe's politicians who betrayed the democratic process by presenting war to their electorates as a fait accompli, rather than submitting war to popular referenda.[52]

While Eugene Debs and Jane Addams were experiencing the cost of dissent, W. E. B. Du Bois was discovering the toll of aligning himself with national sympathy. The American Negro "simply wishes to make it possible for a man to be both a Negro and an American," Du Bois had written in chapter 1 of *The Souls of Black Folk,* "to be a co-worker in the kingdom of culture, to escape both death and isolation, to husband and use his best powers and his latent genius."[53] For most of his young life, Du Bois had been content to take the long road toward racial integration. He would confront white America with its hypocrisy and chastise black and white alike with evidence of the virtue of Negro culture. In World War I, Du Bois took the short road, temporarily relaxing his civil rights campaign and offering his services to the army. Recently, historians have debated Du Bois's behavior in terms of "accommodationism—the strategy," in the words of one historian, "of avoiding confrontation with the racial caste system while seeking to foster goodwill with white America."[54] Such rubric is not only anachronistic, it confines Du Bois to categories that he explicitly rejected. The compelling question is not whether Du Bois's conduct constituted accommodation, but whether it compromised his cosmopolitanism and at what cost. Ideally, cosmopolitanism balances self-interest with particular and universal allegiances. Those who would ascribe Du Bois's actions to egoism overlook the difficulty of that balancing act for an African-American leader at the turn of the twentieth century. Looking back on World War I in *Dusk of Dawn,* Du Bois remarked that he had been "nearer to feeling myself a real and full American than ever before or since," a comment that helps explain, if not excuse, his readiness to commit himself to what he *hoped* would be his country even at the cost of his reputation.[55]

As Du Bois inched closer to a full-blown endorsement of the war, he enlisted sympathetic colleagues to perform editorial advance work. In this way he placed controversial subject matter before his constituents without jeopardizing his credibility. In summer, 1918, Du Bois was chastised for writing the editorial "Close Ranks," which exhorted African American to forget their "special grievances" for the duration of the war. Du Bois defended himself by insisting that "Close Ranks" said nothing that *The Crisis* had not already stated. His adversaries scoffed, accusing him of selling out to the War Department. *The Crisis* vindicates him, revealing not that Du Bois was disinterested in exhorting African Americans to "close ranks" with fellow Americans while the war lasted, but that what he said was indeed familiar to *The Crisis.*[56]

Witness, for example, *The Crisis* of May 1917, which ran an article by Colonel Charles Young, the most prominent African-American officer in the U.S. Army, anticipating Du Bois's sentiment in "Close Ranks" almost to the letter. Young defended the segregated training camp and urged African Americans to serve the nation for which their fathers had fought before them. With so noble a pedigree, would their sons "play the baby-act" and shirk the "citizen's bounden duty?" African Americans should do nothing to divide the country in the face of national exigency, Young maintained. When the war was over, they could renew their campaign for civil rights. Meanwhile, there must be "no Achilles sulking in his tent. Such actions 'cool our friends and heat our enemies,' do no good, and are not in the line of strict loyalty to the flag." Unwilling as yet to commit his editorship to Colonel Young's position, Du Bois reconfirmed the compatibility of patriotism and protest the next month. He published the resolutions of an ecumenical race conference held in Washington, D.C., which both encouraged African Americans to enlist in the war and expressed sympathy for their "reasonable and deep-seated feeling of revolt" at America's unrelenting racism. African Americans had a twofold obligation, the conferees concluded: they must enlist in the battle against international despotism and continue their age-old agitation for the right to serve the nation, attend its schools, enjoy its public domain, and vote in its elections.[57]

The resolutions of the Washington Conference masked division among African Americans. Typically, calls for unanimity in political movements promote the interest of leaders against insurgents. As an insurgent African-American agitator at the turn of the twentieth century, Du Bois had mocked Booker T. Washington's call for black unity. With Washington's death in 1915, Du Bois inherited the mantle as the most visible African-American leader, with which came the burden of constant scrutiny and criticism.[58] Even as Du Bois proclaimed African-American harmony, his sense of how African Americans would benefit in the war began to outpace the sentiment of younger, more militant colleagues. August 1917 seemed a millennial moment to the editor of *The Crisis*. A malleable "new world" unfolded before his eyes. Its "rearrangement" awaited only the initiative and courage of a few individuals willing to step forward. African Americans should either enlist as soldiers or perform analogous civic duties. If the millennium did not materialize, Du Bois did not want African Americans to become scapegoats. With unity the imperative of the hour, he appropriated Washington's rhetoric of teamwork. First he had to purge teamwork of its reactionary connotation. Where "Jim-Crowism" implied un-elected exclusion, teamwork meant the "voluntary coming together of people who have common interests."[59]

Like unity, voluntarism was easier to mandate than maintain. In May 1918, as if to put an official imprimatur on his own opinion, Du Bois called on an NAACP board member named George Bradford to tow *Crisis* readers into line. In the month's lead editorial Bradford declared unequivocally that the conflagration consuming Europe was "Our War and not President Wilson's War," and "no matter how many blunders the administration makes, or how many obstacles it puts in our way we must work the harder to win the war." Privately, Bradford urged Du Bois to promote "War Savings" among African Americans in every way possible, thus aiding the war effort, increasing African Americans' personal wealth, and, most importantly, "putting them on a common footing with other patriotic American citizens and promoting those common bonds that gradually break down prejudice." By seizing the opportunity before them, African Americans could prove their citizenship and thus "score tremendously. When men fight together and work together and save together," Bradford concluded, "this foolishness of race prejudice disappears."[60]

This was the gamble on which Du Bois staked his editorship. Where he had once viewed protest as compatible with patriotism, *The Crisis* now insisted that protest was anathema. Hereafter, talk of common footing and common bonds displaced all mention of civil rights at home. German militarism imperiled the entire world, particularly "darker races," Du Bois announced through Colonel Young in June. German victory would bring "slavery chains for our wives, sweethearts, mothers, fathers, and children, more galling and hopeless than those of ante-bellum days in the United States." With more to win than any group, African Americans were to lead the way "in doing duty, in discipline, in loyalty and leadership." This time the editor did not distance himself from Young's position. Du Bois dedicated May's *Crisis* to "the nearly 100,000 men of Negro descent" enrolled in the U.S. Army, and "to the million dark men of Africa and India, who have served in the armies of Great Britain." With more confidence than ever, Du Bois predicted that the service of colored soldiers would forever change the treatment of the "darker people of the world." It was "written in the stars," he said, that African Americans would return from the war "with the right to vote and the right to work and the right to live without insult."[61]

But it was to the hills and not to the stars that Du Bois looked the following July, when in a controversial editorial he bid African Americans to "forget our special grievances and close ranks shoulder to shoulder with our fellow white citizens and the allied nations fighting for democracy. We make no ordinary sacrifice," Du Bois acknowledged, "but we make it gladly and willingly with our eyes lifted to the hills." Recent scholarship suggests that Du Bois wrote "Close Ranks" to curry favor with the War Department, which was weighing a captain's commission for him as July's *Crisis* went to press. There is also evidence that Du Bois was less than forthcoming about the sequence of events surrounding the pending appointment.[62] Reaction to "Close Ranks" was swift and polarized. Typical was the rebuttal of Byron Gunner, who wrote Du Bois of having difficulty crediting "to your pen the advice." On the contrary, Gunner maintained, now was precisely "the most opportune time for us to push and keep our 'special grievance' to the fore."[63]

In lead editorials in August and September, Du Bois defended the sentiment of "Close Ranks" in portentous rhetoric confirming a conflict of interest. But back of his rhetoric lay a familiar argument: war provided African Americans with an unprecedented opportunity to gain the rights of citizenship. Surely, a nation fighting expressly in the name of democracy would not begrudge democracy's defenders full privileges and immunities. Unless, that is, African Americans gave a racist nation an excuse. "We shall not bargain with our loyalty," Du Bois declared preemptively. "We shall not profiteer with our country's blood." Those who sought to exploit the nation's "tragic predicament" to their own advantage "fatally cheat[ed]" themselves. "God knows we have enough to fight for," he admitted, "but any people who by loyalty and patriotism have gained what we have in four wars ought surely to have sense enough to give this loyalty and patriotism a chance to win in the fifth."[64]

CONCLUSION: THE TWILIGHT OF IDEALS

Like their prowar compatriots who had hearkened to Woodrow Wilson's millennial promise, Debs and Addams had to come to terms after the armistice with the dashing of their prophecies of peace. America's wartime jingoism along with the political reaction and renewed racism that followed the return of American troops from Europe soured the cosmopolitans—as it did so many American intellectuals and cultural critics—to the very concept of patriotism, which never recovered its association with critical vigilance. Released from jail in late 1921, Eugene Debs spent the last five years of his life futilely trying to capitalize on the momentous events of the Russian Revolution; ironically, Debs's focus on Russia robbed his critique of potency by eroding its emphasis on *American* principles. Jane Addams renewed her search for a mechanism by which to end war, but stopped referring to her long-sought "moral substitute" in the language of patriotism. In 1918, Addams helped found the Women's International League for Peace and Freedom, an organization that occupied much of her time during the 1920s, directing her attention away from the problem of American identity toward the issue of international mediation. W. E. B. Du Bois grew increasingly frustrated at America's racial intransigence. Throwing himself back into the fight for civil rights, he expressed less confidence that the United States might become a truly cosmopolitan nation; the thought that the country would one day allow African Americans to vote seemed implausible enough. Meanwhile, John Dewey, apparently overcompensating for his self-described naiveté about the potential benefit of war, embarked on a campaign to "outlaw" war entirely. Dewey had also to come to grips with Walter Lippmann's scathing indictment of mass democratic politics, published as *Public Opinion* in 1922.

In 1922, Jane Addams looked back on her effort to promote a pacifist, cosmopolitan, industrial democracy and concluded that she had not anticipated how stubbornly individuals would cling to the ideal of "separate national existence." By almost any measure, her and Debs's transnationalism had failed abjectly. Except in the minds of a few idealists, war appeared to be as entrenched as ever, the new international order seemed an idle shibboleth, and Americans had become more isolationist, more suspicious of strangers, and readier than ever to erect new barriers to immigration.[1] One cannot fault Debs or Addams for their idealism; but one can critique the assumptions that led them to predict, on the very eve of war, that war had lost its legitimacy and allure. At the heart of their miscalculation lay an indomitable faith in the power of Western principles to promote international comity. They presumed that other cultures would yield obligingly before the advance of Western technology and commerce, never acknowledging that commerce and technology could serve paradoxically as the engine of war. Though pacifist, their imperialism was not benign. By promoting Western principles as the world's salvation, they may have inadvertently encouraged the messianism that spirited America into battle.

Du Bois never really acknowledged the fundamental paradox of warring for democracy. As late as 1942, he remarked that he would not "change a word" of "Close Ranks." In the middle of another war, African Americans were "ready to stand shoulder to shoulder for democracy with soldiers of any race or color and for a democracy of all men."[2] Du Bois's yearning for inclusion overwhelmed the skepticism that had informed "The African Roots of War." In November 1918, Du Bois issued what proved to be his most explicit statement on the subject of patriotism. "Before the war," he observed, "nobody *loved* America. The very phrase seemed maudlin and unintelligent. We loved Justice and Freedom; we sought reform and uplift in politics, health protection; a nobler art, less class dislike, nor race hatred; and we hoped for universal education; but our country? We scarcely had a country—we willed a whole world." Yet in truth, despite rampant injustice, African Americans, socialists, radicals, and immigrants did love America, Du Bois wrote, "because we deemed it capable of realizing our dreams and inspiring the greater world." Was such love incompatible with the "fight for common decency in international affairs?" he wondered, in words designed to give Eugene Debs pause. Was the physical fighting of "beasts" any less necessary than old battles in the "arena of the heart and intellect?" he asked in criticism aimed at Jane Addams. Or "rather is the call of duty infinitely higher when with gun and knife and clenched hand, we are compelled to strive not simply for higher life, but for life itself? On some such foundation is building the new Patriotism in American and in the World."[3]

On some such foundation, indeed, a new patriotism was being constructed—one that celebrated physical wars over battles of conscience. Where once Du Bois equated life without rights as a form of death, he now characterized life devoid of rights as merely one locus on a spectrum between lower and "higher life." The distinction could not have been more crucial, for if rights were no longer akin to life then protest on behalf of those rights could never equal the patriotism of soldiers sacrificing their lives on the battlefield. Thus one of America's great dissidents contributed to the divorce of patriotism and protest, inadvertently jeopardizing his own civil rights campaign.

If the war proved anything, it is that war makes losers of all parties. Undue focus on the cosmopolitans' disappointment of World War I overlooks the cogency of their larger critique. The cosmopolitans wanted Americans to act like "democrats"—to stand on moral principle, to mix freely with those above and below them, to view an attack on others' liberty as an assault upon themselves. From their perspective, the "negative" freedoms of traditional liberalism no longer guaranteed personal autonomy in the face of consolidated corporate and political power. To vindicate the principles of American democracy, they delineated a "positive" model of citizenship that relegated private rights to public duty, while celebrating the "strenuousness" involved in promoting democratic ideals in an era of mounting egoism.

Putting duty before right, the cosmopolitans cut against the grain of a rights-heavy tradition in Anglo-American political thought that stretched back to the Magna Carta. As Linda K. Kerber had noted, even that great republican moment, the American Revolution, represented a fundamentally liberal response to the rule of the British Crown. Kerber's purpose is not to refute the work of Gordon Wood and others who have demonstrated the prevalence of republican ideology in revolutionary discourse. Rather, she helps historians account for the occasional outbreak of republicanism in what has been a predominantly liberal tradition: the Founding Fathers employed republican ideology as the means to a liberal rather than a democratic end. Naturally, individuals with more to gain from hitching their fates to the commonweal sought to exploit republicanism's democratic implications. Hence, there ensued a period of negotiation between liberals and democrats that culminated in America's limited constitutional democracy. The cosmopolitans wanted to reopen that negotiation. To their minds, a century's economic development had skewed the balance between private rights and public duty in favor of property and against democracy. Where traditional liberals viewed the free market as the prerequisite of individual autonomy, the cosmopolitans regarded reciprocity as the precondition of a free market. In an era of proliferating consumer goods and amid the rise of advertising, freedom of choice presumed a critical ability and discerning eye unavailable to individuals struggling at the margin of subsistence. Debs observed back in 1895 that the problem with a corporate economy was not merely that it restricted competition, thereby inflating prices and depressing wages, but that it divided Americans into extremes of rich and poor, yielding the wealthy a lock on critical intelligence. Following Dewey, the cosmopolitans believed that the way to protect private property was to disperse it as broadly as possible—a goal they hoped to accomplish not by redistributing income but by tearing down the barriers of caste and ignorance that impeded reciprocal exchange. To their minds, a society without reciprocity was like a social ladder without rungs. Only by associating with those above them could workers and immigrants learn the virtues required of social mobility; only by sharing ideas and experiences with those beneath them could entrepreneurs and politicians discern the nature and needs of their constituents.[4]

By emphasizing the moral strenuousness of safeguarding democratic principles, the cosmopolitans disassociated republicanism from martial and patriarchal virtues, rendering republicanism itself more "democratic." The strain of defending and promoting democracy was available to anybody—women, African Americans, immigrants, industrial workers—possessing economic independence and intellectual autonomy. Where Roosevelt compared a woman's experience in childbirth to the soldier's "pain and discomfort, self-abnegation, and the incurring of risk of life" (and, conversely, a woman's "flinching" from childbirth to a soldier's cowardice), the cosmopolitans renounced physical exertion as the primary vehicle of heroism. America's bombardment of Manila in 1899 provided fresh evidence—missing amid the monumentalizing of the Civil War—that war could be brutal without promoting valor. Moreover, by elevating moral over physical strain, the cosmopolitans challenged the nineteenth-century dichotomy of separate spheres; in the battle against caste and privilege, men and women would be expected to fight side by side. The effect was to rescue morality from the cloistered world of nineteenth-century domesticity. Rather than emasculating citizenship, as their critics charged, the cosmopolitans hoped to re-imbue citizenship with the notion, dormant since the time of the American Revolution, of egalitarian sacrifice in the name of high ideals.[5]

In *The True and Only Heaven: Progress and Its Critics,* Christopher Lasch charts the development of a Populist/Progressive dialectic in Anglo-American thought. According to Lasch, this dichotomy came to a head at the turn of the twentieth century when Americans submitted to a therapeutic, mass-consumer culture predicated on universal abundance. One of the casualties of progressivism was the republican sensibility, a constellation of ideas centered on the concept of virtue: a commitment to excellence, a sense of civic-mindedness, an appreciation that life is precious and must be lived strenuously, and a humility derived from the acknowledgment of natural and historical limits. Lasch suggests that excellence depends on memory—the recognition that the present and future are indebted to past cultural, moral, and intellectual traditions and achievements. Lasch contrasts memory to nostalgia, really a form of amnesia, which leads individuals disaffected with the present to idealize a lyrical bygone age. Ignoring past obstacles and the effort it took to surmount them, nostalgia cannot sustain a standard of excellence. The cosmopolitans argued that turn-of-the-century America was rife with amnesia. So awed were Americans by their ingenuity and the wealth and power it created, they scarcely reckoned the ways in which material success might compromise the nation's underlying principles. Humble in the face of history, Jefferson and Madison had obsessed about the hazards confronting an expanding republic; by contrast, except for a few anti-imperialists, turn-of-the-twentieth-century Americans assumed that growth and development were evidence of national health. While the cosmopolitans succumbed occasionally to the optimism of their era, their belief in progress did not blind them to the pitfalls of national expansion, to the fundamental principles at stake, to the bracing affect of a good fight, or to the dependence of a favorable outcome on individuals subordinating their private interests to an overarching good. Individually, these aspects of their thought posed no threat to corporate capitalism and mass-consumer culture; but taken together, they constituted a formidable, if unpopular, critique.[6]

In order to inculcate the critical vigilance that would rejuvenate American democracy, the cosmopolitans told stories: Debs of agitators to industrial workers, Addams of democrats to Hull-House audiences, Du Bois of saints and crusaders to students. Of the three, Addams and Du Bois spoke most self-consciously about a democracy's need for heroes. In the winter of 1903, Addams reminded Chicago's Union League that the "lessons of great men are lost unless they re-enforce upon our minds the highest demands which we make upon ourselves; unless they drive our sluggish wills forward in the direction of their highest ideals." Commemorating Lincoln's birthday four years later, Du Bois told Hull-House listeners that the world needed a "real aristocracy"—not a coterie of pampered and privileged elites, but a company of men and women whose "best thought" and "best feeling" could remind us "what it is that is wrong with our ideals." Although the cosmopolitans would point to living examples of individuals clinging heroically to principle, Debs and Du Bois, particularly, appeared concerned to defend a radical reading of the American past from a wave of historical revisionism that had swept through the nation's public school curriculum during the 1890s, and which threatened to transform the likes of Washington and Lincoln from stalwart defenders of principle into sentinels of the status quo.[7]

In volume 2, part 2, chapter 8 of *Democracy in America*, Tocqueville marveled at Americans' propensity to merge individual and collective interest. Although this proclivity made "extraordinary virtues" rarer in American society, it rendered "gross depravity" less common. On balance, Tocqueville concluded, the benefits of self-interest rightly understood outweighed the cost: if fewer Americans were driven by will directly to virtue, more were drawn in virtue's direction. Several chapters later, Tocqueville warned prophetically of the danger confronting a democracy in which avarice erodes the citizenry's commitment to collective self-interest. The more individuals are governed by egoism, the less inclined they become to participate in politics, thus creating the opportunity for an ambitious individual or a tutelary state to usurp the prerogative of the people. According to the cosmopolitans, Tocqueville's fears were in danger of becoming reality by the turn of the twentieth century. Their chronicles of American history recount the evolution of democracy from the dialectical opposition of self-interest rightly and wrongly understood. Although unmistakably progressive in outlook, their narratives can nonetheless be read as odes to human agency: ego drove the mass of mankind to pursue private over public interest; vision inspired a few heroic individuals to reject the private/public dichotomy and to recognize the compatibility of self- and common interest. The cosmopolitans' belief in progress derived from faith not so much that mankind was "good" innately, but that mankind is capable of good. This kind of optimism sustained a critical edge and sense of urgency. If history seemed to move in the right direction, it was only because, every generation or so, there had emerged in American society men and women who viewed democracy as a vulnerable and contingent ideal that had to be constantly renewed. The cosmopolitans accentuated the adjective in the appellation "Founding Fathers." As *founders,* the American revolutionaries had erected the platform on which the edifice of American democracy would be built. Their project was unfinished, dependent on future generations for its realization. Washington's, Jefferson's, and Lincoln's ruminations about the fate of American slavery forecasted that ideas and individuals unwelcome at the time of groundbreaking would one day be admitted. The founders' limited vision did not dim the grandeur of their accomplishment in the cosmopolitans' eyes. As students of history, the cosmopolitans did not hold past generations accountable to contemporary moral standards; as "progressives," they understood that reciprocity was an ideal that would have been unimaginable without the advance work of their progenitors. [8]

NOTES

PREFACE

1. See, among others, Scot M. Guenter, *The American Flag, 1777–1924: Cultural Shifts from Creation to Codification* (Cranbury: Associated University Presses, 1990); Stuart McConnell, *Glorious Contentment: The Grand Army of the Republic, 1865–1900* (Chapel Hill: University of North Carolina Press, 1992); Nina Silber, *The Romance of Reunion: Northerners and the South, 1865–1900* (Chapel Hill: University of North Carolina Press, 1993); Kirk Savage, "The Politics of Memory: Black Emancipation and the Civil War Monument," in John R. Gillis, ed., *Commemorations: The Politics of National Identity* (Princeton: Princeton University Press, 1994); Cecilia Elizabeth O'Leary, " 'Blood Brotherhood': The Racialization of Patriotism, 1865–1918," in John Bodnar, ed., *Bonds of Affection: Americans Define Their Patriotism* (Princeton: Princeton University Press, 1996); and, more recently, David Blight, *Race and Reunion: The Civil War in American Memory* (Cambridge, MA: Harvard University Press, 2001). For a sketch of recent patriotism, see George Lipsitz, "Dilemmas of Beset Nationhood: Patriotism, The Family, and Economic Change in the 1970s and 1980s," in Bodnar, ed., *Bonds of Affection,* 251–72.

2. Oliver Wendell Holmes Jr., "The Soldier's Faith," in Mark De Wolfe, ed., *The Occasional Speeches of Oliver Wendell Holmes* (Cambridge: Harvard University Press, 1962), 20.

3. Douglass quoted in O'Leary, "Blood Brotherhood," 68–9.

4. William James, "Robert Gould Shaw," in *Memories and Studies* (New York: Longmans, Green, and Company, 1912), 42, 57–8. Compare Lincoln: "If destruction be our lot, we must ourselves be its author and finisher. As a nation of freemen, we must live through all time, or die by suicide." Abraham Lincoln, "The Perpetuation of Our Political Institutions," Address before the Young Men's Lyceum of Springfield, Illinois, January 27, 1838, in Roy P. Basler, ed., *The Collected Works of Abraham Lincoln,* vol. 1 (New Brunswick: Rutgers University Press, 1953), 109.

INTRODUCTION

1. United States Attorney to the Attorney General, June 17, 1918, PEVD.

2. Eugene V. Debs, "Statement to the Court," Cleveland, Ohio, September 12, 1918, PEVD.

3. For a convincing account of how these developments are related, see Kevin

Phillips, *Wealth and Democracy: How Great Fortunes and Government Created America's Aristocracy* (New York: Broadway Books, 2002).

4. David A. Hollinger, "How Wide the Circle of the 'We'? American Intellectuals and the Problem of the Ethnos Since World War II," *AHR* 98 (April 1993): 317–37. For a sample of recent writing on liberalism that informs this discussion, see Hollinger, *Postethnic America: Beyond Multiculturalism* (New York: Basic Books, 2000); Charles Taylor, "The Politics of Recognition," in Amy Gutmann, ed., *Multiculturalism: Examining the Politics of Recognition* (Princeton, 1994); Charles Taylor, *Sources of the Self: The Making of Modern Identity* (Cambridge: Harvard University Press, 1989); Richard J. Bernstein, *The New Constellation: The Ethical-Political Horizons of Modernity/Postmodernity* (Cambridge: MIT Press 1992); Richard Rorty, *Contingency, Irony, Solidarity* (Cambridge: Cambridge University Press 1989); Martha Craven Nussbaum, "Patriotism and Cosmopolitanism," in Joshua Cohen, ed., *For Love of Country: Debating the Limits of Patriotism* (Boston: Beacon Press, 1996); Stephen Holmes, *Passions and Constraint: On the Theory of Liberal Democracy* (Chicago: University of Chicago Press, 1995); Peter Berkowitz, *Virtue and the Making of Modern Liberalism* (Princeton: Princeton University Press, 1999); and Mary Ann Glendon, *Rights Talk: The Impoverishment of Political Discourse* (New York: The Free Press, 1991).

5. For contemporary scholars who share this aspiration, see, among others, Hollinger, *Postethnic America;* Michael Lind, *The Next American Nation* (New York: The Free Press, 1995); Yael Tamir, *Liberal Nationalism* (Princeton: Princeton University Press, 1993); David Miller, *On Nationality* (Oxford: Clarendon Press, 1997); Michael Ignatieff, *Blood and Belonging: Journeys into the New Nationalism* (New York: Farrar, Straus, and Giroux, 1993); Will Kymlicka, *Multicultural Citizenship: A Liberal Theory of Minority Rights* (New York: Clarendon Press, 1996); and Richard Rorty, *Achieving Our Country, Leftist Thought in Twentieth-Century America* (Cambridge: Harvard University Press, 1998). For a skeptical perspective on liberal nationalism, see Joan Cocks, *Passion and Paradox: Intellectuals Confront the National Question* (Princeton: Princeton University Press, 2002), chapter 4.

6. On the relationship between public and private rights and duties, see Jean Bethke Elshtain, *Democracy on Trial* (New York: Basic Books, 1995), 5–21; Christopher Lasch, *The Revolt of the Elites and the Betrayal of Democracy* (New York: W.W. Norton, 1995); and Glendon, *Rights Talk.*

7. In this commitment they are supported by evidence from diverse intellectual and political traditions around the world. See Amartya Sen, "East and West: The Reach of Reason," *New York Review of Books* (July 20, 2000) and *Human Rights and Asian Values* (New York: Carnegie Council on Ethics and International Affairs, 1997); Nussbaum, "Patriotism and Cosmopolitanism," in *For Love of Country,* 3–17; and Pratap Bhanu Mehta, "Cosmopolitanism and the Circle of Reason," *Political Theory* 28 (October 2000). Contrast these texts with Hegel's *Lectures on Philosophy of History,* which claim Western proprietorship over not just history but rationality itself.

8. See Michael Walzer, *Thick and Thin: Moral Argument at Home and Abroad* (Notre Dame: University of Notre Dame Press, 1994). Maurizio Viroli, *For Love of Country: An Essay on Patriotism and Nationalism* (Oxford: Clarendon Press,

1995), is also suggestive here. Patriotism, Viroli argues, has taken and can take the form of devotion not to people or nation, per se, but to a set of political principles and the culture that sustains them. Patriotism may constitute what Liberian writer Edward Blyden referred to as "the poetry of politics"—the feeling of "people with whom we are connected." Blyden cited in K. Anthony Appiah, "Cosmopolitan Patriots," in Joshua Cohen, ed., *For Love of Country,* 26.

9. In appropriating the term "cosmopolitan" in this way I am once more trading on the work of Hollinger, *Postethnic America,* 84–6. Adopting Hollinger's historical distinction between universalism, cultural pluralism, and cosmopolitanism does not commit me to his normative ideal of postethnicity, though I find it increasingly compelling in its recent articulations; see, for example, Hollinger's "Nationalism, Cosmopolitanism, and the United States," in Noah M. J. Pickus, ed., *Immigration and Citizenship in the Twenty-First Century* (New York: Rowan and Littlefield, 1998), 85–89; "Not Universalists, Not Pluralists: The New Cosmopolitans Find Their Way," *Constellations* 8 (2001): 236–48; and the postscript to the 2000 edition of *Postethnic America,* a book originally published in 1995. Cf. Werner Sollors, *Beyond Ethnicity: Consent and Descent in American Culture* (New York: Oxford University Press, 1986).

10. Oliver Wendell Holmes Jr., "The Soldier's Faith," in Mark De Wolfe, ed., *The Occasional Speeches of Oliver Wendell Holmes* (Cambridge: Harvard University Press, 1962), 73. On cosmopolitanism as it is conventionally conceived, see Thomas J. Schlereth, *The Cosmopolitan Ideal in Enlightenment Thought* (Notre Dame: University of Notre Dame Press, 1977), Karen O'Brien, *Narratives of Enlightenment: Cosmopolitan History from Voltaire to Gibbon* (Cambridge: Cambridge University Press, 1997); Ross Posnock, "The Dream of Deracination: The Uses of Cosmopolitanism," *American Literary History* (2000): 802–18; and David A. Hollinger, "Ethnic Diversity, Cosmopolitanism, and the Emergence of the American Liberal Intelligentsia," in *In the American Province: Studies in the History and Historiography of Ideas* (Baltimore: Johns Hopkins University Press, 1985), 56–73.

11. See the responses of Robert Pinsky and others to Martha C. Nussbaum's essay, "Patriotism and Cosmopolitanism," in Joshua Cohen, ed., *For Love of Country: Debating the Limits of Patriotism,* as well as Timothy Brennan, *At Home in the World: Cosmopolitanism Now* (Cambridge: Harvard University Press, 1997); and Eric Lott, "The New Cosmopolitanism: Whose America?" *Transition* 72 (fall 1996): 108–35.

12. See Nussbaum, "Patriotism and Cosmopolitanism," 3–17; and Cocks, *Passion and Paradox,* 110. Cocks is actually speaking about the incompatibility of liberalism and nationalism, which, though theoretically distinguishable from cosmopolitanism and patriotism, respectively, are used indistinguishably in her discussion.

13. For contemporary scholarship that recognizes this fact, see not only Hollinger, *Postethnic America;* but also Benedict Anderson, *The Spectre of Comparisons: Nationalism, Southeast Asia, and the World* (New York: Verso, 1998); Jeremy Waldron, "Multiculturalism and Melange," in Robert K. Fullinwider, ed., *Public Education in a Multicultural Society: Policy, Theory, Critique* (Cambridge: Cambridge University Press, 1996), 90–118; Seyla Benhabib, *Situating the Self: Gen*

der, Community and Postmodernism in Contemporary Ethics (London: Routledge, 1992); and Amartya Sen, "Other People: Beyond Identity," *New Republic* (December 18, 2000): 23–30.

14. Michael Walzer, *Thick and Thin: Moral Argument at Home and Abroad* (Notre Dame: University of Notre Dame Press, 1994).

15. In this sense, cosmopolitan patriotism is consistent with the cosmopolitanism described by Ross Posnock, *Color and Culture: Black Writers and the Making of the Modern Intellectual* (Cambridge: Harvard University Press, 1998). See also the broad-ranging, provoking engagement of cosmopolitanism in two edited collections: Pheng Cheah and Bruce Robbins, eds., *Cosmopolitics: Thinking and Feeling Beyond the Nation* (Minneapolis: University of Minnesota Press, 1998); and Vinay Dharwadker, ed., *Cosmopolitan Geographies: New Locations in Literature and Culture* (New York: Routledge, 2001); as well as Pratap Bhanu Mehta, "Cosmopolitanism and the Circle of Reason"; Ulf Hannerz, *Transnational Connections: Culture, People, Places* (New York: Routledge, 1996), chapter 9; Bruce Robbins, *Feeling Global: Internationalism in Distress* (New York: New York University Press, 1999); Samuel Scheffler, *Families, Nations, and Strangers* (Lawrence: University of Kansas, 1995); and Amartya Sen, "Tagore and His India," *New York Review of Books* (June 1997).

16. See Merle Curti, *The Roots of American Loyalty* (New York: Russell & Russell, 1946); and Curti, "Wanted: A History of American Patriotism," *Proceedings of the Middle States Association of History and Social Science Teachers* 36 (1938). As recently as 1991 historian Michael Kammen could cite *The Roots of American Loyalty* as "the best (and almost the only) book to explore [patriotism] in a sustained manner." Kammen, *Mystic Chords of Memory: The Transformation of Tradition in American Culture* (New York: A. E. Knopf, 1991). At long last, historians have begun to answer Curti's call, thanks in part to the impetus of John Bodnar. See Bodnar, *Remaking America: Public Memory, Commemoration, and Patriotism in the Twentieth Century* (Princeton: Princeton University Press, 1992); Bodnar, ed., *Bonds of Affection: Americans Define Their Patriotism;* and Cecilia Elizabeth O'Leary, *To Die For: The Paradox of American Patriotism* (Princeton: Princeton University Press, 1999). Philosophers and political theorists have expressed more interest in patriotism over the last several decades. See John Schaar, "The Case for Patriotism," *American Review* 17 (May 1973): 59–99; Stephen Nathanson, "In Defense of 'Moderate Patriotism,' " *Ethics* 99 (April 1989); Nathanson, *Patriotism, Morality, and Peace* (New York: Rowman and Littlefield, 1993); Alasdair MacIntyre, "Is Patriotism a Virtue?" The Lindley Lecture (Lawrence: University Press of Kansas, 1984); Maurizio Viroli, *For Love of Country: An Essay on Patriotism and Nationalism;* and Rorty, *Achieving Our Country.*

17. Rorty defends a version of liberal patriotism in *Achieving Our Country.* Other efforts include Nathanson, "In Defense of 'Moderate Patriotism' "; Schaar, "The Case for Patriotism"; and Mary G. Dietz, "Patriotism," in Ball, Farr, and Hanson, eds., *Political Innovation and Conceptual Change* (New York: Cambridge University Press, 1989). Dissenting patriotism need not, of course, be liberal. Suggestions of a traditional, counterhegemonic patriotism rooted in the American

working class may be found in Andrew Neather, "Labor, Republicanism, Race, and Popular Patriotism in the Era of Empire," in Bodnar, ed., *Bonds of Affection*, 82–101; Daniel T. Rodgers, *The Work Ethic in Industrial America, 1850–1920* (Chicago: University of Chicago Press, 1974); Gary Gerstle, *Working Class Americanism: The Politics of Labor in a Textile City, 1914–1960* (New York: Cambridge University Press, 1989); and Roy Rosenzweig, *Eight Hours for What We Will: Workers and Leisure in an Industrial City, 1870–1920* (Cambridge: Cambridge University Press, 1983).

18. See James T. Kloppenberg, *Uncertain Victory: Social Democracy and Progressivism* (New York: Oxford University Press, 1986), especially chapters 8 and 9; Eldon Eisenach, *The Lost Promise of Progressivism* (Lawrence: University Press of Kansas, 1994); Kathryn Kish Sklar, *Florence Kelly & the Nation's Work: The Rise of Women's Political Culture, 1830–1900* (New Haven: Yale University Press, 1995); Daniel T. Rodgers, *Atlantic Crossings: Social Politics in a Progressive Age* (Cambridge: Harvard University Press, 1998); and Robert B. Westbrook, *John Dewey and American Democracy* (Ithaca, NY: Cornel University Press, 1991), especially 182–94. On the era's social, economic, and political polarization, see Phillips, *Wealth and Democracy*.

19. Notable among texts addressing globalization is Sayres Rudy, "Subjectivity, Political Evaluation, and Islamist Trajectories," in Birgit Schäbler, ed., *Globalization and the Muslim World* (SUNY Press, forthcoming). See also David Held and Anthony McGrew, eds., *The Global Transformations Reader: An Introduction to the Globalization Debate* (Malden, MA: Blackwell, 2000); David Held, *Global Transformations* (Stanford: Stanford University Press, 1999); James H. Mittelman and Norani Othman, eds., *Capturing Globalization* (New York: Routledge, 2001); James H. Mettelman, *The Globalization Syndrome: Transformation and Resistance* (Princeton: Princeton University Press, 2000); Suzanne Berger and Ronald Dore, eds., *National Diversity and Global Capitalism* (Ithaca: Cornell University Press, 1996); Robert O. Slater, et al, eds., *Global Transformation and the Third World* (Boulder: Lynne Rienner, 1993); Michael Walzer, *Toward a Global Civil Society* (Providence: Berghahn, 1995); Fredric Jameson and Masao Miyoshi, eds., *The Cultures of Globalization* (Durham: Duke University Press, 1998); and George Yudice, "We Are Not the World," *Social Text* 30–33 (1992).

20. I do not mean to imply a lack of sympathy for local cultures imperiled by outside forces; on the contrary, I argue, like others before me, that defending local cultures entails frank acknowledgement of culture's economic and political requisites. This point was made forcefully in a different context by American Marxist historians a generation ago. See, for example, the essays by Eugene D. Genovese and Elizabeth Fox-Genovese in *Fruits of Merchant Capital: Slavery and Bourgeois Property in the Rise and Expansion of Capitalism* (New York: Oxford University Press, 1983). The point is reiterated by, among others, Timothy Brennan in *At Home in the World*.

21. The historical context presented here, by now common knowledge, derives in part from John Higham, *Strangers in the Land: Patterns of Nativism, 1860–1925* (New York: Atheneum, 1968); Alan Trachtenberg, *The Incorporation of America:*

Culture and Society in the Gilded Age (New York: Hill and Wang, 1982); Herbert Gutman, *Work, Culture & Society in Industrializing America* (New York: Vintage, 1977); T. J. Jackson Lears, *No Place of Grace: Antimodernism and the Transformation of American Culture, 1880–1920* (New York: Pantheon, 1981); Robert Westbrook, "Politics as Consumption: Managing the American Election," in Richard Wightman Fox and T. J. Jackson Lears, eds., *The Culture of Consumption: Critical Essays in American History, 1880–1980* (New York: Pantheon, 1983), 143–73; and Martin J. Sklar, *The Corporate Reconstruction of American Capitalism, 1890–1916: The Market, the Law and Politics* (New York: Cambridge University Press, 1988). On the erosion of America's local, voluntary, and religious communities, see Robert S. and Helen Lynd, *Middletown: A Study in Modern American Culture* (New York: Harcourt Brace Jovanovich, 1957).

22. On the economic upheaval here recounted, see Sklar, *Corporate Reconstruction of American Capitalism;* on nativism, see Higham, *Strangers in the Land;* Rogers Smith, *Civic Ideals: Conflicting Visions of Citizenship in U.S. History* (New Haven: Yale University Press, 1997), especially chapters 11 and 12; and Gary Gerstle, *American Crucible: Race and Nation in the Twentieth Century* (Princeton: Princeton University Press, 2001), especially chapters 1 and 2.

23. On populism and the issues at stake in the 1896 presidential election, see Lawrence Goodwyn, *Democratic Promise: The Populist Movement in America* (New York: Oxford University Press, 1978); and Christopher Lasch, *The True and Only Heaven: Progress and Its Critics* (New York: W. W. Norton, 1991), chapter 5. On race and national reconciliation, see David W. Blight, *Race and Reunion: The Civil War in American Memory* (Cambridge: Harvard University Press, 2001).

24. Dewey, *Democracy and Education: An Introduction to the Philosophy of Education* (New York: Macmillan, 1930 [1916]), 96.

25. Hollinger, *Postethnic America,* 83–6.

26. "Radically unfinished society" is Michael Walzer's term; see "What Does It Mean to Be 'American'?" *Social Research* 57 (1990): 614.

27. Walzer, *Thick and Thin: Moral Argument at Home and Abroad,* 1–19.

CHAPTER 1

1. "our ancient national soul": William James to Henry James, June 21, 1899, in *The Correspondence of William James,* vol. 3: *William and Henry, 1897–1910,* Ignas K. Skrupskelis and Elizabeth M. Berkeley, eds. (Charlottesville: University of Virginia Press, 1994), 63–4; "I've lost my country": reported in George Santayana, *The Middle Span* (New York: Charles Scribner's Sons, 1945), 167–70; "Hostile Natives Whipped": *New York Times,* February 6, 1899, in Skrupskelis and Berkeley, eds., 51 n. 6.

2. Recent contributions along these lines include Kristin L. Hoganson, *Fighting for American Manhood: How Gender Politics Provoked the Spanish-American and Philippines-American Wars* (New Haven: Yale University Press, 1998); and Matthew Frye Jacobson, *Barbarian Virtues: The United States Encounters Foreign Peoples at Home and Abroad, 1876–1917* (New York: Hill and Wang, 2000). Many of the contributions to *Cultures of US Imperialism,* Amy Kaplan and Donald E. Pease, eds. (Durham, NC: Duke University Press, 1993), illuminate this con-

nection; see, for example, Walter Benn Michaels's "Anti-Imperial Americanism," 365–91. Hoganson and Jacobson recapitulate what are becoming entrenched historiographical positions. Where Hoganson argues that concerns about masculinity provoked these wars, Jacobson maintains that thirst for export and labor markets fueled American imperialism. While not discounting these influences, I emphasize what we might call classical problems of virtue, citizenship, and national greatness in the writing of James, Theodore Roosevelt, and Woodrow Wilson—problems our current cultural climate has little ear for.

3. See, for example, Edward W. Said, *Orientalism* (New York: Vintage, 1994), 332.

4. Recent literature about American civic identity tends to underemphasize the global context of local and national debates. See Michael Lind, *The Next American Nation: The New Nationalism and the Fourth American Revolution* (New York: The Free Press, 1995); Joshua Cohen, ed., *For Love of Country: Debating the Limits of Patriotism* (Boston: Beacon Press, 1996); Amy Gutmann, ed., *Multiculturalism: Examining the Politics of Recognition* (Princeton: Princeton University Press, 1994); Richard Rorty, *Achieving Our Country: Leftist Thought in Twentieth-Century America* (Cambridge: Harvard University Press, 1998); and Nathan Glazer, *We Are All Multiculturalists Now* (Cambridge: Harvard University Press, 1997). Contrast David A. Hollinger, *Postethnic America: Beyond Multiculturalism* (New York: Basic Books: 2000), chapter 6 and the postscript.

5. For a full expression of the ideal of reciprocity, see Simone de Beauvoir, *The Second Sex* (New York: Vintage, 1989), chapter 11.

6. For a provoking theoretical account of the affinity of liberalism and empire, see Uday Singh Mehta, *Liberalism and Empire: A Study in Nineteenth-Century British Liberal Thought* (Chicago: University of Chicago Press, 1999). See also Hannah Arendt, *Imperialism: Part Two of the Origins of Totalitarianism* (New York: Harvest, 1968), especially chapter 3.

7. For contemporary thought that shares this aspiration, see Judith Butler, "Universality in Culture," in Cohen, ed., *For Love of Country*, 44–52. Cf. Jurgen Habermas, *Theory of Communicative Action*, vol. 2: *Lifeworld and System: A Critique of Functionalist Reason* (Boston: Beacon Press, 1989), especially chapter 8, section 3; Lucius T. Outlaw, *On Race and Philosophy* (New York: Routledge, 1996), especially chapter 5; Hannah Arendt, *Lectures on Kant's Political Philosophy* (Chicago: University of Chicago Press, 1989); and Posnock, "The Dream of Deracination: The Uses of Cosmopolitanism," *American Literary History* (2000): 802–18.

8. The closest approximation of James's, Addams's, and Dewey's nationalism in the political theoretical literature is Maurizio Viroli, *For Love of Country: An Essay on Patriotism and Nationalism* (Oxford: Clarendon Press, 1995), especially 161–87. Whether the ideal of "patriotism" that Viroli describes is really "patriotism without nationalism," as he insists, remains doubtful. The cosmopolitan patriots, while exhibiting Viroli's ideal of patriotism, were not so caught up with labels. Some would equate the cosmopolitan patriotism I describe with "civic," as opposed to "ethnic," nationalism—where civic nationalism correlates with constitutionalism and ethnic nationalism with culture. For scholarship that upholds this distinction, see David Miller, *On Nationality* (Oxford: Clarendon Press, 1997);

Yael Tamir, *Liberal Nationalism* (Princeton: Princeton University Press, 1993); Michael Ignatieff, *Blood and Belonging: Journeys into the New Nationalism* (New York: Farrar, Straus and Giroux, 1993); William Pfaff, *The Wrath of Nations: Civilization and the Furies of Nationalism* (New York: Simon and Schuster, 1993); and Leah Greenfeld, *Nationalism: Five Roads to Modernity* (Cambridge: Harvard University Press, 1992). The view that "civic" nationalism is also "cultural" has been made forcefully by Bernard Yack, "The Myth of a Civic Nation," and Nicholas Xenos, "Civic Nationalism: Oxymoron?" both of which appear in the spring 1996 edition of *Critical Review* (vol. 10, no. 2): 193–211 and 213–31, respectively. See also Will Kymlicka, "Misunderstanding Nationalism," a review in *Dissent* (winter 1995): 131–2. The argument that civic nations are ineluctably cultural is missed not only by Ignatieff and Pfaff, whose work Kymlicka reviews, but also by Stuart McConnell, *Glorious Contentment: The Grand Army of the Republic, 1865–1900* (Chapel Hill: University of North Carolina Press, 1992); and Leah Greenfeld. McConnell argues on pages 221–2 that the GAR's "version of the nation was not based on any linguistic or cultural principle. Rather, it stressed conformity with liberal capitalism; in theory, 'American' was a voluntary identity." Here McConnell hedges his bet; his mitigating distinction between "theory" and reality suggests rightly that liberal capitalism is itself a cultural product. Greenfeld argues on page 7 that "*nationalism is not necessarily a form of particularism. It is a political ideology . . . and as such it does not have to be identified with any particular community.*" This needs amending: nationalism is indeed particular; some nationalisms are simply more particular than others. Benedict Anderson's decade-old recognition that nations are "imagined communities" is for the most part universally accepted by now. See *Imagined Communities: Reflections on the Origin and Spread of Nationalism* (New York: Verso, 1991 [1983]). John Breuilly, *Nationalism and The State* (Chicago: University of Chicago Press, 1993 [1982]), introduction, makes the same observation, as does Eric Hobsbawm, *Nations and Nationalism Since 1780* (New York: Cambridge University Press, 1990). On popular sovereignty as a myth, see Edmund S. Morgan, *Inventing the People: The Rise of Popular Sovereignty in England and America* (New York: W. W. Norton, 1988).

9. Historians tend to accentuate distinctions between antebellum and postbellum American society at the cost of identifying continuities; see, for example, Louis Menand, *The Metaphysical Club* (New York: Farrar, Straus and Giroux, 2001). The persistent interest in the problem of civic virtue is one of the many characteristics of antebellum culture that survived the cataclysm.

10. Alexis de Tocqueville to Ernest de Chabrol, June 9, 1831, in Roger Boesche, ed., *Alexis de Tocqueville: Selected Letters on Politics and Society* (Berkelely and Los Angeles: University of California Press, 1985), 37–8.

11. Alexis de Tocqueville, *Democracy in America*, J. P. Mayer, ed. (New York: Harper Perennial, 1969), vol. 1, part 2, chapter 6, 245.

12. The juxtaposition of democracy to greatness, like that of republicanism to empire, is ancient and extends to classical times. It was scrutinized anew by Machiavelli (via Sallust) and his early-modern followers and interlocutors. See David Armitage, "Empire and Liberty: A Republican Dilemma," forthcoming in Martin van Gelderan and Quentin Skinner, eds., *Republicanism: A Shared European*

Heritage, vol. 2: *The Values of Republicanism* (Cambridge: Cambridge University Press, 2002), 29–46; and Armitage, *The Ideological Origins of the British Empire* (Cambridge: Cambridge University Press, 2000), chapter 5, especially pp. 129–32.

13. Christopher Lasch, *The True and Only Heaven: Progress and Its Critics* (New York: W. W. Norton, 1991), 172–5. Lasch relies heavily on J. G. A. Pocock, *The Machiavellian Moment: Florentine Political Thought and the Atlantic Republican Tradition* (Princeton: Princeton University Press, 1975). On the debate among American historians about the role of republicanism in American history, see, among others, Daniel T. Rodgers, "Republicanism: The Career of a Concept," *Journal of American History* 79 (June 1992): 11–38; Gordon S. Wood, *The Radicalism of the American Revolution* (New York: Vintage, 1991), part 2; Joyce Appleby, *Capitalism and the New Social Order: The Republican Vision of the 1790s* (New York: New York University Press, 1984); Sean Wilentz, *Chants Democratic: New York and the Rise of the Working Class, 1788–1850* (New York: Oxford University Press, 1984); Philip Ethington, *Public City: The Reconstruction of Urban Life in San Francisco, 1850–1900* (New York: Cambridge University Press, 1994); and James T. Kloppenberg, "Premature Requiem: Republicanism in American History," in *The Virtues of Liberalism*.

14. James T. Kloppenberg, *Uncertain Victory,* 171. For characteristics typically associated with liberalism, see Thomas L. Haskell, "Capitalism and the Origins of the Humanitarian Sensibility, Part 2," in Thomas Bender, ed., *The Antislavery Debate: Capitalism and Abolitionism as a Problem in Historical Interpretation* (Berkeley and Los Angeles: University of California Press, 1992), 146–53; Charles L. Griswold, *Adam Smith and the Virtues of Enlightenment* (Cambridge: Cambridge University Press, 1999); and Kloppenberg, *The Virtues of Liberalism*, chapters 1 and 2. For a discussion of the differences between republican and liberal virtues, see Lasch, *True and Only Heaven*, 177–80, where he describes Tom Paine as being neither.

15. Tocqueville, *Democracy in America*, vol. 1, part 2, chapter 5, 225.

16. Ibid., vol. 1, part 2, chapter 6, 235–6.

17. Kloppenberg, *Uncertain Victory,* 173. See also Lasch, *True and Only Heaven*, 175–6, 274–5.

18. James Livingston, *Pragmatism and the Political Economy of Cultural Revolution, 1850–1940* (Chapel Hill: University of North Carolina Press, 1994), 39; see also 34–40.

19. Kloppenberg, *Uncertain Victory,* 155. On the triumph of marginalist economic theory in the 1890s, see Livingston, *Pragmatism,* 49–53; and Martin Sklar, *The Corporate Reconstruction of American Capitalism, 1890–1916* (New York: Cambridge University Press, 1988), 68–72. On the lag time between the emergence of the second industrial revolution and the corporate realization of profits, see Kloppenberg, 153, and Livingston, 41–5. Livingston attributes much of the delay in capitalists' realization of profits to the endurance of a robust republicanism within American culture that perpetuated the labor theory of value. Thus profit making awaited the supplanting of a political culture based on the labor theory of value by one anchored in marginalist economics. This, in turn, awaited the development of solidarity among business leaders, something that did not occur until the 1890s;

see especially 42 and 45. Livingston's argument for republicanism's persistence in mainstream American political economy through the mid-1890s contrasts markedly with the account of republicanism in Christopher Lasch, *True and Only Heaven,* 168–225 (esp. 172–4); Kloppenberg, *Uncertain Victory,* 172–3; and Robert Westbrook, "Fighting for the American Family: Private Interests and Public Obligations in World War II," in Richard Wightman Fox and T. J. Jackson Lears, eds., *The Power of Culture: Critical Essays in American History* (Chicago: University of Chicago Press, 1993), 215. Livingston accords greater power to independent proprietors and small entrepreneurs in inhibiting corporate capitalism. In part this disagreement stems from differing interpretations of republicanism, with Livingston emphasizing the persistence of republican "form" through the nineteenth century, and Lasch, Kloppenberg, and Westbrook signaling the erosion of its "content."

20. These developments are summarized in Kloppenberg, *Uncertain Victory,* 151–2; Livingston, *Pragmatism,* 36–8; and Sklar, *Corporate Reconstruction,* 14–20. The problem of community formation in the late-nineteenth and early-twentieth centuries is treated in Herbert G. Gutman, *Work, Culture, and Society in Industrializing America* (New York: Vintage, 1977); Roy Rosenzweig, *Eight Hours for What We Will: Workers and Leisure in an Industrial City, 1870–1920* (New York: Cambridge University Press, 1989); and Gary Gerstle, *Working-Class Americanism: The Politics of Labor in a Textile City, 1914–1960* (New York: Cambridge University Press, 1989).

21. For Roosevelt, this meant a *return* to politics; he had served two years in the New York State Assembly between 1882 and 1884 and lost a bid for Republican nominee for mayor of New York in 1886. In May 1889, he began a six-year term as U.S. Civil Service Commissioner in Washington, D.C. Wilson's attention, meanwhile, was elsewhere; see Robert M. Saunders, *In Search of Woodrow Wilson: Beliefs and Behavior* (Westport, CT: Greenwood Press, 1998), 21–9.

22. To be fair, Adam Smith anticipated many of the excesses of the free market in book 4 of *The Wealth of Nations.*

23. Kloppenberg, *Uncertain Victory,* 163–70, 173–84. Kloppenberg, it must be said, does not include Roosevelt in his discussion.

24. On James's evolution, see Kloppenberg, *Uncertain Victory,* 181–3; on anti-imperialism as the last gasp of republicanism, see Christopher Lasch, *True and Only Heaven,* 66–7.

25. William James to the Honorable Samuel W. McCall, December 21, 1895, in William James, *Essays, Comments, and Reviews* (Cambridge: Harvard University Press, 1987), 151–2.

26. Ibid.

27. "sheer, hopeless, well-ordered boredom": Rudyard Kipling to William James, August 31, 1896, quoted in Ralph Barton Perry, *The Thought and Character of William James,* vol. 2 (Boston: Little, Brown, and Company, 1935), 276–7. The quote continues: "The other races are still scuffling for their three meals a day. America's got 'em and now she doesn't know what she wants but is dimly realizing that extension lectures, hardwood floors, natural gas and trolley-cars don't fill the bill." On James's reaction to the speed with which Americans changed the course of the nation, see William James to Hon. Samuel W. McCall, and his letter to the

editors of the *Harvard Crimson,* in James, *Essays, Comments, and Reviews,* 151–2, 152–3, respectively.

28. "effective greatness in a nation . . . instinct of obedience": James to Godkin, December 24, 1895, in Henry James, ed., *The Letters of William James,* vol. 1 (New York: Kraus Reprint Co., 1969), 28.

29. Ibid., 28–30.

30. "of a really first class Navy": Theodore Roosevelt quoted in William James, *Essays, Comments, and Reviews,* 578, n. 153.2; "with all our might": William James to the Editors of the *Harvard Crimson,* January 14, 1896, in ibid., 152–3.

31. On the differences and similarities between James and Roosevelt, see Tom Lutz, *American Nervousness, 1903: An Anecdotal History* (Ithaca: Cornell University Press, 1991), chapter 2; and Kim Townsend, *Manhood at Harvard: William James and Others* (Cambridge: Harvard University Press, 1996). On Roosevelt, see Gail Bederman, *Manliness and Civilization: A Cultural History of Gender and Race in the United States, 1880–1917* (Chicago: University of Chicago Press, 1995), chapter 5; and E. Anthony Rotundo, *American Manhood: Transformations in Masculinity from the Revolution to the Modern Era* (New York: Basic Books, 1993), chap. 10.

32. "capacity for ardor , devotion, and joyous action": William James to L. T. Hobhouse, quoted in Lasch, *The True and Only Heaven,* 294–5.

33. On the comparison between Bellamy and James, see Lasch, *The True and Only Heaven,* 302.

34. Oliver Wendell Holmes Jr., "The Soldier's Faith," in Mark De Wolfe Howe, ed., *The Occasional Speeches of Oliver Wendell Holmes* (Cambridge: Belknap Press of Harvard University Press, 1962), 73–83. Like Randolph Bourne attacking John Dewey for his endorsement of World War I, William James repudiated Holmes's and Roosevelt's idealization of war for its refusal to discriminate between the virtues war *might* engender and the havoc war inevitably wrecked. "irremediable flatness": William James, "What Makes a Life Significant?" in *Talks to Teachers on Psychology, and to Students on Some of Life's Ideals* (New York: W. W. Norton, 1958 [1899]), quoted in Kloppenberg, *Uncertain Victory,* 5.

35. See Michael Walzer, "What Does It Mean to Be 'American'?" *Social Research* 57 (1990): 612. On the transatlantic debate between proponents of the Enlightenment and partisans of romanticism, see Christopher Lasch, *The True and Only Heaven,* 129–32, in which Lasch elucidates the conservatism of Edmund Burke; and Frederick C. Beiser, *Enlightenment, Revolution, and Romanticism: The Genesis of Modern German Political Thought, 1790–1800* (Cambridge: Harvard University Press, 1992).

36. Perry, *Thought and Character,* 315–6.

37. "must all work . . . individualism and freedom": William James to William M. Salter, September 11, 1899, in Henry James, ed., *The Letters of William James,* vol. 1, 99–101; "innocence": William James to Miss Frances R. Morse, September 17, 1899, in ibid., 102–3; "bitter bread to eat": William James to Henry James, June 21, 1899, in Skrupskelis and Berkeley, eds., *The Correspondence of William James,* vol. 3, 63. On Boas and Thomas, see R. Fred Wacker, *Ethnicity, Pluralism, and Race: Race Relations Theory in America Before Myrdal* (Westport, CT: Greenwood Press, 1983), chapter 2, especially 17–20.

38. The cultural component of the corporate reconstruction of American capitalism is treated in Livingston, *Pragmatism and the Political Economy of Cultural Revolution,* 45–9; and Sklar, *The Corporate Reconstruction of American Capitalism,* chapter 1. On the rise of the "organic" tradition, see Curti, *The Roots of American Loyalty,* chapter 7, especially 172–8; and George M. Fredrickson, *The Inner Civil War: Northern Intellectuals and the Crisis of the Union* (Urbana: University of Illinois Press, 1993 [1965]), chapter 12, especially 184–9.

39. On Burke's conservatism and its relevance for American society in the postwar period, see Lasch, *True and Only Heaven,* 127–34.

40. Fredrickson, *The Inner Civil War,* 187–8.

41. Thomas Haskell, "The Curious Persistence of Rights Talk in the 'Age of Interpretation,'" *Journal of American History* 74 (1987): 997; and Jeffrey Stout, *Ethics After Babel: The Languages of Morals and Their Discontents* (Boston: Beacon Press, 1988), 288–92, share James's conviction that degraded idioms should be revived, not discarded. Cf. Jurgen Habermas, "Concluding Remarks," in Craig Calhoun, ed., *Habermas and the Pubic Sphere* (Cambridge: MIT Press, 1994), 467; David Harvey, *The Condition of Postmodernity: An Inquiry into the Origins of Cultural Change* (Cambridge, MA: Basil Blackwell, 1988), 116–7; and Leo Marx, "Neglecting History," *Boston Review* 19 (October—November 1994): 20.

42. On the Philippine-American War, see Hoganson, *Fighting for American Manhood: How Gender Politics Provoked the Spanish-American and Philippine-American Wars;* Peter W. Stanley, ed., *Reappraising an Empire: New Perspectives on Philippines-American History* (Cambridge: Harvard University Press, 1984); Stuart Creighton Miller, *"Benevolent Assimilation": The American Conquest of the Philippines, 1899–1903* (New Haven: Yale University Press, 1982). On American anti-imperialism, see Richard Hofstadter, "Cuba, the Philippines, and Manifest Destiny," in *The Paranoid Style in American Politics and Other Essays* (Cambridge: Harvard University Press, 1965); Ernest May, *American Imperialism: A Speculative Essay* (Chicago: Imprint Productions, 1991); Robert L. Beisner, *Twelve Against Empire: The Anti-Imperialists, 1898–1900* (Chicago: University of Chicago Press, 1985); Christopher Lasch, "The Anti-Imperialists, the Philippines, and the Inequality of Man," *Journal of Southern History* 24 (August 1958): 3119–31.

43. "for humanity's sake": unnamed U.S. senator; "he would have saved us": William McKinley; both quoted in Bernard Bailyn, et al., *The Great Republic: A History of the American People,* vol. 2 (Lexington, MA: D. C. Heath, 1992), 264.

44. See, for example, Mark Hulliung, *Citizen Machiavelli* (Princeton: Princeton University Press, 1983).

45. Armitage, "Empire and Liberty: A Republican Dilemma," 2–5; Armitage, *Ideological Origins of Empire,* 127–36.

46. Drew R. McCoy, *The Elusive Republic: Political Economy in Jeffersonian America* (Chapel Hill: University of North Carolina Press, 1980), remains the best account of the American debate about republicanism and empire.

47. "Remarks to the Methodist Delegation, President William McKinley," in Daniel B. Schirmer and Stephen Rosskamm Shalom, eds., *The Philippines Reader:*

A History of Colonialism, Neocolonialism, Dictatorship, and Resistance (Boston: South End Press, 1987), 22–3.

48. Hoar and McKinley quoted in ibid., 265. Rogers M. Smith observes that republican theorists differed about the compatibility of republicanism and foreign conquest. Because of the hazards confronting republican governments, Smith writes, "virtually all republican theorists accepted that a small republic could rule large numbers of non-citizens as slaves, as Sparta did. Some, like Machiavelli, urged further an imperial policy through which martial republics could rule conquered rivals as subject peoples, not as citizens. Less bellicose writers like Montesquieu and Vattel pointed instead to the formation of defensive confederations with other republican regimes." See "The 'American Creed' and American Identity: The Limits of Liberal Citizenship in the United States," *Western Political Quarterly* 41 (1988): 232. Except for Machiavelli, conquest and empire were different matters; empire implied a bigness antithetical to republicanism. As far as William James was concerned, republicanism's ambiguity about the rectitude of foreign conquest *should* have been settled by America's universal principles, which denied, theoretically, individuals and nations the right to rule others.

49. Schirmer and Shalom, eds., *The Philippines Reader,* 266.

50. Roosevelt, "The Stenuous Life," Speech Before the Hamilton Club, Chicago, Illinois, April 10, 1899, in *The Strenuous Life: Essays and Addresses* (New York: Century Co., 1918), "America's Part," 182. Roosevelt does not actually use the term "oriental despotism." But his commentary on China and Turkey closely recapitulates Marx's idea in "The British Rule in India," in Robert C. Tucker, ed., *The Marx-Engels Reader* (New York: W. W. Norton, 1978), 653–8, which, in turn, recapitulates Tocqueville's characterization of both Chinese history itself and "democratic despotism" in general. On Tocqueville's characterization of China, see *Democracy in America,* J. P. Mayer, ed. (New York: HarperPerennial, 1969), vol. 2, part 1, chapter 10, 464; on "democratic despotism," see *Democracy in America,* vol. 2, part 4, chapter 6, 690–5.

51. Roosevelt, "Strenuous Life," 17. (Hereafter, references to this source appear in the text as SL.)

52. Roosevelt, "National Duties," Address to the Minnesota State Fair, September 2, 1901, in *Strenuous Life,* 292–6. (Hereafter, references to this source appear in the text as ND.)

53. Roosevelt, *The Winning of the West,* in DiNunzio, ed., *Theodore Roosevelt,* 53. (Hereafter, references to this source appear in the text as WW.)

54. Contrast my reading of Roosevelt with Jacobson's mischaracterization in *Barbarian Virtues.* Jacobson argues that demand for labor and export markets drove U.S. "imperialism" (at home and abroad). But invoking Roosevelt's account of savages is not the way to substantiate the argument. Labor and export markets were not Roosevelt's salient concern. Nor was the ostensible threat of "immigrants" as Jacobson, apparently following Donna Haraway, maintains. Roosevelt's criticism of barbarism abroad simply did not mirror a fear of immigrants at home. Jacobson, *Barbarian Virtues,* introduction; Donna Haraway, "Teddy Bear Patriarchy: Taxidermy in the Garden of Eden, New York City, 1908–1936," in Kaplan

and Pease, eds., *Cultures of U.S. Imperialism,* 260. The problem with barbarians, from Roosevelt's perspective, was their uncivilized nature; once on the road to civilization, immigrants, like African savages and American Indians, were redeemable. He was "civilizationist," racialist, but not racist. See, for example, his "History of New York City, 1860–1890," in Mario R. DiNunzio, ed., *Theodore Roosevelt: An American Mind* (New York: Penguin, 1994), 69–76.

55. Indeed, one could argue, pace Tom Lutz, *American Innocence, 1903,* that Roosevelt was more concerned with cultural imitativeness than with racial purity ("throughout the continent we . . . find the white, red, and black races in every stage of purity and intermixture," Roosevelt wrote, seemingly unfazed [WW 45]).

56. Henry James was "over-civilized, over-sensitive, over-refined," Roosevelt wrote; this "second rate European" might "write graceful and pretty verses, essays, novels; but he will never do work to compare with that of his brother, who is strong enough to stand on his own feet, and do his work as an American." Roosevelt sensed that James just could not stomach the rough, tumble, and *diverse* world of late-nineteenth-century America. Roosevelt was wrong, as any reading of James's *American Scene* proves. See Henry James, *The American Scene* (New York: Penguin, 1994), especially chapters 2 and 3. Roosevelt's criticism of James and Europeanization comes from "True Americanism," in DiNunzio, ed., *Theodore Roosevelt,* 166–72.

57. "Expansion and Peace, Roosevelt, *Strenuous Life,* 25–8, originally published in the journal *Independent,* December 21, 1899. (Hereafter, references to this source appear in the text as EP.)

58. "The Ideals of America," *Atlantic Monthly* 90 (December 1902): 721–34. (Hereafter, references to this source appear in the text as IA.)

59. *History of the American People* (New York: Harper & Brothers, 1901). (Hereafter, references to this source appear in the text as HAP.)

60. No one exposed Americans' ignorance about the Philippines as devastatingly as Mark Twain. See Jim Zwick, ed., *Mark Twains Weapons of Satire: Anti-Imperialist Writings on the Philippine-American War* (Syracuse: Syracuse University Press, 1992). Twain suggests that accurate accounts of conditions in the Philippines were suppressed in the interest of imperialism.

61. In the *Ancien Régime* Tocqueville challenges this notion that only in England did kings solicit the opinion of the nation. French kings had done so before the advent in France of creeping centralization. See *The Old Regime and the French Revolution* (New York: Anchor, 1983), especially Part 2, chapter 5.

62. William James, "The Philippines Tangle," *Boston Evening Transcript,* March 1, 1899, 16, in *Essays, Comments, and Reviews,* 156.

63. Ibid., 155; and "The Philippines Question," *Boston Evening Transcript,* March 4, 1899, in ibid., 160.

64. "swept away by the overmastering flood": William James, "The Philippines Tangle," *Boston Evening Transcript,* March 1, 1899, 16, in *Essays, Comments, and Reviews,* 154–5; James first remarked "on the way in which history is made" in a letter to his friend Flournoy the previous summer, when what had begun as "perfectly honest humanitarianism, and an absolutely disinterested desire on the part of our people to set the Cubans free" had yielded to abstract and inexorable

war mania: "this whole business . . . has illustrated to perfection the *psychologie des foules!*" James wrote. "We were winning the most extraordinary diplomatic victories, but they were of no use. We were ready (as we supposed) for war and nothing but war has come." William James to Flournoy, June 17, 1898, in Perry, *Thought and Character,* 307.

65. "according to its own ideals.": ibid., 156. James repeated the analogy of America as a "big material corporation against a small one" in "The Philippines Question," *Boston Evening Transcript,* March 4, 1899, in *Essays, Comments, and Reviews,* 160. See also his letter to Mrs. Henry Whitman, June 7, 1899, quoted in Perry, *Thought and Character,* vol. 2, 315; and Cotkin, *William James, Public Philosopher,* 141, where he explains why he is "against bigness and greatness in all their forms. . . . The bigger the unit you deal with, the hollower, the more brutal, the more mendacious is the life displayed," he wrote. Stuart McConnell corroborates James's observation of the "emergence of the flag as a symbol of abstract nationalism" in *Glorious Contentment: The Grand Army of the Republic, 1865–1900* (Chapel Hill: University of North Carolina Press, 1992), 230.

66. "yellow journals . . . the meanness and ignominy of the trick": "The Philippines Tangle," 157.

67. Ibid.

68. Ibid., 155.

69. James's conviction that nations develop "ideals which are a dead secret to other nations" should not be mistaken for a claim about cultural incommensurability. Context is crucial here: James's rhetorical burden in these essays was not to resolve questions about cultural commensurability but to galvanize his readership. "Hands off," as he put it, at the conclusion to "On a Certain Blindness in Human Beings." James, *Talks to Teachers on Psychology* (Cambridge: Harvard University Press, 1983), 149.

70. "entirely different men": William James, "The Philippines Again," *New York Evening Post,* March 10, 1899, 4, in *Essays, Comments, and Reviews,* 161; "the ideals they might be led by": "The Philippines Question," in ibid., 159; "an amount of mere matter in our way": ibid., 160; "to develop in its own way": William James to Miss Frances R. Morse, September 17, 1899, in Henry James, ed., *The Letters of William James,* 102. On James's place among the anti-imperialists, see Beisner, *Twelve Against Empire: The Anti-Imperialists, 1898–1900,* introduction and chapter 3; and Cotkin, *William James, Public Philosopher,* chapter 6, especially 132.

71. James, *Talks to Teachers on Psychology,* 3.

72. Ibid., 4–5.

73. Here James comes remarkably close to anticipating the argument that Josiah Royce would make in *The Philosophy of Loyalty.* There Royce, in promoting "loyalty to loyalty," aims to preserve the opportunity for individuals to remain loyal to *something* (though not, pace Christopher Lasch in *The True and Only Heaven,* to *anything*) in the face of a soul-sapping modernity. See Royce, *The Philosophy of Loyalty* (New York: Macmillan, 1908).

74. "What Makes a Life Signficant," in *Talks to Teachers,* 178.

75. "Address on the Philippines Question," 82.

76. "Secretary Taft a Biased Judge," in *Essays, Comments, and Reviews,* 176.

77. "abroad so long": William James to Miss Frances R. Morse, September 17, 1899, in Henry James, ed., *The Letters of William James, Edited by His Son, Henry James* (Boston: Atlantic Monthly Press, 1969), 102–3; "a real *hero*—a precious possession of any country": William James to Mrs. E. P. Gibbens, August 22, 1899, in ibid., 98; "the prestige of caste opinion": ibid.; "country to possess its ancient soul . . . a positive piece of [their] mind": William James, "The Philippines Tangle," in *Essays, Comments, and Reviews,* 158.

78. "empty abstractions had unrestricted way . . . it is not good enough": William James, "Governor Roosevelt's Oration," *Boston Evening Transcript,* April 15, 1899, in *Essays, Comments, and Reviews,* 165–6; "the life of toil and effort, of labor and strife": Theodore Roosevelt, "The Strenuous Life," quoted in ibid., 159, n. 163.9. For a comparison between Holmes's and Roosevelt's "set pieces," see Christopher Lasch, *The True and Only Heaven,* 296–8.

79. "were pushing and pulling forward": William James, quoted in Perry, *Thought and Character,* vol. 2; also in "Address on the Philippines Question," in *Essays, Comments, and Reviews,* 81; "and to know the truth about ourselves": ibid., 85; "shrill voice lifted in reply": William James, "Governor Roosevelt's Oration," *Boston Evening Transcript,* April 15, 1899, in ibid., 162. The inadequacy of "The Moral Equivalent of War" as the source for national and political rejuvenation is well publicized. Readers familiar with James's oeuvre, however, will recognize that James's death cut short further reflection on that subject. See Perry, *Thought and Character,* 272, and chapter 5 below. On James's distinction between idealism and abstraction, see "Governor Roosevelt's Oration," in *Essays, Comments, and Reviews,* 162, where he writes: "In the hegelian philosophy the worst vice that an orator or any other expression of human nature can have is abstractness. Abstractness means empty simplicity, non-reference to features essential to the case. Of all the carnivals of emptiness and abstractness that the world has seen, our national discussions over the Philippines policy probably bear away the palm."

80. James, "Address on the Philippines Question," 83.

81. Ibid., 85.

82. The place to go for an account of the republican tradition and theories of citizenship in literature about the United States is Rogers M. Smith, " 'The American Creed' and American Identity: The Limits of Liberal Citizenship in the United States," *Western Political Quarterly* 41 (1988): 225–51; and Smith, *Civic Ideals: Conflicting Visions of Citizenship in U.S. History* (New Haven: Yale University Press, 1997), especially chapters 7–9.

83. Roosevelt, "Fellow-Feeling as a Political Factor," in *The Strenuous Life: Essays and Addresses* (New York: Century Co., 1918), 71.

84. Ibid., 80.

85. "On a Certain Blindness in Human Beings," in *Talks to Teachers,* 168.

CHAPTER 2

1. See, among others, Rogers M. Smith, *Civic Ideals: Conflicting Visions of Citizenship in U.S. History* (New Haven: Yale University Press, 1997).

2. For the intellectual schism created by the war, see Louis Menand, *The Metaphysical Club* (New York: Farrar, Straus, and Giroux, 2001).

3. For a theoretical discussion of this, see Charles Taylor, *Sources of the Self: The Making of Modern Identity* (Cambridge: Harvard University Press, 1989), 4–11.

4. See, for example, Amitai Etzioni, ed., *Rights and the Common Good: The Communitarian Perspective* (New York: St. Martin's Press, 1995); Michael J. Sandel, *Democracy's Discontent: American in Search of a Public Philosophy* (Cambridge: Harvard University Press, 1996); Charles Taylor, "The Politics of Recognition," in Gutmann, ed., *Multiculturalism*. Hollinger, *Postethnic America,* 190–3, does not make this mistake.

5. Philip Roth, *The Human Stain* (Boston: Houghton Mifflin, 2000), 121. (Hereafter, references to this source appear in the text as HS.)

6. See also Charles Taylor, "The Politics of Recognition," in Gutmann, ed., *Multiculturalism,* 25–37.

7. See William James, "On a Certain Blindness in Human Beings" and "What Makes a Life Significant?" in *Talks to Teachers on Psychology and to Students on Some of Life's Ideals* (New York: W. W. Norton, 1958 [1899]); and Montaigne's "Of Cripples," in Donald M. Frame, ed., *The Complete Essays* (Stanford: Stanford University Press, 1958), 784–92.

8. The ensuing discussion of Debs's life trades heavily on Nick Salvatore, *Eugene V. Debs: Citizen and Socialist* (Urbana: University of Illinois Press, 1982); and Ray Ginger, *The Bending Cross: A Biography of Eugene Victor Debs* (New York: Russell & Russell, 1969 [1949]). Salvatore's treatment of Debs's critique of American politics and culture as a species of patriotism partly inspired this project. On Debs's genealogy, see Salvatore, *Eugene V. Debs,* 9; and Ginger, *The Bending Cross,* 3–4.

9. Salvatore, *Eugene V. Debs,* 9–10.

10. This account of Addams's life relies on Allen F. Davis, *American Heroine: The Life and Legend of Jane Addams* (New York: Oxford University Press, 1973); and James Weber Linn, *Jane Addams: A Biography* (Urbana: University of Illinois Press, 2000 [1968]). See also Jean Bethke Elshtain, *Jane Addams and the Dream of American Democracy* (New York: Basic Books, 2002), chapter 2 and passim. Elshtain provides a comprehensive review of Addams literature in chapter 1. My biographical account of Addams stops just before the founding of Hull-House in 1889. Readers interested in the life of the mature Addams should consult the preceding references, but also Kathryn Kish Sklar, *Florence Kelley and the Nation's Work: The Rise of Women's Political Culture, 1830–1900* (New Haven: Yale University Press, 1995), especially chapters 7–12. For Addams's genealogy, see Davis, *American Heroine,* 4–6; and Linn, *Jane Addams,* 1–21.

11. This account of Du Bois's life derives from David L. Lewis, *W. E. B. Du Bois: A Biography of a Race, 1868–1919* (New York: Henry Holt, 1993). For two provoking accounts of Du Bois's ideas, see Adolph L. Reed Jr., *W. E. B. Du Bois and American Political Thought* (New York: Oxford University Press, 1997); and Shamoon Zamir, *Dark Voices: W. E. B. Du Bois and American Thought, 1888–*

1903 (Chicago: University of Chicago Press, 1995). On Du Bois's genealogy, see Lewis, 11–4, 20–5.

12. Lewis, *W. E. B. Du Bois,* 21. Lewis nimbly explores Du Bois's contrasting accounts of whether Alfred was already married when he took Mary for a wife.

13. Debs quoted in Salvatore, *Eugene V. Debs,* 3.

14. Ibid., 1–8.

15. Linn, *Jane Addams,* 11–8.

16. Lewis, *W. E. B. Du Bois,* 15–9.

17. Salvatore, *Eugene V. Debs,* 10; Ginger, *The Bending Cross,* 7.

18. Linn, *Jane Addams,* 16–7.

19. "Hapsburg oppression in Italy": Jane Addams, *Twenty Years at Hull-House* (Urbana: University of Illinois Press, 1990), 13; "insofar as it honors the covenant": John Schaar, "The Case for Patriotism," *American Review* 17 (May 1973): 69.

20. Lewis, *W. E. B. Du Bois,* 23–5.

21. Salvatore, *Eugene V. Debs,* 10–12.

22. Ibid., 10–1; Ginger, *The Bending Cross,* 8–11.

23. Davis, *American Heroine,* 7–8; Linn, *Jane Addams,* 22–9.

24. Davis, *American Heroine,* 6–7; Linn, *Jane Addams,* 29–39.

25. Lewis, *W. E. B. Du Bois,* 26–7, 29, 33–4. Perhaps the most impressive aspect of Lewis's scholarship is his painstaking effort to distinguish Du Bois's account of events in his several autobiographies from an approximation of the "truth"; see, especially, p. 28, bottom, and p. 34, top.

26. Ibid., 28–32.

27. Salvatore, *Eugene V. Debs,* 17–8.

28. Ibid., 19–25.

29. Lewis, *W. E. B. Du Bois,* 30–4.

30. Ibid., 35–8.

31. "begging for something to eat": Debs quoted in Salvatore, *Eugene V. Debs,* 18. For Salvatore's and Ginger's differing readings of the effect of the depression on Debs, see Salvatore, *Debs,* 19; and Ginger, *The Bending Cross,* 16.

32. Salvatore, *Eugene V. Debs,* 14.

33. Ibid., 23–55.

34. Davis, *American Heroine,* 10–1; Linn, *Jane Addams,* 40–1.

35. "Christ's mission to you has been fulfilled": Addams quoted in ibid., 15; see also 14–6.

36. "solving the social problems of the world": Addams quoted in ibid., 22; see also 16–23.

37. Lewis, *W. E. B. Du Bois,* 38–9, 47–8.

38. "ten thousand Negroes of every hue and bearing . . . the unhampered self-expression": Du Bois quoted in ibid., 41; "ceremony" and "breeding": Du Bois quoted in ibid., 42.

39. Salvatore, 42, 50–1.

40. Ibid., 53–5.

41. Davis, *American Heroine,* 24–6; Linn, *Jane Addams,* 65–7.

42. See Christopher Lasch, *The New Radicalism in America: The Intellectual as a Social Type, 1889–1963* (New York: W. W. Norton, 1965), chapter 1, es-

pecially 15–8; despite his misgivings about Lasch's argument, the evidence Allen Davis presents for this period of Addams's life corroborates Lasch; see *American Heroine*, 24–31.

43. Lewis, *W. E. B. Du Bois*, 52–3.

44. Salvatore, *Eugene V. Debs*, 58–72.

45. Ibid., 74–80, 88–113.

46. "the softer graces": Addams quoted in Davis, *American Heroine*, 31; see also 29–31.

47. Ibid., 32–7.

48. Lewis, *W. E. B. Du Bois*, 53–5.

49. Salvatore, *Eugene V. Debs*, 61–72, 92–110.

50. "wages . . . boycott and blacklist": Debs quoted in ibid., 116; see also 114–46, for details of the Pullman strike.

51. "necessity": Addams quoted in Davis, *American Heroine*, 37; "superfluity" is Lasch's term, see *The New Radicalism*, 34. On Addams involvement in the Pullman strike, see Davis, *American Heroine*, 112–4; Salvatore, *Eugene V. Debs*, 128; and Addams's essay, "A Modern Lear," in Christopher Lasch, ed., *The Social Thought of Jane Addams* (New York: Irvington, 1982 [1965]), 105–23.

52. "secular outlet . . . for energies essentially religious": Lasch, *The New Radicalism*, 11. On the period between Addams's first and second European tour, see Davis, *American Heroine*, 38–52.

53. Lewis, *W. E. B. Du Bois*, 148–9.

54. "out of bickering peoples": Du Bois quoted in ibid., 77; "upon principles and reason": Frazier paraphrased in ibid., 72–3; "despise [his] . . . color": Du Bois quoted in ibid., 66; see also 60–77.

55. Ibid., 82–115.

CHAPTER 3

1. See Daniel T. Rodgers, "The Twilight of Laissez-Faire," *Atlantic Crossings: Social Politics in a Progressive Age* (Cambridge: Harvard University Press, 1998).

2. "and employ them": *John Dewey, Democracy and Education: An Introduction to the Philosophy of Education* (New York: Free Press, 1966 [1916]).

3. Michael Walzer, "What Does It Mean to be 'American'?" *Social Research* 57 (1990): 596–605.

4. Merle Curti, *The Roots of American Loyalty* (New York: Russell & Russell, 1946), 160–85; George M. Fredrickson, *The Inner Civil War: Northern Intellectuals and the Crisis of Union* (Urbana: University of Illinois Press, 1993), 183–98. "Capacity for loyalty" is Josiah Royce's term; see *The Philosophy of Loyalty* (New York: Macmillan, 1908).

5. James T. Kloppenberg, "Republicanism in American History and Historiography," *Tocqueville Review* 13, no. 1 (1992): 132. Daniel Rodgers, "Republicanism: The Career of a Concept," *Journal of American History* (June 1992): 11–38; and Philip Ethington, *Public City: The Reconstruction of Urban Life in San Francisco, 1850–1900* (New York: Cambridge University Press, 1994) are among the texts dismissive of republican rhetoric.

6. "with other forms of association": John Dewey, *Democracy and Educa-*

tion: An Introduction to the Philosophy of Education, 83. (Hereafter, references to this source appear in the text as DAE.) "of conjoint communicated experience": DAE, 87.

7. Hobbes quoted in Robert B. Westbrook, "Fighting for the American Family: Private Interests and Political Obligation," in Richard Wightman Fox and T. J. Jackson Lears, eds., *The Power of Culture: Critical Essays in American History* (Chicago: University of Chicago Press, 1993), 200.

8. See Samuel Milton Jones to Eugene V. Debs, November 29, 1899, and in response, Eugene V. Debs to Samuel Milton Jones, December 8, 1899, in J. Robert Constantine, ed., *Letters of Eugene V. Debs,* vol. 1: *1874–1912* (Urbana: University of Illinois Press, 1990), 140, 142–3.

9. Lincoln Steffens, "Eugene V. Debs on What the Is In America and What To Do About It," *Everybody's Magazine* (October 1908): 458; Salvatore, *Eugene V. Debs, Citizen and Socialist* (Urbana: University of Illinois Press, 1982), 344.

10. Jane Addams, "The Subjective Necessity for Social Settlements," in Christopher Lasch, ed., *The Social Thought of Jane Addams* (New York: Irvington 1982 [1965]), 29.

11. David L. Lewis, *W. E. B. Du Bois: Biography of a Race, 1868–1919* (New York: Henry Holt, 1993), 150–4; 177–8.

12. "and be an American?": W. E. B. Du Bois, "The Conservation of Races," *American Negro Academy Occasional Papers* 2 (1897): 11; "husband and use his best powers": W. E. B. Du Bois, "Strivings of the Negro People," *Atlantic Monthly* 80 (August 1897): 195.

13. "A child born at Pullman . . . few generations will produce": Eugene Debs, "Verbatim Report of the Lecture Delivered by Eugene V. Debs at Opera House, Fargo, N.D., March 6, 1895" (Fargo, N.D.: T.L.P.U. No. 1): 12; "love of money . . . free institutions": Eugene Debs, "The Significance of Labor Day," *Arena* (October 1895): 303.

14. "Have I not been a father to you?": Eugene V. Debs, "Verbatim Report of the Lecture Delivered by Eugene V. Debs, at Opera House, Fargo, N. D., March 6, 1895" (Fargo: T. L. P. U. No. 1, 1895): 6; "the American principle of arbitration": ibid., 9. On Debs's role in the Pullman strike, see Salvatore, *Eugene V. Debs,* 126–46.

15. Debs, "Verbatim Report," 7, 3.

16. Ibid., 8–9.

17. Ibid., 7.

18. Addams, "The Subjective Necessity for Social Settlements," in Lasch, ed., *The Social Thought of Jane Addams,* 29.

19. Jane Addams, "The Problems of Municipal Administration," *Congress of Arts and Science, Universal Exposition, St. Louis, 1904,* vol. 1 (Boston: Houghton, Mifflin, 1906), 434.

20. For Addams's take on the ambiguous nature of municipal corruption, see "Problems of Municipal Corruption," 438–40; *Democracy and Social Ethics* (Cambridge: Harvard University Press, 1964 [1902]), chapter 7; and "Why the Ward Boss Rules," *Outlook* 58 (April 2, 1898): 879–82, in Lasch, ed., *Social Thought of Jane Addams,* 124–33. On why so much of the citizenry remains indifferent

to politics, see "Problems of Municipal Corruption," 435–40. On the wants of working people, see "The Objective Value of a Social Settlement," *Philanthropy and Social Progress* (New York: Thomas Y. Crowell, 1893), 27–40, in Lasch, ed., *Social Thought of Jane Addams,* 44–61. On young women and the conflicting family claim and social consciousness, see "The Subjective Necessity for Social Settlements," in Lasch, *Social Thought,* 28–43; also in *Twenty Years at Hull-House* (Urbana: University of Illinois Press, 1990 [1909]), chapter 6; *Democracy and Social Ethics,* introduction and chapters 1 and 3. On Addams as anthropologist, see Lasch, ed., *Social Thought of Jane Addams,* 62–3; "the indifferent citizen . . . of the people themselves,": "Problems of Municipal Corruption," 437; "normal and slowly formed ties . . . legitimate objects of political action": ibid., 436.

21. "not be considered . . . only the interests of his 'ring.' ": "The Subjective Necessity for Social Settlements," in Lasch, ed., *Social Thought of Jane Addams,* 30; "a claim upon the public gratitude . . . upon which [political corruption] has grown": "Problems of Municipal Corruption," 438–9; "what headway . . . negative": *Democracy and Social Ethics* (Cambridge: Harvard University Press, 1964 [1902]), 240.

22. "humbler people . . . hardness of heart": "Problems of Municipal Corruption," 438–9. For one urban boss's claims to be democratic, see William Riordan, *Plunkitt of Tammany Hall* (New York: Penguin, 1991 [1905]).

23. "untold capacity, talent, and even genius": "Problems of Municipal Corruption," 446–7; "civic machinery . . . vital forces": ibid., 440.

24. "the greater ideals of the American republic": W. E. B. Du Bois, "Strivings of the Negro People," 197; "the child of emancipation . . . be himself, and not another": ibid., 196; "the Negro problem . . . black man in the land": "Caste: That Is the Root of Trouble," *Des Moines Register Leader,* October 19, 1904, in Herbert Aptheker, ed., *Writings by W. E. B. Du Bois in Periodicals Edited by Others,* vol. 1 (1891–1909) (Millwood, NY: Kraus-Thomson Organization Limited, 1982), 231; "the problem of the twentieth century is the problem of the color-line": *The Souls of Black Folk* (New York: Penguin, 1982), 54. For examples of Du Bois's emphasizing the compatibility of plural allegiances, see *The Souls of Black Folk,* "Strivings of the Negro People," "The Conservation of Races," "The Negro and the Y.M.C.A.," *The Horizon: A Journal of the Color Line* 5 (March 1910): 2, in Aptheker, ed., *Writings in Periodicals Edited by W. E. B. Du Bois: Selections from The Horizon* (White Plains, NY: Kraus-Thomson Limited, 1985), 101–5; and "St. Francis of Assisi," *Voice of the Negro* 3 (October 1906): 419–26, in Aptheker, ed., *Periodicals Edited by Others,* 1, 331–8.

25. Du Bois, "Caste: That Is the Root of Trouble," 231–2.

26. "initiated in the South . . . was a fool": ibid., 232; "good and evil . . . toil and aspiration": ibid., 234.

27. "the worst of each other": *The Souls of Black Folk* (New York: Penguin, 1982), 190; "two great streams": ibid., 204; "point of transference": ibid.

28. "for centuries as slaves . . . the best of modern workingmen": ibid., 191–2. Du Bois addressed the success and failure of the Freedmen's Bureau and other Reconstruction agencies in chapter 2 of *The Souls of Black Folk.*

29. "that close sympathetic and self-sacrificing leadership": ibid., 195.

30. "It is not enough . . . But Vaster' ": ibid., 209.

31. Brandeis, "The Living Law," Address to the Chicago Bar Association, January 3, 1916, in Philippa Strum, ed., *Brandeis on Democracy* (Lawrence: University Press of Kansas, 1995), 60.

CHAPTER 4

1. Henry James, *The American Scene* (New York: Penguin, 1994), 66–7.

2. Ibid., 66. For more on James's response to America's disciplining institutions, see Ross Posnock, "The Politics of Nonidentity: A Genealogy," in Donald F. Pease, ed., *National Identities and Post-Americanist Narratives* (Durham, NC: Duke University Press, 1994).

3. Presumably left political commitments account for this failure of historical, or moral, imagination; the anxiety of empowered elites like James and his peers are unworthy of our attention. Perhaps understandable, such a conclusion is nonetheless regrettable. It both robs us of theoretical and historical insight and diminishes us morally by narrowing the scope of those whose moral and political dilemmas we take seriously. See, for example, Matthew Frye Jacobson, *Barbarian Virtues: The United Sates Encounters Foreign Peoples at Home and Abroad, 1876–1917* (New York: Hill and Wang, 2000), 265 and passim; and Gary Gerstle, *American Crucible: Race and Nation in the Twentieth Century* (Princeton: Princeton University Press, 2001), especially chapters 1 and 2. By contrast, John Higham, *Strangers in the Land: Patter of American Nativism, 1860–1925* (New Brunswick, NJ: Rutgers University Press, 1998 [1955]), eschews a tone of moral superiority partly by taking seriously the political and social problem nativism symbolized. Ditto Philip Gleason, "American Identity and Americanization," in Stephan Thernstrom, ed., *Harvard Encyclopedia of American Ethnic Groups* (Cambridge: Harvard University Press, 1980). For a rich new account of fin de siècle American identity that focuses on politics *and* culture while avoiding the typical sanctimony, see Carrie Tirado Bramen, *The Uses of Variety: Modern Americanism and the Quest for National Distinctiveness* (Cambridge: Harvard University Press, 2000).

4. It is easy to dismiss *The American Scene* as the ranting of a xenophobe. Such a reading misconstrues both the nature of James's project and the author's sensibility. Too many passages in James simply elude the charge. Witness this selection from chapter 3: "Who and what is an alien . . . in a country peopled from the first under the jealous eye of history?—peopled that is, by migrations at once extremely recent, perfectly traceable and urgently required. They are still, it would appear, urgently required—if we look about far enough for the urgency; though of that truth such a scene as New York may well make one doubt. Which is the American, by these scant measures?—which is *not* the alien, over a large part of the country at least, and where does one put a finger on the dividing line, or, for that matter, 'spot' and identify any particular phase of the conversion, any one of its successive moments?" *The American Scene*, 95. For sensitive and discriminating accounts of Henry James that do not fall prey to sanctimony, see Ross Posnock, "The Politics of Nonidentity" and *Trial of Curiosity: Henry James, William James, and the Challenge of Modernity* (New York: Oxford University Press, 1991); and Alex Zwerdling, *Improvised Europeans: American and Literary Expatriates and the Siege of London* (New York: Basic Books, 1998), especially xiv–xvi.

5. For two concise accounts of the nexus between U.S. cultural and civic identity, see Gleason, "American Identity and Americanization"; and Rogers Smith, "The 'American Creed' and American Identity: The Limits of Liberal Citizenship in the United States," *Western Political Quarterly* 41 (1988): 225–51. Smith has extended this argument in *Civic Ideals: Conflicting Visions of Citizenship in U.S. History* (New Haven: Yale University Press, 1997).

6. See, especially, *The American Scene,* chapter 3.

7. Ibid., 90–1.

8. "Corporate reconstruction of American capitalism" is Martin J. Sklar's term and the title of his book by that name. See *The Corporate Reconstruction of American Capitalism, 1890–1916: The Market, The Law, And Politics* (New York: Cambridge University Press, 1988), introduction and part 1. I have drawn on Sklar's work to set the economic context for cultural expression in chapter 1 above.

9. Such an argument is now considered a commonplace. See, for example, Benedict Anderson, *Imagined Communities: Reflections on the Origin and Spread of Nationalism* (New York: Verso, 1991), introduction, chapters 3 and 6; John Breuilly, *Nationalism and the State* (Chicago: University of Chicago Press, 1993), appendix, 404–21; Liah Greenfield, *Nationalism: Five Roads to Modernity* (Cambridge: Harvard University Press, 1992), introduction; and Eric J. Hobsbaum, *Nations and Nationalism Since 1780: Programme, Myth, Reality* (New York: Cambridge University Press, 1990), 10–3.

10. See, among others, R. Fred Wacker, *Ethnicity, Pluralism, and Race: Race Relations Theory in America Before Myrdal* (Westport, CT: Greenwood Press, 1983), introduction and chapter 1.

11. This and the following definitions are indebted to Gleason, "American Identity and Americanization," 31–58; and Michael Walzer, "What Does It Mean to Be an 'American'?" *Social Research* 57 (1990): 591–614, and "Pluralism: A Political Perspective," in Thernstrom, *Encyclopedia;* but especially to David A. Hollinger, "Democracy and the Melting Pot Reconsidered," in *In the American Province: Studies in the History and Historiography of Ideas* (Baltimore: Johns Hopkins University Press, 1985), 92–102, and *Postethnic America: Beyond Multiculturalism* (New York: Basic Books, 1995), 84–6; and John Higham, "Ethnic Pluralism in Modern American Thought," in *Send These to Me: Jews and Other Immigrants in Urban America* (New York: Atheneum, 1975), 197–230.

12. Horace Kallen, "Democracy *Versus* the Melting Pot," *Culture and Democracy in The United States: Studies in the Group Psychology of the American Peoples* (New York: Boni and Liveright, 1924), 67–125.

13. See David A. Hollinger, *Postethnic America,* chapter 4, especially 84–6; Walzer, "What Does It Mean to Be an 'American'?" 614. For a defense of Dewey's democracy against charges of paternalism, see Robert B. Westbrook, *John Dewey and American Democracy* (Ithaca: Cornell University Press 1991), 187–9. Westbrook correctly suggests that Addams, among others, belongs alongside Dewey on "the radical wing of progressivism"; I would number Du Bois among these "others," too.

14. So charge Eric Lott, "The New Cosmopolitanism," *Transition* 72 (fall

1996), 108–35; and Timothy Brennan, *At Home in the World: Cosmopolitanism Now* (Cambridge: Harvard University Press, 1997).

15. See Robert S. and Helen Merrell Lynd, *Middletown: A Study in Modern American Culture* (New York: Harcourt, Brace, Jovanovich, 1929).

16. The writing of Woodrow Wilson and Theodore Roosevelt are cases in point. See, for example, Wilson's "Ideals of America," *Atlantic Monthly* 90 (December 1902), 721–34; and Roosevelt's "Strenuous Life" and "National Duties" in *The Strenuous Life: Essays and Addresses* (New York: Century Co., 1918), 1–21 and 279–97, respectively.

17. The best theoretical accounts of the emergence of racial ideology are Michael Banton, *The Idea of Race* (London: Tavistock, 1977) and *Racial Theories* (Cambridge: Cambridge University Press, 1998). The best historical account of the development of racial ideology in the American context remains Higham, *Strangers in the Land: Patterns of American Nativism, 1860–1925.*

18. In his edition of Alain Locke's *Race Contacts and Interracial Relations: Lectures on the Theory and Practice of Race* (Washington, DC: Howard University Press, 1992), historian Jeffrey C. Stewart credits Locke with "removing race from its biological basis and putting it squarely on a cultural foundation" (xxv). But his etymology ignores evidence that race had long been associated with culture or peoplehood. See, for example, Crevecoeur's *Letters from an American Farmer* (London, 1782); and Emerson's "English Traits" (1856). It was not until the nineteenth century that race became associated primarily with biology, an interpretation challenged by Alain Locke and Du Bois (two decades before him), among others. If Locke can be credited with anything, it is re-associating race not with the vague notion of peoplehood but with Boas's more systematic concept of "culture."

19. Liberal suspicion of the nation is so ubiquitous that documentation seems unnecessary; typical is Gary Gerstle, "Liberty, Coercion, and the Making of Americans," *Journal of American History* (September 1997), 524–58. Exceptions include Richard Rorty, *Achieving Our Country* (Cambridge: Harvard University Press, 1998); Hollinger, *Postethnic America;* Michael Lind, *The Next American Nation* (New York: The Free Press, 1995); and David Miller, *On Nationality* (Oxford: Clarendon Press, 1997).

20. This was Marx's legacy to the socialism of the Second International—it dropped his revolutionary side and kept his uncompromising universalism, which he got from nineteenth-century liberalism. Thus Debs derived his universalism from liberals twice over—once via Marx, once direct from American liberalism. Indeed, intuitively, Debs resembled less orthodox socialists of his party and more the young Marx of "On the Jewish Question" and "The German Ideology"; see Robert Tucker, ed., *The Marx-Engels Reader* (New York: W.W. Norton, 1978).

21. See, for example, "The Social Democratic Party's Appeal," *The Independent* (October 13, 1904), 835–8; "Unionism and Socialism: A Plea for Both" (Terre Haute: Standard Publishing Co., 1904); and "Verbatim Report of the Lecture Delivered by Eugene V. Debs at Opera House, Fargo, N. D." (March 6, 1895), especially 7–8, 11, 16, 21, all in PEVD.

22. See "Verbatim Report," 121, where Debs equates home life with high culture; "Industrial Unionism," in James P. Cannon, ed., *Eugene V. Debs Speaks* (New York: Pathfinder, 1970), 139–40; and "Unionism and Socialism," 43.

23. For examples of scholarly criticism of Debs's alleged "blindness" and "one-dimensionality" on the subject of racial prejudice, see Nick Salvatore, *Eugene V. Debs: Citizen and Socialist* (Urbana: University of Illinois Press, 1982), 226–7; Harold W. Currie, *Eugene V. Debs* (Boston: Twayne, 1976), 108; Ray Ginger, *The Bending Cross: A Biography of Eugene Victor Debs* (New York: Russell and Russell, 1969 [1949]); and David L. Lewis, *W. E. B. Du Bois*, 421.

24. "afflicted by . . . crucible of love": Israel Zangwill, *The Melting Pot: Drama in Four Acts* (New York: Macmillan, 1921 [1909]), 203–4; "contribute[d] its title . . . of the Republic": ibid., 216. (Hereafter, references to this source appear in the text as TMP.)

25. The (justifiable) aversion of liberal scholars to the racist bile of conservatives like William Graham Sumner, Henry Cabot Lodge, and Madison Grant, among others, leads many to ignore the vexing question of the relationship between national culture and civic solidarity. As James, Dewey, Addams, Du Bois, and Brandeis recognized, Progressive-Era attempts to move beyond an ethnic or racial basis for American civic identity would founder unless American civic identity could be reset on a foundation of political culture. This entailed two compromises: first, a cultural cease-fire between old-stock and immigrant Americans—as America's ostensibly universal civic institutions themselves sprang, largely, from an Anglo-Saxon tradition; second, a willingness on the part of individuals and groups to surrender a proportion of their autonomy to national solidarity. For scholars unsympathetic to the problem diversity poses to national cohesion, see Jacobson, *Barbarian Virtues;* Kristin Hoganson: *Fighting of American Manhood: How Gender Politics Provoked the Spanish-American and Philippine-American Wars* (New Haven: Yale University Press, 1988); and Gary Gerstle, "Liberty, Coercion, and the Making of Americans." For more sympathetic accounts of the dilemma, see Smith, *Civic Ideals;* and David A. Hollinger, "National Culture and Communities of Descent," *Reviews in American History* 26 (1998): 312–28. For thinkers who grant the dependence of justice—in an era of nation-states—on an ideal of national solidarity committed to justice, the interesting question becomes how "thick" the political culture can be without impinging on individual autonomy. On this, see K. Anthony Appiah, "Identity, Authenticity, Survival: Multicultural Societies and Social Reconstruction," in Amy Gutmann, ed., *Multiculturalism: Examining the Politics of Recognition* (Princeton: Princeton University Press, 1994), 149–63; Appiah, "Against National Culture," in Laura Garcia-Moreno and Peter C. Pfeiffer, eds., *Text and Nation: Cross-Disciplinary Essays on Cultural and National Identities* (Columbia, SC: Camden House, 1996); and Hollinger, loc. cit., and below.

26. Currie, *Eugene V. Debs*, 107. By 1895, Debs had come to view racism as a product of capitalism's attempt to impede class consciousness; writing from Woodstock (Illinois) prison, he urged workers to unite their ballots without regard to race or of gender. See ibid., 107–8. By 1910, Debs parted ways with the conservative wing of the party over the matter of immigration restriction after Morris Hillquit and

company, courting the support of the American Federation of Labor, endorsed the AF of L's pro-restriction platform. "If Socialism does not stand staunchly, unflinchingly, uncompromisingly for the working class and for the exploited and oppressed masses of all lands," Debs wrote in the *International Socialist Review,* "then it stands for none and its claim is a false pretense and its profession a delusion and a snare." Quoted in Ginger, *The Bending Cross,* 297.

27. "the Negro is . . . same industrial masters": Debs, "The Negro Question," *American Labor Journal* (July 1903), in Currie, *Eugene V. Debs,* 108; "their long training . . . and in society at large": Socialist Party Negro Resolution, quoted in Cannon, ed., *Eugene V. Debs Speaks,* 97–8.

28. "In capitalism . . . capitalist society multiply": Debs, "The Negro in the Class Struggle," *International Socialist Review* (November 1903), in ibid., 94; "no Negro question outside of the labor question": ibid., 93.

29. "fraudulence . . . economic freedom": ibid., 93. "savory bouquet . . . hatred of the Negro race": ibid., 91–2. On the alleged black male assault on white womanhood, see Joel Williamson, *The Crucible of Race: Black-White Relations in the American South Since Emancipation* (New York: Oxford University Press, 1984).

30. "shoot from ambush . . . foolish and fanatical criticism": Debs, "The Negro and His Nemesis," *International Socialist Review* (January 1904), in ibid., 96–7; "you get social . . . member of the Socialist Party": Anonymous to Eugene V. Debs, November 25, 1903, in ibid., 95–6.

31. Debs, "The Negro and His Nemesis," in ibid., 98–104.

32. Ibid., 103.

33. "alone and unguided . . . law, order, and decency": Du Bois, *The Souls of Black Folk* (New York: Signet, 1982), 192. On Du Bois's opinion of Debs, see Lewis, *W. E. B. Du Bois,* 420–1.

34. "institutions of a complexional character . . . essential condition of respectability": Douglass, "An Address to the Colored People of the United States," Cleveland, Ohio, September 29, 1848, in Howard Brotz, ed., *Negro Social and Political Thought: 1850–1920* (New York: Basic Books, 1966), 211. On Douglass's notion of race as a genetic attribute, see "The Claims of the Negro Ethnologically Considered," July 12, 1854, in ibid., 226–44; and "The Future of the Colored Race," May 1886, ibid., 309.

35. "ice . . . common safeguards": Douglass, "The Nation's Problem," April 4, 1889, in ibid., 317–8.

36. "preparation": Washington, "Atlanta Exposition Address," September 18, 1895, in ibid., 359; "yet one in all things essential to mutual progress": ibid., 358.

37. "in God . . . wedlock of the strong": Du Bois, "Credo," *Independent* 57 (October 6, 1904): 787, in Aptheker, ed., *Writings by W. E. B. Du Bois in Periodicals Edited by Others,* vol. 1, 229–30; "absolute . . . self-dependence and self-respect," Jessie R. Fauset to Du Bois, February 16, 1905, in Aptheker, ed., *The Correspondence of W. E. B. Du Bois,* vol. 1: *Selections, 1877–1934* (Amherst: University of Massachusetts Press, 1973), 94–5.

38. Du Bois scholars have exploited the amplitude of his cryptic, occasion-

ally convoluted prose to promote contrasting interpretations. Those excavating the roots of black nationalism, for example, read Du Bois's race consciousness as evidence that he belongs to a nationalist tradition; see Wilson J. Moses, *The Golden Age of Black Nationalism, 1850–1925* (New York: Oxford University Press, 1978); and Brotz, *African-American Social and Political Thought, 1850–1920*. Jeffrey C. Stewart and Nancy Fraser invoke an essentialist Du Bois as foil for Alain Locke's alleged pragmatism; see Stewart, ed., Alain LeRoy Locke, *Race Contacts and Interracial Relations*, xxiv–xxv; and Nancy Fraser, "Another Pragmatism: Alain Locke, Critical 'Race' Theory, and the Politics of Culture," in Morris Dickstein, ed., *The Revival of Pragmatism* (Durham: Duke University Press, 1988). To Ross Posnock, *Color and Culture: Black Writers and the Making of the Modern Intellectual* (Cambridge: Harvard University Press, 1998), Du Bois was a pragmatist; to Shamoon Zamir, *Dark Voices: W. E. B. Du Bois and American Thought, 1888–1903* (Chicago: University of Chicago Press, 1995), Du Bois was a Hegelian idealist; to Adolph L. Reed Jr., *W. E. B. Du Bois and American Political Thought: Fabianism and the Color Line* (New York: Oxford University Press, 1997), Du Bois was a Fabian socialist. I find partial truth in these various accounts, as do David L. Lewis, *W. E. B. Du Bois;* and Herbert Aptheker, editor of the *W. E. B. Du Bois Papers*.

39. "The institutions of the Republic have become the liberating cause and the background for the rise of the cultural consciousness and social autonomy of the immigrant Irishman, German, Scandinavian, Jew, Pole or Bohemian. On the whole, the automatic processes of Americanization have not repressed nationality. These processes have liberated nationality, and more or less gratified it." Kallen, "Democracy *Versus* the Melting Pot," 107. (Hereafter, references to "Democracy *Versus* the Melting-Pot" appear in the text as DVM.)

40. "agonized . . . optimistic": Kallen, "Democracy *Versus* the Melting Pot," 82; "common life": ibid., 78; "like-mindedness . . . ethnic and cultural unity": ibid., 71–2. (Page numbers for further references to DVM appear in the text.)

41. Critical analyses of Kallen's pluralism may be found in Hollinger, "Democracy and the Melting Pot Reconsidered," 93–7; Gleason, "American Identity and Americanization," 43–7; Higham, "Ethnic Pluralism in Modern American Thought," 203–9; and Wacker, *Ethnicity, Pluralism, and Race*, 30–1. For an uncritical perspective, see Walzer, "What Does It Mean to Be an 'American'?" 603–6.

42. Du Bois, "The Conservation of Races" (Washington, DC: Baptists Magazine Print, 1897), 2–15. (Hereafter, references to "The Conservation of Races" appear in the text as COR.) "much to teach the world": ibid., 7; "beg[ging] wedlock of the strong,": Du Bois, "Credo," 229.

43. As Posnock puts it in a passage addressing William James's influence on Du Bois: "we can redescribe more precisely Du Bois's response to invidious racial distinction as thoroughy pragmatist. Faced with the 'pretended absolute' of race, he turned it into a 'program for more work,' a challenge to the 'ready-made compartmentalization' (to borrow Dewey's phrase) that racial distinction inflicts on psyches and on society." Posnock, *Color and Culture*, 115, and 111–21 more generally.

44. In "Strivings of the Negro People," *Atlantic Monthly* (August 1897): 195— "Conservation's" fraternal twin—Du Bois spelled the importance of cultural contact, stating that it was the "end of [Negro] striving . . . to be a co-worker in the kingdom of culture, to escape both death and isolation, and to husband and use his best powers." John Higham cogently captured the distinction between Du Bois and Kallen in "Ethnic Pluralism in Modern American Thought," 209–11.

45. Du Bois reiterated this sentiment in "Strivings of the Negro People," 194–8.

46. "only . . . But vaster' ": *Souls of Black Folk*, 209. Du Bois constantly emphasized the compatibility of racial identity with national and universal affiliation; see, for example, "The Negro Ideals of Life," 268–70; and "The Immediate Program of the American Negro," *The Crisis* 9 (April 1915), in Aptheker, *Selections from The Crisis*, 93–5. David Lewis's suggestion that "Booker Washington would have roundly applauded" Du Bois's distinction between "social equilibrium" and "social equality" ignores the latter's determination to identify an ideal capable of mediating "all the complicated relations of life." If Washington would have applauded Du Bois's sentiment here, that is evidence of his failure to understand it. See Lewis, *W. E. B. Du Bois*, 173; and Du Bois, COR, 15.

47. "If you have heard . . . what a settlement attempts to do": Addams, "The Subjective Necessity for Social Settlements" (1892), in Christopher Lasch, ed., *The Social Thought of Jane Addams* (New York: Irvington, 1982 [1965]), 43. Elsewhere in the same essay, Addams reiterated her sense that the settlement house had to function as a public square. "From its very nature," she wrote, the settlement house "can stand for no political or social propaganda. It must, in a sense, give the warm welcome of an inn to all such propagandas, if perchance one of them be found an angel. The one thing to be dreaded in the Settlement is that it lose its flexibility, its power of quick adaptation, its readiness to change its methods as its environment may demand. It must be open to conviction and must have a deep and abiding sense of tolerance. It must be hospitable and ready for experiment." Quoted in William L. Neumann, ed., *Jane Addams: A Centennial Reader* (New York: Macmillan, 1960), 13–4.

48. This sentiment typified Addams's thought in the thirty years following the founding of Hull-House; for examples, see "Problems of Municipal Administration," in Howard J. Rogers, ed., *Congress of Arts and Science, Universal Exposition, St. Louis, 1904*, vol. 7 (Boston: Houghton, Mifflin, 1906), 434–50; "Ethical Survivals in Municipal Corruption," *International Journal of Ethics* 8 (April 1898): 273–91; "Social Settlement," *Chautauqua Assembly Herald* 25 (August 13, 1900): 2; and Addams's Address at the civic dedication of the Abraham Lincoln Center in "The Tenth General Meeting of the Congress of Religion," *Unity* 55 (July 27, 1905): 364–5, JAP.

49. Randolph Bourne, "Trans-National America," *Atlantic Monthly* 100 (July 1916), in Olaf Hansen, ed., *Randolph Bourne: The Radical Will, Selected Essays, 1911–1918* (Berkeley and Los Angeles: University of California Press, 1977). (Hereafter, references to "The Conservation of Races" appear in the text as TA.)

50. To be fair, Kallen's concluding metaphor in "Democracy *Versus* the Melting

Pot" of America as a symphony of cultures suggests an ideal similar to Bourne's, though Kallen's vision remains extremely vague. See below.

51. Bourne shared this yearning with many others of his generation. See Casey Nelson Blake, *Beloved Community: The Cultural Criticism of Randolph Bourne, Van Wyck Brooks, Waldo Frank, and Lewis Mumford* (Chapel Hill: University of North Carolina Press, 1990).

52. Such scathing indictments of mass culture would become a staple of twentieth-century left cultural criticism. It took books like Janice A. Radway, *Reading the Romance: Women, Patriarchy, and Popular Literature* (Chapel Hill: University of North Carolina Press, 1984), to awaken scholars to the amplitude of popular culture. See also Richard Wightman Fox and T. J. Jackson Lears, eds., *The Culture of Consumption: Critical Essays in American History* (Chicago: University of Chicago Press, 1993), especially the introduction. Jane Addams knew that screeds like Bourne's were often as not the product of ignorance. "We hasten to give the franchise to the immigrant," Addams wrote, "from a sense of justice, from a tradition that he ought to have it, while we dub him with epithets deriding his past life or present occupation, and feel no duty to invite him to our houses." Addams, "The Subjective Necessity for Social Settlements," in Lasch, ed., *The Social Thought of Jane Addams.*

53. Bourne more readily admits the potential for cultural conflict in a pluralist state in his companion essay, "The Jew and Trans-National America," *Menorah Journal* 2 (December 1916): 277–84.

54. Bourne, "The State," in Hansen, ed., *The Radical Will,* 388. (Hereafter, references to this source appear in the text as TS.)

55. "When a country acts as a whole in relation to another country, or in imposing laws on its own inhabitants, or in coercing or punishing individuals or minorities, it is acting as a State" (TS, 358).

56. On James's cosmopolitanism, see chapter 1, above. Historian Ian Tyrell shares my sense that Bourne's cosmopolitanism is, finally, parochial. See "American Exceptionalism in an Age of International History, *AHR* 96, no. 4 (October 1991): 1052–3.

57. "Universal Service as Education," *New Republic* 6 (April 22, 1916), in *Middle Works,* vol. 10, 186.

58. Ibid., 183.

59. "American Education and Culture," *New Republic* 7 (July 1, 1916) in *Middle Works,* vol. 10, 198.

60. Kallen seems to have come up with the term "cultural pluralism" in conversation with Alain Locke, sometime around 1906–7. He first publishes the word in 1924 in *Culture and Democracy in the United States* (New Brunswick, NJ: Transaction, 1998). For a general introduction to Kallen, see Stephen J. Whitfield's introduction to idem, as well as Werner Sollors, "A Critique of Pure Pluralism," in Sacvan Bercovitch, ed., *Reconstructing American Literary History* (Cambridge: Harvard University Press, 1986), 263–73; Philip J. Gleason, *Speaking of Diversity: Language and Ethnicity in Twentieth-Century America* (Baltimore: Johns Hopkins University Press, 1992); and John Higham, *Send These to Me.*

61. Horace Kallen, "Democracy *Versus* the Melting Pot," *The Nation* (February 25, 1915): 220.

62. John Dewey to Horace Kallen, March 31, 1915, in Larry A. Hackman, ed., *Correspondence of John Dewey*, vol. 1 [computer file] (Charlottesville, VA: InteLex Corp., 1999).

63. The longer one pauses over Kallen's metaphor, the more confusing it becomes. How can one reconcile the public unfolding of the symphony of civilization, whose writing is in the playing, with Kallen's conviction that "city life," as he put it in the same essay, is "external, inarticulate, and incidental," whereas the "inalienable" in life, its "intrinsic positive quality," derived from the "psycho-physical inheritance of one's ancestors"? (DVM, 114–5).

64. John Dewey to Horace Kallen, March 31, 1915, in Hackman, ed., *Correspondence of John Dewey.*

65. John Dewey, "Nationalizing Education," *Journal of Education* (1916) in *Middle Works,* vol. 10, 203. (Hereafter, references to this source appear in the text as NE.)

66. Morris R. Cohen, "Zionism: Tribalism or Liberalism," *The New Republic* (March 8, 1919): 182. (Hereafter, references to this source appear in the text as ZTL.) The best account of Cohen remains David A. Hollinger, *Morris R. Cohen and the Scientific Ideal* (Cambridge: MIT Press, 1975). See also Hollinger, "Ethnic Diversity," in *In the American Province,* 61–3.

67. Herder's ideal, of course, antedated German unification.

68. Kallen, "Zionism: Democracy or Prussianism," *The New Republic* (April 5, 1919): 311–3. (Hereafter, references to this source appear in the text as ZDP.)

69. It is interesting to note here that Kallen recognizes creed and nationality, not blood, to have been the basis for Jews historical persecution, confirming the accounts of historians tracing the etymology of the concept of race and careful to discern when the word "race" became associated with blood. See Banton, *The Idea of Race* and *Racial Theories;* and Ivan Hannaford, *Race: The History of an Idea in the West* (Washington, DC: Woodrow Wilson Center Press, 1996).

70. See, for example, Brandeis, "Jews and Arabs," November 24, 1929 (Washington, DC), in *Brandeis on Zionism* (Westport, CT: Hyperion Press, 1942), 150–3; and Allon Gal, "Brandeis, Judaism, and Zionism," in Dawson, ed., *Brandeis and America,* 76–83.

71. Gal, "Brandeis, Judaism, and Zionism," 65–98, especially 67–8.

72. See, for example, Desmond King, *Making Americans: Immigration, Race, and the Origins of the Diverse Diversity* (Cambridge: Harvard University Press, 2000); Jacobson, *Barbarian Virtues: The United States Encounters Foreign Peoples at Home and Abroad, 1876–1917;* and Gary Gerstle, *American Crucible: Race and Nation in the Twentieth Century* (Princeton: Princeton University Press, 2001).

73. Louis D. Brandeis, "True Americanism," in *Brandeis on Zionism: A Collection of Addresses and Statements by Louis D. Brandeis* (Westport, CT: Hyperion Press, 1942), 4. (Hereafter, references to this source appear in the text as TA.)

74. Brandeis, "The Jewish Problem: How to Solve It," in *Brandeis on Zionism*, 22–4. (Hereafter, references to this source appear in the text as JP.)

75. Brandeis, "A Call to the Educated Jew," in *Brandeis on Zionism*, 66. (Hereafter, references to this source appear in the text as CEJ.)

76. See Philippa Strum, ed., *Brandeis on Democracy* (Lawrence: University Press of Kansas, 1995), introduction, 13.

77. Josiah Royce, *The Philosophy of Loyalty* (Nashville: Vanderbilt University Press, 1995 [1908]); and William James, "What Makes a Life Significant?" in *Talks to Teachers on Education and To Students on Some of Life's Ideals* (New York: W.W. Norton, 1958 [1899]).

78. Smith, *Civic Ideals*.

79. Brandeis, "A Call to the Educated Jew," 63–4.

80. "I sit with Shakespeare and he winces not. Across the color line I move arm in arm with Balzac and Dumas, where smiling men and welcoming women glide in gilded halls. From out of the caves of evening that swing between the strong-limbed earth and the tracery of the stars, I summon Aristotle and Aurelius and what soul I will, and they come all graciously with no scorn or condescension." *The Souls of Black Folk* (New York: Penguin, 1982), 139.

81. Kelley quoted in Louis Menand, *The Metaphysical Club* (New York: Farrar, Straus and Giroux, 2001), 310.

82. John Dewey, "American Education and Culture," *New Republic* 7 (1916) in *Middle Works*, vol. 10, 198–9. (Hereafter, references to this source appear in the text as AEC.)

83. Dewey, "The Need of an Industrial Education in an Industrial Democracy," *Manual Training and Vocational Education* 17 (1916), in *Middle Works*, vol. 10, 137–9; and AEC, 200.

84. Dewey, "The Need of an Industrial Education in an Industrial Democracy," 140; and "Learning to Earn: The Place of Vocational Education in a Comprehensive Scheme of Public Education," in *Middle Works*, vol. 10, 147–50. Dewey may not have said enough about race to please some critics, but he was not silent on the matter. See, for example, "Federal Aid to Education," *Child Labor Bulletin* 6 (1917) in *Middle Works*, vol. 10, 125–9, especially 127, 129; and NE, 206.

85. Dewey, "Universal Service as Education," *New Republic* 6 (1916), in *Middle Works*, vol. 10, 186.

86. Nathan Glazer, *We Are All Multiculturalists Now* (Cambridge: Harvard University Press, 1997), chapter 3.

87. Dewey, "Universal Service as Education," 186.

88. Addams, "Problem of Municipal Administration," 443. The ideas outlined in this address became the basis for *Newer Ideals of Peace* (New York: Macmillan, 1907). (Hereafter, references to this source appear in the text as NIP.)

89. Addams, *Democracy and Social Ethics* (New York: Macmillan, 1907), 225–6. Addams uses the phrases "civic virtue" and "commonweal" on p. 269.

90. Ibid., 268–9.

91. Rivka Shpak Lissak, *Pluralism and Progressives: Hull-House and the New Immigration, 1890–1919* (Chicago: University of Chicago Press, 1989), charges

Addams with treating culture instrumentally—that is, as a means to an end rather than as an end in itself. Quite right, Addams would have replied; this stand is perfectly consistent with her and Dewey's sense that a nation founded on abstract political ideals needed a culture derived from civic practices rather than ethnic affiliations. This did not preclude a plurality of ethnic cultures persisting in the United States, though it did preclude the essentialism characteristic of Kallen's cultural pluralism.

92. Addams's idea of dialectical progress toward universalism jibes with Judith Butler's incisive analysis in "Universality in Culture," in Joshua Cohen, ed., *For Love of Country: Debating the Limits of Patriotism* (Boston: Beacon Press, 1996), 45–52.

CHAPTER 5

1. Jane Addams, "What Is the Greatest Menace to Twentieth-Century Progress?" *[Report of] The Sunset Club, One Hundred Eighth Meeting, Palmer House, Chicago* (February 14, 1901): 341, JAP.

2. See, for example, Robert H. Johnson, "Cold War Games Again," *New York Times* (September 23, 1994): A35.

3. Richard Rorty invokes Croly, along with Addams, Debs, and others as an antidote to the unpatriotic left of the late twentieth century. Rorty's reading of Croly is selective, if not naive, ignoring the antidemocratic nature of Croly's domestic and international program. See *Achieving Our Country: Leftist Thought in Twentieth-Century America* (Cambridge: Harvard University Press, 1998), 46–9, passim, and the ensuing discussion.

4. Herbert Croly, *The Promise of American Life* (Cambridge: The Belknap Press of Harvard University Press, 1965 [1909]), 7. (Hereafter, references to this source appear in the text as PAM.)

5. See *Democracy in America,* J. P. Mayer, ed. (New York: HarperPerennial, 1969), vol. 1, part 2, chapter 7, 250, and vol. 2, part 4, chapter 6, 690.

6. On Americans' gratuitous consumption, see Thorstein Veblen, *The Theory of the Leisure Class: An Economic Study of Institutions* (New York, 1899). Cf. Richard Wightman Fox and T. J. Jackson Lears, eds., *The Culture of Consumption: Critical Essays in American History, 1880–1980* (New York: Pantheon, 1983).

7. Debs quoted in Nick Salvatore, *Eugene V. Debs: Citizen and Socialist* (Urbana: University of Illinois Press, 1982), 226–7.

8. "Cuban Rebellion," *Railway Times* (November 15, 1898), PEVD.

9. Eugene V. Debs to Robert M. La Follette, March 3, 1909, in J. Robert Constantine, ed., *Letters of Eugene V. Debs,* vol. 1: *1874–1912* (Urbana: University of Illinois Press, 1990), 299.

10. "Democracy or Militarism," *Liberty Tracts, No. 1* (Chicago: Central Anti-Imperialist League, 1899), 35, JAP. (Hereafter, references to this source appear in the text as DM.)

11. Jane Addams, "What Is the Greatest Menace?" 341.

12. "The Responsibilities and Duties of Women toward the Peace Movement," *Universal Peace Congress, Official Report* (Boston, 1904), 121, JAP. (Hereafter, references to this source appear in the text as RDW.)

13. "Commercialism Disguised as Patriotism and Duty," *St. Louis Post-Dispatch* (February 18, 1900): section 4, p. 4, JAP. (Hereafter, references to this source appear in the text as CD.)

14. "What Is the Greatest Menace?" 340.

15. "Race Friction between Black and White," *American Journal of Sociology* 13 (May 1980): 834–8, in Aptheker, ed., *Writings of W. E. B. Du Bois in Periodicals Edited by Others,* vol. 1, 389; "moral hegemony": Du Bois to President Woodrow Wilson, August 3, 1915, in Aptheker, ed., *Correspondence of W. E. B. Du Bois,* 211–3.

16. "Douglass as a Statesman" Address at Wilberforce University in honor of Frederick Douglass, March 9, 1895, in Aptheker, ed., *Periodicals Edited by Others,* vol. 1, 29–30.

17. "The Future of the Negro Race in America," *The East and The West* 2 (January 1904): 4–19, in Aptheker, ed., *Periodicals Edited by Others,* vol. 1, 190.

18. "The Niagara Movement," *The Horizon: A Journal of the Color Line* 5 (November 1909): 8–9, in Aptheker, ed., *Writings in Periodicals Edited by W. E. B. Du Bois: Selections from* The Horizon (White Plains, NY: Kraus-Thomson, 1985), 84; "that marvelous internal decay . . . its life and government": "The Present Outlook for the Dark Races of Mankind," *Church Review* 17 (October 1910): 95–110, in Aptheker, ed., *Periodicals Edited by Others,* vol. 1, 74. Du Bois explicitly associated unity with "Americanism" in this last essay: "Negro and Filipino, Indian and Puerto Rican, Cuban and Hawaiian, all must stand united under the stars and stripes for an America that knows no color line in the freedom of its opportunities."

19. "The Color Line Belts the World," *Collier's Weekly* (October 20, 1906): 30, in Aptheker, ed., *Periodicals Edited by Others,* vol. 1, 330. "The fountain of all intelligent government . . . the political and social economy of our subjects": *The Horizon* 3 (February 1908): 20–4, in Aptheker, ed., *Selections from* The Horizon, 45.

20. Du Bois to President Woodrow Wilson, August 3, 1915, in Aptheker, ed., *The Correspondence of W. E. B. Du Bois* (Amherst: University of Massachusetts Press, 1973), 211–3. "new standard of national efficiency": "Race Friction Between Black and White," in Aptheker, ed., *Periodicals Edited by Others,* vol. 1, 389. See also "The Present Outlook," in ibid., 77.

21. See "What Makes a Life Significant," in *Talks to Teachers on Psychology: and to Students on Some of Life's Ideals* (New York: W. W. Norton, 1958 [1899]), 170–91.

22. See *David W. Blight, Race and Reunion: The Civil War in American Memory* (Cambridge: Harvard University Press, 2001).

23. "The Moral Equivalent of War," in John K. Roth, ed., *The Moral Equivalent of War and Other Essays* (New York: Harper Torchbooks, 1971), 15. (Hereafter, references to this source appear in the text as MEW.)

24. "Remarks at the Peace Banquet," in *Essays in Religion and Morality* (Cambridge: Harvard University Press, 1982), 122–3.

25. For Bourne's response to James's essay, see "A Moral Equivalent for Universal Military Service," *The New Republic* 7 (July 1, 1916): 217–9, in Carl Resak,

ed., *War and the Intellectuals: Essays, 1915–1919* (New York: Harper & Row, 1965), 144–5.

26. By contrast, witness Roosevelt's response: "Jane Addams—don't talk to me about Jane Addams! I have always thought a lot of her, but she has just written a bad book, a very bad book! She is all wrong about peace." Quoted in James Weber Linn, *Jane Addams: A Biography* (Urbana: University of Illinois Press, 2000), 293.

27. For a sense of Addams's developing thoughts about war and peace preceding the publication of her book, see "Democracy or Militarism," 36; and "Count Tolstoy," *Chautauqua Assembly Herald* 27 (July 11, 1902): 5; "Newer Ideals of Peace," 1 and 2, ibid., 5–7; "The Responsibilities and Duties of Women Toward the Peace Movement," 120–2; "Address of Miss Jane Addams [at the Peace Congress Banquet]," 261–2; "The Interest of Labor in International Peace," 145–6; and "A Moral Substitute for War," 30, all in JAP. Christopher Lasch addresses Addams in the context of these dichotomies in *The New Radicalism in America, 1889–1963* (New York: W. W. Norton, 1986), chapter 1.

28. See also *Newer Ideals of Peace,* 209–19.

29. See Lasch, *The New Radicalism,* 12–3.

30. See also *Newer Ideals of Peace,* 25, where Addams points to the West's battle against tuberculosis as a form of moral equivalency: "This movement has its international congresses," she wrote, "its discoverers and veterans, also its decorations and rewards for bravery. Its discipline is severe; it requires self-control, endurance, self-sacrifice and constant watchfulness."

31. For the moral and masculine components of Debs's ideal of manhood, see, respectively, "Industrial Unionism," an address delivered by Debs at Grand Central Palace in New York City on December 10, 1905, in James P. Cannon, ed., *Eugene V. Debs Speaks* (New York: Pathfinder, 1970), 121–44, especially 133; and "The Gunmen and The Miners," *International Socialist Review* (September 1914), in ibid., 226–30.

32. EVD to Fred D. Warren, February 1, 1910, in Constantine, ed., *Letters of Eugene V. Debs,* vol. 1, 335–8.

33. On his forefathers' military service, see, for example, Du Bois to Wm. P. Pickett, January 16, 1907, in Aptheker, ed., *Correspondence of W. E. B. Du Bois,* 125; and "The Shadow of Years," *The Crisis* 15 (February 1918): 167–71, in Aptheker, ed., *Writings of W. E. B. Du Bois Edited by Himself: Selections from* The Crisis, vol. 1 (New York: Kraus Thomson, 1983), 150–5.

34. Du Bois to Wm. P. Picket; see also Du Bois's letter to Moorfield Storey, October 21, 1907, in Aptheker, ed., *Correspondence of W. E. B. Du Bois,* 136–7.

35. See "Peace," *The Crisis* 6 (May 1913), in Aptheker, ed., *Selections from* The Crisis, 57. "I believe . . . the death of that strength": "Credo," *Independent* 57 (October 6, 1904): 787, in Aptheker, ed., *Periodicals Edited by Others,* vol. 1, 229.

36. "The Present Outlook for the Dark Races of Mankind," *Church Review* 17 (October 1900): 95–110, in Aptheker, ed., *Periodicals Edited by Others,* vol. 1, 81; "Last Crusade . . . heritage of men everywhere": "Godfrey of Bouillon: A Talk to Graduates of the Baltimore Colored High School," *The Horizon* 6 (June 1910): 1–5, in Aptheker, ed., *Selections from* The Horizon, 117.

37. "Negro Ideals of Life," *Christian Registrar* 84 (October 25, 1905): 1197–9, in Aptheker, ed., *Periodicals Edited by Others,* vol. 1, 267–70.

38. "tell of strikes . . . strikers and boycotters": "Verbatim Report of the Lecture Delivered by Eugene V. Debs, at the Opera House, Fargo, N. D., March 6, 1895" (Fargo: T. L. P. U. No. 1, 1895): 7; "Only a semblance of liberty . . . may not perish from the earth": "Political Lessons," *Railway Times* (March 1, 1895), both in PEVD.

39. "Again, I ask . . . the Declaration of Independence": [untitled editorial] *Railway Times* (September 15, 1896); "when liberty itself . . . and their posterity": [untitled editorial] *Railway Times* (July 15, 1895), both in PEVD.

40. [untitled editorial] *Social Democratic Herald* (September 2, 1899), PEVD.

41. [untitled editorial] *Social Democratic Herald* (July 13, 1901); "fetish worship": [untitled editorial] *Social Democratic Herald* (September 2, 1899), both in PEVD.

42. William Everett, "Patriotism: An Oration Delivered Before the Phi Betta Kappa of Harvard College, Commencement, 1900" (Philadelphia: Peace Association of Friends, 1901), 8. (Hereafter, references to this source appear in the text as PAT.)

43. Everett's ideal seems to jibe with Maurizio Viroli, *For Love of Country: An Essay on Patriotism and Nationalism* (New York: Oxford University Press, 1995); and John Schaar, "The Case for Patriotism," *American Review* 17 (May 1973).

44. "Training in Patriotism," *The Nation* 83, no. 2144 (August 2, 1906): 92; "idiotic flag-fetishism": "Patriotism by Manual," *The Nation* 71, no. 1849 (December 6, 1900): 440.

45. "The Passing of the Show," *Social Democratic Herald* (August 22, 1903); "in the capitalist system . . . a rebel and not a patriot": "Debs's Great Speech," *Miner's Magazine* (August 1902), both in PEVD.

46. "Debs's Great Speech," *Miner's Magazine* (August 1902): 33–4; "The chief significance . . . sources of profit": "The Social Democratic Party's Appeal," *The Independent* (October 13, 1904), PEVD.

47. "Christmas Fellowship," *Unity* 42 (December 22, 1898): 309, JAP.

48. "What Is the Greatest Menace?" 339–40.

49. "The Newer Ideals of Peace, 2," *Chautauqua Assembly Herald* 27 (July 10, 1902): 6, JAP. See Michael Walzer, *Thick and Thin: Moral Argument at Home and Abroad* (Notre Dame: University of Notre Dame Press, 1994), introduction.

50. "The Newer Ideals of Peace, 2," 7.

51. "Address of Miss Jane Addams," *Union League Club, Chicago, Exercise in Commemoration of the Birthday of Washington, February 23, 1903* (Chicago: Metcalf Stationery Co., 1903), 6–9, JAP.

CHAPTER 6

1. "means-ends rationality": Robert B. Westbrook, *John Dewey and American Democracy* (Ithaca: Cornell University Press, 1991), 207.

2. Jane Addams, "Statement Endorsing Woodrow Wilson for President"

[October–November] 1916, JAP. "set our house in order . . . people's essential interest": Woodrow Wilson, Second Inaugural Address, March 5, 1917, in Ray Stannard Baker and William E. Dodd, eds., *War and Peace: Presidential Messages, Addresses and Public Papers (1917–1924) by Woodrow Wilson* (New York: Harper & Brothers, 1927), 1.

3. Garry Wills, "It's His Party: Reagan's Legacy," *The New York Times Magazine* (August 11, 1996): 37.

4. "Too Proud to Fight," Naturalization Ceremony, Philadelphia, May 10, 1915, in Baker and Dodd, eds., *The New Democracy: Presidential Messages, Addresses, and Public Papers (1913–1917) by Woodrow Wilson*, vol. 1 (New York: Harper & Brothers, 1927), 318–9. "blood . . . whole globe": "Heroes of Vera Cruz," Brooklyn Naval Yard Address, May 11, 1914, in ibid., 104–5. This sentiment is repeated in "Loyalty Means Self-Sacrifice," Conference on Americanization, July 13, 1916, in ibid., vol. 2, 248–52.

5. "Loyalty Means Self-Sacrifice," Conference on Americanization, Washington, D.C., July 13, 1916, in ibid., vol. 2, 250. "Every one of those flags . . . serving the world": "Men Are Governed by Their Emotions," Address at the Dedication of the Federation of Labor Building, Washington, D.C., July 4, 1916, in ibid., vol. 2, 225.

6. "Outline on the Administration's Program of Preparedness for National Defense," The Manhattan Club, New York, November 4, 1915, in ibid., vol. 1, 385. "orderly and righteous . . . human liberty and human rights": "A Conversation with President Wilson," May 23, 1914, in ibid., 111–3. The sentiment described here was replicated throughout Wilson's preparedness campaign of December 1915—January 1916; see, for example, his speech in Chicago on January 31, 1916, in ibid., vol. 2, 67–8, where he describes the ideals of "reciprocal respect and reciprocal defense" that must govern foreign relations.

7. "The Heroes of Vera Cruz," 105. "The most patriotic man . . . the world is against him": "Be Worthy of the Men of 1776," Independence Day Address, Philadelphia, July 4, 1914, in ibid., 145–6. "active conduct . . . but to regenerate it": "Be Not Afraid of Our Foreign-Born Citizens," Address to the Daughters of the American Revolution, Washington, October 11, 1915, in ibid., 375.

8. For the tensions latent in Wilson's cosmopolitanism, see "Be Not Afraid of Our Foreign-Born Citizens," 381; "Loyalty Means Self-Sacrifice," 248; The League of Nations, Indianapolis, October 12, 1916, in Baker and Dodd, eds., *The New Democracy*, vol. 2, 356; Third Annual Address to Congress, December 7, 1915, ibid., vol. 1, 423; and "A New Kind of Church Life," Federal Council of Churches, Columbus, Ohio, December 10, 1915, ibid., 437. My Wilson accords more closely with the one described by Garry Wills than the one portrayed by Thomas Knock. Compare Wills, "A Theology of Willie Horton," in *Under God: Religion and American Politics* (New York: Touchstone, 1990), 70–2, to Knock, *To End All Wars: Woodrow Wilson and the Quest for a New World Order* (New York: Oxford University Press, 1992), especially chapter 8. Knock writes that Eugene Debs "pronounced the Fourteen Points 'thoroughly democratic,' and deserving of the 'unqualified approval of everyone believing in the rule of the people, Socialists included.' " According to Knock, that quotation, unfamiliar to this author as well as to Debs's biographers, comes from p. 119 of James Weinstein, *The Decline of*

Socialism, 1912–1925 (New York: Monthly Review Press, 1967); p. 119 of Weinstein does not even mention Debs, much less quote him; indeed, nowhere does Weinstein quote Debs speaking on Wilson's Fourteen Points.

9. Call to the Associated Press, New York, April 20, 1915, ibid., 303–7. See also "Be Not Afraid of Our Foreign Born," 378.

10. "The Prospect for Peace," reprinted in *American Socialist* (February 19, 1916), in James P. Cannon, ed., *Eugene V. Debs Speaks* (New York: Pathfinder Press, 1970), 231–3.

11. Debs, untitled editorial in *National Rip-Saw* (November 1914), PEVD.

12. Debs to George D. Heron, January 23, 1917, in J. Robert Constantine, ed., *Gentle Rebel: Letters of Eugene V. Debs* (Urbana: University of Illinois Press, 1995), 118; Allan L. Benson to Debs, March 19, 1915, and Debs in reply, March 22, 1915, in ibid., 98–100.

13. The caution of Addams's circle is captured in JAP. See her correspondence with Paul U. Kellogg, editor of *The Survey*, in mid-September 1914; with Madeline McDowell Breckinridge in late November; and with the German peace activist Rosika Schwimmer, Carrie Chapman Catt, and Lillian D. Wald in December.

14. This and the following four paragraphs come from Jane Addams, *Address Given at the Organizational Conference of the Woman's Peace Party, Washington, DC, January 10, 1915* (Chicago: Woman's Peace Party, 1915), 10–2, JAP.

15. James Atkinson to Jane Addams, May 11, 1917, JAP.

16. Addams, et al., *Women at the Hague: The International Congress of Women and Its Results* (New York: Macmillan, 1915), 60–1. "The enthusiasm for war . . . places of church and state": ibid., 59.

17. Ibid., 62–4.

18. Ibid., 125. "A good patriot . . . with that opinion": ibid., 88.

19. Stanislas d' Halewyn to Jane Addams, July 10, 1915, JAP.

20. Letters from Richard Harding Davis and Everett P. Wheeler, *New York Times* (July 13, 1915): 10, JAP.

21. Compare Addams's Carnegie Hall Address, with its emphasis on reconciling patriotism and internationalism, to her speech in Chicago Auditorium a few weeks later. "I unfortunately gave . . . in connection with bayonet charges": "The Food of War," *The Independent* (December 13, 1915): 431, JAP.

22. On the strain involved in this balancing act, see Du Bois to Mary W. Ovington, April 9, 1914, and Ovington to Du Bois in reply, April 11, 1914; and Joel E. Spingarn to Du Bois, October 24, 1914, and Du Bois to Spingarn in response, October 28, 1914, in Herbert Aptheker, ed., *Correspondence of W. E. B. Du Bois*, vol. 1: *Selections, 1877–1934*, 188–93 and 200–7, respectively.

23. This and the following two paragraphs come from Du Bois, "World War and the Color Line," in Aptheker, ed., *Writings by W. E. B. Du Bois*, vol. 1, 83–5. On Wilson's call for neutrality see "Neutrality" and "American Neutrality—An Appeal by the President," in Baker and Dodd, eds., *The New Democracy*, vol. 1, 151–6, 157–9, respectively.

24. "World War and the Color Line," 84–5.

25. See "The African Roots of War," *Atlantic Monthly* 115 (May 1915): 707–14, in Aptheker, ed., *Periodicals Edited by Others*, vol. 2, 96–104.

26. Du Bois's ducking of the conundrum he himself posed in the "African Roots

of War" should be read not so much as more evidence of double consciousness as a commentary about the tension at the heart of the Enlightenment project between liberty and equality. Compelled to choose between liberty and equality, Du Bois, like so many of his contemporaries (and ours), opted for both. On Du Bois's abiding commitment to Western civilization, see Adolph L. Reed Jr., *W. E. B. Du Bois and American Political Thought: Fabianism and the Color Line* (New York: Oxford University Press, 1997), chapters 4 and 5. On scholars' continued misunderstanding and misappropriation of Du Bois's concept of double consciousness, see idem, chapter 7.

27. Du Bois, "Lusitania," *The Crisis* 10 (June 1915), in Aptheker, ed., *Selections from* The Crisis, vol. 1, 102. For evidence of Du Bois's despair over interference in his editorship of *The Crisis*, see Aptheker, ed., *The Correspondence of W. E. B. Du Bois*, vol. 1: *Selections, 1877–1934*, 188–92, 200–7.

28. Du Bois, "The Battle of Europe," *The Crisis* 12 (September 1916): 216–7, in Aptheker, ed., *Selections from* The Crisis, vol. 1, 126.

29. Wilson at Memorial Hall, Pittsburgh, January 29, 1916, in Baker and Dodd, eds., *The New Democracy*, vol. 2, 26–7. "to put the whole note on very high grounds": Wilson quoted in Wills, *Under God*, 71–2. For Wilson's speech to the Associated Press, see Baker and Dodd, eds., *The New Democracy*, vol. 1, 302–7. For further emphasis of Wilson's mounting idealism and authoritarianism, cf., among other passages, "Outline of the Administration's Program of Preparedness for National Defense," ibid., 384–92; his preparedness campaign speeches, ibid., II, 16–85; "This Nation Is Again to Be Tested," ibid., 207–11; "I Am All Sorts of a Democrat," ibid., 212–6; and "Loyalty Means Self-Sacrifice," ibid., 248–52.

30. Debs to Daniel Hoan, August 11, 1916, and Hoan to Debs in reply, August 15, 1916, in J. Robert Constantine, ed., *Gentle Rebel: Letters of Eugene V. Debs* (Urbana: University of Illinois Press, 1995), 108–10.

31. Debs to Daniel W. Hoan, August 17, 1916, in ibid., 110–1. Publicly, Debs was even harsher. In the *National Rip-Saw*, he renounced Hoan's distinction between a preparedness parade and a demonstration of "patriotic loyalty to the nation and its institutions," declaring it "the same thing by a different name." For ordering Hoan to march, the socialists of Milwaukee could not "be too severely condemned and we are not of those who propose to withhold censure because of cowardly fear that we may injure the party." For the "perfidy" of their "sanction of bourgeois 'patriotism' and the betrayal of principles and ideals," Debs warned that they would be "made to account"; "Patriotism on Parade," *National Rip-Saw* (December 1916), PEVD.

32. Debs to Upton Sinclair, January 12, 1916, in Constantine, ed., *Gentle Rebel*, 106–7; *New York Sun* to Debs, November 28, 1915, and Debs in reply, November 29, 1915, in ibid., 105–6. Privately, Debs's opposition to militarism was more adamant. "I am with you absolutely in the matter of militarism," he wrote his friend, the socialist ex-pat George D. Herron. "I am opposed to any shadow of compromise with the God-damned institution and I would see myself in hell for all eternity before it should receive a word of encouragement or a particle of support in any form from me. Militarism has not a solitary redeeming feature and war is an unmitigated crime and I shall fight both uncompromisingly just as you are doing

while there is a breath in my body." Debs to George D. Herron, November 16, 1916, in ibid., 115.

33. "Toward Internationalism," *Report on the Women's Auxiliary Conference Held in the City of Washington, USA, in Connection with the Second Pan American Scientific Congress, December 28, 1915—January 7, 1916* (Washington: Government Printing Office, 1916), 59–60, JAP.

34. *"Statement [on preparedness] of Miss Jane Addams, of Chicago, Illinois, Representing the Women's Peace Party." In U. S. Congress, House Committee on Military Affairs, *To Increase the Efficiency of the Military Establishment of the United States. Hearing before the Committee on Military Affairs, January 13, 1916*, 4. 64th Congress, 1st Session, 1916, JAP.

35. Ibid., 7–15.

36. "A Conference of Neutrals," *Survey 35* (January 22, 1916): 495, JAP.

37. "Statement [on a Commission of Relations between the United States and the Orient] of Miss Jane Addams, of Chicago, Illinois." In U.S. Congress, House Committee on Foreign Affairs, *United States and the Orient. Hearings before the Committee on Foreign Affairs on H.R. 16661, December 12, 1916*, 10–2. 64th Congress, 2nd session, 1916, JAP.

38. "The War," in "Opinions," *The Crisis* 10 (July 1915): 125.

39. "Of the Sons and Masters of Man," *The Souls of Black Folk*, 197. "patriotism and loyalty . . . common fatherland": "On Booker T. Washington and Others," *The Souls of Black Folk* (New York: Signet Classic, 1982), 91–5.

40. Du Bois, "The Perpetual Dilemma," *The Crisis* 13 (April 1917): 270–2, in Aptheker, ed., *Selections from* The Crisis, vol. 1, 134–5. Du Bois defended the segregated camp again in June 1917; see "Officers," *The Crisis* 14 (June 1917), in Aptheker, ed., *Selections from* The Crisis, vol. 1, 137.

41. "This Is a People's War," Washington, D.C., June 14, 1917, in Dodd and Baker, eds., *War and Peace,* vol. 1, 60. "that the greatest things . . . ready for those things": Second Inaugural Address, March 5, 1917, in ibid., 3.

42. See Ray Ginger, *Eugene V. Debs: A Biography* (New York: Collier, 1962), 365–9. "Whatever the cause," Ginger wrote, "Debs was certainly groping in the dark. He still believed in friendship among workers of the world; he still believed that the war had been inspired by the capitalist pirates; he still longed for peace; but he had no program. He was lost. Month after month he shouted his mighty protests, and they turned out to be frail bleats in an indifferent country." Ginger reports that Debs recovered his voice the following March, when he defended a group of Wobblies on trial in Chicago.

43. Herman Hulman Jr. to Debs, June [?], 1917, and again, June 13, 1917, in Constantine, ed., *Letters of Eugene V. Debs,* vol. 2 (Urbana: University of Illinois Press, 1990), 309–10, 310–1, respectively.

44. Debs to Adolph F. Germer, in Constantine, ed., *Gentle Rebel*, 136–7. "Autocracy is autocracy . . . the people as Elihu Root": Debs to Clarence A. Royce, May 31, 1917, Ibid., 124–5.

45. Debs to Stephen M. Reynolds, April 8, 1918, ibid., 139–40.

46. Debs attributed his knowledge of history to George Bancroft and other "standard" historians; see "Statement to the Court" and "Address to the Jury,"

September 12 and 14, respectively, 9. PEVD. (Hereafter, references to this source appear in the text as SCAJ.)

47. Debs's admiration for Brown et al. went way back. "set an example . . . throne of God": Eugene V. Debs, "December 2, 1859," *Appeal to Reason* (November 23, 1907), PEVD. See also "The Enthusiasm on May Day Was Unbounded," *St. Louis Labor* (May 10, 1902), PEVD; and "Socialism and the Abolition Movement," *Social Democratic Herald* (May 17, 1902), PEVD.

48. Lincoln quoted in Eugene V. Debs, "Verbatim Report of the Lecture Delivered by Eugene V. Debs at Opera House, Fargo, N. D, March 6, 1895" (Fargo: TLPU, 1895): 16–7; and "Lincoln—Champion of Labor," *Debs Magazine* (February 1922), PEVD.

49. Jane Addams, "Patriots and Pacifists in Wartime" (New York: Garland, 1972); this edition is slightly different from the edition in JAP, which appeared originally in the *City Club Bulletin, Chicago* 10, no. 9 (June 16, 1917). "everything we have stood for as a Nation": John Henry Hopkins to Jane Addams, June 11, 1917; "bear the burdens of the real work": James Atkinson to Addams, May 11, 1917; see also the criticisms of Addams in John C. Christie to Addams, June 12, 1917; Judd A. Everett to Addams, June 12, 1917; F. E. Morton to Addams, June 12, 1917; Bryson D. Horton to Addams, June 13, 1917; John Thompson to Addams, June 16, 1917; and Robert L. Henry to Addams, June 21, 1917; all in JAP.

50. James Atkinson to Addams, May 11, 1917, JAP.

51. The only original essay that Addams published between June 1917 and November 1918 was titled "World's Food Supply and Woman's Obligation," in General Federation of Women's Clubs, *Biennial Convention* 14 (1918): 251–63, JAP. "profoundly discouraged": *Peace and Bread in Time of War* (New York: King's Crown Press, 1945 [1922]), 111.

52. See "Address Given at The Hague," May 1915, in *The Overthrow of the War System* (Boston: The Forum Publications, 1915), 6. Addams defended herself in *Peace and Bread in Time of War,* 107–31, much of which reiterated her original sentiment in "Patriots and Pacifists in Time of War." "co-ordinated political activity": *Peace and Bread,* 112; "to a supreme effort": "Patriots and Pacifists," 7.

53. *The Souls of Black Folk* (New York: Signet Classic, 1982), 45–6.

54. See William Jordan, " 'The Damnable Dilemma': African-American Accommodation and Protest during World War I," *Journal of American History* 81, no. 4 (March 1995): 1562–90, especially 1563; and Mark Ellis, " 'Closing Ranks' and 'Seeking Honors': W. E. B. Du Bois in World War I," *Journal of American History* 79, no. 1 (June 1992): 96–124.

55. W. E. B. Du Bois, *Dusk of Dawn: An Essay Toward an Autobiography of a Race Concept* (New York: Harcourt, Brace and Company, 1940), 256.

56. "Of Our Spiritual Strivings," *The Souls of Black Folk,* 45–6.

57. See Du Bois, "Resolutions of the Washington Conference," *The Crisis* 14 (June 1917): 59; and Young, "Loyalty," *The Crisis* 14 (May 1917): 22.

58. For Du Bois's criticism of Washington's silencing of others, see *The Souls of Black Folk,* 33–42; and his exchange with Oswald Garrison Villard in Aptheker, ed., *The Correspondence of W. E. B. Du Bois,* vol. 1, 92–104.

59. Du Bois, "Team Work," *The Crisis* 14 (August 1917): 165–6. See also "The Present," *The Crisis* 14 (August 1917): 165.

60. George G. Bradford to Du Bois, in *The Crisis* 16 (May 1918): 7.

61. Du Bois, "The Black Soldier," *The Crisis* 16 (June 1918): 60; Young, "A Comrade to Comrades," *The Crisis* 16 (June 1918): 59–60.

62. On Du Bois's writing of "Close Ranks" and the pending captain's commission, see Ellis, " 'Closing Ranks' and 'Seeking Honors,' " 96–124; and William Jordan, " 'The Damnable Dilemma,' " 1562–90. On Du Bois's disingenuous response to the allegations uncovered by Ellis and Jordan, compare Du Bois's letter to Lafayette M. Hershaw, August 5, 1918, in Aptheker, ed., *The Correspondence of W. E. B. Du Bois,* vol. 1, 229, in which Du Bois tells Hershaw that he had first heard of the proposed captaincy "two weeks after the July *Crisis* was in print," to the evidence presented in Ellis (" 'Closing Ranks' and 'Seeking Honors,' " 105–6) that has Du Bois in Washington on June 4 in Spingarn's own office at Military Intelligence.

63. Byron Gunner to Du Bois, July 25, 1918, in Aptheker, *Correspondence of W. E. B. Du Bois,* vol. 1, 228.

64. "A Philosophy in Time of War," *The Crisis* 16 (September 1918): 216–7, in Aptheker, ed., *Selections from* The Crisis, vol. 1, 162–3.

CONCLUSION

1. Jane Addams, *Peace and Bread in Time of War* (New York: King's Crown Press, 1945), 110–5.

2. "Closing Ranks Again," *Amsterdam News* (February 14, 1942), in David Levering Lewis, ed., *W. E. B. Du Bois: A Reader* (New York: Henry Holt, 1995), 739.

3. Du Bois, "Patriotism," *The Crisis* 17 (November 1918): 10.

4. See Linda K. Kerber, "A Constitutional Right to Be Treated Like American Ladies: Women and the Obligations of Citizenship," in Linda K. Kerber, Alice Kessler-Harris, and Kathryn Kish Sklar, eds., *U.S. History as Women's History: New Feminist Essays* (Chapel Hill: University of North Carolina Press, 1995), 19–20; and Gordon S. Wood, *The Creation of the American Republic, 1776–1787* (New York: W. W. Norton, 1967), especially chapters 10 and 13. The debate over the liberalism or republicanism or liberal-republicanism of the founding era is summarized in James T. Kloppenberg, "The Virtues of Liberalism: Christianity, Liberalism, and Ethics in Early American Political Discourse," *Journal of American History* 74, no. 1 (June 1987): 9–33; and "Republicanism in American History and Historiography," *The Tocqueville Review* 13, no. 1 (1992): 119–36.

5. Roosevelt quoted in Kerber, "A Constitutional Right to Be Treated Like American Ladies," 33.

6. Lasch uses the term "sensibility" to avoid the reifying effect of "intellectual tradition"; "sensibility" is more protean, more commodious; see *The True and Only Heaven: Progress and Its Critics* (New York: W. W. Norton, 1991), 17; on the "republican" sensibility Lasch delineates, see 49–52, 168–76; on memory and nostalgia, see 82–3.

7. "real aristocracy . . . wrong with our ideals": W. E. B. Du Bois, "Abraham

Lincoln," *Voice of the Negro* 4 (June 1907): 242–7, in Aptheker, ed., *Others,* vol. 1, 373; "the lessons of great men . . . of their highest ideals": "Address of Miss Jane Addams [on George Washington]," Union League Club, Chicago (Chicago: Metcalf Stationary Co., 1903), 9, JAP. Addams refers to Du Bois's speech in *Twenty Years at Hull-House,* chapter 11, remarking that his Greek audience listened "with apparently no consciousness of that race difference which color seems to accentuate so absurdly"; see 149.

8. See Alexis de Tocqueville, *Democracy in America,* 527, 539–41. Tocqueville's notion of "self-interest rightly understood" jibes with Thomas L. Haskell's analysis of the role of contracts in the expansion of "recipe knowledge" in the eighteenth and nineteenth centuries. See "Capitalism and the Origins of Humanitarian Sensibility, Part 2," in Thomas Bender, ed., *The Antislavery Debate: Capitalism and Abolitionism as a Problem in Historical Interpretation* (Berkeley and Los Angeles: University of California Press, 1992), 136–60.

WORKS CITED

Addams, Jane. *Democracy and Social Ethics*. Cambridge: Harvard University Press, 1965 [1902].

———. *The Jane Addams Papers*. Ann Arbor: University Microfilms International, 1984. (JAP)

———. *The Long Road of Woman's Memory*. New York: Macmillan, 1917.

———. *Newer Ideals of Peace*. New York: Macmillan, 1911 [1907].

———. *The Overthrow of the War System*. Boston: Forum, 1915.

———. *Peace and Bread in Time of War*. New York: King's Crown Press, 1945 [1922].

———. *The Social Thought of Jane Addams*. Ed. Christopher Lasch. New York: Irvington, 1965.

———. *Twenty Years at Hull House*. Urbana: University of Illinois Press, 1990 [1909].

———. *Women at the Hague: The International Congress of Women and Its Results*. New York: Macmillan, 1915.

Anderson, Benedict. *Imagined Communities: Reflections on the Origin and Spread of Nationalism*. New York: Verso, 1991.

———. *The Spectre of Comparisons: Nationalism, Southeast Asia, and the World*. New York: Verso, 1998.

Appiah, K. Anthony. "Against National Culture." In Laura Garcia-Moreno and Peter C. Pfeiffer, eds., *Text and Nation: Cross-Disciplinary Essays on Cultural and National Identities*. Columbia, SC: Camden House, 1996.

———. "Cosmopolitan Patriots." In Joshua Cohen, ed., *For Love of Country: Debating the Limits of Patriotism*. Boston: Beacon Press, 1996.

———. "Identity, Authenticity, Survival: Multicultural Societies and Social Reconstruction." In Amy Gutmann, ed., *Multiculturalism: Examining the Politics of Recognition*. Princeton: Princeton University Press, 1994.

———. "Race, Culture, Identity: Misunderstood Connections." Pp. 30–105 in Appiah and Amy Gutmann, eds., *Color Conscious: The Political Morality of Race*. Princeton: Princeton University Press, 1996.

———. "The Uncompleted Argument: Du Bois and the Illusion of Race." In Henry Louis Gates Jr., ed., *"Race," Writing, and Difference*. Chicago: University of Chicago Press, 1986.

Appleby, Joyce. *Capitalism and the New Social Order: The Republican Vision of the 1790s*. New York: New York University Press, 1984.

Arendt, Hannah. *Imperialism: Part Two of the Origins of Totalitarianism.* New York: Harvest Books, 1968.

———. *Lectures on Kant's Political Philosophy.* Chicago: University of Chicago Press, 1989.

Armitage, David. "Empire and Liberty: A Republican Dilemma," forthcoming in Martin van Gelderan and Quentin Skinner, eds., *Republicanism: A Shared European Heritage,* vol. 2: *The Values of Republicanism* (Cambridge: Cambridge University Press, 2002).

———. *The Ideological Origins of the British Empire.* Cambridge: Cambridge University Press, 2000.

Banton, Michael. *The Idea of Race.* London: Tavistock, 1977.

———. *Racial Theories.* Cambridge: Cambridge University Press, 1998.

de Beauvoir, Simone. *The Second Sex.* New York: Vintage, 1989.

Bederman, Gail. *Manliness and Civilization: A Cultural History of Gender and Race in the United States, 1880–1917.* Chicago: University of Chicago Press, 1995.

Beiser, Frederick C. *Enlightenment, Revolution, and Romanticism: The Genesis of Modern German Political Thought, 1790–1800.* Cambridge: Harvard University Press, 1992.

Beisner, Robert L. *Twelve Against Empire: The Anti-Imperialists, 1898–1900.* Chicago: University of Chicago Press, 1985.

Benhabib, Seyla. *Situating the Self: Gender, Community and Postmodernism in Contemporary Ethics.* London: Routledge, 1992.

Berger, Suzanne, and Ronald Dore, eds. *National Diversity and Global Capitalism.* Ithaca: Cornell University Press, 1996.

Berkowitz, Peter. *Virtue and the Making of Modern Liberalism.* Princeton: Princeton University Press, 1999.

Bernstein, Richard J. *The New Constellation: The Ethical-Political Horizons of Modernity/Postmodernity.* Cambridge: MIT Press, 1992.

Blake, Casey Nelson. *Beloved Community: The Cultural Criticism of Randolph Bourne, Van Wyck Brooks, Waldo Frank, and Lewis Mumford.* Chapel Hill: University of North Carolina Press, 1990.

Blight, David W. *Race and Reunion: The Civil War in American Memory.* Cambridge: Harvard University Press, 2001.

Bodnar, John. *Remaking America: Public Memory, Commemoration, and Patriotism in the Twentieth Century.* Princeton: Princeton University Press, 1992.

———, ed. *Bonds of Affection: Americans Define Their Patriotism.* Princeton: Princeton University Press, 1996.

Boesche, Roger, ed. *Alexis de Tocqueville: Selected Letters on Politics and Society.* Berkeley and Los Angeles: University of California Press, 1985.

Bourne, Randolph. "The Jew and Trans-National America." *Menorah Journal* 2 (December 1916): 277–84.

———. *The Radical Will: Randolph Bourne Selected Writings, 1911–1918.* Ed. Olaf Hansen. New York: Urizen Books, 1977.

———. "Trans-National America." *Atlantic Monthly* 100 (July 1916): 86–97.

———. *War and the Intellectuals: Essays by R. S. Bourne, 1915–1918.* Ed. Carl Resek. New York: Harper and Row, 1965.

Bramen, Carrie Tirado. *The Uses of Variety: Modern Americanism and the Quest for National Distinctiveness.* Cambridge: Harvard University Press, 2000.

Brandeis, Louis. "A Call to the Educated Jew." Pp. 59–69 in *Brandeis on Zionism: A Collection of Addresses and Statements by Louis D. Brandeis.* Westport, CT: Hyperion Press, 1942.

———. "The Jewish Problem, How to Solve It." Pp. 12–35 in *Brandeis on Zionism.*

———. "Jews and Arabs." Pp. 150–153 in *Brandeis on Zionism.*

———. "True Americanism." Pp. 3–11 in *Brandeis on Zionism.*

Brennan, Timothy. *At Home in the World: Cosmopolitanism Now.* Cambridge: Harvard University Press, 1997.

Breuilly, John. *Nationalism and the State.* Chicago: University of Chicago Press, 1993.

Brotz, Howard, ed. *Negro Social and Political Thought: 1850–1920.* New York: Basic Books, 1996.

Butler, Judith. "Universality in Culture." In Joshua Cohen, ed., *For Love of Country.* Boston: Beacon Press, 1996.

Cheah, Pheng, and Bruce Robbins, eds. *Cosmopolitics: Thinking and Feeling Beyond the Nation.* Minneapolis: University of Minnesota Press, 1998.

Cocks, Joan. *Passion and Paradox: Intellectuals Confront the National Question.* Princeton: Princeton University Press, 2002.

Cohen, Joshua, ed. *For Love of Country: Debating the Limits of Patriotism.* Boston: Beacon Press, 1996.

Cohen, Morris R. "Zionism: Tribalism or Liberalism." *The New Republic,* March 8, 1919, 182.

Cotkin, George. *William James, Public Philosopher.* Urbana: University of Illinois Press, 1994.

de Crèvecoeur, J. Hector St. John. *Letters from an American Farmer and Sketches of Eighteenth-Century America.* New York: Penguin, 1981 [1782].

Croly, Herbert. *The Promise of American Life.* Cambridge: Harvard University Press, 1965 [1909].

Currie, Harold W. *Eugene V. Debs.* Boston: Twayne, 1976.

Curti, Merle. *The Roots of American Loyalty.* New York: Russell and Russell, 1946.

———. "Wanted: A History of American Patriotism." *Proceedings of the Middle States Association of History and Social Science Teachers* 36 (1938).

Davis, Allen F. *American Heroine: The Life and Legend of Jane Addams.* New York: Oxford University Press, 1973.

Debs, Eugene V. *Eugene V. Debs Speaks.* Ed. James P. Cannon. New York: Pathfinder, 1970.

———. *Letters of Eugene V. Debs.* Ed. J. Robert Constantine. 3 vols. Urbana: University of Illinois Press, 1990.

———. *The Papers of Eugene V. Debs, 1834–1945.* Sanford, NC: Microfilming Corporation of America, 1982. (PEVD)

Dewey, John. *Correspondence of John Dewey.* Ed. Larry A. Hackman. Vol. 1 [computer file]. Charlottesville, VA: InteLex Corp., 1999.

————. *Democracy and Education: An Introduction to the Philosophy of Education.* New York: Free Press, 1966 [1916].

————. *The Middle Works, 1899–1924.* Ed. Jo Ann Boydston. 15 vols. Carbondale: Southern Illinois University Press, 1981–90.

Dharwadker, Vinay, ed. *Cosmopolitan Geographies: New Locations in Literature and Culture.* New York: Routledge, 2001.

Dietz, Mary G. "Patriotism." In Terence Ball, James Farr, and Russell L. Hanson, eds., *Political Innovation and Conceptual Change.* New York: Cambridge University Press, 1989.

Douglass, Frederick. "An Address to the Colored People of the United States." In Howard Brotz, ed., *Negro Social and Political Thought: 1850–1920.* New York: Basic Books, 1996.

————. "The Claims of the Negro Ethnologically Considered." In Howard Brotz, ed., *Negro Social and Political Thought: 1850–1920.* New York: Basic Books, 1996.

————. "The Future of the Colored Race." In Howard Brotz, ed., *Negro Social and Political Thought: 1850–1920.* New York: Basic Books, 1996.

————. "The Nation's Problem." In Howard Brotz, ed., *Negro Social and Political Thought: 1850–1920.* New York: Basic Books, 1996.

Du Bois, W. E. B. "The Conservation of Races." *American Negro Academy Occasional Papers* 2 (1897): 5–15.

————. *Correspondence of W. E. B. Du Bois.* Ed. Herbert Aptheker. Amherst: University of Massachusetts Press, 1973.

————. *The Papers of W. E. B. Du Bois, 1868–1963.* Sanford, NC: Microfilming Corporation of America, 1979.

————. *The Souls of Black Folk.* New York: Signet Classic, 1982 [1903].

————. "The Strivings of the Negro People." *Atlantic Monthly* 80 (August 1897): 194–8.

————. *Writings by W. E. B. Du Bois in Periodicals Edited by Himself: Selections from* The Crisis. Ed. Herbert Aptheker. Millwood, NY: Kraus-Thomson, 1983.

————. *Writings by W. E. B. Du Bois in Periodicals Edited by Himself: Selections from* The Horizon. Ed. Herbert Aptheker. White Plains, NY: Kraus-Thomson, 1985.

————. *Writings by W. E. B. Du Bois in Periodicals Edited by Others.* Ed. Herbert Aptheker. Millwood, NY: Kraus-Thomson, 1982.

Eisenach, Eldon. *The Lost Promise of Progressivism.* Lawrence: University Press of Kansas, 1994.

Elshtain, Jean Bethke. *Democracy on Trial.* New York: Basic Books, 1995.

————. *Jane Addams and the Dream of American Democracy.* New York: Basic Books, 2002.

Emerson, Ralph Waldo. "English Traits." In Brooks Atkinson, ed., *The Selected Writings of Ralph Waldo Emerson.* New York: The Modern Library, 1992.

Ethington, Philip. *Public City: The Reconstruction of Urban Life in San Francisco, 1850–1900.* New York: Cambridge University Press, 1994.

Etzioni, Amitai, ed. *Rights and the Common Good: The Communitarian Perspective.* New York: St. Martin's Press, 1995.

Everett, William. "Patriotism: An Oration Delivered Before the Phi Betta Kappa of

Harvard College, Commencement, 1900." Philadelphia: Peace Association of Friends, 1901.

Fox, Richard Wightman, and T. J. Jackson Lears, eds. *The Culture of Consumption: Critical Essays in American History*. Chicago: University of Chicago Press, 1993.

Fraser, Nancy. "Another Pragmatism: Alain Locke, Critical 'Race' Theory, and the Politics of Culture." In Morris Dickstein, ed., *The Revival of Pragmatism*. Durham: Duke University Press, 1988.

Fredrickson, George M. *The Inner Civil War: Northern Intellectuals and the Crisis of the Union*. Urbana: University of Illinois Press, 1993.

Gal, Allon. "Brandeis, Judaism, and Zionism." Pp. 76–83 in Nelson L. Dawson, ed., *Brandeis and America*. Louisville: University Press of Kentucky, 1989.

Genovese, Eugene D., and Elizabeth Fox-Genovese. *Fruits of Merchant Capital: Slavery and Bourgeois Property in the Rise and Expansion of Capitalism*. New York: Oxford University Press, 1983.

Gerstle, Gary. *American Crucible: Race and Nation in the Twentieth Century*. Princeton: Princeton University Press, 2001.

———. "Liberty, Coercion, and the Making of Americans." *Journal of American History* (September 1997): 524–58.

———. *Working Class Americanism: The Politics of Labor in a Textile City, 1914–1960*. New York: Cambridge University Press, 1989.

Geunter, Scot M. *The American Flag, 1777–1924: Cultural Shifts from Creation to Codification*. Cranbury: Associated University Presses, 1990.

Ginger, Ray. *The Bending Cross: A Biography of Eugene Victor Debs*. New York: Russell and Russell, 1969.

Glazer, Nathan. *We Are All Multiculturalists Now*. Cambridge: Harvard University Press, 1997.

Gleason, Philip J. "American Identity and Americanization." In Stephan Thernstrom, ed., *Harvard Encyclopedia of American Ethnic Groups*. Cambridge: Harvard University Press, 1980.

———. *Speaking of Diversity: Language and Ethnicity in Twentieth-Century America*. Baltimore: Johns Hopkins University Press, 1992.

Glendon, Mary Ann. *Rights Talk: The Impoverishment of Political Discourse*. New York: The Free Press, 1991.

Goodwyn, Lawrence. *Democratic Promise: The Populist Moment in America*. New York: Oxford University Press, 1978.

Greenfeld, Leah. *Nationalism: Five Roads to Modernity*. Cambridge: Harvard University Press, 1992.

Griswold, Charles L. *Adam Smith and the Virtues of Enlightenment*. Cambridge: Cambridge University Press, 1999.

Gutman, Herbert. *Work, Culture, and Society in Industrializing America*. New York: Vintage, 1977.

Gutmann, Amy, ed. *Multiculturalism: Examining the Politics of Recognition*. Princeton: Princeton University Press, 1994.

Habermas, Jurgen. "Concluding Remarks." In Craig Calhoun, ed., *Habermas and the Pubic Sphere*. Cambridge: MIT Press, 1994.

————. *Theory of Communicative Action,* vol. 2: *Lifeworld and System: A Critique of Functionalist Reason.* Boston: Beacon Press, 1989.

Hannaford, Ivan. *Race: The History of an Idea in the West.* Washington, DC: Woodrow Wilson Center Press, 1996.

Hannerz, Ulf. *Transnational Connections: Culture, People, Places.* New York: Routledge, 1996.

Haraway, Donna. "Teddy Bear Patriarchy: Taxidermy in the Garden of Eden, New York City, 1908–1936." In Kaplan, Amy and Donald E. Pease, eds. *Cultures of US Imperialism.* Durham, NC: Duke University Press, 1993.

Harvey, David. *The Condition of Postmodernity: An Inquiry into the Origins of Cultural Change.* Cambridge, MA: Basil Blackwell, 1988.

Haskell, Thomas L. "Capitalism and the Origins of the Humanitarian Sensibility, Part 2." In Thomas Bender, ed., *The Antislavery Debate: Capitalism and Abolitionism as a Problem in Historical Interpretation.* Berkeley and Los Angeles: University of California Press, 1992.

————. "The Curious Persistence of Rights Talk in the 'Age of Interpretation.'" *Journal of American History,* 74 (1987), 984–1012.

Held, David, and Anthony McGrew, eds. *The Global Transformations Reader: An Introduction to the Globalization Debate.* Malden, MA: Blackwell, 2000.

————. *Global Transformations.* Stanford: Stanford University Press, 1999.

Higham, John. "Ethnic Pluralism in Modern American Thought." Pp. 197–230 in *Send These to Me: Jews and Other Immigrants in Urban America.* New York: Atheneum, 1975.

————. *Strangers in the Land: Patterns of Nativism, 1860–1925.* New York: Atheneum, 1968.

Hobsbawm, Eric. *Nations and Nationalism since 1780.* New York: Cambridge University Press, 1990.

Hofstadter, Richard. "Cuba, the Philippines, and Manifest Destiny." *The Paranoid Style in American Politics and Other Essays.* Cambridge: Harvard University Press, 1965.

Hoganson, Kristin L. *Fighting for American Manhood: How Gender Politics Provoked the Spanish-American and Philippines-American Wars.* New Haven: Yale University Press, 1998.

Hollinger, David A. "Democracy and the Melting Pot Reconsidered." *In the American Province: Studies in the History and Historiography of Ideas.* Baltimore: Johns Hopkins University Press, 1985.

————. "Ethnic Diversity, Cosmopolitanism, and the Emergence of the American Liberal Intelligentsia." *In the American Province: Studies in the History and Historiography of* Ideas. Baltimore: Johns Hopkins University Press, 1985.

————. "How Wide the Circle of the 'We'? American Intellectuals and the Problem of the Ethnos Since World War II," *American Historical Review* 98 (April 1993): 317–37.

————. *Morris R. Cohen and the Scientific Ideal.* Cambridge: MIT Press, 1975.

————. "National Culture and Communities of Descent." *Reviews in American History* 26 (March 1998): 312–28.

————. "National Solidarity at the End of the Twentieth Century: Reflections on the United States and Liberal Nationalism." *Journal of American History* 84 (September 1997): 559–69.

———. "Nationalism, Cosmopolitanism, and the United States." In Noah M. J. Pickus, ed., *Immigration and Citizenship in the Twenty-First Century.* New York: Rowman and Littlefield, 1998.

———. "Not Universalists, Not Pluralists: The New Cosmopolitans Find Their Own Way." *Constellations* 8 (2001).

———. *Postethnic America: Beyond Multiculturalism.* New York: Basic Books, 2000.

Holmes, Oliver Wendell, Jr. "The Soldiers Faith." *The Occasional Speeches of Oliver Wendell Holmes.* Ed. Mark De Wolfe. Cambridge: Harvard University Press, 1962.

Holmes, Stephen. *Passions and Constraint: On the Theory of Liberal Democracy.* Chicago: University of Chicago Press, 1995.

Hulliung, Mark. *Citizen Machiavelli.* Princeton: Princeton University Press, 1983.

Ignatieff, Michael. *Blood and Belonging: Journeys into the New Nationalism.* New York: Farrar, Straus, and Giroux, 1993.

Jacobson, Matthew Frye. *Barbarian Virtues: The United States Encounters Foreign Peoples at Home and Abroad, 1876–1917.* New York: Hill and Wang, 2000.

James, Henry. *The American Scene.* New York: Penguin, 1994.

James, William. *Talks to Teachers on Psychology: and to Students on Some of Life's Ideals.* New York: W. W. Norton, 1958 [1899].

———. "Robert Gould Shaw." Pp. 37–61 in *Memories and Studies.* New York: Longmans, Green and Co., 1912.

———. *Essays, Comments, and Reviews.* Ed. Frederick H. Burkhardt. Cambridge: Harvard University Press, 1987.

———. *The Correspondence of William James.* Ed. Ignas K. Skrupskelis and Elizabeth M. Berkeley. Charottesville: University Press of Virginia, 1994.

———. *The Letters of William James.* Ed. Henry James. New York: Kraus Reprint Company, 1969.

———. *The Moral Equivalent of War, and Other Essays.* Ed. John Roth. New York: Harper and Row, 1971.

———. *The Writings of William James.* Ed. John McDermott. Chicago: University of Chicago Press, 1967.

Jameson, Fredric, and Masao Miyoshi, eds. *The Cultures of Globalization.* Durham: Duke University Press, 1998.

Kallen, Horace. *Culture and Democracy in the United States.* New York: Boni and Liveright, 1924.

———. "Democracy *Versus* the Melting Pot." *The Nation,* February 18 and 25, 1915, 190–4, 217–20.

———. "Zionism: Democracy or Prussianism." *The New Republic,* April 5, 1919, 311–3.

Kammen, Michael. *Mystic Chords of Memory: The Transformation of Tradition in American Culture.* New York: A. E. Knopf, 1991.

Kaplan, Amy, and Donald E. Pease, eds. *Cultures of U.S. Imperialism.* Durham, NC: Duke University Press, 1993.

Kerber, Linda K. "A Constitutional Right to Be Treated Like American Ladies: Women and the Obligations of Citizenship." In Linda K. Kerber, Alice Kessler-Harris, and Kathryn Kish Sklar, eds., *U.S. History as Women's History: New Feminist Essays*. Chapel Hill: University of North Carolina Press, 1995.

Kloppenberg, James T. "Republicanism in American History and Historiography." *Tocqueville Review* 13, no. 1 (1992): 119–136.

———. *Uncertain Victory: Social Democracy and Progressivism*. New York, Oxford University Press, 1986.

———. *The Virtues of Liberalism*. New York: Oxford University Press, 1998.

———. "The Virtues of Liberalism: Christianity, Liberalism, and Ethics in Early American Political Discourse," *Journal of American History* 74, no. 1 (June 1987): 9–33.

King, Desmond. *Making Americans: Immigration, Race, and the Origins of the Diverse Diversity*. Cambridge: Harvard University Press, 2000.

Knock, Thomas. *To End All Wars: Woodrow Wilson and the Quest for a New World Order*. New York: Oxford University Press, 1992.

Kymlicka, Will. "Misunderstanding Nationalism." *Dissent* (winter 1995): 130–7.

———. *Multicultural Citizenship: A Liberal Theory of Minority Rights* (Oxford: Clarendon Press, 1995.

Lasch, Christopher. "The Anti-Imperialists, the Philippines, and the Inequality of Man." *The World of Nations: Reflections on American History, Politics, and Culture*. New York: Vintage, 1972, 70–9.

———. *The New Radicalism in America: The Intellectual as a Social Type, 1889–1963*. New York: W. W. Norton, 1965.

———. *The Revolt of the Elites and the Betrayal of Democracy*. New York: W. W. Norton, 1995.

———. *The True and Only Heaven: Progress and Its Critics*. New York: W. W. Norton, 1991.

———, ed. *The Social Thought of Jane Addams*. New York: Irvington, 1982 [1965].

Lears, T. J. Jackson. *No Place of Grace: Antimodernism and the Transformation of American Culture, 1880–1920*. New York: Pantheon, 1981.

Lewis, David L. *W. E. B. Du Bois: A Biography of a Race, 1868–1919*. New York: Henry Holt, 1993.

Lincoln, Abraham. "The Perpetuation of Our Political Institutions." Pp. 108–15 in Roy P. Basler, ed., *The Collected Works of Abraham Lincoln*, vol. 1. New Brunswick: Rutgers University Press, 1953.

Lind, Michael. *The Next American Nation: The New Nationalism and the Fourth American Revolution*. New York: The Free Press, 1995.

Linn, James Weber. *Jane Addams: A Biography*. Urbana: University of Illinois Press, 2000.

Lipsitz, George. "Dilemmas of Beset Nationhood: Patriotism, The Family, and Economic Change in the 1970s and 1980s." Pp. 250–72 in John Bodnar, ed., *Bonds of Affection: Americans Define Their Patriotism*. Princeton: Princeton University Press, 1996.

Lissak, Rivka Shpak. *Pluralism and Progressives: Hull House and the New Immigration, 1890–1919*. Chicago: University of Chicago Press, 1989.

Livingston, James. *Pragmatism and the Political Economy of Cultural Revolution, 1850–1940*. Chapel Hill: University of North Carolina Press, 1994.

Locke, Alain. *Race Contacts and Interracial Relations: Lectures on the Theory and Practice of Race*. Ed. Jeffrey C. Stewart. Washington, DC: Howard University Press, 1992.

Lott, Eric. "The New Cosmopolitanism: Whose America?" *Transition* 72 (fall 1996): 108–35.

Lutz, Tom. *American Nervousness, 1903: An Anecdotal History*. Ithaca: Cornell University Press, 1991.

Lynd, Robert S. and Helen Lynd. *Middletown: A Study in Modern American Culture*. New York: Harcourt Brace Jovanovich, 1957.

MacIntyre, Alasdair. "Is Patriotism a Virtue?" The Lindley Lecture. Lawrence: University Press of Kansas, 1984.

Marx, Karl. "The German Ideology." In Robert Tucker, ed., *The Marx-Engels Reader*. New York: W. W. Norton, 1978.

———. "On the Jewish Question." In Robert Tucker, ed., *The Marx-Engels Reader*. New York: W. W. Norton, 1978.

Marx, Leo. "Neglecting History." *Boston Review* 19 (October—November 1994).

May, Ernest. *American Imperialism: A Speculative Essay*. Chicago: Imprint Productions, 1991.

McConnell, Stuart. *Glorious Contentment: The Grand Army of the Republic, 1865–1900*. Chapel Hill: University of North Carolina Press, 1992.

McCoy, Drew R. *The Elusive Republic: Political Economy in Jeffersonian America*. Chapel Hill: University of North Carolina Press, 1980.

McLaren, Peter. "White Terror and Oppositional Agency: Towards a Critical Multiculturalism. In David Theo Goldberg, ed., *Multiculturalism: A Critical Reader*. Cambridge, MA: Blackwell, 1996, 45–74.

Mehta, Pratap Bhanu. "Cosmopolitanism and the Circle of Reason." *Political Theory* 28 (October 2000): 619–39.

Mehta, Uday Singh. *Liberalism and Empire: A Study in Nineteenth-Century British Liberal Thought*. Chicago: University of Chicago Press, 1999.

Menand, Louis. *The Metaphysical Club*. New York: Farrar, Straus, and Giroux, 2001.

Mercer, Kobena. "Welcome to the Jungle: Identity and Diversity in Postmodern Politics." In Jonathan Rutherford, ed., *Identity: Community, Culture, Difference*. London: Lawrence and Wishart, 1990.

Miller, David. *On Nationality*. Oxford: Clarendon Press, 1997.

Miller, Stuart Creighton. *"Benevolent Assimilation": The American Conquest of the Philippines, 1899–1903*. New Haven: Yale University Press, 1982.

Mittelman, James H., and Norani Othman, eds. *Capturing Globalization*. New York: Routledge, 2001.

———. *The Globalization Syndrome: Transformation and Resistance*. Princeton: Princeton University Press, 2000.

Montaigne, Michel de. *The Complete Essays*. Ed. Donald M. Frame. Stanford: Stanford University Press, 1958.

Morgan, Edmund S. *Inventing the People: The Rise of Popular Sovereignty in England and America*. New York: W. W. Norton, 1988.

Moses, Wilson J. *The Golden Age of Black Nationalism, 1850–1925*. New York: Oxford University Press, 1978.

Nathanson, Stephen. "In Defense of 'Moderate Patriotism,' " *Ethics* 99 (April 1989): 535–52.

———. *Patriotism, Morality, and Peace*. New York: Rowman and Littlefield, 1993.

Neather, Andrew. "Labor, Republicanism, Race, and Popular Patriotism in the Era of Empire." Pp. 82–101 in Bodnar, ed., *Bonds of Affection: Americans Define Their Patriotism*. Princeton: Princeton University Press, 1996.

Neumann, William L., ed. *Jane Addams: A Centennial Reader*. New York: Macmillan, 1960.

Nussbaum, Martha Craven. "Patriotism and Cosmopolitanism." In Joshua Cohen, ed., *For Love of Country*. Boston: Beacon Press, 1996.

O'Brien, Karen. *Narratives of Enlightenment: Cosmopolitan History from Voltaire to Gibbon*. Cambridge: Cambridge University Press, 1997.

O'Leary, Cecilia Elizabeth. " 'Blood Brotherhood': The Racialization of Patriotism, 1865–1918." Pp. 53–81 in John Bodnar, ed., *Bonds of Affection: Americans Define Their Patriotism*. Princeton: Princeton University Press, 1996.

———. *To Die For: The Paradox of American Patriotism*. Princeton: Princeton University Press, 1999.

Outlaw, Lucius T. *On Race and Philosophy*. New York: Routledge, 1996.

Perry, Ralph Barton. *The Thought and Character of William James*, vol. 2. Boston: Little, Brown, 1935.

Pfaff, William. *The Wrath of Nations: Civilization and the Furies of Nationalism*. New York: Simon and Schuster, 1993.

Phillips, Kevin. *Wealth and Democracy: How Great Fortunes and Government Created America's Aristocracy*. New York: Broadway Books, 2002.

Pocock, J. G. A. *The Machiavellian Moment: Florentine Political Thought and the Atlantic Republican Tradition*. Princeton: Princeton University Press, 1975.

Posnock, Ross. *Color and Culture: Black Writers and the Making of the Modern Intellectual*. Cambridge: Harvard University Press, 1998.

———. "The Dream of Deracination: The Uses of Cosmopolitanism." *American Literary History* (2000).

———. "The Politics of Nonidentity: A Genealogy." In Donald F. Pease, ed., *National Identities and Post-Americanist Narratives*. Durham, NC: Duke University Press, 1994.

———. *The Trial of Curiosity: Henry James, William James, and the Challenge of Modernity*. New York: Oxford University Press, 1991.

Radway, Janice A. *Reading the Romance: Women, Patriarchy, and Popular Literature*. Chapel Hill: University of North Carolina Press, 1984.

Reed, Adolph L., Jr. *W. E. B. Du Bois and American Political Thought*. New York: Oxford University Press, 1997.

Riordan, William. *Plunkitt of Tammany Hall*. New York: Penguin, 1991.

Robbins, Bruce, and Pheng Cheah, eds. *Cosmopolitics: Thinking and Feeling Beyond the Nation*. Minneapolis: University of Minnesota Press, 1998.

———. *Feeling Global: Internationalism in Distress*. New York: New York University Press, 1999.

Rodgers, Daniel T. *Atlantic Crossings: Social Politics in a Progressive Age.* Cambridge: Harvard University Press, 1998.

———. "Republicanism: The Career of a Concept." *Journal of American History* 79 (June 1992): 11–38.

———. *The Work Ethic in Industrial America, 1850–1920.* Chicago: University of Chicago Press, 1974.

Rogers, Howard J., ed. *Congress of Arts and Science, Universal Exposition, St. Louis, 1904,* vol. 7. Boston: Houghton Mifflin, 1906.

Roosevelt, Theodore. *The Strenuous Life: Essays and Addresses.* New York: The Century Co, 1918.

———. *Theodore Roosevelt: An American Mind.* Ed. Mario R. DiNunzio. New York: Penguin, 1994.

———. *The Winning of the West: The Spread of the English-Speaking Peoples.* New York: G. P. Putnam's Sons, 1889–96.

Rorty, Richard. *Achieving Our Country: Leftist Thought in Twentieth-Century America.* Cambridge: Harvard University Press, 1998.

———. *Contingency, Irony, Solidarity.* Cambridge: Cambridge University Press, 1989.

Rosenzweig, Roy. *Eight Hours for What We Will: Workers and Leisure in an Industrial City, 1870–1920.* Cambridge: Cambridge University Press, 1983.

Roth, Philip. *The Human Stain.* Boston: Houghton Mifflin, 2000.

Rotundo, E. Anthony. *American Manhood: Transformations in Masculinity from the Revolution to the Modern Era.* New York: Basic Books, 1993.

Royce, Josiah. *The Philosophy of Loyalty.* New York: Macmillan, 1908.

Rudy, Sayres. "Subjectivity, Political Evaluation, and Islamist Trajectories." In Birgit Schäbler, ed., *Globalization and the Muslim World.* SUNY Press, forthcoming.

Said, Edward W. *Orientalism.* New York: Vintage, 1994.

Salvatore, Nick. *Eugene V. Debs: Citizen and Socialist.* Urbana: University of Illinois Press, 1982.

Sandel, Michael J. *Democracy's Discontent: America in Search of a Public Philosophy.* Cambridge: Harvard University Press, 1996.

Santayana, George. *The Middle Span.* New York: Charles Scribner's Sons, 1945.

Saunders, Robert M. *In Search of Woodrow Wilson: Beliefs and Behavior.* Westport, CT: Greenwood Press, 1998.

Savage, Kirk. "The Politics of Memory: Black Emancipation and the Civil War Monument." In John R. Gillis, ed., *Commemorations: The Politics of National Identity.* Princeton: Princeton University Press, 1994.

Schaar, John. "The Case for Patriotism." *American Review* 17 (May 1973): 59–99.

Scheffler, Samuel. *Families, Nations, and Strangers.* Lawrence: University Press of Kansas, 1995.

Schirmer, Daniel B., and Stephen Rosskamm Shalom, eds. *The Philippines Reader: A History of Colonialism, Neocolonialism, Dictatorship, and Resistance.* Boston: South End Press, 1987.

Schlereth, Thomas J. *The Cosmopolitan Ideal in Enlightenment Thought.* Notre Dame: University of Notre Dame Press, 1977.

Sen, Amartya. "East and West: The Reach of Reason." *New York Review of Books* (July 20, 2000).

———. *Human Rights and Asian Values*. New York: Carnegie Council on Ethics and International Affairs, 1997.

———. "Other People: Beyond Identity." *New Republic,* December 18, 2000, 23–30.

———. "Tagore and His India." *New York Review of Books* (June 26, 1997).

Silber, Nina. *The Romance of Reunion: Northerners and the South, 1865–1900.* Chapel Hill: University of North Carolina Press, 1993.

Simone, Timothy Maliqualim. *About Face: Race in Postmodern America.* Brooklyn, NY: Autonomedia, 1989.

Sklar, Kathryn Kish. *Florence Kelly and the Nation's Work: The Rise of Women's Political Culture, 1830–1900.* New Haven: Yale University Press, 1995.

Sklar, Martin J. *The Corporate Reconstruction of American Capitalism, 1890–1916: The Market, the Law and Politics.* New York: Cambridge University Press, 1988.

Slater, Robert O., et al., eds. *Global Transformation and the Third World.* Boulder: Lynne Rienner, 1993.

Smith, Adam. *An Inquiry into the Nature and Causes of the Wealth of Nations.* Ed. R. H. Campbell and A. S. Skinner. Oxford: Clarendon Press, 1976.

Smith, Rogers. "The 'American Creed' and American Identity: The Limits of Liberal Citizenship in the United States." *Western Political Quarterly* 41 (1988): 225–51.

———. *Civic Ideals: Conflicting Visions of Citizenship in U.S. History.* New Haven: Yale University Press, 1997.

Sollors, Werner. *Beyond Ethnicity: Consent and Descent in American Culture.* New York: Oxford University Press, 1986.

———. "A Critique of Pure Pluralism." In Sacvan Bercovitch, ed., *Reconstructing American Literary History.* Cambridge: Harvard University Press, 1986.

Stanley, Peter W., ed. *Reappraising an Empire: New Perspectives on Philippines-American History.* Cambridge: Harvard University Press, 1984.

Stout, Jeffrey. *Ethics After Babel: The Languages of Morals and Their Discontents.* Boston: Beacon Press, 1988.

Tamir, Yael. *Liberal Nationalism.* Princeton: Princeton University Press, 1993.

Taylor, Charles. "The Politics of Recognition." Pp. 25–73 in Amy Gutmann, ed., *Multiculturalism: Examining the Politics of Recognition.* Princeton: Princeton University Press, 1994.

———. *Sources of the Self: The Making of Modern Identity.* Cambridge: Harvard University Press, 1989.

de Tocqueville, Alexis. *Democracy in America.* Ed. J. P. Mayer. New York: Harper Perennial, 1969.

Townsend, Kim. *Manhood at Harvard: William James and Others.* Cambridge: Harvard University Press, 1996.

Trachtenberg, Alan. *The Incorporation of America: Culture and Society in the Gilded Age.* New York: Hill and Wang, 1982.

Tucker, Robert C., ed. *The Marx-Engels Reader.* New York: W. W. Norton, 1978.

Tyrell, Ian. "American Exceptionalism in an Age of International History." *American Historical Review* 96, no. 4 (October, 1991): 1031–55.

Veblen, Thorstein. *The Theory of the Leisure Class: An Economic Study of Institutions.* New York, 1899.

Viroli, Maurizio. *For Love of Country: An Essay on Patriotism and Nationalism.* Oxford: Clarendon Press, 1995.

Wacker, R. Fred. *Ethnicity, Pluralism, and Race: Race Relations Theory in America Before Myrdal.* Westport, CT: Greenwood Press, 1983.

Waldron, Jeremy. "Multiculturalism and Melange." In Robert K. Fullinwider, ed., *Public Education in a Multicultural Society: Policy, Theory, Critique.* Cambridge: Cambridge University Press, 1996.

Walzer, Michael. "Pluralism: A Political Perspective." In Stephan Thernstrom, ed., *Harvard Encyclopedia of American Ethnic Groups,* 1980.

———. *Thick and Thin: Moral Argument at Home and* Abroad. Notre Dame: University of Notre Dame Press, 1994.

———. *Toward a Global Civil Society.* Providence: Berghahn, 1995.

———. "What Does It Mean to Be 'American'?" *Social Research* 57 (1990): 591–614.

Washington, Booker T. "Atlanta Exposition Address." In Howard Brotz, ed., *Negro Social and Political Thought: 1850–1920.* New York: Basic Books, 1996.

Weinstein, James. *The Decline of Socialism, 1912–1925.* New York: Monthly Review Press, 1967.

Westbrook, Robert B. "Fighting for the American Family: Private Interests and Public Obligations in World War II." In Richard Wightman Fox and T. J. Jackson Lears, eds., *The Power of Culture: Critical Essays in American History.* Chicago: University of Chicago Press, 1993.

———. *John Dewey and American Democracy.* Ithaca, NY: Cornell University Press, 1991.

———. "Politics as Consumption: Managing the American Election." In Richard Wightman Fox and T. J. Jackson Lears, eds., *The Culture of Consumption: Critical Essays in American History, 1880–1980.* New York: Pantheon, 1983.

Whitfield, Stephen J., ed. *Culture and Democracy in the United States.* New Brunswick, NJ: Transaction, 1998.

Wilentz, Sean. *Chants Democratic: New York and the Rise of the Working Class, 1788–1850.* New York: Oxford University Press, 1984.

Williamson, Joel. *The Crucible of Race: Black-White Relations in the American South Since Emancipation.* New York: Oxford University Press, 1984.

Wills, Garry. "A Theology of Willie Horton." *Under God: Religion and American Politics.* New York: Touchstone, 1990.

Wilson, Woodrow. "Democracy and Efficiency." *Atlantic Monthly* 87, no. 521 (March 1901): 289–99.

———. *History of the American* People. New York: Harper and Brothers, 1901.

———. "The Ideals of America." *Atlantic Monthly* 90, no. 542 (December 1902): 721–34.

————. *War and Peace: Presidential Messages, Addresses, and Public Papers* (1917–1924). Ed. Ray Stannard Baker and William E. Dodd. 2 vols. New York: Harper and Brothers, 1927.

Wood, Gordon S. *The Radicalism of the American Revolution.* New York: Vintage, 1991.

Xenos, Nicholas. "Civic Nationalism: Oxymoron?" *Critical Review* 10, no. 2 (spring 1996): 213–31.

Yack, Bernard. "The Myth of a Civic Nation." *Critical Review* 10, no. 2 (spring 1996): 193–211.

Yudice, George. "We Are *Not* the World," *Social Text* 30–33 (1992).

Zamir, Shamoon. *Dark Voices: W. E. B. Du Bois and American Thought, 1888–1903.* Chicago: University of Chicago Press, 1995.

Zangwill, Israel. *The Melting Pot: Drama in Four Acts.* New York: Macmillan, 1921 [1909].

Zwerdling, Alex. *Improvised Europeans: American Literary Expatriates and the Siege of London.* New York: Basic Books, 1998.

Zwick, Jim, ed. *Mark Twain's Weapons of Satire: Anti-Imperialist Writings on the Philippine-American War.* Syracuse: Syracuse University Press, 1992.